Anonymous

Report and Record of the Operations of the Stafford House

Committee

For the Relief of sick and wounded Turkish Soldiers

Anonymous

Report and Record of the Operations of the Stafford House Committee
For the Relief of sick and wounded Turkish Soldiers

ISBN/EAN: 9783337135508

Printed in Europe, USA, Canada, Australia, Japan

Cover: Foto ©ninafisch / pixelio.de

More available books at **www.hansebooks.com**

REPORT AND RECORD

OF THE OPERATIONS OF THE

Stafford House Committee

FOR THE RELIEF OF SICK AND WOUNDED

TURKISH SOLDIERS

CHAIRMAN—THE DUKE OF SUTHERLAND, K.G.

RUSSO-TURKISH WAR, 1877-78

PART I. FINAL REPORT OF THE COMMITTEE
PART II. RECORD OF OPERATIONS AT THE SEAT OF WAR, BY MR. V. B. BARRINGTON-KENNETT, M.A., LL.M., CHIEF COMMISSIONER
PART III. MEDICAL REPORT BY THE SUB-COMMITTEE, SIR J. FAYRER, K.C.S.I., M.D., F.R.S., CHAIRMAN
PART IV. ACCOUNTS
APPENDIX—OBITUARY

Printed by
SPOTTISWOODE & CO., NEW-STREET SQUARE, LONDON
1879

STAFFORD HOUSE COMMITTEE FOR THE RELIEF OF SICK AND WOUNDED TURKISH SOLDIERS.

THE DUKE OF SUTHERLAND, K.G., *Chairman.*

H.E. THE NAWAB SIR SALAR JUNG BAHADUR OF HYDERABAD, G.C.S.I.
THE DUKE OF PORTLAND.
THE MARQUIS OF TWEEDDALE.
THE MARQUIS OF HERTFORD.
THE MARQUIS OF ORMONDE.
THE MARQUIS OF LONDONDERRY.
THE MARQUIS OF ABERGAVENNY.
THE MARQUIS OF STAFFORD, M.P.
THE EARL OF DENBIGH.
THE EARL OF DUNMORE.
THE EARL OF FEVERSHAM.
THE EARL OF CHARLEMONT, K.P.
GENERAL THE EARL OF LUCAN, G.C.B.
THE EARL OF ORFORD.
THE EARL OF HARROWBY, K.G.
THE EARL OF SHEFFIELD.
THE EARL OF RAVENSWORTH.
THE EARL OF WHARNCLIFFE.
THE LORD HENRY LENNOX, M.P.
THE LORD CLAUD J. HAMILTON, M.P.
CAPT. LORD CHARLES BERESFORD, R.N., M.P.
GENERAL LORD WILLIAM PAULET, G.C.B.
LIEUT.-GENERAL LORD ALFRED PAGET.
THE LORD BLANTYRE.
THE LORD FORESTER.
MAJOR-GENERAL LORD ABINGER, C.B.
THE LORD DE L'ISLE AND DUDLEY.
THE LORD CAMPBELL AND STRATHEDEN.
THE LORD STANLEY OF ALDERLEY.
THE VISCOUNT HOLMESDALE.
THE VISCOUNT MELGUND.
THE HON. EDWARD WILLIAM DOUGLAS.
THE HON. THOMAS CHARLES BRUCE, M.P.
ADM. THE HON. SIR HENRY KEPPELL, G.C.B.
COLONEL SIR FREDERIC ARTHUR, BART.
MAJOR-GENERAL THE HON. P. FEILDING.
THE HON. PERCY WYNDHAM, M.P.
REAR-ADMIRAL THE HON. CARR GLYN, R.N., C.B., C.S.T., A.D.C.
SIR EDWARD SULLIVAN, BART.
SIR WILLIAM FRASER, BART, M.P.
SIR FRANCIS GOLDSMID, M.P.
SIR MOSES MONTEFIORE, BART.
SIR PHILIP ROSE, BART.
SIR E. H. LECHMERE, BART.
SIR CHARLES MORDAUNT, BART.
SIR HENRY HOARE, BART.
BARON M. DE HIRSCH.

BARON HENRY DE WORMS.
GEN. SIR JOHN LINTORN SIMMONS, G.C.B.
GENERAL SIR CHARLES REID, K.C.B.
ADMIRAL SIR ADOLPHUS SLADE, K.C.B.
ADMIRAL SIR CHARLES EDEN, K.C.B.
LIEUT.-GENERAL SIR ARNOLD KEMBALL, R.A., K.C.B., K.C.S.I.
REAR-ADMIRAL SIR EDMUND COMMERELL, V.C., K.C.B.
MAJOR-GEN. SIR HENRY GREEN, K.C.S.I., C.B.
SIR JOSEPH FAYRER, K.C.S.I., M.D.
SIR ALBERT SASSOON.
LIEUT.-GENERAL H. S. ROWAN, C.B., R.A.
MAJOR-GENERAL FOSTER, C.B.
MAJOR-GENERAL F. MARSHALL.
MAJOR-GENERAL DE HORSEY.
COLONEL OWEN WILLIAMS, R.H.G.
COL. JAMES FARQUHARSON, of Invercauld.
COLONEL NASSAU LEES.
COLONEL REGINALD BULLER.
COLONEL MALCOLM GREEN, C.B.
COLONEL BORTHWICK.
MAJOR POORE.
CAPTAIN F. BURNABY.
CAPTAIN JOHN CLARK.
HENRY CHAPLIN, ESQ., M.P.
M. BUTLER-JOHNSTONE, ESQ., M.P.
SAUL ISAAC, ESQ., M.P.
ALFRED AUSTIN, ESQ.
V. B. BARRINGTON-KENNETT, ESQ.
W. L. BIRKBECK, ESQ.
A. BORTHWICK, ESQ.
T. GIBSON BOWLES, ESQ.
GEORGE CRAWSHAY, ESQ.
H. W. FREELAND, ESQ.
DR. GUY.
GEORGE LOCH, ESQ., Q.C.
H. B. LOCH, ESQ., C.B.
W. MacCORMAC, ESQ.
A. MACKELLAR, ESQ.
M. LAING MEASON, ESQ.
THE REV. R. PHELPS, D.D.
STEWART ERSKINE ROLLAND, ESQ.
JOHN ROSS, ESQ., of Bladensburg.
W. A. ROSS, ESQ.
E. R. PRATT, ESQ.
W. H. RUSSELL, ESQ., LL.D.
W. J. STANIFORTH, ESQ.
HENRY WRIGHT, ESQ.

Hon. Treasurer —MAJOR-GENERAL SIR HENRY GREEN, K.C.S.I., C.B.
Hon. Secretary—HENRY WRIGHT, ESQ.

STAFF OF THE STAFFORD HOUSE COMMITTEE AND LORD BLANTYRE ENGAGED AT THE SEAT OF WAR.

(With Places where Services were rendered.)

V. B. BARRINGTON-KENNETT, M.A., LL.M., Chief Commissioner.

E. R. PRATT, M.A., Assistant-Commissioner for Bulgaria.

W. L. STONEY, C.E., Assistant-Commissioner for Roumelia.

SURGEONS OF THE STAFFORD HOUSE COMMITTEE.

F. L. ATTWOOD, M.R.C.S.—Karabounar, Tirnova, Adrianople, Eskisaghra, Shipka, Kesanlik, Otloukeui.

F. R. BARKER, M.R.C.S.—Roumelian Railway Transport Service, Gallipoli.

W. H. BERESFORD, M.R.C.S., L.R.C.P., Lond.— Lom Campaign, Rustchuk, Salonica.

— CALFOGLOU—Philippopolis.

S. F. CLEMENTS—Stamboul, Salonica, Gallipoli.

CULLEN, M.R.C.S. (subsequently transferred to Red Crescent)—Varna.

A. S. ECCLES, M.R.C.S. (formerly Imperial Ottoman Service) - Philippopolis, Salonica, and Gallipoli.

W. EDMUNDS, M.A., M.B., M.C. Cantab, F.R.C.S. Eng., L.S.A.—Rustchuk, Lom Campaign, Elena.

T. E. D. HAYES, M.R.C.S., L.K.Q.C.P.I., L.S.A.— Rustchuk-Varna Railway Transport Service, Varna, Tchifout-Burgas.

F. N. HUME, M.R.C.S. — Karabounar, Tirnova, Adrianople, Shipka, Kesanlik, Philippopolis, Stanimaka, Suleiman Pacha's Retreat.

KOUVARAS (subsequently transferred to Red Crescent)—Varna.

W. LAKE, M.R.C.S., L.S.A.—Lom Campaign, Rustchuk, Stamboul.

R. MacIVOR, M.D., M.Ch. Qu. Univ. Irel.— Adrianople.

T. MacQUEEN, M.D., C.M. Edin. — Lom Campaign, Elena, Stanimaka, Suleiman Pacha's Retreat.

S. MINASSIAN—Philippopolis.

B. MOORE, M.R.C.S., L.R.C.P. Lond., L.S.A.— Adrianople, Plevna.

J. NEYLAN, L.S.A.—Philippopolis, Stamboul.

C. ROE, L.R.C.S.I., L.K.Q.C.P.I. (late Imperial Ottoman Service)—Salonica, Stamboul.

C. RYAN, M.B., and C.M. Edin. Univ. (late Imperial Ottoman Service, Servian Campaign and Plevna)—Erzeroum.

F. M. SANDWITH, M.R.C.S., L.R.C.P. Lond.— Karabounar, Tirnova, Shipka, Kesanlik, Adrianople, Stanimaka, Suleiman Pacha's Retreat.

E. W. F. STIVEN, M.B., C.M. Edin. (late Imperial Ottoman Service) — Rustchuk, Erzeroum, Stamboul.

G. STOKER, L.K.Q.C.P.I., L.R.C.S.I. (late Imperial Ottoman Service, Servian Campaign, and Soukoum Kalé)—Shipka, Kesanlik, Sofia (subsequently transferred to Red Crescent), Philippopolis, Erzeroum.

J. WELLER, M.R.C.S., L.S.A.—Kesanlik, Philippopolis.

SURGEONS SENT OUT BY LORD BLANTYRE ATTACHED TO STAFFORD HOUSE SECTIONS, AND SUBSEQUENTLY TRANSFERRED TO THE SERVICE OF THE STAFFORD HOUSE COMMITTEE.

A. R. BUSBY, M.R.C.S., L.S.A.—Lom Campaign, Sofia.

G. KIRKER, M.R.C.S., M.D. Qu. Univ. Irel.— Adrianople.

C. L. WATTIE, M.B., C.M.—Lom Campaign, Sofia.

A. A. WOODS, M.D., M.Ch. Qu. Univ. Irel.— Adrianople, Erzeroum.

SURGEONS SENT OUT BY LORD BLANTYRE AND ATTACHED TO HIS SECTIONS IN ASIA.

R. G. BUCKBY, L.R.C.P. Edin., L.R.C.S.I.—Erzeroum, Kars.

J. H. CASSON, M.R.C.S.—Erzeroum, Kars.

J. DENNISTON, M.B. Glasg., C.M. — Erzeroum, Stamboul.

C. FETHERSTONHAUGH, B.A., M.B., M.Ch. Dub., L. and L.M.R.C.S.I.—Erzeroum.

W. G. GUPPY, L.R.C.S. Edin.—Erzeroum.

J. PINKERTON, M.B., C.M. Glasg.—Erzeroum.

STAFF OF STAFFORD HOUSE COMMITTEE.

SURGEONS SENT OUT BY LORD BLANTYRE AND ATTACHED TO SECTIONS OF THE
RED CRESCENT SOCIETY.

A. O. MACKELLAR, F.R.C.S.—Plevna, Balkans.
R. MACPHERSON, M.B., M.C.—Orkhanie, Sofia.

R. PINKERTON, M.B., M.C. (Glasgow.)—Orkhanie, Philippopolis (subsequently attached to S.H.)

ASSISTANT-SURGEONS.

R. BOYD—Lom Campaign, Sofia (Lord Blantyre's, transferred to S. H. C.)
C. SKETCHLEY—Adrianople, Samakov, Stanimaka, Makrikeui, Suleiman Pacha's Retreat.
W. STEWART—Adrianople (Lord Blantyre's).
AZZOPARDI — Adrianople, Makrikeui, Stamboul.

COSLOWSKI—Adrianople.
HADJI EFFENDI—Erzeroum.
ISMAEL EFFENDI—Erzeroum.
MEHEMET EFFENDI—Rustchuk.
A. MICHÆLEDIS—Adrianople, Salonica.

HOSPITAL DISPENSERS.

T. AKESTORIDES—Philippopolis.
M. W. BEYLIKGY—Stamboul.
J. GÖRLITZ—Sofia, Gallipoli.

SPANOPOULOS—Adrianople.
TAMOLINI—Tchifout-Burgas.
(And others.)

TRANSPORT STAFF.

E. H. BANFATHER—Shipka, Samakov.
C. E. CULLEN—Philippopolis, Sofia.
H. HARVEY—Plevna District, Erzeroum, Tchekmedje.

LIEUT. MORISOT—Adrianople, Plevna District, Erzeroum.
R. WILLIAMS—Sofia, Kesanlik, Gallipoli, Samakov. (and others.)

INTERPRETERS AND DRESSERS.

J. ATKINSON—Salonica.
J. BARBERICK.
A. COLLEY—Adrianople.
J. COLLEY—Roumelian Railway Transport.
G. CONSTANTINE—Lom.
J. COWAN—Adrianople, Gallipoli.
J. CUMMINGS—Lom Campaign.
B. FORTUNATO—Erzeroum.
G. MONTÉ—Philippopolis.
C. NICHOLAS.

C. PAVALEDI—Lom Campaign, Sofia.
T. RENNISON—Erzeroum, Kars.
G. STAMOS—Roumelian Railway, Plevna.
G. TAMOLINI—Erzeroum.
A. VANZIAN.
C. VITALIS—Varna.
J. D. WILLIAMS—Erzeroum.
W. WILLIAMS.
WOLLOUSKI—Varna Railway.
(And others.)

CENTRAL OFFICE.

R. ISIDORE, Manager, Stamboul Depôt.
A. LANZONI, Stamboul Depôt.
R. A. WILLIAMS, Accountant.

G. SKLIRAKIS, First Dragoman — Danube, Balkans.

N.B.—The Committee also sent out to the seat of war three surgeons and five assistant-surgeons, who transferred their services to the Red Crescent Society by a special arrangement.

CONTENTS.

	PAGE
I. FINAL REPORT OF THE COMMITTEE . . .	1
II. RECORD OF OPERATIONS AT THE SEAT OF WAR .	5
General Sketch of Operations in relation to Military Events. . .	8
General Report on Returns of Sick and Wounded . . .	10
General Report on the Distribution of Stores . . .	12
General Statement of Accounts in Turkey . .	13
Chief Commissioner's Reports	14
Rustchuk Hospital	46
Rustchuk-Varna Railway Transport . . .	53
First Ambulance of the Lom . .	57
Second Ambulance of the Lom . .	59
Shipka Ambulance . . .	62
Adrianople Hospital . .	68
Philippopolis Hospitals . .	71
Roumelian Railway Transport	75
Plevna District Ambulance .	82
Sofia Hospital	83
Stamboul Mundy Barrack Hospital . . .	85
Samakov Transport	87
Tchifout-Burgas Dispensary	88
Tchekmedje and Makrikeui Hospitals and Dispensary . . .	89
Salonica Hospital	90
Gallipoli Hospital	92
Boulair Lines Dispensary . .	94
Stamboul New Barrack Hospital . .	96
Kesanlik Relief Section . . .	98
Erzeroum Stafford House Hospital . .	99
Trebizond Relief Section . .	105
Erzeroum English Hospital . . .	107
Kars District Ambulance	113
Various Reports and Letters—Sections worked in co-operation with Red Crescent Society	121
Reports from Surgeon Buckle, R.N.	124
Constantinople Mosques	127

CONTENTS.

III. MEDICAL REPORT BY THE SUB-COMMITTEE:—

	PAGE
Sir J. Fayrer's Introductory Remarks	132
Dr. McIvor's Account of Four Hundred Surgical Cases	133
Mr. Barker's Surgical Report of Roumelian Railway Transport	139
Mr. Weller's Cases of Gunshot or Shell Wounds	145
Mr. Eccles' Report on Malarial Poisoning	146
Dr. R. Pinkerton's Surgical Experiences, Observations, &c.	153
Mr. Mackellar's Surgical Report	164
Mr. Eccles' Report of Hospitals at Constantinople	177
Mr. Stiven on the Rustchuk Hospital	179
Mr. Pratt on the Organisation of Field Ambulance and Transport	180

IV. ACCOUNTS:—

Abstract of Receipts and Payments by the Honorary Treasurer	183
Abstract of Expenditure of Funds remitted to the Chief Commissioner	184
Cash Statement	185
Table showing Monthly Expenditure on every section, and on salaries, purchase of stores, &c.	186

APPENDIX.—LETTERS OF THANKS . . . 187

OBITUARY . 192

INDEX . . . 195

TABULATED SUMMARY OF SICK AND WOUNDED TREATED . *to face page* 5

CHART SHOWING TOTAL NUMBERS TREATED EVERY MONTH *to face title*

MAPS

ILLUSTRATING OPERATIONS IN EUROPEAN TURKEY	*to precede chart*
DITTO OPERATIONS IN ASIATIC TURKEY	,,

PART I.

FINAL REPORT OF THE STAFFORD HOUSE COMMITTEE.

On December 12, 1876, the Duke of Sutherland invited some friends to Stafford House to consider what steps could be taken to alleviate the great sufferings which prevailed amongst the Turkish soldiers. From well-informed sources it was ascertained that the hardships these men were patiently enduring were extreme: without tents or other covering than their ragged uniforms, they had to pass days and nights incessantly exposed to rain, sleet, and snow; while the medical arrangements for the sick were of the worst description, and the medicines scanty and ill-assorted.

Under these circumstances it was decided to form a Committee, of which the Duke of Sutherland was unanimously elected Chairman, for the purpose of inviting subscriptions from the public with a view to supplying the sick and wounded Turkish soldiers with warm clothing and medicines.

At a general meeting of the Committee it was decided that the undertaking should bear the name of 'The Stafford House Committee for the Relief of Sick and Wounded Turkish Soldiers.'

About this time it became known that another Committee, under the Chairmanship of Lord Stanley, of Alderley, having similar objects, was in existence, and the gentlemen composing it offered their co-operation, which was cordially accepted. The funds, however, which they had collected, amounting to £1,100, had already been forwarded to Turkey, and placed at the disposal of Ahmed Vefyk Pacha.

Major-General Sir Henry Green was requested to act as Treasurer, and Mr. Thomas Gibson Bowles as Honorary Secretary. The latter, however, owing to pressure of other important business, retired in the following July, and Mr. Henry Wright continued to perform the duties of the office.

Messrs. Drummonds, Smith Payne & Smith, Barnett Hoare & Co., and King & Co. kindly consented to receive subscriptions.

Messrs. Taylor, of the Depository, Pimlico, undertook to store, free of charge, any goods sent to their care.

Messrs. C. Hanson & Co., of Constantinople, also offered their services to receive and distribute any stores and money entrusted to them, and Mr. Alexander Carnegie to convey gratuitously goods belonging to the Committee by his steamers to Constantinople, while the Turkish Government agreed to pass all goods free of duty.

The proper distribution of the stores on arriving in Turkey was a matter of considerable importance, and the Committee did not feel justified, until they ascertained the amount of support they might receive from the public, in sending out an agent of their own. In addition to the service of Messrs. Hanson, they were fortunate enough to obtain the assistance of Ahmed

Vefyk Pacha, a Turkish gentleman personally well known to many members of the Committee, esteemed for his integrity and possessing the confidence of his countrymen.

The above arrangements having been completed, the Committee made its first appeal to the public for subscriptions, which brought in a sum of £4,515; the first list of subscribers was published in December, 1876.

Further subscriptions were received, and the amount remitted in cash and stores (chiefly blankets and quinine) to Constantinople up to the month of May, 1877, was about £5,700.

On the 25th of the same month the Hon. Treasurer announced at a general meeting that the sum of £5,300 had been received from India, subscribed by the inhabitants of Hyderabad, and transmitted through H.E. Salar Jung.

At this date the fund amounted to £12,045 and the expenditure to £5,746, leaving such a balance in hand as justified the Committee in carrying into effect an object they had long had under consideration—viz., that of sending a Commissioner of their own to the seat of war for the purpose of attending exclusively to the organisation of the relief.

It was felt that neither Ahmed Vefyk Pacha (who had been appointed Speaker to the Turkish Parliament) nor Messrs. Hanson could fairly be asked to continue a work which necessarily involved more labour and time than they could devote to it. With this view the Committee gladly accepted the offer of Mr. V. Barrington-Kennett, a gentleman who, under the Red Cross Society, had gained great experience in the Franco-German, Carlist, and Servian wars, from which latter he had recently returned.

Mr. Barrington-Kennett placed himself entirely at the disposal of the Committee, without requiring any remuneration beyond his actual personal expenses, and, having been appointed Chief Commissioner, left for Constantinople on June 11.

On his departure he took medical stores to the value of £1,118, and a credit for £2,000 was placed at his disposal with Messrs. Hanson & Co.

Soon after Mr. Barrington-Kennett's arrival in Turkey the following telegram was received by the Duke of Sutherland from H.I.M. the Sultan's First Secretary:—

'It is with great pleasure that I convey to your benevolent Committee, through your Lordship, the sincere thanks and gratitude of His Imperial Majesty the Sultan, and of all Osmanlis, for the help your Committee have rendered to the wounded Turkish soldiers. You can well imagine how grateful we all feel here for your help, particularly when most needed.'

On July 3 Mr. Barrington-Kennett telegraphed for the services of four surgeons and for a further supply of stores.

The Committee at once sanctioned his request, and, at the recommendation of Mr. MacCormac, of St. Thomas's Hospital, four surgeons were selected, their salaries being fixed at £1 per diem, with £50 for the passage out and home. Subsequently as the funds at the disposal of the Committee permitted of it, the number of surgeons was augmented to 38, which, with those sent out by Lord Blantyre, made a total of 53. In addition to the above surgical staff, there were permanently employed by the Committee the following : 5 hospital dispensers, 5 transport agents, 19 dragoman dressers, and a staff of assistants at the stores. This list does not include a number of dressers and others temporarily engaged at the large hospitals. Mr. Barrington-Kennett's duties had now become most arduous, and one of his personal friends, Mr. E. R. Pratt, having volunteered to join him, his offer was accepted, and he was appointed an Assistant-Commissioner.

In addition to the above gentlemen, the services of Mr. Stoney, a civil engineer at Constantinople, were obtained, who was likewise appointed an Assistant-Commissioner.

For the account of the work performed in Turkey after the arrival of Mr. Barrington-

Kennett the Committee refer the subscribers to his 'Record of Operations at the Seat of War,' Part II., wherein will be found full details of the work of every hospital, ambulance, and transport, with the names of the Staff, and tables annexed showing the returns of patients treated, and distribution of expenditure.

The Committee believe that, from the perusal of this record, the subscribers to the Stafford House Fund will best be able to judge of the manner in which the fund has been administered, and the Committee feel sure that they will read with feelings of pride an account, showing the courage, devotion, and resolution which have been displayed by their Hospital and Ambulance Staff under circumstances unparalleled in any war of late years. Many of these gentlemen, while still suffering from severe illness, nevertheless continued their duties.

It has been the pleasurable duty of the Committee frequently to convey special thanks to individual surgeons for their admirable conduct under exceptional circumstances, and they feel assured that the subscribers will unite with them in thinking that such acknowledgments have been well merited.

To Mr. Barrington-Kennett the Committee feel that very much of the success which has attended their efforts is due. Uniting, as that gentlemen does, untiring energy with great tact and administrative ability, he has been able to organise a practical system of voluntary field ambulance and hospital relief work, under circumstances of exceptional difficulty, and to maintain in harmonious working the many discordant elements with which he has had to deal.

To Mr. E. R. Pratt, and to Mr. Stoney, the thanks of the Committee are also due for the loyal manner in which they supported and carried out the system of administration and accounts established by Mr. Barrington-Kennett; and to Mr. Stoney the Committee are further indebted for the admirable manner in which he superintended the closing of the work after the departure of the Chief Commissioner.

The Committee's thanks are due to Rear-Admiral Sir Edmund Commerell, V.C., K.C.B., commanding the British Squadron stationed off Gallipoli, to whose personal exertions, and to those of several of the naval and medical officers under his command, the success which attended the working of the hospital established at that station is greatly to be attributed.

The Committee are likewise much indebted to the ladies and gentlemen who aided the fund by organising concerts, theatrical entertainments, &c. Very valuable aid was given by those who so kindly forwarded old clothes, lint, blankets, &c., all of which articles assisted greatly to alleviate the sufferings of the wounded.

Mr. Barrington-Kennett has frequently brought to the notice of the Committee the great assistance which he received from the Turkish authorities, and the Staff of the Imperial Ottoman and the Rustchuk-Varna Railway Companies, to all of whom the thanks of the Committee have been conveyed.

The Committee are happy to be able to state that throughout the war their work was carried on in cordial co-operation with that of the British National Aid and the Ottoman Red Crescent Societies.

The balance-sheet will be found in Part IV., containing a detailed account of the receipts and expenditure, from which it will be seen that the total sum received by the Stafford House Committee amounts to £39,293 8s. 11d., and that £38,384 15s. 1d. have been by it expended, leaving a balance of £908 13s. 10d.

Amongst the subscriptions the Committee consider it their duty to mention the munificent donation of £6,000 by his Grace the Duke of Portland.

The Committee record with pleasure that a considerable sum was received in subscriptions of small amount from working-men's committees.

In furtherance of the same objects, Lord Blantyre, one of the members of the Committee, has generously expended a sum of £3,357 3s. 5d., the disbursement of which, however, has been entirely in his own hands. This sum, together with the £1,100 provided by Lord Stanley of Alderley's Committee, makes a total of £43,750 12s. 4d. subscribed as above explained for the relief of the Turkish soldiers.

The Committee would call the attention of the subscribers to the fact that their labours have extended over a period of upwards of two years, and that no expenses beyond those for advertisements, printing, and postage have been incurred in this country, the whole of the correspondence and other office work having been gratuitously performed by members of the Committee.

The Committee feel it their duty to record the valuable assistance received on all occasions from Sir Henry and Lady Layard.

The Committee have received repeated assurances from the Sultan, expressive of he feelings of gratitude which have been engendered in the minds of the Turkish people towards the English nation by the work of the Committee; and in giving audience to Mr. Barrington-Kennett before his departure from Turkey, H.I. Majesty warmly thanked him, and the Committee which he represented, for their generous exertions in aid of the Turkish soldiers. The Sultan desired that the Stafford House surgeons might also be thanked in his name, and that a list of them should be given to him. He further stated that he had been much touched by the kindly and charitable efforts of the British nation, and felt deeply grateful for all that had been done for his suffering people and troops.

In conclusion, the Committee would state that this Report has been published not only with a view of showing to the subscribers the manner in which the fund has been expended, but also in order to record the services which have been performed by Englishmen in alleviating suffering humanity under difficulties and amidst scenes which the Committee believe are almost unprecedented, and in the performance of which services the English characteristics of courage, devotion, and endurance have been conspicuous. This history of the work performed will also, it is thought, be of essential service as a reference in affording data for any association of a similar nature which may be called together in future wars.

SUTHERLAND,
Chairman.

April, 1879.

ICK AND WOUNDED TRE

bulance. A patient evacuated from a hospital

NAME OF SECTION	NOVEMBER, 1877				DECEMBER, 1877			
	Treated during month			Average per day	Treated during month			Average per day
	Sick	Wounded	Total		Sick	Wounded	Total	
RUSTCHUK HOSPITAL	...	310	310	171	...	197	197	165
FIRST LOM AMBULANCE	...	...	...	...	...	...	...	...
SECOND LOM AMBULANCE	833	5	838	83	33	477	510	20
RUSTCHUK-VARNA RAILWAY TRANSPORT	439	1105	1544	51	305	1637	1942	63
SHIPKA AMBULANCE	70	...	70	5	25	...	25	2
ADRIANOPLE HOSPITAL	20	441	461	206	40	369	409	246
„ RAILWAY STATION	120	380	500	16	80	220	300	9
ROUMELIAN RAILWAY TRANSPORT ...	63	1396	1459	49	243	2242	2485	80
PHILIPPOPOLIS HOSPITALS	64	95	159	106	62	93	155	79
SOFIA HOSPITAL	...	...	...	...	...	214	214	130
STAMBOUL MUNDY BARRACK HOSPITAL	...	...	...	...	...	30	30	12
SAMAKOV AMBULANCE								
TCHEKMEDJE & MAKRIKEUI HOSPITALS & DISPENSA	...	...	...	...	...	...	...	...
TCHIFOUT-BURGAS DISPENSARY ...	...	...	...	...	...	...	...	...
SALONICA HOSPITAL	...	...	...	...	...	...	...	...
GALLIPOLI HOSPITAL	...	...	...	...	...	...	...	...
BOULAIR LINES DISPENSARY ...	...	...	...	...	...	...	...	...
TRANSPORT	...	...	...	...	...	...	...	...
VARIOUS	...	...	...	...	...	...	...	...
STAMBOUL NEW BARRACK HOSPITAL ...	...	...	...	...	...	...	...	...
ERZEROUM STAFFORD HOUSE HOSPITAL	84	251	335	75	108	322	430	312
Combined service with Lord Blantyre's Sections in Asia.								
ERZEROUM ENGLISH HOSPITAL	7	1759	1766	191	4	246	250	152
KARS DISTRICT AMBULANCE ...	...	...	...	...	...	...	...	...
TOTALS	1700	5742	7442	953	900	6047	6947	1270

Total number of rations supplied at seven sou

TABLE OF ESTIMATED TOTAL NUMBER OF *DIFFERENT** CASES.

NAME OF SECTION	TOTAL NUMBER OF DIFFERENT CASES TREATED			
	Sick	Wounded	Total	Average per day
RUSTCHUK HOSPITAL ...	...	441	441	124
FIRST LOM AMBULANCE ...	2430	921	3351	89
SECOND LOM AMBULANCE	2322	689	3011	57
RUSTCHUK-VARNA RAILWAY TRANSPORT	3157	6108	9265	61
SHIPKA AMBULANCE ...	756	3013	3769	35
ADRIANOPLE HOSPITAL ...	200	983	1183	200
„ RAILWAY STATION	630	2550	3180	22
ROUMELIAN RAILWAY TRANSPORT	810	10443	11253	80
PHILIPPOPOLIS HOSPITALS	322	2084	2406	140
SOFIA HOSPITAL		269	269	130
STAMBOUL MUNDY BARRACK HOSPITAL		77	77	23
SAMAKOV AMBULANCE	...	1265	1265	63
TCHEKMEDJE & MAKRIKEUI HOSPITALS & DISPENSARY	2888		2888	182
TCHIFOUT-BURGAS DISPENSARY ...	800	...	800	65
SALONICA HOSPITAL	...	248	248	123
GALLIPOLI HOSPITAL ...	259		259	61
BOULAIR LINES DISPENSARY ...	19241		19241	545
TRANSPORT ...	2684		2684	26
VARIOUS	1192	...	1192	20
STAMBOUL NEW BARRACK HOSPITAL ...	...	131	131	83
ERZEROUM STAFFORD HOUSE HOSPITAL ...	521	353	874	293
Combined service with Lord Blantyre's Sections in Asia.				
ERZEROUM ENGLISH HOSPITAL ...	137	2613	2750	172
KARS DISTRICT AMBULANCE	150	587	737	26
TOTALS	38499	32775	71274	—

* See remarks on pages 6, 11. [*To face Part II., page 5.*

PART II.

RECORD OF OPERATIONS AT THE SEAT OF WAR.

BY MR. V. B. BARRINGTON-KENNETT.

THE following is a record of operations carried out at the seat of war, from June 1877 to September 1878, under myself as Chief Commissioner, assisted by Mr. E. R. Pratt and Mr. W. L. Stoney, Assistant-Commissioners for Bulgaria and Roumelia. One or other of these two gentlemen acted for me whenever I was obliged to be absent from our head-quarters at Constantinople, and I think it my duty, in the first place, to state how much I am indebted to them for their valuable assistance. *Preliminary remarks.*

I have divided the subject matter of this record as follows :—

(1)—A short sketch of the Stafford House operations in relation to the military events of the war.

(2)—General Report on the Returns of Sick and Wounded treated by the Stafford House sections.

(3)—General Report on the Distribution of Stores.

(4)—General Statement of Accounts in Turkey, having special reference to the expenditure under various heads and during the different months.

(5)—Reports from the seat of war, subdivided as follows :—

    (A) Reports to the Committee from the Chief Commissioner.
    (B)   ,,   ,,   Chief Commissioner from the Bulgaria sections.
    (C)   ,,   ,,   ,,   ,,   Roumelia ,,
    (D)   ,,   ,,   ,,   ,,   Asia ,,
    (E) Various reports and letters.

The section reports from Bulgaria, Roumelia, and Asia are selections I have made of the surgeons' reports. These I have grouped according to sections, prefacing every group with a concise statement of the section's period of service, list of working staff, number of patients treated, and other details.*

For convenience of reference and statistics two maps, a chart, and five tabular statements are annexed, to the following purport :—

    Two maps to illustrate operations in European and Asiatic Turkey. *Preceding chart.*

    Chart showing by a diagram the estimated total numbers treated every month from August 1, 1877, to September 15, 1878, by every section. *Facing title.*

    A list of the staff of the Stafford House Committee and of Lord Blantyre's engaged at the seat of war, with services, *p.* v.

* Lord Blantyre's Asia sections are included in this record.

RECORD OF OPERATIONS.

Tabulated return of sick and wounded treated in hospitals, ambulances, and during transport, showing estimated totals and daily averages under treatment by every section during the several months from August 1, 1877, to September 15, 1878. *Facing p. 5.*

Abstract of Expenditure extracted from the Chief Commissioner's 'General Account,' showing the distribution of the funds remitted to him in Turkey among the different Stafford House hospitals, ambulances, transport services, &c. (p. 184).

General Cash Statement extracted from the 'General Account,' showing the total amount of cash paid into the Chief Commissioner's account at Constantinople from the Hon. Treasurer, or other sources, and the disbursements every month. As the accounts were necessarily kept in Turkish currency, the Cash Statement is also in that currency (p. 185).

Table of monthly disbursements to every section, and monthly expenditure for salaries, purchase of stores, &c. (p. 186).

I have devoted considerable attention to making the returns of sick and wounded treated as accurate as possible. The figures are based on the original reports written on the spot by the surgeons. These reports were many of them drawn up under circumstances of great pressure of work and other difficulties, but where any doubt arose, the lowest estimate has been invariably adopted. The numbers mentioned may therefore safely be taken as being, if anything, below the mark.

The following is a capitalised summary of the 'totals' extracted from the tables and statements annexed. I have set it out in this place for the purpose of immediate reference in illustrating the remarks which follow, on the subject of the returns during the various months and relative disbursements. The monthly expenditure in the last column is extracted from the Cash Statement, the Turkish pound being taken at about eighteen shillings. It must be remembered that these disbursements do not include the value of the stores sent from England.

Recapitulation of Totals extracted from the Tabular Statements.

Months	No. of sections engaged	Total sick treated	Total wounded treated	Total treated	Average under treatment per day	Disbursements made every month during which the S. H. sections were engaged
1877						£ s. d.
August	5	355	3529	3884	412	2711 0 5
September	10	1008	10526	11534	981	1490 8 2
October	10	5542	3202	8744	1004	1422 5 10
November	9	1700	5742	7442	953	2305 15 8
December	11	900	6047	6947	1270	3121 2 0
1878						
January	11	1816	5712	7528	1152	2130 13 10
February	6	2346	690	3036	1003	2643 12 10
March	9	2132	622	2754	959	2809 19 10
April	6	788	512	1300	535	1675 17 10
May	3	594	123	717	217	1229 17 5
June	3	7804	93	7897	664	1581 13 2
July	1	6724	...	6724	583	294 7 0
August	1	4915	...	4915	535	84 19 2
September	1	2684	...	2684	258	238 12 2

PRELIMINARY REMARKS.

In all our operations we endeavoured to make our organisation as elastic as possible, so as to be able rapidly to place the sections where any sudden influx of wounded was overpowering the medical staff at the disposal of the authorities; and also by soup-kitchens, improved systems of transport, and other means to fill up the gaps left by the Government in its medical administration. We hoped thus to extend the benefit of the Committee's work over as large an area as possible. This is entirely opposed to the system of establishing *model* transports or ambulances in the strict sense of the word.

In my reports I have frequently had occasion to point out the great advantage of establishing a principle of co-operation in the work of voluntary Societies. The Stafford House transport services, in combination with the Rustchuk-Varna Railway Company and the Imperial Ottoman (Roumelian) Railway Company, afforded good examples of the beneficial results of such a system. Again, in most of our Stafford House hospitals, by falling in with the general arrangements of the Government authorities, great economy was effected, as under these circumstances the Government would generally provide soldiers, infirmiers, rations, and part of the heavier matériel.

To Sir H. A. Layard, H.M. Ambassador to the Porte, I feel personally grateful for the sound advice and powerful support which he was always ready to give me. And I desire also to record my sincere thanks to Rear-Admiral Sir E. Commerell and the officers of H.M. Fleet at Gallipoli for their valuable assistance; also to Lieut.-Gen. Sir A. Kemball for the assistance which he gave to our sections in Asia. I have to thank the representatives of the National Aid and Red Crescent Societies for their friendly co-operation. I frequently attended the meetings of the latter, and received every kindness and courtesy from its members. Among them was Baron Mundy, one of the highest authorities on all matters connected with military hygiene. To him we all felt grateful, not only for his valuable advice on ambulance matters, but also for the unremitting care and attention he bestowed on two of our surgeons whom he successfully treated through long and dangerous illnesses.

I beg to thank the Stafford House Committee most sincerely for the confidence they reposed in me, and for the liberty of action allowed me at the seat of war. This enabled me to carry out many large operations for the relief of distress, which would have lost much of their value, had it been necessary to await the decision of a Committee before taking action. The prompt attention paid to every communication I made to the executive officers of the Committee secured that rapidity of action which is of the very greatest importance in time of war.

In acknowledging the kind way in which the Committee has referred to any services I may have rendered, I do so not only on my own behalf, but as representative of my two Assistant-Commissioners, and the whole working Staff of the Committee. These gentlemen ably and loyally supported me at the seat of war, and to them I feel is due a large share of the thanks of the Committee.

V. B. BARRINGTON-KENNETT,
Chief Commissioner.

May 18, 1879.

(1) GENERAL SKETCH OF OPERATIONS.

OUR first operations took place early in August, in Eastern Roumelia and the Danube districts, where hospitals were established at Rustchuk (July 20) and Varna (August 3)—the two extremities of the Rustchuk-Varna Railway—the Varna Hospital being carried on for two months in co-operation with the Red Crescent Committee. At the same time a railway transport service was organised along that line, with soup-kitchens at convenient intervals, and a special service of improvised ambulance carts was established at Varna to transport the wounded between the railway station, the town hospitals, and the pier. The First and Second ambulances of the Lom were formed on August 3 and 25, and attached to divisions in the front. This completed our organisation for Bulgaria. At seven out of the eight battles which took place in the district, surgeons of the Stafford House ambulances were engaged on the field.

As soon as news arrived that the Russian forces had crossed the Balkans, a field ambulance (the Shipka section) was sent to the front (July 24th), and attached to Suleiman Pacha's head-quarters. A hospital was established at Adrianople (August 12), on which town the wounded from the fighting at Yenisaghra and Eskisaghra were concentrated. Soon afterwards the grand attack on Shipka (August 21 to 27) crowded Philippopolis with wounded, in consequence of which the Philippopolis Hospital section was at once despatched to that town (September 1). After treating large numbers of the wounded who were scattered about in private houses, this section formed two permanent hospitals. At the same time the Roumelian Railway transport service, with a system of soup-kitchens, was organised on the Imperial Ottoman line, along which the wounded were transported from Philippopolis and Adrianople to Constantinople.

On September 20 a field ambulance was attached to the Sultan's Circassian Guard on its expedition to Plevna in advance of Chefket Pacha's relieving column.

Early in November the First Lom ambulance was withdrawn from the Danube district and sent to Sofia, where a Stafford House Hospital was at once established. Great distress was prevalent in that town, owing to the large number of wounded crowded there from Plevna and Orkhanie.

The Second Lom ambulance, attached to Fuad Pacha's head-quarters, after their service on the Lom, joined in the expedition against Elena, December 4, and subsequently retreated with the Turkish army across the Northern Balkans to Slivno and Yamboli, and thence to Philippopolis.

On December 4, the Mundy Barrack Hospital in Stamboul was handed over to a Stafford House staff, by whom it was kept up for over six months.

On the general retreat of the Ottoman forces necessitated by the fall of Plevna (December 10), the Stafford House work entered on a new phase. The Samakov section was formed and despatched with all haste to the front (December 26) to assist in the evacuation of the wounded. The occupation of Sofia and Philippopolis by the Russians rapidly followed (January 3 and 15). In accordance with their instructions the staffs of the Stafford House Hospitals established in those towns remained at their posts to protect the wounded in their hospitals (there being no time for them to be evacuated), while the Stafford House field ambulances retired with the divisions to which they were severally attached.

The Second Lom ambulance, attached to Fuad Pacha's division, and the Shipka and Samakov sections, attached to the head-quarters of Suleiman and Osman Nouri Pachas respectively, united at Philippopolis in the general retreat. After handing over their heavy and valuable stores to the Stafford House Hospital established in that town, these three sections retired with Suleiman's army across the Rhodope Balkans to Port Lagos, and thence by sea to Constantinople, attending to large numbers of wounded who followed the army in its retreat.

The Stafford House Hospital at Rustchuk was bombarded by the Russians on December 30 and 31, and completely destroyed. The patients were gallantly rescued by our Hospital Staff. The explanation given for this flagrant breach of the customs of civilised warfare was that the Russian authorities thought that the hospital was being used as a barrack. Some of the patients were wounded a second time during the bombardment, and died of the injuries received.

On January 20, 1878, Adrianople was occupied by the Russians, but the whole of the wounded in the Stafford House Hospital had been evacuated on Constantinople the night before, accompanied by our staff, while the valuable stores were placed under the protection of the British Consul, and came in usefully afterwards for the relief of the wounded Turks taken prisoners at Kesanlik.

The rapid advance of the Russians on Constantinople and Varna followed the evacuation of Adrianople. Our railway transport services kept up their work as long as the lines were open, the Rustchuk-Varna service until January 31, and the Roumelian until January 20, while the soup-kitchens established along those lines were the means of relieving many hundreds of sick and wounded who were rapidly sinking from want of nourishment and from exposure to the cold during that terrible winter retreat.

In the months of February and March much illness broke out among the Turkish troops crowded in the unhealthy suburbs of Constantinople on the St. Stefano side. In order to relieve the distress thus occasioned the hospitals and dispensaries of Tchekmedje, Makrikeui, and Tchifout-Burgas were established.

On February 15 I commissioned Mr. Harvey, a young English engineer, to raise a corps of 150 able-bodied refugees to bury the thousands of decomposed carcases of horses, oxen, and other cattle, which were lying in ditches and watercourses in immediate proximity to the quarters of the troops in the environs of Constantinople. These carcases poisoned the water supplies, and were considered by our surgeons to be the cause of much of the prevailing sickness. As the Turkish authorities would not act, I thought myself justified in undertaking this sanitary measure on the principle of prevention being better than cure.

The Salonica Hospital section was formed on March 1, to alleviate the great distress in that town, overcrowded as it was with the wounded from the battles fought to cover Suleiman Pacha's retreat. Soon afterwards (March 11), the Gallipoli section was established and served in that town and the neighbouring Boulair Lines until the middle of September.

In April 1878 a resumption of hostilities seemed imminent, and it became necessary to prepare for the possibility of a Russian advance on Constantinople. We had a large collection of valuable stores in our depôt at Galata, and it would have been an exceedingly difficult matter, perhaps quite impossible, to remove them to any place of safety had a panic occurred in the town. To guard against this danger I chartered a small Greek brig, and shipped the most valuable stores on board, making of her, as it were, a floating depôt, ready at any moment to drop down to Gallipoli and anchor under protection of the British fleet.

With regard to the relief furnished to Asia, large supplies of medical stores from the Committee had been distributed at Batoum and elsewhere before my appointment, through the medium of Ahmed Vefyk Pacha (afterward Prime Minister), who then represented the Committee in Turkey.

In July 1877, soon after my arrival, Lord Blantyre's surgeons, assisted by M. Zohrab, H.B.M. Consul at Erzeroum, established a hospital in that town, which was largely subsidised with money and stores, of which some were purchased in Constantinople and others selected from our depôt at Galata.

On August 22, the Erzeroum staff having been reinforced by a fresh batch of surgeons, a field ambulance under Lord Blantyre's surgeons was organised and attached to Mukhtar Pacha's head-quarters in the Kars district.

In consequence of the increasing distress in Asia, a strong Stafford House staff, with a large supply of stores, was despatched from Constantinople on November 12, and within a fortnight was hard at work at Erzeroum in charge of a large hospital. This was kept up until the middle of April 1878, when the united Stafford House and Lord Blantyre's staffs were withdrawn from Asia.

During the months of March, April and May, 1878, Vice-Consul Biliotti on our behalf undertook a system of distributing relief in small sums of money among the convalescent soldiers who were passing through Trebizond in large numbers on the road home, many in a state of extreme poverty and distress. This work was well carried out and relieved a great deal of suffering.

For further particulars and all details of the different hospitals, ambulance and transport services, I beg to refer to the selection of 'Reports from Seat of War,' p. 14, and to the statements at the head of every section's report.

(2) RETURNS OF SICK AND WOUNDED TREATED.

REFERRING to the recapitulation of totals on p. 6, it will be seen that during August 1877 the number of sick and wounded treated by the three sections of Stafford House and two of Lord Blantyre's was 3,884, the proportion of sick to wounded being as 1 to 10, and the average treated per day 412. In September the number of sections was increased to ten, and the number of different patients amounted to 11,534; the relative proportion of sick to wounded remained about the same as in August. The average under treatment per day was 981. During October, with the same sections the numbers treated fell off to 8,744, the sick being more than half as numerous again as the wounded, a result which is accounted for by the large number of sick treated by the Lom ambulances and transported by the Rustchuk-Varna railway section. In spite of this decrease, the average under treatment per day rose to 1,004, which shows that the patients were longer under the surgeons' care.

In November, with nine sections at work, 7,442 patients were treated, the proportion of sick to wounded being about as 1 to 3, and the daily average 953. In

December eleven sections treated 6,947 patients, the proportion of sick to wounded being as 1 to 7. The daily average rose during this month to 1,270, which shows that the length of treatment of the cases still further increased.

The first month of the New Year saw eleven sections at work, and 7,528 patients pass through the hands of our surgeons, the proportion of sick to wounded being as 1 to 3, and the average 1,152. In February the number of our sections was reduced to six, and the total number of cases treated was 3,036, the sick being more than three times as numerous as the wounded. The daily average, however, only fell to 1,003. In March nine sections treated 2,754 patients, the relative proportion remaining about the same, the daily average falling to 959. In April, the Asia sections having been withdrawn, there remained only six Stafford House sections. These treated 1,300 cases, the proportion of sick to wounded being about as 3 to 2, and the daily average 535. In May three sections treated 717, the sick being nearly five times as numerous as the wounded. The daily average in this month fell to its minimum, 217. In June the Boulair Lines Dispensary was established at Gallipoli. This section, with the two others which remained, treated 7,897 patients, of which only 93 were wounded; the daily average increasing again rapidly to 664.

In July, August, and September 1878, the Boulair section, Gallipoli, was the only one left, but was worked on a large scale by means of the assistance of the officers of H.M. fleet at Gallipoli. The numbers treated by our section during these three months were 6,724, 4,915, and 2,684, respectively—all sick; and the corresponding daily averages were 583, 535, and 258. The large majority of these cases were slight.

The maximum total number treated in any one complete month was 11,534, in September 1877, and the minimum was 717, in May 1878. The average number of cases treated per month was 5,436. The maximum daily average for any one complete month was 1,270 in December 1877, and the minimum 217 in May. The average number of patients under treatment daily calculated for the entire period from August 1877 to September 1878 was 751.

The total number of cases treated during the whole period was 38,499 sick and 32,775 wounded, making a final total of 71,274 cases. Of these 11,526 were treated in hospitals, 12,133 by field ambulances, 21,233 by dispensaries, and 26,382 attended to during transport.

Necessarily many of the sick and wounded were treated by more than one of our sections. This fact tended to multiply the aggregate total of different cases treated, as the same man might be evacuated from one of our sections in the front to another in the rear, and thus count as a 'case' in the books of both. One case came particularly under my notice, that of a man wounded at Shipka. He was first treated by our Shipka ambulance and counted as one of their cases. He was subsequently transported to a Stafford House hospital at Philippopolis in one of Surgeon Stoker's Red Crescent carts, and was entered in the books of that hospital, where he went through a long course of treatment. When well enough to stand transport he was handed over to our Roumelian Railway section, and was taken to the Stafford House Adrianople hospital, where he was treated for a considerable period, and ultimately sent up to Constantinople convalescent. This of course was a rare case, but it was by no means unusual for the same man to pass through two or three of our sections in the course of his treatment and evacuation to the rear. Thus the number of *cases recorded* exceeds considerably the number of *different men treated*.

The number of rations issued at the soup-kitchens of the Stafford House Committee were as follows :—

At the soup-kitchens established at Bazardjik, Tirnova, Tchorlou, and Stamboul Terminus (Roumelian Railway Transport)	39,904
At the soup-kitchens established at Sheitanjik and Tchervenavoda (Rustchuk-Varna Railway Transport)	8,659
At the Boulair Lines	58,377
Total rations issued	106,940

A ration consists of a bowl of broth with meat and rice, half a pound of bread, and where practicable a cup of coffee or milk; sometimes also a packet of tobacco and cigarette papers.

1708 convalescents were relieved by small money donations at Trebizond to assist them in returning to their homes.

(3) STORES.

THE amount spent on the purchase of stores in England was 8,265l. 11s. 7d., and in Turkey 2,398l. 3s. 8d.; making a total of 10,663l. 15s. 3d., being above one-fourth of the entire funds of the Committee.

During the early part of the war our stores were warehoused in a depôt kindly placed at our disposal by the Red Crescent Society. This depôt became subsequently too small for us, and in consequence we transferred the stores to a very convenient warehouse in the Ottoman Post Office Buildings, Galata. The greater portion of the stores sent out to Turkey by the Committee after my appointment were required for the Committee's sections. Considerable supplies, however, were furnished to the Red Crescent Society from time to time, especially for its hospitals on the Bosphorus, at Begler Bey and Kavak. Chests of selected stores were also supplied to such English doctors in the Turkish service as required them for the treatment of their patients in the Government hospitals, a system which was found to work well.

On the transfer of a Stafford House hospital to the Government or Red Crescent, we usually handed over with the sick and wounded all the heavy matériel, and a certain supply of medical stores, so that the change of administration might be effected with as little inconvenience as possible to the patients, or those to whose care they were delivered. A responsible supercargo was sent with every supply of stores forwarded to the different sections when it was possible to do so. By these means alone we could secure their rapid and safe delivery in the general confusion of traffic which the war entailed. It was our practice never to hand over stores without receiving an acknowledgment from some responsible person entitled to give it. Also, in order to keep an accurate register of the stores, strict orders were given to the storekeeper never to allow any stores to be taken from the depôt, even by the chiefs of sections, without a written order from one of the Commissioners, except of course in cases of urgency.

Mr. Stoney, Assistant-Commissioner, exercised a general control over the business at the depôt, which was carried on by an active and responsible staff. Before finally delivering over the remaining stores to the care of Rear-Admiral Commerell, Mr. Stoney made a careful inspection of them, and also examined the depôt books of account, inventories, &c. He reported that all was correct and in order.

(4) ACCOUNTS.

THE total amount remitted to me in Turkey by the Hon. Treasurer was 22,394*l*. 9*s*. (see the Committee's Abstract of Receipts and Expenditure, p. 183), which, together with a sum of 122*l*. 11*s*. received by private subscriptions, and on the transfer of Lord Blantyre's surgeons, makes a total of 22,517*l*.

The expenditure of this sum between the different hospitals, field ambulances, railway transports, &c., is set forth in a tabular form in the Chief Commissioner's Abstract of Expenditure, p. 184. Referring to this it will be seen that, exclusive of salaries of surgeons and cost of stores sent from England, the working expenses in Turkey of the fixed hospitals was 6,797*l*. 13*s*. 3*d*. ; the field ambulances, 2,473*l*, 5*s*. 9*d*.; and of the railway transport services, including soup-kitchens, 1,541*l*. 15*s*. 9*d*. The amount paid on account of salaries of surgeons and others was 6,806*l*. 0*s*. 5*d*., and for the purchase of medical stores and other hospital and ambulance matériel, &c., 2,398*l*. 3*s*. 8*d*. The cost of transport of personnel and matériel was 732*l*. 8*s*. 7*d*. For other details I beg to refer to the Abstract of Expenditure itself. In comparing the *relative* expenditure of the different sections, it must be borne in mind that some sections were obliged to purchase articles which in others were gratuitously supplied by the Government, or provided from our depôts.

With regard to the expenditure during the different months, referring to the table, p. 6, it will be seen that the expenditure up to the end of August 1877 was 2,711*l*. 0*s*. 5*d*. This was heavy owing to considerable purchases of stores. During September the expenditure was 1,490*l*. 8*s*. 2*d*., and during October, 1,422*l*. 5*s*. 10*d*. The increased expenditure during the next five months, reaching a maximum of 3,121*l*. 2*s*. in December, was owing to the organisation of new sections, and the operations being conducted on a large scale (see returns of numbers treated). The number of sections and consequent expenses was reduced in April and May, in the latter month the expenditure being but 1,229*l*. 17*s*. 5*d*. In June, owing to several payments made on account of salary, the expenditure was raised to 1,581*l*. 13*s*. 2*d*. The expenses of the last three months, July, August and September, were small, there being only one section employed.

The General Account presented to the Committee was kept in Turkish currency, and shows the details of expenditure of all the funds remitted to me in Turkey. References are made in this account to the 'vouchers' which accompany it, and which are grouped according to the several months. In order to secure an accurate record of the details of expenditure of funds paid through me to the different sections, the following system was pursued :—The chief surgeon of every section was supplied by me with money from time to time, the several items of which were entered in the General Account, and he was held responsible to me for its expenditure. On his section being dissolved, his account was made up in a special 'Section Account-book,' and the balance, if any, refunded. Cross-payments between the different sections were at the same time carefully recorded to secure the accuracy of the final estimate of total expenditure of the different sections. The Depôt Account-book was kept in a similar manner. The surgeons' salary accounts were kept distinct from the accounts of their sections. For further particulars I beg to refer to the books and vouchers themselves, which I have placed in the hands of the Hon. Treasurer.

No little difficulty was experienced by the chiefs of section in keeping their accounts accurately under the trying circumstances in which they often found themselves placed. This difficulty was increased in some parts of the country by the carrying on of business transactions in Cäime (Turkish bank-notes). The rapid fluctuations in the value of these notes as against gold made prices very unsteady, and also caused considerable trouble in the final settlement of some of the section accounts. The currency of debased silver was also very inconvenient. It was our practice in settling up section accounts to convert into gold currency all accounts kept in Cäime or debased silver, with a view to securing uniformity. The whole of the accounts (including the section accounts) and the vouchers, up to July 31, 1878, were submitted to Mr. Scaife, an auditor appointed by Messrs. Hanson and Co., the Constantinople Bankers of the Committee. In my absence from Constantinople Mr. Stoney undertook to act for me in the matter.

The following is the report of the Auditor :—

Constantinople, Jan. 18, 1879.

I have examined the accounts and original vouchers of the Stafford House Committee at Constantinople, presented to me by Mr. W. L. Stoney, Assistant-Commissioner, and hereby certify that the accounts are correct, and that the vouchers correspond with the amounts charged in the accounts to which they respectively refer. Further, that the rates of exchange are correct, and calculations accurately made. I have signed the books and sheets of accounts presented to me as correct.

(Signed) A. H. SCAIFE, *Auditor*.

Witness to Signature of A. H. Scaife—
W. WELLESLEY HANSON, of Chas. S. Hanson & Co.,
Constantinople.

The expenditure after July 31, which was small, owing to being mainly confined to the work in the Boulair Lines and the business of closing the accounts, is contained in the supplementary accounts, which have been audited by Mr. Culverwell.

Lord Blantyre's expenditure on account of the salaries of the fifteen surgeons whom he sent to the seat of war, and expenses connected with the British hospital at Erzeroum and the Kars District Ambulance, amounted to the sum of 3,357*l*. 3*s*. 5*d*. The disbursement of this sum was controlled by Lord Blantyre.

(5) REPORTS FROM THE SEAT OF WAR.

(A).—*Reports from* MR. V. B. BARRINGTON-KENNETT, *Chief Commissioner.*

Varna, July 4, 1877.

Mr. BARRINGTON-KENNETT'S reports.

On arriving in Paris, I enquired at Walcter's manufactory about stretchers and cacolets, and put him into communication with the committee. I consulted with the committee of the Red Cross of France as to the help they were sending to Turkey. At the request of the Turkish Red Crescent, they are sending 10,000 francs' worth of stretchers and ' tentes d'abri.'

I arrived in Constantinople on Saturday, June 20. On the 21st I sent telegrams to Sir Arnold Kemball at Erzeroum, Dr. Crookshank at Rustchuk, and Dr. Roy at Shumla. I received the answers enclosed from the two former. As Drs. Casson and Fetherstonhaugh were going direct to Erzeroum, I bought at Constantinople at wholesale price a large selection of medicines, bandages, &c., which I consigned to the care of Casson, who will take them to Erzeroum, and distribute them personally under Sir A. Kemball's general directions. A similar selection will arrive here on Saturday, and be handed over to Dr. Crookshank, to whom I shall also give a money subsidy of 50l. for further relief. I have telegraphed to Dr. Williams, of Sienitza, but have not as yet received an answer.

Mr. BARRINGTON-KENNETT'S reports.

On June 25 I called on Ahmed Vefyk Pacha and Mr. Layard. The former received me very well, and offered me every assistance. He told me that he had spent all the 2,000l. entrusted to him by our Committee, except 600l., and had distributed all the stores. I had a long conversation with Mr. Layard on the 25th, and also on the 28th. His advice agreed with the general plan of action which I had laid out.

I presented my letter of introduction to Safvet Pacha, and was introduced by him to the Grand Vizier. They both received me well, and gave me papers to facilitate my work ; the latter recommending me to act under protection of the Red Crescent. I attended two meetings of the Red Crescent Society on June 27 and 30, which were held in the Dolma Bagtché Palace. I decided to accept the honorary post on the committee offered me, and find it a great help to me and beneficial to our Stafford House position and work. I have subsidised with money and materials many local committees. I shall give particulars in my next report. I am hard at work organising relief here, and Mr. Reade, the Consul of Rustchuk, who has gone on to Kustendje, has at his disposition 50l. of ours to distribute there, in supplying wants of wounded.

Red Crescent Society.

Our help is received with the greatest gratitude. I find I can buy many things cheap in Constantinople, as people are anxious to realise. Several violations of the Red Crescent on the part of Russians are reported. I helped Drs. Casson and Fetherstonaugh in every way in my power. The former was very glad to take on the stores to Erzeroum, as it will make his position stronger.

Supplies sent to Erzeroum.

Constantinople, July 18, 1877.

I have lately returned from my visit to Shumla and Rustchuk. I am sending a second large supply of stores purchased here to Erzeroum, under the supervision of the Consuls of Trebizond and Erzeroum ; an American missionary acquainted with the language and country will accompany them. Infirmiers and a further supply of stores are being sent by me to Rustchuk and Varna. Lord Melgund has kindly taken charge of some money to be spent in relief in the Osman Bazar district. Mr. Reade, Consul at Rustchuk, informs me that he has made satisfactory arrangements at Kustendje about the expenditure of the remittance he received from me for the relief of the sick and wounded from the Dobrutscha district. I saw Mr. Layard yesterday, and am acting with his approval in my operations with regard to establishing hospitals and transport services. When our stores arrive from England I shall at once devote myself to their distribution. They are much wanted. I have received nothing but kindness and assistance from the authorities, and the deepest gratitude from the sick whose evacuation I assisted in carrying out from Shumla.

Further supplies sent to Erzeroum.

Constantinople, July 20, 1877.

As I informed you by telegram, hospitals have been established at Varna and Rustchuk, and I have guaranteed keeping them up for two months, putting a limit of from 250l. to 300l. each. The hospital site at Rustchuk is so good that the Government authorities have applied for a portion of the building not occupied by us, with a view of forming their own hospital there. It is situated about three-quarters of a mile outside the town, so there will be no fear of any but an intentional bombardment. In addition, notice is being sent to the Russian authorities that a hospital is established there.

Establishment of Varna and Rustchuk hospitals.

On Tuesday last I sent to Varna by steamer six infirmiers, whom I engaged from the Scutari hospital, at about 10s. a month, and uniforms at about 30s. each ; four of these have gone on to Rustchuk in charge of a Mr. Johnson, who will assist Crookshank, and the other two will remain for the Varna hospital. I also sent a further supply of stores. Our hospital is the only one in Rustchuk ; the others have been completely destroyed or abandoned, owing to their dangerous position in the centre of the town.

Rustchuk.

	RECORD OF OPERATIONS.

Mr BARRINGTON-KENNETT'S reports.
Drs. Crookshank and Stiven buy beds and bedding at a low price in Rustchuk. Some of the former are even given for nothing, the owners thinking that the Red Crescent flag over the Stafford House hospital will be respected. The medicines, &c., I have bought of Della Sudda in Stamboul, a large wholesale druggist, who supplies medicines under the strict surveillance of Dr. Sarell, a leading English surgeon here. Crookshank reports that with the 200*l*. I have placed at his disposal he can, in addition to fitting up 100 to 150 beds, organise a field ambulance to follow the Rustchuk division in any sorties should the position be blockaded, which is expected to be the case. I had engaged Dr. Stiven, who speaks Turkish, and has had eleven months' active service in the Servian and in this campaign, as Crookshank's assistant. Crookshank had accepted service from the National Society, but, not having received any definite instructions, placed himself at my disposal until such should arrive. [N.B.—Before the hospital was finished, Dr. Crookshank's services were required by the National Aid Society, and Dr. Stiven succeeded him.]

Varna.
The Varna hospital is established in a newly erected mill. It required about 80*l*. to put it in good order for receiving wounded. The site is the best in the town, being on the rising ground at the north-west corner, with large open spaces on every side. One of our doctors will be in charge there. I have not received any report from Col. Borthwick yet, but Mr. Layard, Col. Baker, and all authorities seem to think that I have been very lucky to secure his services under such good conditions.

Kustendje.
Mr. Reade reports that he left the 50*l*. put at his disposal by me for Kustendje in the hands of the director of the railroad, who will employ an English doctor, Mr. Ball, when necessary. Kustendje is now occupied by the Russians, but I hope that good was done during the rapid evacuation which took place. Lord Melgund undertook to employ 40*l*. in relief of

Osman Bazar.
the wounded in the Osman Bazar district. He could not have left money in better hands, as he will be where the fighting actually takes place. A large supply of stores is being

Relief to Asia.
shipped for Trebizond for Casson's distribution at Erzeroum, subject to the direction of any of our doctors who may arrive there. Until one arrives Casson will distribute, assisted by the British Consul, M. Zohrab, and Sir A. Kemball. Lieut. Drummond, R.N., here on leave, has kindly consented to accompany personally these stores through to Erzeroum. Protection is necessary, owing to the many delays which will occur if sent alone. An American missionary will probably accompany them up country. Mr. Drummond goes at his own expense, but, through the Red Crescent, we can secure free passage for him and for all our goods.

Ladies' committees.
I am supplying bandages, mattresses, shirts, &c., to the hospitals made by the different ladies' committees on the Bosphorus, especially Mrs. Layard's. I subsidise them with money and materials, and they work up the things exceedingly rapidly and well.

Diary.
The following is my diary during my last journey:—July 3.—Started from Constantinople by steamer after purchasing stores, &c., and spent night in ship. July 4.—Arrived at Varna. Well received by Ali Bey, civil governor; arranged about scheme for hospital and relief with Mons. Court, the director of the Ottoman branch bank. July 5.—Meeting of Red Crescent Committee, who offered all help; scheme met with approval. Started by evening train, where spent night. July 6.—Rustchuk. Arrived at Tchervenavoda at 2 P.M., drove on to Rustchuk with Col. Lennox, met Crookshank, decided on site of hospital so much required. Soldiers with fever, &c., under hot bell-tents. Well received by Muchir Eskreff Pacha. Found Stafford House stores (Vefyk's) in possession of Ohannes Bey, head surgeon in tent hospital. Expressed wishes of Committee. July 7.—Arranged details with Crookshank. Returned towards Shumla with Dr. Stiven. (Slept in train). July 8.—(Shumla). Arrived daybreak. Called on Commander-in-Chief, Abdul Kerim, Borthwick, and hospital authorities. Visited hospitals; 1,000 sick. Well received by everybody; had conversation with Nedjib Pacha as to our operations. July 9.—Started in evening after further consultations with medical board and Borthwick. (Slept in train). July 10.—(Varna). Arrived in morning, and settled site of Stafford Hospital; arranged details. July 11.—Returned towards Shumla, after arranging contract about site of hospital and alterations in house. Report of heavy fighting between Shumla and Rustchuk, which proved false. (Slept in train). July 12.—(Shumla). Called again at camp. Long conversation with medical board

and others. Received well by Abdul Kerim, Commander-in-Chief, &c. Arranged about transport service under Borthwick. Began by undertaking evacuation of 500 sick (invalided) from Shumla; accompanied them from the station. Supplied them with refreshments and help. Namyk Pacha inspected hospitals with me. Took list of requirements. July 13.—(Slept in train and at Varna). Arrived in Varna at 2 A.M. with 100 sick. Arranged with civil governor for gates of town to be opened, and carts sent to bring sick to hospital for the night. Five dangerously ill. July 14.—(On s.s. *Austria*). Arranged details about Varna hospital, and left further money for Borthwick and Crookshank at Ottoman Bank. Embarked late. 150 sick on board. July 15.—(Constantinople). Arrived in afternoon. Supplied sick with necessary comforts, lemonade, syrup, &c. They were taken off on arrival. July 16.—(Therapia). Called on Mr. Layard, after purchasing stores, &c., for Asia, Varna, and Rustchuk. July 17 to 20.—(Constantinople). Arranging expedition of stores, hire of infirmiers, selected stretchers, and assisted in committee meetings of Red Crescent. Assisted in getting papers required for National Society staff just arrived. Made designs for new ambulance carriage for Red Crescent, &c.

Mr. BARRINGTON-KENNETT'S reports.

First convoy of sick.

* * * * * * * * * *

I shall take care that the stores which I buy here or you send me from England shall be distributed under the control of our own or other English doctors, or such responsible men as the staff of the Ottoman Bank, &c. The National Society staff arrived about two or three days ago. They offered to carry our stores, and co-operate with us in every way; of course, I agreed to work as far as possible in co-operation with them, and thus all hands will be strengthened. I have drawn up to the present moment 1,158 Turkish pounds, including provision for Rustchuk for two months (300*l*.), transport service, Borthwick (200*l*. and stores), Varna (50*l*. and stores), Reade, for Kustendje district (50*l*.), Melgund (40*l*.), Casson (100*l*.), and large supply of stores; Mrs. Layard's committee (100*l*.) I shall have to provide for Casson's second 100*l*., and for further stores for Varna and Asia.

Arrival of National Aid Society's staff.

Pera, July 31, 1877.

I have occupied myself with forwarding Lord Blantyre's surgeons, and providing them with papers, firmans, diplomas, dragomans, and, when necessary, money, in the same way as Stafford House surgeons. This, I believe, is in accordance with the wish of the Committee. Five out of these fourteen surgeons sent out have served with me in Servia, and they will be most valuable, owing to their previous practice in gunshot wounds. On July 12 I sent Mr. Johnson with stores and infirmiers to Rustchuk. On July 23 I sent Lieut. Drummond with stores to Erzeroum according to list sent by British Consul at Erzeroum. I obtain now free passages for personnel and matériel. The *Brightman* bringing our stores is delayed at Malta owing to the death of her captain. I have been appointed one of the Committee of Installation of Red Crescent hospitals. Owing to your letter about funds, I shall leave further expenses for matériel at Varna to the Red Crescent Society, which has now in hand nearly 16,000*l*. I have been very much occupied with the Installation Committee, and the Red Crescent will in return furnish our Stafford House and Lord Blantyre's surgeons with matériel for flying ambulances, should they require it. All the societies, the National Aid, Red Crescent, Stafford House, and Lord Blantyre's surgeons, are working hand in hand. It is the first time I have seen so much good feeling and sensible co-operation, from which immense benefits for the great end, the good of the wounded, will inevitably result. The Government authorities are assisting us in every way. I go to the front to-day with Hayes, Wattie, and Boyd. The Red Crescent are most anxious that I should establish a transport service for them also, and have voted a credit for it. I may do so if I have a good opportunity, and place one of our surgeons in charge. I engaged two surgeons here for Varna hospital. All is going well. The non-arrival of the ship with our stores from England is a great *contretemps*, but we shall make the best of it. Attwood and party are already in the front beyond Adrianople, and Edmunds and party somewhere in the front near Rasgrad or Rustchuk. I send al telegrams *free*, and they are not examined; this makes me doubly careful in not giving you war news. You will easily understand how necessary is this precaution. I am expect

Lord Blantyre's surgeons.

All societies co-operating

Mr. BARRINGTON-KENNETT'S reports.

ing Pratt by the next mail, and shall ask him to remain at Pera until my return from the front. I supplied Attwood and party with 200 liras; Edmunds and party with 50 liras; Buckby and Guppy with 10 liras. I have also bought large supplies of stores from the firm of Della Sudda; these have all gone to the front, to Asia and the Rustchuk district. I called last Sunday on Mr. Layard and informed him of our work; he seemed quite satisfied. Dr. Sarell and Dr. Bartoletti of the Quarantine assisted me in purchasing stores before Attwood came; the latter chose his own stores for Adrianople, as also Edmunds for those he took to Shumla. I consult the doctors who are proceeding to the front as to the stores they require, as different doctors like different selections of medicines.

Report from MR. E. R. PRATT

(*Acting as Chief Commissioner*).

Pera, Aug. 8, 1877.

Mr. PRATT's report.

Arrival of stores from England.

The stores you entrusted to me were landed and placed in the Red Crescent magazine last Saturday. Kennett arrived here from Varna on Sunday, and left for Adrianople on Monday. Operating cases, bandages, lint, splints, and quinine have been sent to Adrianople. Operating cases and sheets were sent to Varna yesterday; some medicines are ready to go on Friday. Splints have been sent to Erzeroum.

Reports from MR. BARRINGTON-KENNETT, Chief Commissioner.

(*Continued.*)

Constantinople, Sept. 12, 1877.

Mr. BARRINGTON-KENNETT's reports.

Organisation of Roumelian railway transport and soup-kitchen.

All our sections have been hard at work since my last report. At one time, three sections were at work upon the field at once. Our soup-kitchens at Tchorlou and Constantinople work very well, and every two or three days trains pass full of wounded who are supplied with the nourishment of which they are in such need. At the last two arrivals of wounded, Nouri Pacha, President of the Medical Council of the War Office, and other members of the Council, came down to inspect our arrangements, and they one and all expressed themselves highly satisfied. It was difficult to make the wounded men believe that it was the Stafford House Committee which was providing them with soup, coffee, tobacco, &c.; they think that no one but the Sultan could supply them with such good things. At Constantinople, the cost per head for soup, coffee, bread, and, if necessary, milk, is one piastre and a half (threepence), all included. At Tchorlou it is slightly more. My original opinion was that the greatest want likely to be experienced by the Turkish ambulances would be the absence of any proper organisation for transporting wounded on a large scale, and that we ought to come to their aid in this important branch of their ambulance service. The Stafford House transport services already in work are doing excellent work. Dr. Barker has just arrived with a train of 401 wounded. Four waggons of the train were fitted up with eight beds each for the most seriously wounded. The train was accompanied by the special ambulance brake-van of Stafford House. At Adrianople every man's wounds were dressed, and the worst cases were dressed again to-day by Dr. Barker and his staff. The whole of the wounded received soup and other refreshments at the Stafford House soup-kitchen establishments at Tirnova, Tchorlou, and Stamboul.

Constantinople, Sept. 17, 1877.

I enclose you some extracts of reports received since my last. I shall write you fully next week on money matters, sending you detailed accounts and estimates to the end of

CHIEF COMMISSIONER'S REPORTS.

August. I am practising every economy, but my estimates cannot be kept below 1,000*l.* per month, and, if I am to support Lord Blantyre's surgeons, my outlay must be more. I have to give up an important service which I was organising for removing the heavily wounded from Philippopolis to Constantinople for want of funds. I hope that you can put this before the Committee. It is such a pity that I have to reduce my operations at this critical moment simply for want of funds. Our sections in the Danube district are doing capitally, working on the field, while the transport services attached to them remove the wounded to the line; they are here taken up by our railway transport.

_{Mr. Barrington-Kennett's reports.}

Constantinople, Sept. 19, 1877.

I enclose you herewith some extracts of reports received. I enclose also the extract from my general account up to the end of August. The reports speak for themselves. I need not comment upon the awful misery and distress among the wounded in every district. It is with feelings of the greatest reluctance that, for want of funds, I find myself unable to extend or even strengthen our different sections. Please make every exertion to secure further subscriptions at this critical moment. All our sections are working extremely well; Dr. Neylan at Philippopolis has secured for our staff a high and responsible position.

I regret to have to report that Neylan is returning temporarily invalided with dysentery, as also Drs. Beresford and Lake, but I hope they will be able to resume their positions.

_{Illness of Drs. Neylan, Beresford and Lake.}

Mr. Pratt is working well and energetically in the Varna and Shumla district. Our soup-kitchens are still working well; over 4,000 wounded have been received and attended to at each of them. The ranks of the Red Crescent have just received a great addition in the person of Baron Mundy.

_{Mr. Pratt's district.}

Constantinople, Sept. 21, 1877.

I find myself obliged to restrict my operations for want of funds, so much so that I cannot supply a properly equipped field-ambulance for the last batch of our surgeons sent out. I might attach them to Turkish military hospitals, but as I consider that under existing circumstances the services of these surgeons can be best employed *in the field*, I have with their consent transferred their services to the Red Crescent Society. These surgeons will form the personnel of the largest and most important field-ambulance yet attached to any of the Turkish armies. It will be under the direct command of Baron Mundy, M.D., Professor of Military Hygiene, Imperial University of Vienna, and Head Surgeon of the Order of Malta. The ambulance will consist of five sections, each containing one surgeon, two dressers, and twenty-five stretcher-bearers. There will be one surgeon-in-chief, and perhaps some supernumerary surgeons. The medical staff will be mounted, and the sections will be accompanied by convoys of native waggons. It will work under the Red Crescent, but will be subsidised by Stafford House stores. In my quality of member of the 'Committee of Organisation' of the Red Crescent, I do not lose all control over the operation and management of this ambulance. The Mundy ambulance will operate in the Plevna district, which I agreed to leave to the care of the Red Crescent. Eight surgeons of the Stafford House Committee and of Lord Blantyre left this morning for Philippopolis, on their way to the front. Mr. Cullen and Dr. Sketchley are waiting for them at Philippopolis, with the horses and conveyances which they had purchased for our Stafford House Plevna ambulance and transport, but which will now be handed over to the Red Crescent at cost price. Want of means, and *this alone*, compelled me to abandon the Plevna ambulance, which is sure to do splendid service. It is, however, a consolation to me to know that it will be in good hands, and worked by men chosen by Stafford House. The Red Crescent hospitals of Doyler Boy (300 wounded), Kavac (250 wounded), and Dr. Sarell's hospital established at the Ecole Militaire (80 wounded) have been supplied with nearly the whole of their medical stores, blankets, &c., from the Stafford House depôt. These hospitals are in full working order under European surveillance. In conclusion, I beg to make an earnest appeal for further funds for Stafford House. It is heartrending to be cramped in one's work at such a terrible crisis. With our organisation in good working order, as it now is, every 100*l.* will relieve an immense amount of misery, and save the lives of many brave men.

_{Transfer of S. H. surgeons to the Red Crescent Society.}

_{Large supplies of stores given to Red Crescent society.}

RECORD OF OPERATIONS.

Constantinople, Sept. 26, 1877.

Mr. Barrington Kennett's reports.

Plevna ambulance.

Dr. Moore has gone towards Plevna, and has probably arrived there by this time. Chefket Pacha, to whom he is attached, is very desirous that we should form a hospital at Orkhanie, where large numbers of wounded are expected, and no provision has been made. I am sending up stores and what money I can spare. Mr. Pratt, who has just come down to Constantinople from the army of Mehemet Ali, reports that our surgeons are doing good work with the several divisions to which they are attached. Drs. Lake and Beresford, who have been for some time on the sick list, are recovering. I regret to state that Dr. Weller is seriously ill. He is, however, receiving every care at Philippopolis.

Constantinople, Sept. 28, 1877.

Dr. Sarell.

I enclose reports. All our sections continue working well. Dr. Moore is at Orkhanie, between Sofia and Plevna. I am sending Dr. Sketchley to assist him, and forwarding him large supplies of stores. The last two batches of doctors whom you sent out are now at Philippopolis, on their way to the front under the Red Crescent. Dr. Sarell takes command of this English Red Crescent ambulance in the place of Baron Mundy, who remains at Constantinople for the present, and is superintending the construction of a hospital barrack, floating hospital, and railway ambulance wagons. Dr. Beresford is better, and also Dr. Lake.

Constantinople, Oct. 10, 1877.

Sickness among surgeons.

Dr. Weller is here seriously ill with fever and diarrhœa. He is being attended by Dr. Baron Mundy, Dr. Patteson, of the English hospital, and Dr. Neylan. I am glad to say that to-day's report is much more favourable. Dr. Beresford is convalescent. The report from Sofia is that Dr. Sketchley is recovering. Nearly all our doctors have been more or less ill from fever.

Explosion at Makrikeui.

There was a large explosion yesterday morning at Makrikeui (a village a little distance from Constantinople) in the Government powder manufactory. Immediately on hearing it I ordered an ambulance section to proceed to the spot; it consisted of Dr. Neylan, Mr. Williams (storekeeper), and other assistants, with ten stretchers and all necessary medical stores. Mr. Kuhlman, the director of the railway line, put a special train at our disposal, which brought us to the scene of the disaster. Unfortunately nearly all the victims (120) were blown to atoms, so there was but little work for us to do. Fifteen survivors were taken to a hospital close by.

Constantinople, Oct. 24, 1877.

Transfer of Varna staff and Dr. Stoker.

Mr. Pratt is remaining in the Shumla district, and will devote especial attention to the Rustchuk hospital. I am shortly going to hand over Drs. Cullen and Kouvaras to the Red Crescent Society, as the Varna hospital, of which they have charge, is supported entirely at the cost of that society. For a similar reason I am handing over Dr. Stoker. There has been a lull in active operations in Bulgaria. Our sections have carried out their instructions and devoted their services to the sick as well as wounded, as you will see from reports enclosed.

Dr. Neylan.

Dr. Neylan has been appointed surgeon at the hospital established in the Military School, Stamboul. He will hold a high position there, with Turkish medical students under him.

Relief to Asia.

Drs. Pinkerton and Denniston (Lord Blantyre's) left last Monday by steamer for Trebizond, en route to strengthen Casson's section. Dr. Weller is now quite out of danger, but I think he ought to leave Turkey as soon as he can travel. Dr. Woods has arrived here from Philippopolis, temporarily invalided, as also Dr. Sketchley from Sofia. The Stafford House medical staff at Adrianople has been provided with excellent quarters in the hospital itself, which is well situated about a mile from the town. They are on good terms with the chief medical officers, and are frequently called in to perform operations in the Turkish hospitals. I have forwarded quinetum and brandy to Silistria to Dr. Niamara,

Relief to Silistria.

an English chief surgeon of the 1st and 2nd divisions, at his urgent request. 1,800 sick of his two divisions are under treatment, for malarian fever principally.

CHIEF COMMISSIONER'S REPORTS. 21

I have forwarded other stores to Dr. Milligan, Batoum, at his request. Dr. McCormac particularly recommended Dr. Milligan to me when the latter accepted his appointment in the Imperial Service.

Mr. BARRINGTON-KENNETT's reports.

Constantinople, Nov. 2, 1877.

Dr. Weller is still lying in a very precarious state. He is being nursed at Mrs. Cullen's house (the wife of Dr. Cullen of the Varna hospital). Dr. Barker has returned to Constantinople temporarily invalided. Dr. Sketchley has returned to duty at Adrianople. I regret to state that I have received a letter from the British Embassy, informing me that Buckby, being still ill with typhoid fever, Casson and he had been left behind in Kars.

Relief to Batoum. Illness of doctors.

Constantinople, Nov. 7, 1877.

I have detached Sandwith from Dr. Attwood's section, and appointed him to the S.H. section at Adrianople, an increased medical staff having become necessary, on account of the 200 beds we are taking over. Drs. Pinkerton and Denniston have arrived safely at Erzeroum.

Adrianople.

Constantinople, Nov. 14, 1877.

In consequence of a telegram from Sir Arnold Kemball, forwarded to me by Mr. Layard on Saturday night, and urgently requesting immediate help in Asia, I despatched by Monday's boat to Trebizond en route to Erzeroum, a field ambulance, consisting of Dr. Ryan, lately returned from Plevna, Dr. Woods (Lord Blantyre's), a dragoman and two volunteers who have already done good service in our ranks, Mr. Morisot and Mr. Harvey. A full supply of medical and surgical stores, blankets, &c., were also sent off. In addition, Dr. Ryan took with him 150*l*. I shall take care that nothing is wanting to ensure the efficiency of this ambulance.

Departure of Dr. Ryan's staff for Asia.

Constantinople, Nov. 21, 1877.

I beg to report that on Nov. 18, an ambulance section started for Sofia, consisting of the following personnel, viz. :—Dr. Busby, surgeon-in-chief ; Dr. Wattie, surgeon ; Dr. Boyd, assistant-surgeon ; Mr. Cullen, secretary ; Constantin, dragoman ; one groom (with three horses) ; an ambulance wagon, &c., also 33 cases of matériel. The exact destination of this section will be decided by Dr. Busby on his arrival at Sofia, where he will have the choice, either of attaching himself to Mehemet Ali Pacha's newly formed army, which will shortly move towards Plevna, or of taking over a wing of the military hospital at Sofia. I am glad to be able to report to you that the medical authorities at the Seraskeriat afforded me every facility in despatching this ambulance section to its destination.

Departure of Sofia section.

Captain Burnaby called to see me on his arrival at Constantinople. I have given him a letter to take to Osman Pacha in case he should visit Plevna. The letter enquires after the state of the wounded, and offers to send medical help if necessary. I supplied Admiral Hobart with a selection of medical stores to be distributed under his personal supervision on the occasion of his last leaving for the fleet. I have received information from Trebizond stating that Dr. Ryan's party with some of the stores started for Erzeroum immediately after their arrival, and Williams followed them with the remaining stores yesterday. I have to-day received a telegram from Dr. Stiven, Rustchuk, informing me that a battle took place yesterday near Kadikeui, that he and Dr. Lake served on the field, while Dr. Beresford attended to the wounded on their arrival at the Stafford House hospital, 180 beds of which were filled with serious cases. This hospital has been of great service during all the recent engagements near Kadikeui and Pyrgos. It is within range of the Russian batteries, but being nearly a mile distant from the town, there is no danger of any shells falling into it by accident during the periodical bombardments which take place.

Supplies to Turkish fleet. Dr. Ryan. Battle of Kadikeui.

Letter from MR. BARRINGTON-KENNETT to SIR A. H. LAYARD.

(*On the evacuation of the Turkish wounded from Plevna.*)

376 Grand Rue, Nov. 27, 1877.

SIR,—The circumstances attending the departure of the English surgeons from Plevna having been much commented upon, I think it my duty to lay before your Excellency the facts of the case founded upon the reports of Dr. Ryan, Dr. Mackellar, and Dr. Bond Moore, and also the opinion I have formed on these and verbal reports from other members of the Stafford House Plevna ambulance.

Dr. Bond Moore, with an ambulance section, was attached to the Sultan's Circassian Guard, commanded by Kiazim Pacha, and accompanied them in the Plevna district, in advance of Shefket Pacha's relieving column. He was accompanied by Dr. Mackellar, one of Lord Blantyre's surgeons, whose services had been lent to the Red Crescent Society. Dr. Bond Moore, when at Tillich, hearing of the great distress in Plevna, detached his ambulance from the Circassian Guard, and proceeded to Plevna, where he arrived late at night, and where it appears that he was somewhat badly received by the Caïmacam (Governor of the town), when he called to ask him for quarters.

The following day the whole party had an interview with Osman Pacha, who received them courteously, and thanked them for their offer of remaining in Plevna to attend to the wounded. He however requested them, rather than remain in Plevna, to proceed to Sofia, on which town he intended evacuating at once nearly all his wounded, and where he considered that their services would be most required.

I wish here to call special attention to the fact that all the three surgeons agree in stating that Osman Pacha personally was courteous and polite to them.

There may have been coolness, amounting to incivility, on the part of the Caïmacam, whose position is invariably a most unenviable one, and perhaps the interrogations of Tahir Bey, the head of the staff, were felt by the surgeons to be superfluous under the circumstances of Dr. Bond Moore having a 'Boyourouldon' from the Grand Vizier, and all his other papers in order. Foreign surgeons, however, entering a fortified position of the importance of Plevna in the middle of the night, and without previous notice being given of their arrival, must be prepared to put up with little annoyances of this description, so trifling in comparison with the momentous events occurring round them.

With regard to the telegram of Osman Pacha, mentioned by Dr. Mackellar, requesting for Austrian and French but not English surgeons, I should remark that this information was based on hearsay, and, even if confirmed, cannot be construed as a discourtesy towards the English as a nation.

Osman Pacha has been severely and, I think, unjustly criticised on account of his decision to evacuate all his wounded from Plevna—a measure which, owing to the rude means of transport at his disposal, entailed undoubtedly an immense amount of human suffering, and many deaths amongst the severest cases. But I beg here to call attention to the fact that the majority of the cases were slight (see Dr. Ryan's report). This decision of Osman Pacha may be looked upon from two points of view—viz. *military* and *sanitary*.

From a *military* point of view, it must be remembered, he had before him the prospect of a siege, and it was therefore his imperative duty to reduce, as far as possible, the number of mouths to be fed. In addition, there was every probability of an epidemic breaking out amongst the wounded, which might extend beyond the hospitals, and seriously diminish the number of fighting men. About this there can be no difference of opinion.

With reference to the *sanitary* point of view opinions differ. Dr. Ryan, who had been fifteen months in the Turkish service, and had been during the last five of them in Plevna itself, and who was therefore far better acquainted with the conditions of the wounded than any of our surgeons could be, considers Osman Pacha justified. He gives as his reasons the

impossibility of providing proper food and surgical appliances, and the unhealthy over- Mr.
crowded state of the hospitals, impregnated as they were with septic germs, making it BARRINGTON-
extremely probable that some serious epidemic would break out. He also calls attention to Letter to Sir
the outbreak of cholera at Plevna about seventeen years ago. Dr. Mackellar, of St. A. Layard.
Thomas's, who has had the experience of three campaigns, speaking as a professional
man, considers that Osman Pacha was not justified in evacuating, without splints or other
apparatus, certain severe cases of fracture which he observed; and he complains, moreover,
of his offer of extemporising some such apparatus not being accepted by the medical
authorities (not Osman Pacha).

Great allowance must be made for the hurry and confusion which attended this evacuation; those responsible for its execution being in hourly expectation of their retreat being cut
off. It must also be remembered that Dr. Mackellar's services were so far highly appreciated
by these same Turkish medical authorities that they invited him to a consultation on many of
the most important cases, and paid him the highest compliment for which a medical man
could wish, in requesting him to operate on any cases he might select as being of special
difficulty. Dr. Mackellar accordingly performed several major operations in presence of the
principal members of the medical staff.

Dr. Bond Moore in his report agrees with Dr. Mackellar in condemning the evacuation
of the severe cases, and protested strongly against it in a letter addressed to Osman Pacha,
a copy of which is in your Excellency's hands. On the other hand, he states that Osman
Pacha so far acceded to his suggestions as to order the wounded to be taken as far as
Orkhanie only, instead of to Sofia, as originally ordered by him.

I have been associated with the working of six field ambulances, four hospitals, and two
systems of railway transport, during the greater part of the present war, and consider that
the Stafford House staff, including myself, have always received kindness and courtesy at the
hands of the Commanders-in-Chief, and (with very few exceptions), at those of the other
military officials. Jealousies and bad feeling have occasionally arisen between doctors of
different nationalities and different schools, and difficulties in consequence arisen, but I can
state from an experience of four campaigns that this is by no means peculiar to Turkey.

I have the honour to enclose the reports of Dr. Ryan, also an extract of Dr. Bond
Moore's report, and have notified in the margin the passages most important to the subject
of this letter.

Apologising for having troubled you at such length,
I have the honour to remain, &c.
V. BARRINGTON-KENNETT,
Chief Commissioner representing the Stafford House Committee.

To His Excellency the Right Hon. A. H. Layard.

Reports of MR. E. R. PRATT.

(*Acting as Chief Commissioner.*)
Tatar-Bazardjik, Dec. 20, 1877.

I arrived at Adrianople on Wednesday, Dec. 5. Dr. McIvor and the surgeons with him Mr. PRATT's
were working well. There had been several deaths from exhaustion, apparently owing to reports.
exposure during transport and want of necessary food. I brought up a large quantity of
stores, including blankets, and, with a few trivial exceptions, these surgeons are well supplied.
Dr. Barker still appears to render great service to the wounded during their railway transport. Dr. Calfoglou has entered the Committee's service, and assists Dr. Minassian at the
Philippopolis hospital. Hearing from Dr. Barker the condition in which he received the Soup-kitchen
wounded arriving from Sofia at Tatar-Bazardjik, I immediately had built a small wooden at Bazardjik.

Mr. Pratt's reports.	barrack as a soup-kitchen, and five days afterwards the next convoy of wounded received soup before starting on their railway journey. On repassing to-day I saw that 450 sick and
General report on S. H. relief in Bulgaria.	wounded from Sofia (who had arrived under the care of one of the Red Crescent surgeons) received soup, tobacco, firing, and other requisites. A similar ration will be given to-morrow morning, before embarking on Dr. Barker's transport. Drs. Busby, Wattie, and
Sofia.	Boyd are working well at Sofia, having three Turkish houses, with about 50 wounded in each, under their charge. They had, however, several difficulties to combat with regard to administration. 150 beds, with all requisites, are now ready, and, owing to the kindness of Kirkor Bey, the médecin-en-chef, a large hospital pavilion has been placed at their service. I herewith enclose Dr. Busby's report. Before arriving at Sofia I met a convoy of bullock arabas with 180 wounded proceeding to Tatar-Bazardjik. On seeing their condition I immediately attached to the convoy J. Görlitz, a Stafford House pharmacien, who was with me. He was of great assistance in insuring their proper housing at night, and in purchasing soup and bread whenever it was possible to do so. Hearing from Captain Burnaby at Sofia that three English surgeons in the Turkish service were in great need of medicines and other necessaries, I took up to the front the next morning two cases and one bale of selected stores. Undoubtedly here the great deficiency is that of properly organised transport. The sick and
Sufferings during transport.	wounded men are carried in bullock arabas over bad roads in snow and rain, with no further covering than their thin greatcoats, and often with an insufficient ration of bread ; owing to the exigencies of the case, many men are transported who are physically unfit to bear the fatigue of so long a journey—some absolutely dying on the road, and others arriving at their destination in a sinking condition. I commenced arrangements for the amelioration of this transport, but at the special request of Dr. Sarell, of the Red Crescent Society, I have ceded this work to him. He sent me yesterday an official answer to the effect that he has two surgeons, with dressers, and hospital servants, supplied with money, clothing, and necessary requisites, already engaged for this service. I shall supplement his work if necessary. I find I could save a great amount of suffering with blankets, socks, and woollen underclothing.
Distribution of ambulances.	There are 5,200 wounded in Sofia. The district is at present well supplied with European surgeons, there being at the front at Kamarli three English surgeons in the Turkish service, two Red Crescent surgeons and three National Aid Society's surgeons, five Red Crescent surgeons at Tashkesen (between Kamarli and Sofia) ; in Lady Strangford's hospital at Sofia, one surgeon, and four nurses ; on the transport between Sofia and Tatar-Bazardjik two Red Crescent surgeons, and eleven German surgeons in Turkish service. The Egyptian and Turkish Government hospitals are doing good service, the former with two surgeons and three dressers. I shall inspect the Philippopolis and Adrianople hospitals and Dr. Attwood's ambulance, and report their condition to you before returning to Constantinople.

Constantinople, Dec. 26, 1877.

Formation of Surgeon Sketchley's section.	Assistant-Surgeon Sketchley and Messrs. Banfather and Williams will start immediately to Tatar-Bazardjik, and the district beyond, with a supply of waterproofed sheeting, blankets, clothing, sheets, and money, to ameliorate as far as possible the condition of the wounded during their transport. Dr. Attwood's ambulance has gone to Ichtiman, to follow wherever fighting is probable. Dr. McQueen's ambulance, which has crossed the Balkans with Fuad Pacha's division, will remain attached to it, and proceed in the same direction.

Reports from MR. STONEY

(*Acting as Chief Commissioner*).

Constantinople, Jan. 16, 1878.

I have just received your telegram of 15th inst. enquiring if Stafford House funds are being disbursed on any other charity than the relief of sick and wounded Turkish soldiers, and have telegraphed reply:—'Stafford House funds expended only on sick and wounded Turkish soldiers. Write to-day.' Our soup contractor has a contract to supply, on the same terms as ourselves, the Committee of the Turkish Compassionate Fund and the representative of Baron Hirsch's Committee. The trains arrive crowded with wounded soldiers and fugitives. The soldiers are served first, the refugees after. Stafford House pays for the rations served to the soldiers, the other societies for the fugitives. The soup-kitchen and boilers are the property of Stafford House. The service is paid for by the contractor. Trains arrive at all hours without sufficient, sometimes without any, notice—such is the confusion on the line. The plan adopted of having one contractor for all three societies insures a supply of soup always ready day and night, a result which could not be so economically and so satisfactorily arrived at in any other manner.

Mr. Stoney's reports.

Co-operation with Compassionate Fund and Baron Hirsch.

Constantinople, Jan. 19, 1878.

No information from Erzeroum since Dec. 31 until last night, when a letter dated 2nd inst. was received from Dr. Denniston. Dr. Stoker, who happened to be here, at once volunteered to go up to the assistance of his friend Dr. Ryan, and as I can spare Dr. Stiven for a time, he will go too. They sail this afternoon for Trebizond, taking with them medical comforts and such stores as they consider may be useful. Mr. Layard will give them letters to Sir Arnold Kemball, who can perhaps facilitate their movements. I cannot obtain information about any of our sections in Roumelia, with the exception of Adrianople, where the hospitals have all been evacuated to make room for fresh cases in the event of further fighting.

Relief to invalided staff in Asia.

Constantinople, Jan. 25, 1878.

My letters of last week will in part have prepared you for the sad news contained in the letters of Mr. Biliotti and Dr. Denniston. I very much fear poor Ryan will not pull through. If he should, however, Stoker and Stiven will soon be with him, and their instructions are to bring the survivors out of Erzeroum at once, and return to Constantinople with them as quickly as their condition will allow. There is no use wasting more valuable lives in a pest-house. Since Jan. 12 I have no news of the western sections, but suppose Sketchley's, Attwood's, and McQueen's to be falling back with Suleiman's army, which by latest report is supposed to be near Lagos, on the southern coast. Of Busby's sections you may perhaps have had news through Russian sources; we have had none. McIvor's party from Adrianople have arrived here, and will remain for a few days until it shall be determined whether we are to have further fighting or not. If a resistance should be made on the lines of Constantinople, they will go out as an ambulance party. Having heard that a large influx of wounded was expected at Salonica, I telegraphed to the British Consul there to know if assistance was required. His reply was—'Authorities say no need now of assistance for wounded soldiers.'

Critical position of staff at Erzeroum.

376 Grand Rue, Pera, Feb. 1, 1878.

Herewith I beg to forward (1) a tabulated statement of the total expenditure on the various sections up to date; (2) a statement of our liabilities to date; (3) a rough estimate for the month of February; (4) an abstract of doctors' accounts for salary to date; (5) the cash account for the month past. The tabular statement will eventually be considerably modified when the final accounts are received from the several sections, but the total amount will remain the same. I have sent out two ambulance sections to the lines of Constantinople

Ambulances sent to the lines of defence.

RECORD OF OPERATIONS.

Mr. Stoney's reports. near Haidemkeui—Dr. McIver with Dr. Kirker and Dr. Barker with Dr. Edmunds. Their base of operation is at Hademkeui, where they have two railway wagons on a siding. The soldiers, sick, weary, and worn from the retreat from Bazardjik, arrive in a deplorable condition, barefooted and half clad. I had 250 blankets in store, which I have sent out, and would have purchased more, but that your letter advised me of the dispatch of 2,000 from England. I hope they will arrive soon, as the want of covering is severely felt by the poor fellows. The three ambulance sections—Attwood's, McQueen's, and Sketchley's—are still with the army of Suleiman at Port Lagos, or on the way up attending to the wounded at his request.

Pera, Feb. 8, 1878.

Sufferings of surgeons taken prisoners. Suleiman Pacha's generals, Chakir, Baker, Osman Nouri, and Fuad, like to have our surgeons attached to their divisions. It was clearly their duty, as attached to flying ambulances, to stick to their divisions as they did. Dr. Kirkpatrick (one of those transferred to the Red Crescent by Stafford House), Drs. Leslie and Neville, of the Red Cross, and Mr. Bell, artist (*Illustrated London News*), arrived yesterday from Adrianople in wretched plight. They had been taken prisoners at Tashkessen, and have suffered terribly at the hands of the Russians, who robbed them of everything, and marched them on foot through Bulgaria and over the Shipka Pass to Adrianople. There Consul Blunt had them liberated, and took their depositions, which go by this mail from Mr. Layard to Lord Derby.

Reports from MR. BARRINGTON-KENNETT, *Chief Commissioner.*

(*Continued.*)

Constantinople, Feb. 22, 1878.

Mr. Barrington-Kennett's reports. I have the honour to report to the Committee my arrival here on Feb. 16. Several of our ambulances have been broken up during the recent disasters. The surgeons of these, with few exceptions, returned to Constantinople shortly before my arrival. I cannot praise too highly the skill and energy with which Mr. Stoney has conducted our affairs during the crisis through which they have just passed, and at the same time I am glad to report that all the members of our staff, both in the front and at Constantinople, have done their duty to a man, under difficult and trying circumstances.

The following is a short *résumé* of the operations and routes of some of our sections during the retreat of the Turkish armies. I follow the order of the accompanying printed monthly list.

Bombardment of Rustchuk hospital. *Rustchuk section* (Drs. Stiven, Lake, and Beresford, with assistants).—The Stafford House hospital at Rustchuk was bombarded on Dec. 29 and 30; patients removed to Rustchuk, and on Jan. 5 evacuated to Varna. On 9th matériel sent to Varna, and steps taken to form a hospital there.

Relief to Erzeroum section. On Jan. 19 Dr. Stiven was sent, together with Dr. Stoker, to the assistance of our Erzeroum section. Owing to the large number of refugees flocking into Varna, and occupying every available building, and the presence of a great many surgeons of the Turkish service who had retired from the front, it was not considered expedient to form a hospital at Varna, and accordingly, on Feb. 10, Drs. Lake and Beresford returned to Constantinople, leaving all our outstanding matériel in charge of Dr. Hayes, who has since forwarded the greater part to Constantinople. No matériel lost.

Erzeroum section (Drs. Ryan and Stoker, Capt. Morisot, T. Williams).—Affairs went on well at Erzeroum until the end of December, when there were in full working order, the Stafford House hospital under Dr. Ryan, with over 300 patients, and the English hospital under Dr. Fetherstonhaugh, with 100 patients. Dr. Fetherstonhaugh then fell ill, and giving over the hospital to Dr. Denniston, returned to England. Dr. Pinkerton, who was suffering at the same time from the fever which ended fatally, was too ill to be moved. Subsequently Dr. Ryan, Mr. Morisot, and Williams their dragoman, were taken ill with the same fever, and Dr. Denniston, with Turkish surgeons, took charge of both hospitals until Drs. Stiven and Stoker came to the rescue; since then the three invalids have partially recovered, and Drs. Ryan, Stoker, and Denniston are carrying on our work with their hospitals full. Dr. Stiven and Mr. Morisot are on their way home. Mr. BARRINGTON-KENNETT'S reports.

Adrianople section (Drs. McIvor, Kirker, Sandwith, Stewart, and Azzopardi, Dispenser Spanopoulos, J. Cowan).—Everything went on smoothly until Jan. 18, when official information was given of the impending occupation of the town by the Russians. Dr. McIvor evacuated his 130 remaining wounded by rail; left his matériel in charge of the British Consul; sent horses and hospital attendants by road to Constantinople. All matériel saved except beds, which could not be transported. Hospital burnt.

Philippopolis (late Eccles') section (Drs. Minassian and Calfoglou, Dispenser Theodore Akestorides).—On retreating through Philippopolis (Jan. 14), Suleiman Pacha asked the British Consul if any Stafford House doctors would volunteer to remain there with those wounded who could not be evacuated in time to escape capture. Dr. Minassian at once volunteered, and two English doctors in the Turkish service being placed under his immediate orders, he was left in charge of all military and civil hospitals. He was well supplied with Stafford House stores by Drs. Hume and Sandwith, who were passing through Philippopolis with the retreating army, and who thus saved their heavy stores from capture by the Russians. Communications are interrupted with Dr. Minassian, but I have every reason to believe that he and his wounded are doing well. I am sending Dr. Hume with further stores to his aid.

Sofia section (Drs. Busby and Wattie, Dispenser Görlitz, A. Colley).—The Stafford House hospital at Sofia consisted of 150 beds, and was well supplied with matériel. During the last few days of December as many of the wounded as possible were evacuated in compliance with orders from head-quarters, while fresh wounded came in from the actions at Tashkessen. On the night of Jan. 2 the town was evacuated, and on the following morning a panic took place among the wounded at this and the other hospitals, and all who could leave their beds rushed out from the hospital; those who did not perish from the cold were captured by the Russians and brought back. The town was occupied by the Russians on the 3rd. Dr. Busby and staff remained and attended to their wounded, as well as to others brought in by the Russians, many of them frost-bitten; in addition they tended the wounded, in some of the Turkish hospitals, who had been deserted in the panic, and were left in a most miserable condition. Order was subsequently restored. At the end of the month Dr. Busby considered that there was a sufficient number of surgeons, exclusive of his staff, to look after the remaining wounded in Sofia, and accordingly handed over his wounded and matériel to the Turkish medical authorities, whom the Russians left at liberty to discharge their duties. Dr. Busby, with his staff, returned to Constantinople by the only route permitted to him, namely, by Nisch, Belgrade, and Trieste. I may here add that General Gourko, who visited our hospital, highly complimented Dr. Busby on its condition. All matériel saved. Panic among wounded. Occupation by Russians.

Stamboul section (Dr. Neylan, with clinical class of Turkish medical students).— Dr. Neylan has been steadily employed at the Mundy barrack-hospital. His clinical class of students has been dispersed among different hospitals, but he expects a new class shortly. This hospital is always full of the severest cases. On the occasion of the railway accident near Tchataldja he proceeded immediately to the spot with Baron Mundy, and brought back the wounded.

Shipka section (Dr. Attwood, Dr. Sandwith, Dr. Hume).—Several other ambulances having been stationed at Shipka and the neighbourhood, I had given orders to this section to proceed to the front in the Sofia district where hostilities were imminent. Dr. Attwood and staff, with horses and matériel, proceeded, *viâ* Philippopolis and Bazardjik, to Ichtiman on the Sofia road, where they arrived on Jan. 5, after sending back Dr. Hume to recover his health and fetch money and stores from Constantinople. They here met Zabit Pacha, who informed them of the occupation of Sofia.

Leaving Ichtiman as the Russians entered it on the opposite side, they retired to Yetrena,

Mr. BARRINGTON-KENNETT's reports.

Retreat from Ichtiman.

where, at the request of Muchir Safvet Pacha, they obtained possession of some houses for a hospital and visited sick and wounded soldiers. They subsequently fell back on Bazardjik, and on Jan. 10 proceeded to Otloukehi, on which Chakir Pacha's and Baker Pacha's divisions had retired. They were able to assist very materially the ambulances of those divisions which had lost all their stores. The same night the retreat was made upon Bazardjik, which was extremely difficult, owing to the state of the roads and the wagons in consequence breaking down. Sandwith reached Bazardjik on the evening of the 11th, and, by advice of Baker Pacha, proceeded to Philippopolis. [Note.—It was afterwards ascertained that the party separated on the retreat from Otloukeui, Dr. Attwood remaining behind at the village of Pepensey in order to save the stores in the broken-down wagon. He was captured the following day by Cossacks, and, after suffering great hardships, was marched back to Otloukeui.]

On Jan. 14 Dr. Hume reached Philippopolis after a perilous journey along the line on a 'trolly' during the night, the Russians being in close proximity to the line, and all trains having in consequence stopped running. In the meantime Drs. Hume and Sandwith had joined at Bazardjik Dr. McQueen (from Elena) and Dr. Sketchley, with Banfather and Williams (from Samakov), and the united staff worked on the field during the three days' battle of

Battle of Stanimaka.

General retreat of ambulances across Rhodope Balkans.

Stanimaka at the foot of the Rhodope Balkans, south-east of Philippopolis. Under circumstances of great difficulty and no little danger they retreated with the beaten Turkish army over the mountains to the sea-coast at Porto Lagos. During the whole of the five days' weary march they attended to the 500 sick and wounded under their charge. With the exception of those who succumbed on the way, the whole of these were shipped on board the transport steamer *Sultanie* on Jan. 27. Our surgeons accompanied them as far as Constantinople, where they arrived on Feb. 2, bringing with them twelve of our ambulance horses. Mr. Young, Chief Commissioner of the National Aid Society, met our ambulance most opportunely at Porto Lagos, and supplied them with provisions, bandages, and warm clothing, of all of which our staff were in great want. I beg to call the special attention of the Committee to the great services rendered by these sections during the above retreat. Portions of the matériel, including heavy stores, were left with our section at Philippopolis ; a few cases were abandoned in the mountains at Stanimaka, owing to the impossibility of the transport up the mountain paths, covered, as they were, with ice.

Second Lom Ambulance section (Dr. McQueen, Dr. Edmunds).—After the battle of Elena Drs. McQueen and Edmunds accompanied their division (Fuad Pacha's) over the Balkans to Yamboli, where it was intended to form an ambulance, this being the terminus of the railway line nearest the Shipka army. Dr. Edmunds had returned to Constantinople to get money and stores, but in the meantime, about Jan. 11, the Russians cut off communications with Yamboli. Dr. McQueen accordingly joined Dr. Sketchley's section at Bazardjik on Jan. 11. and Dr. Edmunds, with stores, remained working with McIvor's section at Adrianople.

Rustchuk-Varna Railway Transport (Dr. Hayes, with assistants at two soup-kitchens).— Dr. Hayes continued accompanying the trains of wounded from the Danube district to Varna, until the destruction of the Rustchuk hospital, when he joined Stiven's staff and superintended the transport of his matériel and wounded to Varna. He remains there now to collect our matériel, distribute some of it, and forward the rest to Constantinople, and generally to wind up our affairs in his district.

Roumelian Railway Transport (Dr. Barker, with assistants at four soup-kitchens).—Dr. Barker was incessantly employed during the large influx of wounded to Constantinople, accompanying the trains, dressing the wounded *en route*, and superintending the soup-kitchens up the line. During the latter part of the great rush when there was such need at Stamboul, Dr. Barker, with Colley, by night, and Dr. Azzopardi with Monté by day, were engaged attending the wounded at the terminus. They all showed great devotion in this work.

Samakov section (Dr. Sketchley, E. H. Banfather, Roderick Williams).—This section arrived at Samakov on Jan. 4 with instructions to assist in the evacuation of wounded which had been ordered on the rapid advance of the Russians. On the 9th an action took place

Battle of Samakov.

near Samakov, and this section was engaged on the field till 2 A.M. the following day, and did great service, being the only ambulance with the army. After the battle they retreated with the army in charge of 110 wounded and 200 sick. They accompanied these during a

CHIEF COMMISSIONER'S REPORTS. 29

march, which lasted 20 consecutive hours, and arrived safely at Bazardjik, where they were joined by Drs. McQueen, Hume, and Sandwith, as stated above, and finally returned to Constantinople with their wounded. Part of matériel lost.

Mr. BARRINGTON-KENNETT'S reports.

We are now entering upon a new phase of our work. The following are the changes in our personnel and operations, namely :—Drs. McIvor, Kirker, and Woods returned to England, having concluded their service and being desirous of returning home. Dr. Wattie returned to England from Trieste on Feb. 9, for the same reasons. Drs. Busby, McQueen, and Sandwith will return to England next Saturday, Feb. 23, for the same reasons.

Re-organisation of sections.

I have begun the following new operations which I consider desirable in the altered state of circumstances :—1. Owing to the extreme poverty of the Government, it cannot afford to supply milk to the hundreds of cases of typhoid fever and dysentery among the soldiers in hospital here. I have therefore established a system of providing this in locked cans, sent to English doctors in the service of the Government. 2. I am giving each of such doctors a locked-up chest containing medical stores, which he will use for his own ward and also distribute to others under his own observation. 3. I have established an hospital in two new barracks erected by the Government in the gardens of Marco Pacha's hospital—150 beds. 4. Also an evacuation hospital and soup-kitchen at Kutchuk-Tchekmedje [afterwards transferred to Makrikeui], the head-quarters of Mukhtar Pacha in the lines before Constantinople. In the event of the Government sending a transport ship to fetch its wounded from Galatz or any other Danube port, I have offered to fit it up as a hospital-ship with mattresses, &c., and some medical stores.

I should add that the Government hospitals are in great want of every description of matériel, and we can sensibly ameliorate this bad position of affairs in the way I have indicated. To-day I had an interview with Prince Vladimir Mestchersky, President of the Russian Red Cross, on the subject of our ambulances left in Russian lines. This interview does away with the necessity of my visiting the Russian lines for the present, which is most fortunate, as I have plenty of work to do here. I am sending Dr. Hume with relief to Dr. Attwood and our Philippopolis section next Sunday. He is bearer of a letter of introduction from Prince Vladimir Mestchersky which will facilitate his journey up country. I have lent Dr. Barker's and Dr. Edmunds' services for a few days to the Compassionate Fund. They are engaged in discovering and isolating cases of small-pox and typhoid fever among the masses of fugitives crowded in the mosques, and also in vaccinating.

Assistance to Dr. Attwood.

Constantinople, March 1, 1878.

As the Committee is aware, Drs. Stiven and Stoker had been sent to Erzeroum by Mr. Stoney on receiving the bad news that Dr. Ryan and Messrs. Morisot and Williams were ill with typhus. Dr. Stoker in his report gives a graphic account of the journey up country, which was accomplished with great rapidity under most trying circumstances. Arrangements had been made by the British Consul at Trebizond, Mr. Biliotti, which enabled the party to start from that town two hours after they arrived by steamer from Constantinople. In a private letter from Dr. Ryan to Mr. Stoney, the former says, in reference to the arrival of the party : 'I can't tell you what a pleasure and unexpected surprise it was. Stoker is assisting me in the hospital and seems to be waiting orders before deciding whether he will remain or not; there's lots of work to do, but, if he is much wanted, I can and will get on without him. He himself is anxious to remain and assist me. There are great rumours here of peace. I wrote to the Russian General about twelve days ago asking him if he had any of our letters to send them in. I received in reply a very polite letter telling me that he very much regretted that a post with letters for us was intercepted and destroyed, but he added that since the occupation of Erzeroum by our troops was a question which would be settled in a few days, we could then make arrangements for our correspondence. In the event of peace being declared, there will be lots of work for us for a month or six weeks at least. Of course in such an event, and when the line is open, I await your orders. Everything is quiet ; we have had several parlementaires (Russian), but what has been their business I don't know.'

Surgeons at Erzeroum.

Interception of mails by Russians.

Dr. Hayes returned from Varna on Feb. 27. To-day he begins his new work as head of

RECORD OF OPERATIONS.

Mr. Barrington-Kennett's reports.

Dr. Hayes' section in lines of defence.

Unburied carcases.

a section to relieve the numerous sick in the battalions in the lines outside Constantinople. Mr. Harvey began his work to-day as head of a section to distribute fresh milk to the hospitals and to bury the masses of dead oxen and horses in the neighbourhood of the encampments. For the latter purpose we have called for volunteers among the refugees and found over 200 willing to work for a loaf of bread and sixpence a day. We provide them with spades and pickaxes. The bodies will be buried, having previously been covered with quicklime. The existence of these unburied carcases has caused a great deal of fever and other illness amongst the troops stationed in the outlying villages. In some places during a recent visit of inspection, I found the roads literally blocked with dead horses, oxen, and donkeys, within a hundred yards of the encampment, all in a state of putrefaction. Raouf Pacha, the Minister of War, expressed himself very much pleased at this useful work which we are undertaking, and has promised us every assistance. The two new barrack hospitals are progressing rapidly. The bedding for 150 beds will be ready in a day or two. Dr. Neylan, with Drs. Lake, Barker, and Clements (the latter I have recently engaged), will form the working staff. I shall reserve all details of the new barracks until they begin work. The Government gives us the building, 140 beds, hay to fill the mattresses, and rations. We supply the rest. Dr. Stiven and Mr. Morisot arrived from Erzeroum yesterday. Drs. Barker, Clements, and Edmunds are devoting their spare time to the refugees, until our new hospitals are full. The greatest exertions are required to prevent an epidemic, which would be a terrible scourge to the army. Dr. Hume started 24th ult. to the assistance of Dr. Attwood. I regret to report that I received a telegram to-day from him, dated Philippopolis, Feb. 28, in which he states that Dr. Attwood was seriously ill and also Dr. Calfoglou; the latter, however, is recovering. He also states that our hospital at Philippopolis is working well, with over 200 patients. I have received further very bad accounts of the state of the wounded at Salonica. Our ambulance section sent there under Dr. Eccles will be of the greatest service.

New barrack hospitals.

Relief to refugees.

Dr. Attwood's illness.

Constantinople, March 8, 1878.

Formation of Gallipoli section.

I beg to report to the Committee the following ambulance operations:—Dr. Barker starts to-day for Gallipoli to take over the hospital of the National Society established there, Mr. Young having decided to withdraw his staff from that place. Dr. Clement, with a dresser and storekeeper, starts to-day for Salonica, taking selection of stores in compliance with a telegraphic request from Dr. Eccles. I regret to report the illness of Dr. Beresford, attached to this section. Dr. Eccles reports that there is frightful want in Salonica, and that typhus is raging there. Dr. Neylan starts to-day for Philippopolis with a special wagon kindly put at our disposal by the Red Crescent Society for conveyance of Dr. Attwood to Constantinople. I have no recent information as to the state of Dr. Attwood, but he is under good medical advice, and will have every comfort during his transport. Mr. Morisot will leave next Monday to rejoin Dr. Ryan's section in Asia in charge of money and instructions. This section will follow the wounded to whatever station they are evacuated, and assist in their transport, establishing, if necessary, soup-kitchens on the line of march. We anticipate great loss of life among the troops in retiring from Erzeroum, owing to the insufficient supply of food and the intense cold. There is a report that a great disaster has fallen on a large body of the Erzeroum garrison on their march to Erzinghian, owing to its being overwhelmed in a snowstorm. Particulars are wanting. All our surgeons being now required for our own ambulance work, I have withdrawn them from the mosques. Major de Winton, who is administering the relief of the Compassionate Fund, has expressed himself extremely satisfied with the good services they have rendered. Five English surgeons in the Turkish service working at the hospitals of Selimie, Kulelee, Medjidie, and Coumbarkhané are now provided with large chests of stores from our depôt, sufficient for the treatment of the sick and wounded in their respective wards. Average number of patients to each surgeon 80. We have also supplied blankets when necessary for their wards, and extra stores as occasions arise. The surgeons report very satisfactory results. One of our stablemen, who had served in McQueen's section during the Lom campaign, died on March 1. His funeral was attended by Dr. Edmunds and some other members of our staff here. The horses of the Committee

Subsidies to Asia.

Relief to Government Hospitals.

in the Constantinople district are now all in active use, except those invalided. Most of them   Mr.
suffered terribly during the retreat across the Rhodope Balkans, but they have been well   BARRINGTON-
taken care of since, and are now, with the above exceptions, in fair condition. Dr. Langdon   KENNETT's
has just called. He was under Dr. Minassian at Philippopolis. He saw Dr. Attwood on   reports.
Tuesday last (March 5) at 6 P.M. He was then suffering from typhoid fever, and was delirious at intervals. He was considered in a critical condition. Dr. Hume was attending him.

Constantinople, March 17, 1877.

Many Turkish wounded are being brought in by rail from the Russian lines. The Red Crescent sanitary train is in full work, and will continue running between Bazardjik and Stamboul until all the Turkish wounded are brought here. As our two new barracks are close to the railway station, the wounded can be brought in upon stretchers from the carriages themselves. We are fortunate in having Dr. Stiven here; I have appointed him head of the new barrack hospital. His knowledge of Turkish, and the long experience he has had in managing Rustchuk hospital, fit him particularly well for the post.

With regard to my having lent four surgeons temporarily to the Compassionate Fund,   Relief to re-
the following are my reasons:—There was no proper staff of medical men attending the   fugees in
masses of refugees in the mosques of Sultan Achmet and St. Sofia; small-pox and typhoid   mosques.
fever were rapidly on the increase, and a great epidemic of these diseases appeared imminent.
In the meantime, surgeons came in batches to Constantinople from their broken-up sections,   Epidemic
and I had a few to spare while making new arrangements for the redistribution of our staff.   imminent.
An epidemic in the town would be a terrible danger to the troops, as it would be sure to extend to them. To check this as far as lay in my power, I lent the services of four surgeons, which were gladly accepted by the Compassionate Fund Committee. By all accounts they have been doing excellent work, searching for the cases of small-pox and typhoid among the masses of people huddled together, and isolating them until they are sent to the hospital established for those diseases. At the same time I supplied out of our stores a few disinfectants and some common medicines, of which we have an abundant supply. In exchange we have received a large supply of bandages, &c., from the Compassionate Fund, which were not required by it. This I consider a most satisfactory arrangement for both societies.

We have just received more reports from Drs. Ryan and Stoker, dated Feb. 18. There   Erzeroum sec-
are 260 patients now in the Stafford House hospital. The Turkish soldiers are leaving   tion.
Erzeroum to make way for the Russians. Ryan is in some difficulties, as several of his Turkish employés, and one Turkish surgeon, have deserted their posts in his hospital at the approach of the Russians, and have gone to Erzinghian; I hope that Ryan will catch them and have them punished.

Should the Turkish hospitals be evacuated our united Erzeroum sections will assist in the evacuation, establish soup-kitchens on the road, and attend generally to the wounded. There is still great need of Stafford House help, owing to the extreme poverty of the Government and, I am sorry to say, some apathy on the part of certain of the hospital authorities as to the state of the wounded.

Lady Strangford is here; I shall supply her with some stores from our depôt, and   Lady Strang-
give her what other help we can afford.   ford.

The English doctors in the Turkish service have terminated their contracts with the Government, but some will stay on, and so we can continue our system of supplying them with stores for their own wards.

Constantinople, March 20.

I enclose reports from our sections at Erzeroum, Salonica, Philippopolis, Tchifout-   Condition of
Burgas (lines of defence), Makrikeui, and Gallipoli, also copy of official despatches from   ambulances.
Suleiman Bey, chief surgeon of the Government hospital at Kesanlik, containing upwards of 900 Turkish sick and wounded.

Erzeroum section.—The reports from Erzeroum are very interesting, and show how well the Stafford House and British hospitals are working. At the same time these reports show that there is no longer any great necessity for us to keep up our sections there. The Turkish

32   RECORD OF OPERATIONS.

Mr. BARRINGTON-KENNETT'S reports.	Government hospitals have been evacuated, and the remaining sick and wounded placed in our hospitals, in consequence of which there are many Government surgeons to spare. After due consideration, and consulting with Mr. Stoney and Dr. Stiven, the latter of whom has recently returned from Erzeroum, we have unanimously come to the conclusion that we
Withdrawal of staff.	should withdraw our hospital staff from that town. The following telegram has accordingly been sent to Dr. Ryan through Mr. Biliotti, Trebizond :—' If you consider advisable, hand over both hospitals, assist transport where practicable, give remaining stores to American Mission for distribution to Turkish sick and wounded ; return yourselves by Trezionbd.' I should add that the recent arrival of a large Red Crescent ambulance at Erzeroum has influenced our decision. Sir Arnold Kemball, who has personal knowledge of the work of our Asia section, speaks in the highest terms of Dr. Ryan and his energetic staff.
Great distress at Salonica.	*Salonica section.*—Dr. Eccles' report gives a terrible account of the distress among the sick and wounded at Salonica. Large numbers continue to arrive, and, in spite of the high rate of mortality, all the hospitals are overcrowded. He states that ' the suffering at this present time is increased tenfold compared with what it was during the war.' In accordance with a request from Dr. Eccles I have increased his medical staff, and sent him Dr. Roe (recently retired from the Imperial service), Dr. Aristides Michaelides (a Greek surgeon, who was working for six months under our staff at Adrianople), and also a good dresser and storekeeper. I also sent a second large supply of stores. I instructed Dr. Eccles to extend his operations to Volo, should he find it desirable, and he is accordingly going to inspect that town immediately. Three surgeons of the National Aid Society were sent to Salonica a short time after the despatch of our section, and a fourth has since followed. I understand from Mr. Young that they have taken over some wards of the Government hospitals there, a system which we found to answer so well and economically at Adrianople. There is a vast field for the operations of both societies at Salonica, and I am very glad to have the powerful co-operation of the 'National Aid' there. Dr. Beresford has so far recovered from the fever from which he was suffering as to be able to resume his duties.
Turkish wounded prisoners under Dr. Minassian	*Philippopolis section.*—On March 18 Dr. Hume arrived here from Philippopolis in charge of Dr. Attwood, who remains dangerously ill from exhaustion consequent upon recurrent fever. Dr. Neylan also returned by the same train. It appears from what these doctors report, as also from a letter which I have received from Dr. Minassian, that our work at Philippopolis has been carried on under very great difficulties. The Russian authorities recognised Dr. Minassian as the head of the Turkish hospitals, and accordingly allowed him a certain sum per head for ration money. By supplementing this from our funds in his possession, he has provided fairly well for the nourishment of all the sick and wounded left behind in Philippopolis, nearly 400 in number. Unfortunately, however, his hospital
Illness of hospital attendants.	attendants were all attacked with fever, as also his colleague Dr. Calfoglou, while he himself was at the most critical moment severely indisposed. He was obliged to employ some Bashi-Bazouks for infirmiers, and struggle on as well as he could. We had arranged that the Red Crescent sanitary train should take away the Philippopolis wounded, but, owing to some difficulties, this train never arrived, and the Russian authorities requisitioned another train, by which all, except 50, severe cases have been removed to Constantinople. These 50 cases have been left at our Philippopolis hospital, and yesterday, when I was at the War Office, some of the authorities expressed their sincere thanks that our section had remained behind to look after them. I have given instructions to Dr. Minassian to bring these 50 cases up, and close our operations at Philippopolis as soon as possible. The town is a hotbed of fever and dysentery, and the Russian commandant has ordered his sick and wounded to be at once removed to neighbouring villages.

Tchifout-Burgas (Dr. Hayes') section.—I have but little to add to Dr. Hayes' report. He is working steadily and well, and, by treating the sick promptly on the spot, saves many of them from coming into the crowded and impoverished hospitals of Constantinople.

Makrikeui.—I rode out and inspected Dr. Sketchley's section last Sunday. I found everything going on well in the hospital, and was pleased to see that he had established a system of outdoor relief as well. The hospital is always full.

Daoud Pacha section (Mr. Harvey's).—This section is composed of Mr. Harvey, an energetic young engineer, accustomed to manage Turks, and speaking their language fluently, with a body of 100 Turkish refugees, who volunteered to accompany him. These are divided into parties of ten men, who elect their own chiefs. Mr. Harvey superintends all their operations. The Government provides Mr. Harvey with tents, and affords us every facility for our work. The carcases are buried one metre below the surface, being previously covered with quicklime. Nearly 1,000 have now been buried. In some places in the immediate vicinity of the villages hundreds of dead animals were lying in the ditches in groups of from four to ten. They had died on the road, and been pushed into the nearest ditch, where they lay in hideous heaps, damming up the stream and poisoning the water, which would probably be drunk by other animals farther down. I need not describe to you the horrible stench emanating from these masses of decaying animal matter, spreading fever and pestilence around. The soldiers, worn out with the long campaign and insufficiently nourished at the present moment, are most apt to catch fevers and dysentery. No doctors are attached to his section. It costs us about 130*l*. a month, including pay.
_{Mr. BARRINGTON-KENNETT'S reports. Burial of carcases of animals.}

Gallipoli.—Dr. Barker's report does not give a very favourable view of the Gallipoli hospital which we have just taken over. Another house has now been chosen for our hospital, into which the sick will be removed. I am sending Dr. Barker another doctor and a large supply of medical stores for which he has written. Sir E. Commerell strongly approves of our establishing a good hospital there, as also a transport service from the 'lines' to the hospital. This, however, we cannot do at present from want of means. I am afraid that our present expenditure will be considered very high, though the strictest economy is practised in all our sections.
_{New hospital.}

Kesanlik.—I received Suleiman Bey's urgent appeal for help officially from the War Office on the 9th. On the 11th Mr. Stoney prepared a large selection of stores, which were forwarded for Kesanlik the following day in charge of R. Williams, formerly our storekeeper, and since attached to Sketchley's and Harvey's section. His instructions are to proceed to Kesanlik as fast as possible *viâ* Philippopolis; he will receive other stores from our depôt there should he not have sufficient with him. There being no want of medical men at Kesanlik, we are not sending a *section* there; the more so as the Red Crescent surgeons are sending some of their surgeons to relieve the Government surgeons; the latter will then return to Constantinople. Except at Philippopolis, we have not as yet furnished any help to the Turkish wounded in Russian hands. This case, however, was very urgent, and in consequence I considered it my duty to send help without an hour's delay.
_{Relief to Turkish wounded prisoners.}

Dr. Hayes has just come in from Tchifout-Burgas since I began this report. There are no rations allowed the troops but biscuits; those very sick cannot eat them, and consequently often go without eating at all. He has come to fetch some beds, and also soup, and other provisions, to supply this urgent want. There are six battalions of infantry at Tchifout-Burgas, besides artillery, and Dr. Hayes is the only medical man there. In addition to those duties, Dr. Hayes distributes necessary medicines to some of the doctors in the neighbouring divisions, who are completely destitute of some of the most essential medical supplies.
_{Distress in the Lines.}

On the whole, the Turkish sick and wounded are in a miserable condition. The Government cannot afford to purchase the most necessary requirements for their hospitals, and the medical staff have to work under great disadvantages. In addition to this, the hospitals are over-crowded, and in too many the most ordinary sanitary precautions are neglected. Never, perhaps, during the whole course of the campaign, was help more needed than now. The number of sick and wounded is as great as ever, while the means of the Government to meet the torrent of misery which has overwhelmed them are less than ever. I earnestly hope that those who backed up and sympathised with the brave fellows who fought so hard during the recent campaign, will not forget them now, when many of the bravest of them are lying in agony and want, their wives and children outcasts and refugees. Can one imagine greater misery than this?
_{General condition of Turkish wounded.}

F

Mr. BARRINGTON-KENNETT's reports.

Constantinople, March 27, 1878.

Since writing my last report I have received your second telegram, dated March 23, informing me that, in addition to the 2,000*l.* credit which I asked for, I could count on another 2,500*l.* for winding up. Under these altered circumstances, I have decided as follows :—To keep up Gallipoli, Salonica, Tchifout-Burgas, and Harvey's section to the end of April ; to keep up barrack hospitals, Stamboul, until end of May ; to evacuate Philippopolis on Constantinople ; to hand over Makrikeui to Red Crescent ; to hand over Erzeroum to Government. I estimate that we shall be able to do this on the 2,500*l.* winding-up allowance. I shall, however, keep a sharp look-out, and hand over Salonica, Hayes', and Harvey's sections should I find myself running too near the limit of our expenses. I enclose reports from the following sections :—Stamboul, Salonica, Stamboul Mosques, and Tchifout-Burgas ; also copy of letters from Sir E. Commerell relating to Gallipoli, and from M. Biliotti relating to the convalescents in Asia.

Stamboul (barrack hospital).—Dr. Stiven's report is very satisfactory. I inspect the hospital nearly every day, and find everything going on well. The Saxon Sisters of Charity (professed) are working from morning until night. I have handed over the depôt of the hospital to them, including the case of linen, &c. We have everything ready for the second barrack, but it is not yet cleared of convalescents. I have had the greatest difficulty in persuading the authorities to remove them into an adjacent house hired by us for the purpose.

Salonica.—Dr. Eccles' report is satisfactory. He has since started for the Volo district with a few stores, leaving Dr. Beresford in charge of the hospital. Our funds will not permit us to build a barrack as suggested in his report, but we are applying to the Government for some tents which will, no doubt, be lent to us.

Stamboul Mosques.—As the Committee is aware, I lent for a short period to the Compassionate Fund the services of Drs. Barker, Lake, Clement, and Edmunds. Their duty was to detect and send to hospital any cases of small-pox or typhoid, and to treat in the mosques those of the sick whom they considered it safe to leave there. For this purpose I supplied them with medicines from our store. I enclose Dr. Clements' report on his work ; it serves as an example of what they all did. It was an understood thing that the services of these surgeons were lent only during the period which was required to redistribute our medical staff. Mr. Bartlett, the Commissioner of the Compassionate Fund, begged me to convey to the Committee his sincere thanks for the services our doctors rendered to his society.

Tchifout-Burgas.—Dr. Hayes continues his work steadily, and is gradually extending his operations. Intermittent fever seems to be now the prevailing complaint.

Gallipoli.—As will be seen from Sir E. Commerell's letter, the Stafford House hospital is now established in a new house, and all seems going on well. Here as everywhere else where we have been engaged, the soldiers are extremely grateful to us. The authorities also assist us when they can, and whenever I have any communication with them, express sincere thanks for the work of the Committee.

Convalescents in Asia.—Mr. Biliotti, the British Vice-Consul at Trebizond, has been of the greatest service to us during the whole war, and lately he has formed our means of communication with the Erzeroum section. Hearing that a large number of convalescents were likely to be sent to Trebizond, I had telegraphed a credit of LT. 200, in favour of Mr. Biliotti, to be administered as he thought best. His letter will show how much he appreciated having the disposition of the money. He will make it go as far as possible, and alleviate the immediate wants of some of the poor fellows who are returning to their homes in poverty and bad health. Yesterday I visited the new Turkish encampment in the vicinity of the Bosphorus (northern shore). A great many sick were continually on the road finding their way, mostly on foot, to Constantinople. I shall try and organise some sort of transport for these poor fellows. The Government has plenty of available omnibuses and horses for this purpose. The noise being very warlike, I am making arrangements to meet the contingency of hostilities breaking out again.

CHIEF COMMISSIONER'S REPORTS.

Constantinople, March 29, 1878.

I have to-day received yours of March 20. With regard to the burying of the dead horses, you may be certain that it is a good work—a work rather of prevention than cure. I acknowledge that the Turkish Government ought to have done this work; but, as I could not persuade the authorities to move in the matter, I thought it my duty to undertake it myself. We have now buried 3,600 horses and oxen, at a cost of 5d. or 6d. each, including Harvey's salary and the pay of the refugees. The burial of a horse or ox costs us less than the treatment of a wounded or sick man for one day. This work will be quite finished in a week or so.

Mr. BARRINGTON-KENNETT's reports.

I enclose a report from Dr. Buckle, who has lately been visiting our hospitals at Stamboul and Makrikeui. With regard to our future movements, much will depend upon whether or not war breaks out between England and Russia. I have prepared as far as possible for this contingency, in keeping our hospitals at Salonica and Gallipoli well supplied with all requisites, and in recalling our Erzeroum staff. Also in arranging to hand over the Makrikeui hospital to the Red Crescent, as I think that the first move of the Russians might be to occupy that village, and facilitate their communications with Constantinople, if they did not occupy Constantinople itself.

Preparations in case of hostilities between England and Russia.

The sections of Harvey and Hayes could be withdrawn at a day's notice, and they have neither of them any valuable material to lose. I calculate that, if we were pressed, we could clear our depôt at Galata in a single night, and ship off our stores to Princes Islands or Scutari the following day. Williams duly arrived at Kesanlik with the stores, and has telegraphed for a further supply, which under the circumstances will not be sent. He has been ordered back to Constantinople. The line of railway being obstructed owing to an accident, Dr. Minassian cannot evacuate his wounded from our Philippopolis hospital for a few days. However he will come with the wounded on the first opportunity. Dr. Attwood continues to improve, and we hope that he will be sufficiently restored to bear removal to Italy a fortnight hence.

Constantinople, April 10, 1878.

I beg to report to the Committee that on Saturday, March 30, I proceeded to inspect our hospital at Gallipoli, and subsequently visited the old Crimean war hospitals at Nagara Point, near the town of the Dardanelles. My object was to find some convenient place on which we could concentrate remaining stores and staff in the event of hostilities breaking out, and rendering it necessary for us to evacuate Constantinople.

Inspection of Gallipoli hospital.

At Gallipoli I was most kindly received by Admiral Sir E. Commerell, and also by the civil and military Governor. I found everything most satisfactory at our hospital. It is established in a Greek house in the upper part of the town. The wards are of a convenient size, well ventilated, and perfectly clean. The hospital can contain 120 patients, and more than half the beds were occupied on the occasion of my visit. Dr. Barker has a good supply of wines, soups, and other medical comforts, which have done more than medicine towards curing the sick and worn-out soldiers.

The moral effect of this hospital is extraordinary. There is scarcely a man among the 15,000 troops in the Gallipoli lines who does not look upon it as a sign of English sympathy, for which he is deeply grateful. Admiral Commerell considered it most important that we should not close the hospital for the present, and to show how strongly he felt on this subject, he promised a subscription of 25l. towards keeping it up.

Gratitude of Turkish soldiers.

On Tuesday I went to the Dardanelles in H.M.S. *Sultan*. I visited the military governor, who seemed well acquainted with the Stafford House work. I made myself acquainted with the different sites convenient for a hospital, in the event of a resumption of hostilities, and subsequently visited Nagara Point, and made a careful inspection of the old Crimean war hospitals, English and French. The old English hospital is in a very bad condition. It consists of two long barracks, containing eight wards in each barrack, 22 paces long by 10 paces wide, the whole surrounded by a high wall. All the offices are in ruins. I do not consider that restoring this building would be worth the expense. The French hospital

Proposed hospital at the Dardanelles.

Old Crimean war hospitals.

Mr. BARRINGTON-KENNETT's reports.

consists of an oblong block of low barracks, divided off into 28 wards, 6½ paces square each. There is a convenient house for the personnel, and other buildings have been erected in the barrack square. The system of ventilation is as bad as it can be. However, with some considerable alterations, the barracks would be serviceable, and I have accordingly secured the refusal of them in the event of hostilities breaking out again and the committee continuing operations.

Harvey's section.—This section was wound up Thursday, April 4. The 120 volunteers were paid off, each man receiving his blanket and the spade or pick which he used. Though serving under most unfavourable sanitary conditions, their general health was good. Mr. Harvey started on Saturday, April 6, to Sofia to bring back some stores which have been left there by Dr. Busby in charge of the French Consul, and on his return through Adrianople to pick up the Stafford House stores left there by Dr. McIvor in charge of the British Consul.

Mukrikeui section.—The hospital is doing excellent service, though there have been lately several deaths owing to an outbreak of typhus fever. Ghazi Osman Pacha visited the hospital on Friday, April 5, and expressed himself highly satisfied. The hospital will be transferred as it stands to the Government at the close of this week.

Rustchuk-Varna Transport.—This section was wound up on Saturday, April 6. Some of the medicines were distributed by Dr. Hayes to the military surgeons in the neighbourhood of his ambulance, for which he has taken official receipts from the regimental committees. The remaining and most valuable medicines he has returned to depôt. Dr. Hayes leaves the Stafford House service to-day.

Gallipoli section.—Dr. Clement takes the place of Dr. Barker, temporarily invalided, and returning to Constantinople on leave.

Salonica section.—Dr. Eccles' two reports are very satisfactory. I have heard several independent authorities speak in high terms of his hospital, and the good services it has rendered. Dr. Beresford returns home on private affairs, and leaves the Stafford House service to-day.

Erzeroum section.—Dr. Ryan's report shows good work being done. I hope that by this time his hospital has been transferred or evacuated, and that he and his staff are on their return home. I regret extremely to have to report an act of unjustifiable cruelty towards the wounded in Dr. Denniston's hospital, an act for which Hussein Effendi, the head surgeon of Erzeroum, seems to be responsible. I beg to refer you to Dr. Denniston's report of the occurrence, dated March 20, and also to his spirited protest to the Turkish governor, Hakki Bey, which has resulted in the imprisonment of Hussein Effendi. Dr. Attwood's condition is so far improved that he is enabled to leave Constantinople by the Messageries steamer to-day. He will be accompanied by Dr. Hume, who leaves the Stafford House service to-day, and a dragoman. We all consider that he owes his life completely to Dr. Hume, who, since he found him lying insensible and in a dying state at Philippopolis, has scarcely ever left his side.

Turkish wounded prisoners.

Kesanlik section.—Roderick Williams has returned here after a successful mission to Kesanlik and Carlovo. He arrived safely at Kesanlik with a large supply of stores from our depôt here, and with a further selection from our depôt at Philippopolis. He found that Suleiman Bey's report, which was sent to the committee on March 20, was only too true. There were plenty of doctors at Kesanlik, but no stores; his arrival was, therefore, a godsend to those poor fellows left behind and almost forgotten. After distributing the stores, Williams took an active part in the evacuation to Philippopolis of the greater part of these wounded, by means of Russian ambulance waggons lent for this purpose, and established temporary soup-kitchens on the line of evacuation. It is right to state that the Russian authorities rendered every assistance in their power. On their arrival at Philippopolis, Dr. Minassian took charge of 200 of the wounded, and there being a good supply of stores remaining in our Philippopolis depôt, he was enabled to meet all necessary wants. Dr. Minassian will hand over these wounded, as also the old patients of the Stafford House hospital, to the Red Crescent on our closing operations at Philippopolis, which will take place at the end of next week. I have given instructions for all our stores at Salonica and here to be ready for removal at 24 hours' notice, so that we are not unprepared for any emergency that may arise. All the accounts up to recent date (general and section accounts) have been copied out in duplicate, and one copy with original vouchers deposited at Hanson's bank for security.

Mr. BARRINGTON-KENNETT'S reports.

I am taking care to keep well within the sum allowed by the committee for winding up. I consider that it is most desirable to keep up one or two hospitals till the present crisis is over. The effect of our suddenly closing all our hospitals would be very bad, the more so as the National Society have now practically brought their operations to a close. It is most important at this moment that we should not do anything which might be construed as showing a diminution of British sympathy. Further reports have been received and will be sent by next Friday's mail.

Constantinople, April 12, 1878.

I enclose reports from Dr. Eccles, Dr. Hayes, and R. Williams, also general cash account for the months of Feb. and March. Dr. Eccles' reports show that the sanitary state of the wounded in Salonica has been rapidly improving, while large numbers have been evacuated on Constantinople. Under these circumstances, I have thought it desirable that our hospital should be transferred at an earlier date than I had anticipated. Accordingly Dr. Eccles, with his staff of surgeons and hospital assistants, with a selection of stores, not immediately wanted, will embark for Constantinople on a Government ship next Sunday. Few things in this war have been more satisfactory in their results than the missions of the National Society and Stafford House to Salonica. Dr. Crookshank, chief surgeon of the former, very kindly handed over to our section eight cases of hospital stores, when he left Salonica. As will be seen from his report, Dr. Eccles was able to render good service in an action which took place recently on the eastern slope of Mount Pelion on the Greek frontier. Dr. Hayes' report shows that the sickness in the lines of defence is decreasing, which is most satisfactory, especially when compared with the rapid increase of sickness in the Russian lines. I do not doubt that this result is partially due to the good work done by Harvey's section in burying 3,600 carcases of horses and oxen, which were poisoning the air and the water of the immediate neighbourhood. Hundreds of carcases are lying in the Russian lines opposite, and, as long as they remain unburied, sickness is sure to be prevalent among their troops. I have received a telegram from Trebizond to the effect that Dr. Ryan and party had arrived there safely yesterday afternoon, and are coming here by next Saturday's steamer. I assume that Dr. Denniston will be with them. Dr. Attwood, accompanied by Dr. Hume, left for Naples last Wednesday; satisfactory arrangements were made on board the ship for his comfort. Lady Strangford has established a hospital at Scutari with English nurses, and Dr Stevenson as head surgeon; I have supplied her with a few medicines and other things which we could spare, including some bedsteads, which we had ordered for the second barrack, and which she took at cost price. Dr. Barker has arrived here for a little change of air, but returns to Gallipoli to-morrow; he reports that everything is going on satisfactorily there; we have 200 mattresses and bedding, with complete hospital stores for 200 wounded, ready to be sent down at a few hours' notice to Gallipoli, should hostilities recommence. We shall also have sufficient money over, to start a new ambulance. With regard to money matters, you may rely upon me to keep well within the mark, especially now that there is some chance of our being able to relieve wounded 'allies.' Should affairs take a decidedly peaceful turn, we shall be able to fit up a hospital ship for the Government to send to Russia, for transporting here the Turkish sick. According to advices from Baron Mundy, now on a tour of inspection in Russia, there are 20,000 sick and wounded Turks there and in Roumania. There are over 22,000 here in Constantinople.

Improved state of Salonica.

Estimated number of Turkish prisoners.

I regret to say that Mr. Bartlett, the commissioner of the Compassionate Fund, and Drs. Tritton and Leslie serving under him, have been attacked with typhoid fever. Atkinson, our Salonica dragoman, who is also suffering from typhoid, is doing as well as can be expected. The new barrack at the Ecole Militaire is working well; the medical comforts, such as soup, tobacco, &c., are distributed by German sisters, sent by the Queen of Saxony, who also have charge of the linen and stores. Between 20 and 30 Turkish medical students

Mr. BARRINGTON-KENNETT'S reports.

have been placed, by Marco Pacha, the director of the school, under Dr. Stiven's orders, in order to learn English hospital practice with regard to the treatment of wounds and sanitary arrangements.

Constantinople, April 19, 1878.

Return of staff of Erzeroum hospital.

Acting on my instructions, the Stafford House staff left Erzeroum on March 31, having handed over the Stafford House hospital with 250 patients and a complete supply of stores to Ismail Bey, chief doctor of the Imperial Hospitals in Asia. Hakki Bey, Civil Governor of Erzeroum, gave an official receipt for the matériel handed over, and offered his warmest and most grateful thanks for the services rendered to the Turkish soldiers by the Stafford House Committee.

Dr. Denniston, after the evacuation of the English hospital (Lord Blantyre's), attached himself to the Stafford House staff at our hospital, and returned with them to Constantinople.

Gallant conduct of Dr. Denniston.

To Dr. Denniston more than one of our staff owes his life. Single-handed, he stuck to his post after seeing two of his colleagues die, and three others almost at death's door. Dr. Stiven's report of the work in the new barrack hospital at Stamboul is very satisfactory; 35 medical students from the Government medical school have been appointed to study under him the English system of treating wounds. Though all of these do not attend as regularly as might be wished, yet there is no doubt that Dr. Stiven's instruction will be of immense value, not only to them, but to the wounded whom they may be called upon to treat hereafter. The wounded in this hospital are doing very well. Out of the 105 patients 13 have been discharged cured, and only one has died. When they first came under our care, they were all in very bad condition, suffering, not only from old wounds, but also from insufficient nourishment and rough transport.

Thanks from Turkish authorities.

Tahir Bey, chief of the Gendarmerie in the lines of defence, an officer well known in India and the Crimean War, was deputed by the Turkish authorities of the outlying districts of Constantinople, where our sections have been recently working, to express their thanks and deep gratitude for the assistance given by those sections to the sick and wounded Turkish soldiers. The sections referred to were those of Dr. Sketchley, Dr. Hayes, and Mr. Harvey. We continue supplying Lady Strangford's hospital at Scutari, as also the compassionate and international funds, with such medicines as we can spare from our depôt. On the other hand, we have received great assistance from Mrs. Layard's ladies' committee.

Constantinople, May 2, 1878.

I have the honour to forward to the Committee two reports from Dr. Eccles, relating to the transfer of our Salonica hospital; a report from Biliotti, H.M. Vice-Consul at Trebizond, concerning distribution of relief to convalescents; a report from Dr. Stoker containing statistical account of the work done by his ambulance; and two reports of the Stafford House hospitals at Stamboul and Gallipoli respectively.

Transfer of Salonica hospital.

Salonica.—248 patients have been admitted into this hospital, of whom 128 have been discharged cured, and 87 are convalescent—a most satisfactory result. On April 13, 103 of the convalescents, accompanied by Dr. Roe, were shipped on board a Turkish transport for Constantinople, en route for their homes. On April 15, the hospital building, with the greater portion of the stores and matériel, was formally handed over to the Imperial Ottoman Government, and placed under the superintendence of Dr. Rutledge, a British medical officer in the Ottoman service. The letter of thanks from the governor of Salonica, and by other authorities, copies of which are enclosed, testify how much the Committee's work has been appreciated at Salonica.

Trebizond.—Mr. Biliotti gives a detailed report of his distribution of money relief to convalescent soldiers passing through Trebizond. Though the amount given to each man is small, yet it goes far in that country. The total amount at Mr. Biliotti's disposal is about 120*l*. His report contains the name of almost every man who has received help, and the district in which he lives.

Stoker's Report.—Dr. Stoker's tabular statement of work done shows that in four months he transported in the Red Crescent wagons over 2,000 wounded with only eight deaths. In addition to this, Dr. Stoker's section, consisting of himself, Dr. Weller, Mr. Banfather, and Mr. Smith, dressed hundreds of the worst cases during transport, and organised soup-kitchens,&c. *Stamboul Hospital.*—Dr. Stiven's report shows that everything is going on satisfactorily. Gangrene has almost disappeared from the hospital. I have repeatedly visited the barrack, and can say that I never saw wounded men better treated in any military hospital in Turkey or elsewhere.

Gallipoli.—Though everything is going well at the Stafford House hospital, yet I am sorry to report that many complaints reach me of the state of the wounded in the Turkish hospitals. Mr. Layard forwarded me yesterday the following telegram from Admiral Commerell:—' There are 1,000 sick soldiers here, and the Turkish medical officers complain they have no medicines or stores ; can you do anything with Turkish Government ? ' I had partially anticipated this telegram by sending stores last Saturday to Admiral Commerell ; and Dr. Eccles will proceed with a further large supply of stores next Saturday. I shall also try to put pressure on the medical authorities at the War Office, to induce them to pay more attention to these important hospitals. At the request of the governor of Gallipoli, I sent ground plans, and also elevations and sections of a system of hospital barracks to contain about 800 wounded in all. I distributed these barracks in double echelons, which experience has shown to be the best system to prevent the spread of infectious diseases. These hospital barracks will be constructed at the expense of the Government ; a portion of them will be delivered over to Stafford House.

Dr. Eccles is preparing a report of the state of the sick and wounded in Constantinople. There are 23,000 in hospital, of whom 4,000 are wounded. A great many of the generals, with whose divisions the Stafford House sections were engaged, are now in the neighbourhood of Constantinople ; they all express their satisfaction and gratitude for the good services rendered by those sections.

Mr. BARRINGTON-KENNETT's reports.

Condition of Turkish hospitals.

Constantinople, May 8, 1878.

I enclose a copy of Dr. Eccles' report of the military hospitals in the Constantinople district, and a copy of letter from Rechid Pacha, governor of Gallipoli, conveying his thanks to the Committee.

Dr. Eccles' Report.—Acting on my instructions, Dr. Eccles made a careful enquiry into the state of Constantinople hospitals ; his knowledge of the Turkish language, and his long services as a surgeon of the Imperial Ottoman army, fitted him peculiarly for this duty. There are 22,000 patients in the 27 hospitals, of whom 4,000 are suffering from wounds received in battle, 3,000 from other wounds, such as frostbites, and the remainder, with few exceptions, from fever, dysentery, and diarrhœa. The prevailing fever is typhoid or intermittent. A few cases of small-pox are reported, and no mention is made of typhus. I quite endorse all that Dr. Eccles states as to the causes of the unsatisfactory sanitary state of the patients, and also the remedies which he suggests. It is most important that soldiers who are only suffering from complaints such as cold, diarrhœa, ague, &c., should not be sent to hospitals full of severe fever cases, where they run the risk of catching some new diseases, instead of being cured of a slight complaint. The question of diet is also most important. Some of our surgeons have been surprised at the rapid recoveries of patients in our hospitals, who have been many months under treatment elsewhere, and attribute their recovery mainly to the more delicate and varied diet which they received when under our care. We have endeavoured to carry out the principle of camp hospitals on the Lom, Tchekmedje, Tchifout-Burgas, and Makrikeui. These hospitals did excellent work, especially when the small expenses which they incurred are taken into consideration. Of course we were unable to supplement the diets of many of the large Government hospitals, but in certain cases where we have done so, as at Selimnie and Medjidieh, the surgeons of those hospitals report a great change for the better. I hope to be able to establish a system of supplementing diets at the Government hospitals of Gallipoli. It consists in supplying milk, soups (and occasional stimulants), and other medical comforts not provided in the Government diet.

General condition of Turkish wounded and sick in Constantinople.

Gallipoli.—Dr. Eccles arrived at Gallipoli on May 5, accompanied by a chemist, and in charge of a large selection of stores. He will take the place of Dr. Barker, who is returning

RECORD OF OPERATIONS.

Mr. BARRINGTON-KENNETT's reports.

to England, after having rendered most valuable service during nine months. Dr. Eccles will take charge of our operations at Gallipoli, and will open a second hospital there, besides superintending distribution of stores to out-patients. I have lately experienced great difficulty in sending off at short notice stores by the steamers from here, owing to the rapid exodus of passengers and goods, whenever the news looks very warlike. It is easy to foretell that, in the event of the recommencement of hostilities, and our wishing to send any considerable quantity of stores to Gallipoli or elsewhere, the freight would be ruinous, if indeed we should be enabled to transport the stores at all. To provide for this contingency, I have chartered a brig, the 'St. Nicholas,' at the rate of 35l. per month, for three months, with right to terminate the contract at the expiration of the first or second month. 10l. per month extra to cover all expenses, port dues, lighthouse, &c., if she goes to sea; salaries of captain and crew are included in above sum. Ship sails under a Turkish flag, crew is composed of Greeks very well disposed. The ship is to be painted white with red ports, in conformity with the 13th additional article of the Geneva Convention, paragraph 3. One month's stores have been selected from depôt, and sent to our Stamboul barrack hospital. The whole of the remainder, consisting of 200 cases and bales, have been shipped on board the 'St. Nicholas,' where they are under the charge of M. Isidore, director of our depôt. The stores have been valued by Drs. Stiven and Eccles at about 1,500l., and will be insured (through the agency of Messrs. Hanson & Co.) up to that value.

Stafford House hospital ship.

Constantinople, May 17, 1878.

Sanitary condition of Gallipoli.

I enclose a report from Dr. Eccles, on the sanitary condition of the Turkish troops at Gallipoli. The principal causes of the prevailing illnesses there seem to be bad water, insufficient transport, want of accommodation for those slightly sick, and entire absence of extra diet and medical comforts, without which the best doctor's work is almost thrown away. We shall endeavour to supply these wants as far as is in our power by establishing a camp hospital and dispensary, with soup-kitchens annexed, in the Boulair lines, also a transport service of two light wagonettes (and any other country carts we may pick up on the spot), between the lines and Gallipoli, under Roderick Williams. Dr. Eccles will superintend the whole. I am very sorry to report the severe illness of Dr. Stiven. He is now being nursed by his friend Dr. Stevenson, at Lady Strangford's hospital. His illness has not yet declared itself, but it is probably typhus or typhoid accompanied by congestion of some of the organs. Dr. Blake takes Stiven's place at the barrack hospital. I have been urgently requested by General Baker Pacha to send a field ambulance to his corps d'armée. In the present state of our funds I regret that I am unable to comply with his request, but I shall send him some medical stores which we can spare.

Illness of Dr. Stiven.

Naples, June 8, 1878.

Transfer of Stamboul barracks.

I beg to report to the Committee that I left Constantinople on Wednesday last, June 5, to return home. Before leaving I made all arrangements for the transfer of our Stamboul barracks to Marco Pacha, the director of the Ecole Militaire, in the grounds of which institution the two barracks were constructed. Mr. Stoney will visit Gallipoli to-day, to settle an important question about a change in our plans there. We have decided to move the whole of our staff from the town into the lines of Boulair, on the recommendation of Sir E. Commerell and Dr. Eccles. Dr. Sketchley will return home shortly, as also Drs. Roe and Lake.

Statistics of mortality and sickness among medical staff.

It may interest the Committee to know that, out of 35 surgeons who have served on the Stafford House and Lord Blantyre's staff, there have been thirteen cases of typhus, typhoid, or other dangerous illness, including two deaths. Out of 45 surgeons who have served in the Red Crescent, there have been fourteen cases of dangerous illnesses, seven of which terminated fatally. In the Red Cross (British National) Society, there were fourteen surgeons employed. I am informed that there were three cases of dangerous illnesses, one of which terminated fatally. In the Turkish Compassionate Fund there were eleven doctors employed, of whom three suffered from dangerous illnesses. There were also 40 French sisters of charity in the service of this society, of whom 13 died of fevers; the number of sick I do not know exactly, but 30 is a minimum. The result of the above numbers is that 31·4 per cent. of the doctors engaged by the four societies suffered from dangerous illnesses, and 9·5 per cent. of them died. If we take the sisters into calculation, 15·9 per cent. of doctors and sisters died.

Mr. Barrington-Kennett's reports.

Before leaving Constantinople, I was formally requested to convey to the Stafford House Committee the sincere thanks of the Red Crescent Society for the great assistance rendered to the latter during the formation of their hospitals at the beginning of the war, and also for the transfer of some of the Stafford House surgeons to their service, when it was found necessary to increase the medical staff of their ambulances. The President gave me a letter to the chairman of our Committee expressing these thanks. Ghazi Osman Pacha sent me a message the same day, expressing his gratitude and thanks, and stating that he would have come to the ship to see me off had he not been detained by important business. Namyk Pacha, Nedjib Pacha, and many others of the authorities desired me to convey their thanks to the Committee. Last Monday I called on Safvet Pacha, now Grand Vizier, and on Ahmed Vefyk Pacha, late First Minister; they both desired me to convey to the Committee their feelings of sincere gratitude, on behalf of themselves and the whole Ottoman people.

Thanks from Turkish authorities.

Reports from MR. STONEY

(Acting as Chief Commissioner).

Gallipoli, June 21, 1878.

We have handed over the hospital at Gallipoli to the Turkish medical staff, and transferred the section to the lines of Boulair, where more effective service can be rendered without increased expense. Drs. Eccles and Clement have pitched their tents in the Sultan Fort, which crowns the ridge between the two seas. Close by is a large barrack, now empty, as the troops are all under canvas. One large room in this barrack is devoted to receiving and examining the sick, who to the number of about 300 per day present themselves for inspection. About five per cent. are sent to the hospitals in Gallipoli, and the remainder are treated on the spot. The room is divided by barricades, as shown in the rough sketch enclosed. And the men according to their brigades, following the course of the arrows, are examined by one or other of the doctors, as they pass his table. Each man has a sheet of paper, which he receives on his first visit, and which he hands back on his last. The doctor marks on this paper the medicine to be given, and passes the man on to the pharmacien, who administers the dose, and turns the man into the compounds, either to the right or left, to wait for his soup. A clerk at the table of each doctor fills into a book the particulars written by the doctor on each paper, and thus a complete register of the work is kept. The inspection begins at 7 A.M., and generally lasts till after 12 o'clock. The men ordered to hospital are then packed into carriages or mounted on horses and sent to Gallipoli. The average number treated each day is about 300, many of whom are not fresh cases. To give you an instance of one day when I was present (June 15):—

Mr. Stoney's report.

Inspection of Boulair ambulance.

Dr. Eccles:		Dr. Clement:	
1st Brigade	84	2nd Brigade	79
3rd ,,	127	4th ,,	10
Artillery	17	5th ,,	9
5th Brigade	3		
	231		98

Total 329, of whom 154 were fresh cases; 18 were sent to hospital. The following day 306 were examined and 11 sent to hospital.

A glance at his register book shows the doctor in which brigade exists the greatest amount of sickness, and in his afternoon ride he visits the camp of such brigade to examine

Mr. STONEY'S reports.

into the cause of the evil, and if possible arrest it. Already the sanitary arrangements are considerably improved, and consequently the health of the camp is becoming daily better. Osman Nouri Pacha, commander-in-chief, is so much pleased with the excellent work done, that he has sent all the regimental surgeons into Gallipoli to look after the hospital, and given over to the care of the Stafford House section the entire force at the lines, amounting to more than 15,000 men. The cost of the section, now that it is in working order, does not exceed 150*l*. per month. It was with great regret that I telegraphed yesterday to Dr. Eccles to prepare to close the end of June. Admiral Commerell, who takes a great interest in our work, and lends us every assistance in his power, has expressed his entire satisfaction with the work now being done.

Constantinople, July 4, 1878.

The 'winding up' is progressing, but not so fast as I could wish. The brig will be given up to-day, and all stores embarked on board the 'Frasinet' steamer. Isidore will go down with them on Saturday, and hand them over to Admiral Commerell. He and Lanzoni spent the day yesterday repacking the cases, as many of them had been opened from time to time since they went on board the brig. There are some 76 cases in all, I believe, besides bales. I am in constant communication with the Admiral, by letter and telegraph, and he is quite prepared to receive the stores and look after the sections at the lines. I will pay everything up to July 1, and hand over to him any cash balance I may have. I have already advised him that the sections can be maintained to end of July. Writing on the 1st inst., he says, 'I do most devoutly hope that the field hospital will be kept on. Eccles and Clements are doing splendid work for minimum of cost. So strong are the doctors about it, that Clements offers to serve without pay.

Death of Mr. Masters.

Poor Masters was buried last Sunday. All Stafford House staff attended the funeral. We all liked him very much. He worked well last winter when the trains used to come in crammed with fugitives and soldiers, pell mell and half frozen.

Constantinople, July 15, 1878.

Isidore, in charge of the depôt, returned from Gallipoli on Saturday, having delivered over all our remaining stores to Admiral Commerell. He brought me letters from which I send you extracts.

To do the work we have undertaken at Gallipoli, we ought properly to have at least double the staff we have at present, which is of course out of the question, so I very much fear the poor fellows will get seriously knocked up. They certainly deserve every credit for sticking to their work so well. Eccles was determined to make it a success, and has been most ably backed up by Clements and the entire staff. It would be a gracious act on the part of the Committee to pass them a vote of thanks. Poor Williams is, I fear, very ill. I sent his brother John (of Erzeroum fame) down on Saturday to nurse him. He had typhus, as you know, at Erzeroum, and therefore does not run so much risk as others might.

As regards the winding-up, I had hoped to have got all finished by to-day, but you know how difficult it is to calculate on anything in this country. And there has been a great deal of accountant's work, which must all pass through Williams' hands. I must retain him till the end of this month, as also the office, and Sklerakis ; but the sale of our furniture will cover these expenses.

(B)—BULGARIA DISTRICT.

FOUR SECTIONS.

Reports to the Chief Commissioner from MR. E. R. PRATT, *Assistant-Commissioner of District.*

General Report of District.

The Committee employed in Bulgaria, for which I was Assistant-Commissioner during the campaign under Mehemet Ali and Suleiman Pacha, eleven surgeons (and about ninety assistants), four of whom were engaged in fixed hospitals, six in flying ambulances, and one in charge of a railway transport.* There were, during the advance and retreat from Biela, eight battles fought, where the wounded averaged from two hundred to eight hundred, and of those the Stafford House surgeons were fortunately able to be present at seven—Kara-hassan-keui, Kaselevo-Ablava, Sinankeui, Kadikeui, Giovan-tchiflik, Pyrgos, Elena—and at the eighth, that of Cherkovna, more than half of the wounded were dressed by surgeons of the National Aid Society. <small>Mr. PRATT's reports. General report of Eastern Bulgaria and Danube district. Battles during campaign. Number of wounded.</small>

The average daily number of sick treated by each of our two ambulances at the front were thirty in August, but rose to nearly three hundred per diem in the month of November. In fact, it appears that nearly all the sick within a radius of two miles came to the Stafford House ambulances, inasmuch as the Turkish surgeons were not sufficiently provided with medicines. To these two ambulances were attached a transport of twenty and twelve light wagons respectively; these wagons were employed in bringing provisions and surgical stores up to the front, and taking sick and wounded to the Turkish village hospitals in rear. <small>Number of sick treated.</small>

Of the two hospitals in this district, Rustchuk, situated in the railway workshops, was able to be of the greatest use. The hospital was nearly always full; its height, excellent ventilation, isolated position, and the fact that the sick came straight from the battle-fields, caused the comparative mortality to be very much less than that of any other hospitals in Turkey. The Varna hospital, supported by the Red Crescent Society, under our surgical control, also remained in full employment while in our hands; it was transferred entirely to the Red Crescent in November. <small>Hospitals.</small>

The system of relief to wounded during railway transport was similar to that on the Roumelian railway under Dr. Barker; but it was not found necessary to have a van fitted up for the surgery, owing to the shortness of the distance traversed, and the fact that depôts of stores were placed at various points on the line—i.e. at Rustchuk, Tchervenavoda, Rasgrad, Shumla, and Varna. There was such a scarcity of railway wagons on the line that none could be spared to be fitted up for ordinary ambulance purposes. It was more convenient, therefore, to improve the ordinary trucks by means of mattresses and so relieve larger numbers at less cost. Nearly all the wounded were accompanied by Dr. Hayes to Varna, and many thence in his ten ambulance wagons to the hospitals; the only other means of transport being the town hackney carriages engaged for the occasion. The soup given at Tchervenavoda and Sheitandjik (and by the National Aid Society in Rasgrad) was of the greatest benefit, sick men never being provided by the Government with more than biscuit. <small>Railway transport.</small>

The aim of the Stafford House Committee here, as in other parts of Turkey, instead of instituting model systems of relief in a limited area, was rather to subsidise quickly the

---

* Four of these surgeons were for several months in the pay of Lord Blantyre, but were subsequently transferred to the service of the Stafford House Committee.

RECORD OF OPERATIONS.

Mr. PRATT's reports.

Turkish system wherever its weakness was most apparent and the necessity most pressing, and thus perhaps obtain the maximum of result with the minimum of cost; and in pursuance of this object the Commissioner in charge of the district distributed both money and stores when he found such necessity.

The greatest distress was as elsewhere during transport from the front to the railway. With but little exception the bullock-arabas were the only means of transport used by the Turks, and these were incapable of improvement in the way of comfort on an emergency. Had regular ambulance wagons been provided they would have proved utterly useless in such a roadless country. Corps of stretcher-bearers would have been useful at intervals, as very severely wounded men seldom left the battle-field; but it is questionable whether the benefit occasionally derived would in any way have corresponded with the cost of their maintenance.

Shumla, Sept. 1, 1877.

I left Constantinople with medicine and stores for Varna, accompanied by Drs. Beresford and McQueen. Mr. Young very kindly gave us a passage on board the National Aid Society's steam-ship *Belle of Dunkerque*. I found the Varna hospital, under Drs. Cullen and Kouvaras, in every way satisfactory; but at that time no wounded had been sent by the authorities. On Aug. 31, I saw Raouf Pacha, who at once telegraphed that wounded should be sent from Rasgrad, which wounded came down the line at last with many others, under the charge of Dr. Hayes. The authorities at Shumla and Prince Hassan having requested the formation of a Red Crescent transport, Dr. Hayes and myself thought it better to send his Varna transport to the front; and, M. Court having most expeditiously placed at my disposal twelve horses, I formed a small transport, which left Varna Aug. 26, and arrived in camp at Shumla at 11 P.M. on that day. It consists of two surgeons, nine wagons, twenty cacolets, brancards, and mattresses, &c., and eighteen men. After waiting Monday for orders, we proceeded at 5 A.M. on Tuesday, Aug. 28, to Eski-Djuma; and on the road thither overtook his Excellency Mehemet Ali Pacha, who courteously requested that we should diverge to Yenikeui, where we arrived on Wednesday morning. The village of Yenikeui having been evacuated by the Russians four days previously and the houses empty, we made what arrangements were possible for receiving wounded. There were nine sick and wounded at Yenikeui; and, as there was no hospital accommodation for them, I took them to Eski-Djuma, arriving Thursday morning. The Government hospital is inadequately provided in every respect; it is in the Bulgarian school—gangrene, fever, and healthy wounded are side by side.

For mation of Second Lom ambulance.

Head-quarters of Mehemet Ali, Sept. 12, 1877.

I beg to inform you that I left Shumla on the date of my last report (Sept. 1), for Varna, by a train in which there were 80 severely wounded men. There were no Turkish surgeons to meet them on their arrival at Varna, and Dr. Hayes and myself had, with the aid of his transport drivers, with our own hands carried out of the trucks and placed on the transport wagons more than two-thirds of their number before the Turkish surgeons and their carriages arrived.

The Red Crescent hospital under Drs. Kouvaras and Cullen (Stafford House surgeons) is full and working well.

Wounded after battle of Kaselevo.

On Sept. 4 I left Varna for Rasgrad, and thence on horseback to the front with Drs. Cheyne and Jolly (National Aid Society). We arrived late—the fighting at Ablava and Kaselevo was just over; we had time, however, to collect some twelve severely wounded men, and place them in a tent, out of the rain for the night. Next morning their wounds were dressed by Dr. Wattie. We on the same morning found a large number of slightly wounded men at Cherissa; we dressed some of their wounds, the remainder were attended to by Drs. Wattie, Busby, and Lake, after their severer cases had been disposed of. The same day I rode to Yenikeui, and brought back with me Drs. McQueen and Beresford and their transport to Cherissa. We found Messrs. Wattie and Busby. Before night the lighter cases remaining were dressed and transported to the Turkish hospital, and the severer ones not admitting removal remain at present under the care of Drs. McQueen and

BULGARIA DISTRICT.

Beresford, an empty house having been prepared as a temporary hospital. During the few days that Drs. McQueen and Beresford were at Yenikeui they were not allowed to perform any operations by the Turkish surgeons there; men with undressed wounds being sent to Shumla and Eski-Djuma. Dr. McQueen will report, however, to you with regard to this.

 I visited Dr. Wattie's ambulance in camp opposite Ablava. Dr. Lake was suffering severely from dysentery. He was very anxious to remain, in expectation of more work, but as Drs. Wattie and Busby both agreed that it was not advisable that he should do so, he left the next morning for Varna with a convoy of sick. He has since written to offer his services at the Imperial hospital at Varna, where help is very much required. He has stipulated for the care of wounded men only, and for independent action with regard to treatment in his own wards. Dr. Busby will report to you as to the large number of wounded that have passed through their hands lately. I have appropriated an empty house at Yenikeui as a store for Dr. Crookshank (National Aid Society) and Stafford House ambulances. As this village is protected by a very strong and fortified position, it is not likely to be again in possession of the Russians.

 I have sent the stores destined for Eski-Djuma to Yenikeui. I visited the Government hospital yesterday, and as several very bad cases had disappeared, it did not appear to be in such an offensive condition as I described in my last report. They are still without disinfectants. On the two chief doctors writing me that they were in great need of certain medicines, which they could not procure immediately, I gave them a small quantity, and some hospital requisites that they were obviously in need of. I have done the same at Yenikeui.

 The voluntary aid given to Mehemet Ali Pacha's army may be thus described:—Drs. Crookshank, Cheyne, and Jolly (National Aid Society), in camp with south wing; Drs. Wattie, Busby, and Mr. Boyd (First Lom ambulance), with their transport, in camp with north wing; Drs. Beresford and McQueen (Second Lom ambulance), with transport, in village in rear of centre, with orders to move forward in whatever direction the fighting next takes place; Dr. Hayes, in charge of railway transport from Rustchuk to Varna, which is doing excellent service. The Varna and Rustchuk hospitals are both now full. I proceed to the latter to-morrow.

Mr. Pratt's reports.

Dr. Lake's illness.

Depôt at Yenikeui.

Distribution of ambulances.

Constantinople, Sept. 27, 1877.

 I left Varna on Friday, Sept. 12, the date of my last report, and proceeded to Rustchuk, doing the latter part of the journey on horseback. The Stafford House hospital there was full, and working most satisfactorily under the care of Drs. Stiven and Edmunds. The building is peculiarly well suited for a hospital, the ventilation perfect, the attendance and food good, and the patients most contented and grateful. I saw Ohannes Bey, the 'chirurgien en chef' of the Turkish ambulance, and, after some discussion, thought fit, with Dr. Stiven's advice, to make him a proposition to the following effect, viz.: That the necessaries for 100 additional beds, sheets, mattresses, coverlets, and other hospital matériel, shall be provided, as far as possible, and the building cleaned, by the Stafford House; and that the Turkish authorities, on their part, shall undertake to provide all the 'personnel,' that is, assistant-surgeons, pharmaciens, infirmiers, and servants of all descriptions, entirely at their own cost; also oil, coals, &c. The whole to be under Drs. Stiven and Edmunds; they having entire liberty of treatment, subject only to the supreme medical authorities. On Monday, Sept. 17, I rode by Kadikeui and Senankeui to Nankeui, where I found Drs. Wattie, Busby, and Boyd, with their ambulances. On the 19th, I arrived at Cherissa. Dr. Beresford had left for Varna, owing to a severe attack of dysentery. Dr. McQueen and I decided that we should take his ambulance and transport, and work with Dr. Wattie till Dr. Beresford's return. The next day I left for Costova, where I found Dr. Crookshank and ambulance (N.A.S.), and also the Heinrich ambulance (Red Crescent). I saw Dr. Roy (Turkish service) at Kaselevo; he assured me that the wounded in his charge, and shot in the face, had only hard biscuit given them. I, therefore, gave him two liras to purchase sheep, which are very cheap, to boil down for broth. On Saturday, 21st, I arrived at Osman Bazar, and the next day crossed the Balkans to Islimyeh, thence to Eski-Saghra and Constantinople, where

Enlargement of Rustchuk hospital.

Mr. Pratt's reports.	I arrived on Monday, Sept. 24. Upon the whole, the work being done under Stafford House doctors is most satisfactory. I may state that I have seen no sign of distress among the Bulgarians north of the Balkans.

Shumla, Oct. 18, 1877.

I left Constantinople on Oct. 2 for Varna, taking with me 42 cases of stores of all kinds. The Red Crescent hospital, under Drs. Kouvaras and Cullen (S. H.), was working satisfactorily. The former has reported to you the necessary details. Dr. Lake had just recovered from his recent illness, and accompanied me to Rustchuk, where he has taken Dr. Edmunds' place in the S. H. hospital; the latter has gone to the S. H. ambulance with Nedjib Pacha's division at Kadikeui, under Dr. McQueen. I left nine cases of stores at the S. H. depôt at Shumla Road; they contain medicines of various descriptions, and remain in reserve under my charge. I brought 26 cases for Dr. Stiven. On Tuesday, Oct. 9, I found the two S. H. Lom ambulances at Kadikeui, within half a mile of each other; Dr. Busby with Assaf Pacha's division, and Dr. McQueen with that of Nedjib Pacha. They were each treating more than 100 sick daily—dysentery, fever, and camp sores being the most prevalent complaints. They told me that they had all the medicines they required, and had no complaints to make. On arriving at Tchervenavoda I found that 150 sick were without a doctor, and sent at once to Dr. Stiven at Rustchuk to send over a surgeon, medicines, and soup, until they could be evacuated.

Shumla Road depôt.

I arrived at Shumla yesterday, and this morning surrounded a house with police, and seized some S. H. stores, which had been stolen by an ambulance chemist—blankets, quinine, &c., which are now in my possession.

Shumla, Oct. 27, 1877.

On Oct. 19 Nedjib Pacha's division retired to Rasgrad, and Drs. McQueen and Edmunds and ambulance accompanied it. Both this and Dr. Busby's ambulance are well supplied with all necessaries. On Oct. 24 I was present at the battle of Giovan-Tchiflik (the attack on the Turkish camp at Kadikeui); the wounded were carried to the Verbandplatz, in rear of the village, where the Turkish and S. H. surgeons—Drs. Busby, Beresford, Wattie, and Boyd—were at work. The wounded were immediately attended to, and carried to the village of Kadikeui. We volunteered to go over the battle-field that night, but the Turkish surgeon-in-chief, after enquiry, assured us that there were no wounded remaining. Drs. Busby, Boyd, and I afterwards went into the village, but found nothing but Russian dead.

Battle of Giovan-Tchiflik.

I accompanied the wounded next morning to Rustchuk, where all, with the exception of three Turkish officers and nine Russian prisoners, were received by the S. H. hospital there. In less than two hours we had them all dressed and in their beds. Some of the wounds were most serious, one man dying at the hospital door; others, on the contrary, were very slight indeed. Dr. Stiven had everything prepared, and worked most assiduously with Drs. Lake, Beresford, and Boyd. On Oct. 27 I procured the remainder of the amputation cases sent by Ahmed Vefyk Pacha, from the central hospital at Shumla. Six I have already accounted for; six I have now, and six more are distributed to the Turkish ambulances at Shumla, Rasgrad, Eski-Djuma, Solanitz, and Osman Bazar.

Rustchuk Hospital.

This hospital was established in the depôt of the Rustchuk-Varna Railway Company, conveniently situated at the head of the line, about three-quarters of a mile from the town, and was organised and fitted up by Surgeon Stiven. In addition to their ordinary hospital work, the Staff were engaged in the field in the actions of Kadikeui and Pirgos. On the occasion of the bombardment of the hospital

(Dec. 30), Surgeons Stiven and Beresford displayed great gallantry in rescuing their wounded, for which services a high distinction was conferred on them by the Sultan.

Period of service: July 20 to Dec. 30.—Average number of beds occupied, 124; total number treated, 441. The following served at different times on the staff of this section: Surgeons Stiven, Lake, Beresford, and Edmunds, and Turkish assistants.

The following are extracts from the Reports to the Chief Commissioner:—

Rustchuk, Sept. 9, 1877.

After anxiously waiting from day to day for something to do for the sick and wounded, we have at last received all at once all the work that two doctors can undertake. On Aug. 31 there was a reconnaisance here, at which date our hospital was prepared to receive 50 patients. The other 50 beds were partially prepared, but, for want of coverlets or blankets and small soft pillows, were not fit to receive wounded men in. Having no patients to attend to, we thought it advisable that we should make ourselves useful in going out to the scene of this reconnaissance and doing what lay in our power in the shape of ambulance work. Taking bandages, splints, &c., with us, we went out and attended to the wounded as they were brought out from action; some 30 to 40 men, comprising Turkish soldiers and Circassians, passing through our hands. We fully expected to receive our first instalment of patients that same evening, but were disappointed in that respect; still, we had the satisfaction of having done something in the shape of work. We have now been in full swing for five days, and I am thankful to say that everything is going on satisfactorily, and, as far as the wounded are concerned, they seem very contented, happy, and comfortable. On the morning of the 7th instant, on account of our having about 20 to 25 Egyptian soldiers among our wounded, we received a visit from the Egyptian General Osman Pacha, who, after he had walked round and inspected all the patients, in a nice little speech complimented us on the appearance of our hospital, and thanked us for our attention to the wounded, and hoped we would continue our care of them, &c. On the afternoon of the same date the 'Vali' Ahmet Kaïsserli Pacha paid us the honour of a visit to the hospital, which he inspected, and personally expressed his satisfaction and thanks to me, in Turkish, for our efforts and attention to the soldiers. Early next morning we received a visit from the Caimakan, who also expressed himself satisfied, and again repeated that the 'Vali' Pacha had informed him that he was exceedingly well pleased with our hospital.

Dr. Stiven's reports.
Action near Rustchuk.
Attending wounded at front.
Egyptian wounded.

Rustchuk, Oct. 1, 1877.

On Sept. 4 a fight took place at Kadikeui, of which we had been previously advised by the Caimakan of the military hospital. As he said all the wounded would come direct to our hospital, we thought it advisable to stay at home and receive them. The first wounded man arrived about 11 A.M., and from that time up to 5 P.M. they were brought into our hospital in batches of twos and threes. During that time Dr. Edmunds and myself attended to the wounded, redressing their wounds, and getting them into their beds that were all ready to receive them. The total number of wounded we received and attended to was 110; but the latter ten we were obliged to send to the military hospital, as we had only accommodation for 100. Six of these, however, did not go, but returned to their tents, and came two days afterwards to us, whom we took in, as some of the more seriously wounded died shortly after admission. On Sept. 7 we received another wounded man; he was suffering from a shell-wound received during the bombardment of Rustchuk. The servants at present in the hospital and paid by us are—one barbor, two water-carriers, two dressers and poultice-makers, and two women for washing, one for sewing and repairing sheets, one lad to assist apothecary, and the cook. On account of want of accommodation and the inclemency of the weather, it has been necessary to build wooden barracks for the kitchen and washing-house. With a view to the winter coming on, brick stoves are being built, which will not only keep their heat longer, but save expense in the consumption of fuel. The number of patients received up to the present date is 107; of these, fourteen have died, and 27 have been already discharged to their battalions, leaving at present 66 patients in hospital. The number of deaths may seem large, but when one considers that all the wounded received were brought direct from the battle-field, and many of these mortally wounded, only reaching the hospital to die within its walls, and that, had the hospital been more distant from

Battle at Kadikeui.
Arrival of wounded.

Dr. Stiven's reports.	the scene of fight, they would never have reached it alive, the mortality is not above the average, Most of these were seriously wounded in the abdomen and chest, and died within 24 or 36 hours of admittance. Putting aside these cases, the wounded have done exceedingly well. The patients have been kept in a perfectly healthy condition, showing the aptness of the *fabrique* for a military hospital.

Rustchuk, Oct. 6, 1877.

Extension of hospital.	On Oct. 5, one patient was admitted, being a case of fracture of the leg, sent in from Dr. Busby's ambulance at Kadikeui. Four patients were sent back to their battalions. No deaths have occurred during this week. Total number of patients left in hospital 63. On Mr. Pratt's arrival, on 5th inst., I received orders to make the wards ready to receive the additional 100 beds, which work has already been entered into. Dr. Lake arrived here on the 7th to take Dr. Edmunds' place in the hospital, as the latter leaves to join Dr. McQueen.

Rustchuk, Oct. 13, 1877.

The two new wards have been cleaned and white-washed, the floors repaired, and engine pits boarded, stoves built in all three wards, and the lower parts of the windows boarded so as to exclude all possible draught. The 100 straw mattresses and pillows, soft woollen mattresses, and thick yorgans all now ready, and as we have been supplied with the necessary number of sheets, shirts, &c., brought lately by Mr. Pratt, the hospital is now ready for 200 wounded. No wounded have been entered into the books this week. Fourteen have been discharged for duty, seven transferred to Constantinople for change of air; one death from gangrene of the lungs. Total number left in hospital 41.

Rustchuk, Oct. 20, 1877.

The total number of patients treated in hospital has been 42. Of these sixteen have been discharged fit for duty. There have been no deaths. The number of patients under treatment is 26.

Rustchuk, Oct. 27, 1877.

Wounded from Giovan-Tchiflik.	On the 25th, about two o'clock, the major part of the wounded from the battle of Giovan-Chiflik arrived, 129 in number, who were all carefully redressed and put into bed before 5.30 in the evening; a large number have been seriously wounded, but I am glad to say are doing well, and exceedingly satisfied with their lot in getting into the hands of the English doctors.

Rustchuk, Nov. 3, 1877.

Bombardment of Rustchuk.	Since my last report we have received ten more wounded, two of these during a bombardment; the other eight were brought in from Kadikeui, being principally due to accidents in camp. The sum total of patients left in our hospital before this was 148, thus bringing the number treated during this week to 158. Of this number two have died, eight have been discharged fit for duty; thus leaving our numbers up to the end of this week once more 148 in all.

Rustchuk, Nov. 10, 1877.

Further extension of hospital.	During this past week we have admitted into the hospital three other patients, thus bringing the total number of patients treated up to 151. From this number three patients have died, two of whom had perforating wounds of chest and lungs, and the third was wounded in the leg, but succumbed, not from his wound, but from a severe attack of typhoid fever. The patients discharged and fit for duty have been eight, thus leaving a total of 140 patients at present in hospital under treatment. A separate ward of ten beds is being prepared for the reception of officers, but the actual number of beds from 200 has not been increased. There not being sufficient room in the *fabrique* buildings for all the infirmiers to occupy one room and be always near the ward, I have formed a 'Zimlik,' or mud-house, for their accommodation. A second will also be formed for the cook and kitchen servants, as they at present occupy a tent, which will not be sufficient protection during the winter.

Rustchuk, Nov. 18, 1877.

New arrivals of wounded.	The beginning of this week saw 140 wounded still under treatment in this hospital, and this number was not increased by any new arrivals. Twenty patients have been discharged to their battalions fit for service. We had three deaths this week- one a case of severe wound of the

RUSTCHUK HOSPITAL. 49

knee-joint; one a case where the ball entered the shoulder-joints, death being caused by an attack of acute bronchitis; and the third a case of wound in the leg, death being caused by pyæmia. Beyond these deaths everything continues satisfactory. The total number of patients under treatment is at present 117.

Dr. Stiven's reports.

Rustchuk, Nov. 20, 1877.

We are now as hard at work as we possibly can be. Our hospital contains 180 patients, and I expect the other empty beds to be filled to-morrow, as 44 wounded are at present lying at Kadikeui in the Turkish hospital, ready to be passed on to us.

Rustchuk, Nov. 24, 1877.

This is now the third occasion that the Stafford House hospital, Rustchuk, has been of value to the Turkish wounded, in affording accommodation and treatment to the victims of the fight of the 19th inst. at Pyrgos and Giovan-Tchiflik. Being informed that a great battle was taking place at Pyrgos and in the vicinity of Kadikeui, Dr. Lake and myself started for the scene of action to assist in helping the wounded, leaving Dr. Beresford in charge to receive any wounded that might arrive on that day. Finding that the Turkish doctors were short of hands, I left Dr. Lake with them, who stayed all night at Kadikeui, and assisted the dressing of the wounded. Fearing that wounded might arrive at our hospital, I returned in the evening to Rustchuk, and found Dr. Beresford with the assistants, Mehemet Effendi, a Turkish surgeon (who, I may add, has done exceedingly good work in connection with the hospital since its opening), busily engaged in attending to a large number of wounded that had just arrived. Taking up my share of the work, we got them all (65 in number) safely into bed about 6 P.M. On the following day Dr. Lake returned to his duties at the hospital, as no farther fighting was expected on that day, the weather being unfavourable for any field operations. Our hospital was very nearly full then, only some eighteen beds being vacant for the service of any fresh wounded that might arrive on the following day. On the 21st inst. the 32 wounded and two officers were sent down to our hospital from Kadikeui, from which number we took in 22 of the graver cases, and the two officers, who were both severely wounded in the arm. The ten that remained were slight finger cases, and were sent to the military hospital, where they were admitted. The hospital has now for the first time been filled up to its full complement of beds, excluding the ten beds of the officers' ward, of which two are occupied. At the close of last week the hospital contained 117 patients; on the 19th it admitted 65 patients; on the 21st, 22; and on the 23rd, one; it also admitted on the 21st two officers into the lately-made ward for the latter patients. During the week five patients have died, three of which were severe cases from the fresh arrivals. Those discharged to duty number three. Thus the hospital at the close of this week contains 197 wounded soldiers and two wounded officers.

Battle of Pyrgos.

Hospital filled.

Rustchuk, Jan. 1, 1878.

The Stafford House hospital, Rustchuk, instituted in the workshops belonging to the railway company, after extending its benefits to 438 Turkish wounded, received within its walls during the space of four months, has been obliged to evacuate its patients on account of being deliberately bombarded by the Russians.

On Dec. 29, while Dr. Beresford and myself were engaged dressing the wounded in the third ward of the hospital, we were surprised to hear a shell burst in the grounds adjacent to the hospital. I immediately sent a messenger to see where the shell had fallen, and before he had time to return a second shell fell into the second ward of the hospital containing 54 patients, and burst in the midst. Five patients were wounded by the bits of shell that flew about, three on the head, one on the face, and one on the thigh, though I may add not seriously. The shock received has considerably retarded their recovery. Dr. Beresford and myself immediately left our dressing and repaired to the second ward, and assisted in getting the patients removed into the third ward, which was then nearly empty of patients. We had just successfully accomplished our task, and were attending to the freshly wounded cases in the third ward, when a second shell came into our hospital and burst in the midst of the lately removed patients and ourselves. By the bursting of this shell one patient was struck on the chest by a large portion of shell, and died shortly afterwards. Dr. Beresford and myself miraculously escaped from being struck, large portions of shell having fallen just at our feet. After this shell no more were fired at the hospital that evening, and we were enabled to afford comfort to the patients for the night by putting them all in the first and third wards. The extent of damage received from these two shells was considerable; the second ward was completely untenable, a large portion of the roof being

Bombardment and destruction of hospital by Russians.

Patients wounded in their beds.

Narrow escape of medical staff.

H

50   RECORD OF OPERATIONS.

Dr. Stiven's reports.

damaged, several frameworks of the windows being broken to bits, and not a single pane of glass was left.

Effect of shells.

As regards the property of the hospital, six beds were completely torn to rags. The damage done to the third ward was not so great, the shell which entered not being of such a large calibre, the loss sustained being chiefly in the peculiar property of the hospital; four other bedsteads being broken to fragments, and several mattresses, coverlets, blankets, and sheets being reduced to shreds. After the second shell fell into our hospital, we went to see if there was any probable cause for the firing, and observed some cannon on their way to Rustchuk from Maratin had stopped behind the slaughter-house, a building on the banks of the Danube some 400 metres distant from our hospital. I demanded that these cannon should be removed at once, as that was the probable cause of the Russians firing in our direction, but was unsuccessful in getting them removed. The darkness had set in, however, by the time the Russian battery ceased firing. During the night these cannon were removed, and nothing remained on the following day that could give any cause for the Russians firing in the direction of our hospital. We waited anxiously on the following day, Dec. 30, to see if the Russians had intentionally fired on our hospital on the preceding day, for if so they would be certain to open fire again upon the hospital buildings, as there was no other cause in our neighbourhood which could give them any ground to direct their cannon towards our hospital. At about 2.30 P.M., while returning from our duties at the hospital, we observed the Russian battery

Second bombardment of hospital.

called 'Menschikoff' open fire, and the shell passed directly over our hospital. This was followed immediately afterwards by two shells from the 'Esmurda' battery, which fell in the immediate vicinity of the hospital. Dr. Beresford and myself immediately returned to the hospital to do what lay in our power to place the patients, who were unable to move out of the wards for themselves, into positions affording the greatest amount of safety from the entry of the shells. There was no doubting now the intention of the Russians as regarded our hospital, as shell after shell fell in our vicinity while we were busily engaged in placing the patients under the protection of the centre wall of the first ward. So great was the panic caused by the first three shells that were fired, that all the patients that were able to walk took flight into the open plain, where the snow is at present lying over three feet deep, and not only they, but all the domestics and other officers of the hospital, so that Dr. Beresford and myself were quite alone with some 80 patients to

Removal of patients.

do what best we could for their safety. We went to our work, nevertheless, and lifted the patients in our arms, and placed them on mattresses under the wall for protection, which I am thankful to say we had just accomplished in time when the first shell struck and burst in the empty ward of our hospital. The Russians kept on firing till sunset, up to which time they had fired between 30 and 40 shells at our hospital, eight of which entered into the different wards of the hospital, and three into the private dwelling, one into our own premises, another completely destroying the room and goods belonging to the interpreter, and the third entering the house of the apothecary. No further accident occurred to the patients, though several have received a severe shock; two of whom have already died from its effects.

After the bombardment on the evening of Dec. 29, I informed the governor of the vilayet, Ahmed Kaïsserli Pacha, of the occurrence by letter, who immediately sent down an officer to see the extent of damage done, and forwarded for us a telegram of the occurrence to Mr. Layard, at Constantinople. On the evening of the 30th, the staff officer from Ahmed Kaïsserli Pacha again paid us a visit after the bombardment, and took notes of the occurrence. That evening, in company with the officer, we paid a visit to Ahmed Kaïsserli Pacha, who received us with all kindness, and immediately forwarded for us another telegram to Mr. Layard and to the Sublime Porte; and we have to thank him exceedingly for the assistance he afforded us in pro-

Removal of patients to town.

curing wagons for the removal of our wounded that night. We pressed that a *parlementaire* should be immediately instituted to enquire into the cause of the firing on our hospital; but up to the time I write one has not been formed. Having procured some 40 or 50 wagons, Dr. Beresford and myself started to get our patients removed into the town, which we were obliged to do during the night, the thermometer at that time standing at 9 deg. F., and in the early morning at 2 deg. F., a severe trial indeed for our wounded patients to suffer. Nevertheless, it had to be done, as our hospital was totally destroyed and untenable, and in twelve hours we had removed all the patients and property of the hospital (except the wooden bedsteads), along with private goods, &c., into the town. The patients, numbering in all at present 131, are distributed in ten different houses in one quarter of the town, and are as comfortable as possible after the trying circumstances they have had to pass through. I may as well add before closing this report, that the workshops belonging to the railway company are about fully two kilometres out of the town, in the midst of a large plain, perfectly isolated from all buildings, and not in the immediate

RUSTCHUK HOSPITAL. 51

neighbourhood of any one Turkish battery. Two large hospital flags bearing the Red Crescent were flying at the time the Russians fired on the hospital, and were moved up and down to show that the hospital had been struck, but no notice was taken of it.

Dr. Stiven's reports.

Rustchuk, Jan. 12, 1878.

After the bombardment of our hospital on the 29th and 30th ult. our patients were all removed into the town and quartered temporarily in ten different houses. I then immediately set about making arrangements to procure a train to convey them to Varna, and on Jan. 5 we sent off 109 under charge of Dr. Hayes, Dr. Lake, and our Turkish surgeon, Mehemet Eifendi; three were sent to the military hospital, as they were too weak to stand removal; 30 cases, which were light, were, after a week's treatment, discharged to their battalions. Six patients died from the shock received from the bombardment and the removal into the town during the extreme cold. On the 9th Dr. Beresford left for Varna with the greater part of the hospital property, and I followed him on the 10th with the remainder.

Removal of patients to Varna.

Rustchuk, Jan. 17, 1878.

In the *Times* dated Jan. 7 I have seen the following extract, taken from an official Russian report, regarding the bombardment of the Stafford House hospital at Rustchuk:—' On the 29th ult. the Giurgevo batteries opened fire upon a Turkish detachment of 2,000 men with four guns marching from the south-east in the direction of Rustchuk. One shell struck the horses attached to the guns, whereupon the whole body took shelter behind the heaps of stones which were thrown up by the side of the road. Upon their reappearance in the road the Russian batteries fired unceasingly, when a ball accidentally hit a house on which a flag bearing the Red Crescent was flying. The consequence,' says the report, ' was that 300 armed soldiers rushed out of the house, which proves that the Turks hoist the flag with the Red Crescent upon their barracks. On the 30th ult., therefore, our Giurgevo batteries again opened fire upon the said house and upon the quarantine building. The Turks replied from two batteries and from Fort Subtabla.' I have already written a report concerning the bombardment of the Stafford House hospital at Rustchuk, and the plain and simple facts connected with it; but on seeing such an utterly false statement as is contained in the official Russian report, I feel it my duty to write a few lines in reply, and expose the utter disregard the Russians have for the truth, and the shameful manner in which they attempt to throw a cloak over their acts of cruelty and barbarity. As regards the first portion of the report, I can confidently assert that there was no detachment of 2,000 men marching from the south-east in the direction of Rustchuk. As to the four guns, I have already reported that they came along the shores of the Danube from Maratin to Rustchuk, and had been seen for miles by the Russians before they came into the vicinity of our hospital, and not a shell was fired in their direction. These guns stopped behind the slaughter-house, a building on the shore of the Danube, 400 metres distant from our hospital. I demanded (unsuccessfully) their removal from the Egyptian colonel in command, as that might have given cause to the Russians to fire in our direction. They were removed in the night. Not one shell fell in the vicinity of the slaughter-house or guns during the whole time that the Russians fired, but all without exception fell in the grounds of the hospital and its immediate vicinity, and two (not one) burst in the wards of our hospital, killing one patient and wounding five others. ' The consequence,' says the report, ' was that 300 armed soldiers rushed out of the house, which proves that the Turks hoist the flag with the Red Crescent upon their barracks.' The statement is utterly false. If from a distance of three to four kilometres the Russians could give the exact number of men, and see that they were armed, they might have seen that they were dressed in white shirts, white cotton drawers, white nightcaps, stockings, and slippers, and with nothing further than a blanket thrown over their shoulders to protect them from the cold. Indeed, they were more like a number of old women than an 'armed force,' and instead of 300 only 70 patients out of the 150 then in hospital were able to take flight for safety on the neighbouring plain.

In conclusion, I give an unqualified denial of the statement. I state on my honour as a gentleman that never since the building was handed over to us on July 9, 1877, has it been used as barracks for Turkish soldiers or for any other military purposes than those of a military hospital for the wounded; that it has never at any time contained soldiers but those wounded and those employed as infirmiers and servants; and from the month of July to the date of the bombardment, on the 29th and 30th ult., it has always showed its nature by the display of two large hospital flags bearing the Red Crescent on a white ground.

Denial of Russian statement that hospital was used as a barrack for troops.

Dr. Stiven's reports. [The Rustchuk hospital staff was disposed of as follows :—Dr. Stiven was sent to Erzeroum to the relief of Dr. Ryan; Dr. Beresford returned home, and Dr. Lake was attached to the Stafford House barrack hospital at Stamboul.]

July 13, 1878.

WOUNDED RECEIVED INTO HOSPITAL, WITH PARTS OF BODY INJURED.

Statistical report of wounded from Sept. 1 to Dec. 30, 1877.

Wounds of the head 11	Wounds of the upper extremities . . 140
„ „ face 24	„ „ lower extremities . . 182
„ „ neck 8	Wounds with perforation of the large
„ „ chest 34	joints 7
„ „ abdomen 18	
„ „ back and spine . . . 11	Total . . 441
„ „ perineal and genital organs 6	

TOTAL NUMBER OF DEATHS THAT OCCURRED IN HOSPITAL, WITH PARTS OF BODY INJURED.

Wounds of the head 1	Wounds of the lower extremities . . 13
„ „ neck 2	Wounds with perforation of the large
„ „ chest 13	joints 5
„ „ abdomen 12	
„ „ upper extremities . . 11	Total . . 57

Note.—(1) *Two* from the above total of deaths occurred from shock on account of the bombardment. (2) Fourteen from the above total occurred within twelve hours of their admission.

TOTAL NUMBER OF PATIENTS DISCHARGED FIT FOR DUTY.

Wounds of the head 9	Wounds of the perineal and genital organs 2
„ „ face 13	„ „ upper extremities . . 73
„ „ neck 5	„ „ lower extremities . . 100
„ „ chest 10	
„ „ abdomen 4	Total . . 221
„ „ back and spine . . 5	

TOTAL NUMBER OF PATIENTS TRANSFERRED FROM HOSPITAL.

Wounds of the head 1	Wounds of the upper extremities . . 56
„ „ face 11	„ „ lower extremities . . 69
„ „ neck 1	Wounds with perforation of the large
„ „ chest 11	joints 2
„ „ abdomen 2	
„ „ back and spine . . . 6	Total . . 163
„ „ perineal and genital organs 4	

Note.—32 from the above total were convalescents sent to Constantinople; the remainder were transferred to Varna after the bombardment.

MAJOR OPERATIONS PERFORMED, WITH RESULTS.

Amputations.	No.	Results.	
1. Middle third of thigh	1	Death from shock from bombardment.	Dr. STIVEN'S reports.
2. Lower third of thigh	2	Died.	
3. Disarticulation at shoulder	1	Cured.	
4. Upper third of upper arm	2	Died (one from shock).	
5. Middle third of fore arm	1	Cured.	
Total	7		
1. Excision at shoulder	2	Died.	

MINOR OPERATIONS PERFORMED.

1. Number of bullets extracted 44
2. Pieces of shells extracted 3
3. Number of fingers amputated 23

Note.—Several other minor operations were performed, of which no accurate account was kept.

PERCENTAGE OF DEATHS OCCURRING IN HOSPITAL: 12·92 per 100.

Wounds of the head . . . . . 9·09	Wounds of the perineal and genital organs 0·	
,, ,, face . . . . . 0·	,, ,, upper extremities . . 7·85	
,, ,, neck . . . . . 25·	,, ,, lower extremities . . 7·14	
,, ,, chest . . . . . 38·23	Wounds with perforation of the large joints . . . . 71·42	
,, ,, abdomen . . . . . 66·66		
,, ,, back and spine . . 0·		

Note.—This percentage is of newly-wounded patients, no chronic case ever having entered into hospital.

RUSTCHUK-VARNA RAILWAY TRANSPORT.

(*Combined Service with the Rustchuk-Varna Railway Company.*)

This service was formed in connection with the hospitals of Rustchuk and Varna and the two ambulances of the Lom. Every facility was given to our Staff by the railway authorities. Soup-kitchens were established at Sheitandjik and Tchervenavoda. A service of improvised ambulance wagons was organised at Varna, to run between the railway station, the town hospitals, and the pier.

The transport operations of this section were terminated on January 31, when the Russians cut the line about thirteen miles from Varna.

A large depôt of stores was established at Varna under Surgeon Hayes, from which supplies were sent to the Lom Ambulances, the Rustchuk hospital, and, in cases of urgent necessity, to some of the Government hospitals, especially during the early part of February. Sub-depôts were established at Rustchuk, Tchervenavoda, Rasgrad, and Shumla.

Period of service: Aug. 15, 1877, *to* Jan. 31, 1878.—Total number of sick and wounded transported and attended to during 62 railway journeys, 9,265; by Stafford House wagon transport, 2,100; total number of rations of soup, &c., given at soup-kitchens, 8,659. Surgeon Hayes, with Turkish assistants, was in charge of this section.

The following are extracts from Reports to the Chief Commissioner:—

NUMBERS OF MEN EVACUATED TO VARNA FROM THE LOM ARMY, ATTENDED BY THE STAFFORD HOUSE STAFF, AND SUPPLIED WITH SOUP, TOBACCO, AND MATTRESSES, WHERE NECESSARY.

Date		Number and Description		From	Died during transport
September	1	462	wounded	Rasgrad	—
„	2	73	„	„	—
„	4	65	„	„	—
„	6	56	„	„	—
„	8	200	„	„	—
„	9	553	„	„	—
„	10	229	„	„	—
„	11	69	„	„	—
„	20	87	sick	Tchervenavoda	—
„	24	448	sick and wounded	Shumla	—
„	26	66	wounded	„	—
„	27	122	„	„	—
„	28	126	sick and wounded	„	—
October	1	107	„ „	„	—
„	3	108	wounded	„	—
„	6	117	„	„	—
„	7	75	sick and wounded	„	—
„	7	30	sick	Rasgrad	—
„	8	290	Egyptian sick	„	—
„	8	90	sick	„	—
„	9	120	„	„	—
„	10	140	„	„	—
„	11	42	„	„	—
„	15	130	„	„	—
„	16	310	„	„	—
„	19	72	„	„	—
„	23	59	sick and wounded	„	—
„	27	40	sick	„	—
„	28	50	wounded	„	—
November	3	27	sick	„	—
„	5	200	„	Rasgrad (to Shumla)	—
„	16	150	sick and wounded	Rasgrad	—
„	23	180	„ „	„	—
„	26	147	„ „	„	—
„	28	89	wounded	Tchervenavoda	—
,	29	482	„	„	—
„	30	260	sick and wounded	„	—
	Total	5,884			

		Sick	Wounded		
December	1	—	44	Tchervenavoda	—
„	6	6	40	„	—
„	8	76	9	„	—
„	13	61	5	„	—
„	14	4	466	„	1
„	15	—	6	„	—
„	16	—	400	„	2
„	17	—	273	„	1
„	26	90	208	„	2
„	27	50	116	„	1
„	28	18	70	„	—
January	3	25	66	„	1
„	6	140	145	„	—
„	7	40	36	„	—
„	13	14	6	„	—
„	14	74	120	„	—
„	15	25	81	„	—
„	16	40	56	„	—
„	17	40	12	„	—
„	18	50	6	„	—
„	20	7	—	„	—
„	21	50	17	„	—
„	22	54	—	„	—
„	25	85	—	„	—
„	27	185	65	„	—
	Total	1,134	2,217		

[TOTAL . . . . . . 9,265]

RUSTCHUK-VARNA RAILWAY TRANSPORT. 55

Varna, August 30, 1877.

I made a careful inspection of Ohannes Bey's military hospital at Rustchuk; and, though only a temporary one of wood, it has room for 500 or 600 beds, and is well organised in all its details, except sanitary matters, which are generally much neglected by the medical officers of the Turkish army. There were about 500 sick here; but none of them (or rather very few) looked really ill. At Shumla there is a very large military hospital, in which, at the time of my visit, there were 1,290 sick, including 100 wounded. The hospital makes up 2,000 beds, and there are other buildings in the town which can be adapted to hospital purposes. I have had curtains made and rings fixed in the railway carriages to place beds on for wounded. Yesterday evening 94 sick arrived from Rasgrad; the military authorities were more on the alert this time than last, but they had only a few miserable carts, so they actually took hold of the town carriages, forcing the people that were in them and their luggage to get out, and then they placed sick, vermin-covered soldiers in them. For this there was no excuse, as almost all the sick were in a condition to have waited an hour or two without harm. I sent the only two really bad cases in one of our carts, and the stretchers had only to be used for one man. The Stafford House stores, of which we have got some, and which we guard, are really beautifully packed. Still, there is a lack of those useful astringents catechu and rhatany.

Dr. HAYES' reports.

State of Turkish hospitals. Arrival of sick at Varna.

Varna, Sept. 3, 1877.

On Friday last, Aug. 31, at 8.30 P.M., I received information, through the kindness of the railway officials, that a number of wounded were to come from Rasgrad on Saturday, and that a special train was being made up to fetch them. After a delay of nearly three hours, caused by the Turkish authorities making difficulties about our going through the gates, I left at 11.45 P.M., taking a number of beds and carriage-cushions I have had made. We arrived at Rasgrad station at 8 A.M. on Sept. 1, and were told that the wounded were at the hospital near the town. It is nearly two miles from the station. I went there immediately, and found a wretched state of affairs. The chief doctor, Hayreddin Bey, a most intelligent Turk, was up to his eyes in work; he seemed the only competent surgeon there. I went to work along with him at once, and stayed till after 2 P.M., when I visited our doctors' tent, which was, of course, empty, they being at the front with Nedjib Pacha's division, where they had done right good service, as I have learnt from quite independent sources; and the Turkish soldiers themselves, 49 of whom are now in the Red Crescent hospital, speak feelingly of the kind and prompt attention they received at the hands of the English doctors. At 4 P.M. we had 462 wounded placed in the train on mattresses, stretchers, and straw. A surgeon in the Turkish service, a Greek, was supposed to be in charge of the men, but he seemed to know nothing about the nature of their injuries, nor the number of the men, though he had come from the hospital with them. One man died on the road, just as the train was stopping at Ishiklar station; he was removed on a stretcher and given over to some zaptiehs to be buried. The men had bread with them, and they were given water at each station on the road. We arrived at Varna about 11.45 P.M., and, after a good deal of heavy work, got them out of the train, and the worst cases were placed in our wagons. I think they were all in hospital by 1.30 A.M. Last evening 78 more arrived; and, on the part of the Turkish authorities (medical), there was no one to receive them. We went to work and got them out of the train, and sent as many as we could in our wagons. After we nearly had finished this work, a species of Turkish doctor arrived with some bearers; and, with the aid of them and some of the town carriages, the rest of the wounded were got to the hospital by 10 P.M. I have already established at Rasgrad and Shumla Road depôts where there are beds, cushions, &c., under the charge of competent persons; and I can easily make an arrangement to have some soup ready for the Rasgrad wounded at Sheitanjik. As for those from Shumla, there are no stations on the road where food can be got. The soldiers have always bread with them.

Relief to wounded during transport.

Varna, Sept. 10, 1877.

On Sept. 4, 65 wounded came in by train, and on the 6th 56 wounded and sick more. On the evening of the 7th, I started for Rasgrad; and on the 8th, at Rasgrad, superintended the placing of 200 wounded in the train, and escorted them to Varna, and supervised their removal to hospitals here. On the 9th, 553 wounded arrived here by train, escorted by one of my transport people. I was at the station, and supervised their removal to hospitals. I am informed that above 120 more will arrive this morning. On all occasions wagons and bearers have attended and

RECORD OF OPERATIONS.

Dr. Hayes' reports.

rendered good service in removing the most severely wounded. I have given instructions to have soup ready at Sheitanjik for those coming from Rasgrad. The railway authorities continue to afford us every facility in their power.

Varna, Sept. 13, 1877.

Sheitanjik soup-kitchen

I have arranged that at Sheitanjik soup-kitchen the wounded have soup ready for them, and they have already partaken of it, and enjoyed it much. On the night of the 9th I received 553 wounded at the station here; on the 10th, 229; on the 11th, 69 very badly wounded. On all these occasions I personally assisted and superintended the matter, and our wagons were of much service. Dr. Lake is now here; he arrived on the night of the 11th. The trains conveying wounded often arrive after 10 P.M., and we have been at the station as late as 1.30 A.M. next day before we could get all the wounded away. My reasons for having established the local transport service were, that when I came here every one was loud in complaining of the way in which the sick and wounded were received here on their arrival; that they were left all night in the station, &c. So I set to work to remedy this, and since we have been here no wounded have been left; they have always all been carefully removed. Often have I been down when there was no one on the part of the civil or military authorities to receive them, and our people have carried them to the ambulance wagons. I must say that, stimulated perhaps by the example of others, the authorities seem to be working out of their lethargy now, and to be becoming alive to the fact that badly wounded men cannot walk, and require somewhat tender removal.

List of staff and matériel.

Rasgrad: One man permanent and three occasional bearers; one man to travel with train to see after soup, &c. Shumla Road: One man. Varna: One chaoush, seven drivers, four bearers, Vitalæs Piperes as agent, thirteen horses, six pair-horse wagons, one single-horse wagon, twenty-two mattresses, twelve stretchers. On the railway line: Eight stretchers, eighty carriage-cushions, thirty-five mattresses.

Note.—Five pair-horse wagons take two persons each; one wagon, one man full length or three sitting; one wagon, six men sitting. The wagons have sometimes to make four trips per diem from station to hospital.

Varna, Sept. 27, 1877.

On 20th inst., 87 sick came from Tchervenavoda; on the 23rd we were advised of a train of 448 sick and wounded from the Shumla hospitals. We waited at station till 4 P.M. on 24th, and transported a great number to the pier. By 6 A.M. they were all removed; but they remained at the pier some hours in the cold, and did not leave Varna till the next day. On the same day I went to Rasgrad, and on the 25th escorted 55 wounded to Varna. The soup at Sheitanjik is much appreciated by the soldiers. On the 26th 280 wounded arrived. We were detained till 1 A.M. to-day before they could be removed. On all these occasions our transport-wagons have been of much service.

Varna, Dec. 24, 1877.

Soup has been given from Sept. 11 to Nov. 30 to 4,927 sick and wounded soldiers. The contractor's price per tin of soup is one piastre metallic, or a fraction over one penny English money, which I venture to think can hardly be called expensive when the difficulties of obtaining meat for soup for 200 or 300 men, at three hours' notice, in the middle of this country, are con-

Soup-kitchen at Tchervenavoda.

cerned. Our soup-room at Tchervenavoda has now been opened since the end of October, and about 400 wounded have been supplied with soup there, when often they have had to wait several hours, or even a night, for the train. I have made twenty journeys by railway, either with the wounded or on the Stafford House Committee's business. On no occasion have sick or wounded travelled by train since the beginning of August without a Stafford House transport employé accompanying them. The Stafford House ambulance carts here stationed have on all but two occasions of the above-mentioned dates been on duty, and sometimes our bearers and carts are the only ones at the station. They have carried upwards of 1000 sick and wounded from the station to the town hospitals, and have on many occasions carried convalescents from the hospitals to the pier for embarkation. Before our work was begun here last August, the wounded and sick often remained all night without shelter in the station. Since we have been at work this has never happened, though I and my helpers have often to wait at the railway till 2 A.M. before all can be got away.

Railway-line blocked with snow.

I visited McQueen's ambulance at a village called Marian, near to Elena; since then I have been to Rustchuk, and have been very busy attending to the transport of 1,081 wounded; many of these had never been dressed, and I had much to do for three days in that way. The railway line is blocked with snow, and there is no communication with Rustchuk.

Dr. Hayes' reports.

Varna, Dec. 1877.

The weather at the beginning of December was fine, but on the 9th it became very cold and continued so without intermission till end of month. Much snow fell, and at times the line of railway was blocked; in places the snow was piled higher than the carriage roofs. The trains were greatly delayed, and sometimes the wounded were sixteen hours in the train. They were supplied with soup often twice on the journey, and when required tobacco was given to them. As will be seen, remarkably few deaths occurred—seven. The temperature was on some occasions as low as 12 deg. below zero, Réaumur.

Our large depôt at Tchervenavoda, where there were beds and a stove, and where soup and tobacco were distributed, was of immense service after the severe battle of the 12th on the Lom near Metchka and Kadikeui. On the 14th and 15th I was occupied in dressing large numbers of them, many of whom had never been touched since they were wounded. Had it not been for our depôt, many of these most severely wounded men must have perished from cold and hunger. There was much snow at the time. All the transport trains were accompanied by me or one of my agents, and our ambulance carts at Varna were always at the Varna station to receive the sick and wounded and transport them to the hospitals—a work which frequently occupied the whole of the night in most inclement weather. Frequently none but the bearers and carts were to be found, and they transported 650 sick and wounded. It is hardly necessary to mention that all the trains were provided with mattresses, and were accompanied by men who attended to the wants of the soldiers, gave them water, &c.

Tchervenavoda depôt.

Varna, Jan. 1878.

The weather at the beginning of this month most severe, much snow, and line blocked. On one occasion we were seventeen hours coming with a train of wounded from Tchervenavoda to Varna. On another occasion we took nearly fifteen hours to reach Rasgrad, a distance usually run in seven to eight hours. The cold was most intense, temperature 11 deg. Réaumur. The soldiers were taken every possible care of, and only one death occurred. The trains were always accompanied by some of our bearers, myself, or conductors. Our ambulance carts were always ready to receive the wounded, and often had to be at work the whole night. I may mention here that our ambulance carts have been at work at the Varna hospital daily, transporting wounded from one hospital to another or to the bath, for the past three months, besides transporting large numbers of sick and wounded from the hospitals to the steamers for embarkation. From the station to the hospitals, and from the hospitals to the pier, they have carried more than 1,500 men. Our ambulance carts rendered also great service in carrying refugees from the station to the town, in number 600. On Jan. 31 traffic was suspended on the line, the Russians having broken it about thirteen miles from Varna.

Severe cold.

Occupation of line by Russians.

Varna, Feb. 1878.

There was no railway transport this month. My time was chiefly occupied in sorting the Stafford House stores at Varna and distributing a large quantity of them to the military hospitals there; for them there is a masbuta or acknowledged list given. They were received with much gratitude, and many of them were much wanted; for instance, they had neither bandages nor charpie to dress the wounded with. I forwarded a large quantity of stores to Constantinople, and having paid off all the employés in my section, left Varna on the 25th for Constantinople, where I arrived on the 26th. I may mention that our ambulance-carts were employed in carrying refugees, and our men in aiding to give soup to these greatly distressed and most unfortunate people during a great part of this month.

Distribution of stores to Turkish hospitals.

[Dr. Hayes was subsequently appointed to take charge of the Tchifout-Burgas section.]

First Ambulance of the Lom.

This ambulance was despatched from Constantinople at the end of July. It was first attached, under Surgeon Busby, to Nedjib Pacha's division, and subsequently to Assaf Pacha's division. It served at the battles of Karahassankeui, Kaselevo,

I

Senankeui, Kadikeni, and Giovan-Tchiflik, and in addition attended to large numbers of sick of the divisions to which it was attached.

Period of service: Aug. 3 to Nov. 1, 1877.—Number of sick treated, 2,430 ; number of wounded treated, 921—total number, 3,351. The following served on the staff of this section : Surgeons Busby, Wattie, Assistant-Surgeon Boyd, and one dispenser.

The following are extracts from reports to the Chief Commissioner :—

Assaf Pacha's Camp, Senankeui, Sept. 18, 1877.

Dr. WATTIE'S report.

I beg to forward some details of the work we have done since we left Varna. We reached Rasgrad on Aug. 2, and after some days we went on to Shumla, where we were courteously received by Mehemet Ali, the Commander-in-Chief, who promised us all assistance, and telegraphed to the different stations as to where our services would be most urgently wanted. Accordingly, on Aug. 14, we set out for Rasgrad, and, joining with Drs. Busby and Lake, became attached to the division under Nedjib Pacha. For the next nine days, we treated, on an average, 30 sick cases a day, mostly ague and dysentery. On Aug. 24, we moved along with Nedjib Pacha's division up to Spagalar. Here we remained till Aug. 30, the sick-list averaging 40 per day, all of which were treated by us, while we transported some of the more urgent cases to Rasgrad. There were also occasional wounded brought in by reconnoitring parties from day to day. On

Battle of Karahassankeui.

Aug. 30, we were present, with twenty ambulance wagons, at the battle of Karahassan, where nearly, if not all, the Turkish wounded fell into our hands. During that day and the following night and morning, we attended to (including operations) 251 wounded ; remaining with them during the night, and transporting as many of the more urgent cases as possible to Rasgrad, the Turkish ambulance helping with the remainder. Next day we passed on with the army to Karahassan, and there remained a few days, the sick-list averaging 35 per day. On Sept. 4, the army advanced to Yenikeui, where we spent the night ; and next day, 165 wounded were attended to by

Battle of Kaselevo.

us at the battle of Kaselevo. During that day and the following, we remained with the wounded, also throughout the night, making them as comfortable as possible beside a stack of barley. The night was very wet and cold ; the wounded suffered terribly. Next day, after the wounded were transported to different places, we went forward to the village of Kaselevo to look for more wounded, but finding none, we went on to Cherissa, where, during that day and the following, 225 wounded soldiers passed through our hands ; these being collected from the left bank of the Lom by the Turkish ambulance, Mr. Boyd at this time working with the Turkish ambulance. Our wagons here did good work in transporting the wounded to the Turkish hospital at Salonica. During the afternoon of the following day, we were joined by Mr. Pratt at Cherissa, accompanied by Drs. Beresford and McQueen, who attended to the remainder, we returning to the camp of Safvet Pacha. During the next few days, we were engaged in attending to the usual number of sick cases, about 40 a day, chiefly ague and dysentery, with occasional wounded ; and on Sept. 13 we advanced with Assaf Pacha 12 miles in a westerly direction, and at night encamped near the

Battle of Senankeui.

village of Senankeui. Mr. Lake, who had suffered severely from dysentery, had, two days previously, left us to recruit at Varna. Next day, Sept. 14, at the battle of Senankeui, we attended 180 wounded men, employing our ambulances in transporting the wounded from the field. Next day we asked his Excellency Assaf Pacha to lend us help in the transportation, which he at once did, sending for 50 wagons to help us to send them to Rasgrad. In this battle, as at Karahassan, almost all of the wounded were attended to by us. The wounded suffered badly in the night, which was very cold, we doing our best in making large fires and collecting fuel from the neighbouring woods. We have received many severely wounded which had been dressed by Turkish surgeons previously. In none of these cases whatever have we seen a splint used or the bullets extracted. We are glad to say we have received the greatest courtesy from all the authorities with whom we have come in contact.

Assaf Pacha's Camp, Oct. 20, 1877.

Dr. BUSBY'S report.

After the battle of Senankeui, the ambulance remained with Assaf Pacha's division at that place till Sept. 26, when it retreated with the army to Kaselevo. During its stay at Senankeui, we treated about 70 sick a day, but only an occasional wounded man from the outposts. We remained at Kaselevo till Oct. 1. On account of the continual rain, our sick average rose to 120 and 130 a day, rheumatism becoming very prevalent. On Oct. 2 we camped on the Lom, and on Oct. 3 came here to Kadikeui. The number of sick has steadily increased to about 180 a day, but these numbers vary much, and have amounted to 300 occasionally. As far as we can gather, sick come to us from Fuad Pacha's division, a mile off, as well as from that of Assaf Pacha. The men suffer from camp-sores, which have considerably increased, dysentery, diarrhœa, ague, rheumatism, bronchitis, and œdema of the legs. Scurvy has apparently decreased. We do not consider that the sick-rate is large considering that the men are insufficiently clothed, badly housed, and that the weather lately has been most inclement.

Dr. Busby's report.

[After this ambulance was dissolved, Drs. Busby, Wattie, and Assistant-Surgeon Boyd were sent to form a hospital at Sofia.]

SECOND AMBULANCE OF THE LOM.

This ambulance was organized by Mr. Pratt at Varna at the end of Aug. 1877, and placed under Surgeon McQueen, with a transport service of nine improvised country carts. The Red Crescent Society supplied twelve horses for this section.

The section attended to the wounded after the battle of Kaselevo, and subsequently was attached to Nedjib Pacha's division. On Dec. 1 it was attached to Fuad Pacha's division, with which it served in the expedition against Elena, and subsequent retreat across the Northern Balkans to Slivno. It served in the fighting near Tatar-Bazardjik, and retreated with Fuad Pacha's division over the Rhodope Balkans to the sea-coast, in company with the Shipka and Samakov ambulances.

Period of service: Aug. 25, 1877, to Jan. 31, 1878.—Number of sick treated, 2,322; number of wounded treated, 689—total, 3,011. The staff consisted of Surgeons McQueen and Edmunds, with assistants for transport. Colonel Borthwick (Mahir Bey) rendered great assistance to this section.

Cherissa, Sept. 13, 1877.

On Aug. 29 Dr. Beresford and myself, accompanied by Mr. Pratt, arrived at Yenikeui to form a temporary hospital there, using our wagons to transport the wounded from the field to our hospital, and from there as soon as possible to the nearest large hospital in the rear. We found a Turkish hospital already established in the best houses of the village, so that we had some difficulty in securing suitable places for our hospital, but at last fixed upon a house capable of containing twelve beds, and a large hay-shed, which we had cleared out, capable of containing 20 or 25 beds. On the 31st we set out with our arabas, cacolets and horses, and worked over the battle-field of the previous day along with Dr. Crookshank and Dr. Roy, but found no wounded. The few sick or wounded that came into the village were taken to the Turkish hospital, where they lay without anything being done for them—several cases of gunshot wounds with bullets unextracted, smashed fingers requiring amputation, &c. When asked why they did not operate, they said they had not proper instruments, and afterwards that they had received orders not to operate; and though we begged to be allowed to operate or to take charge of the cases, we were always put off for a day or two, and then the cases were sent off to Eski-Djuma untouched. On the 4th we had five sick soldiers in our hospital. We transported from the Turkish hospital of Yenikeui to Eski-Djuma on the 30th nine sick and wounded, and on the 3rd twenty sick and wounded. On the evening of the 6th Mr. Pratt arrived from Cherissa, where he had seen numbers of wounded unattended to, so, as there was no work at Yenikeui, we started off early next morning, and arrived here late in the afternoon. We found numbers of wounded lying about the streets in a deplorable state, with undressed wounds and unset fractures. We got them as comfortably housed as possible, with mattresses and blankets for the bad cases, and distributed bread. Early next morning we dressed seven fresh cases and performed amputation of the thigh on a poor fellow we found the evening before, lying on the bare floor of a room, suffering great agony from a gunshot smash of the leg, the wound being in a bad state, swarming with maggots. We fortunately were able to buy a supply of bread from a passing cart; sent off an araba to Rasgrad for

Dr. McQueen's reports.

Wounded attended after the battle of Kaselevo.

Transport of wounded.

60   RECORD OF OPERATIONS.

Dr. McQueen's reports. Transport to Rasgrad.

two sheep to make soup for the wounded. On the 9th we were able to secure seven arabas, and transported fourteen sick and wounded to Rasgrad (six or seven hours from here), and in the course of the day we treated thirteen sick and wounded, and sent them off the next morning to Rasgrad. On the 10th we treated seven fresh sick cases, and on the 11th one. To-day Dr. Beresford has taken all the cases from here to Rasgrad. These include the amputation case, which has been doing famously.

Nedjib Pacha's Division, Oct. 20, 1877.

Illness of Dr. Beresford.

After writing my last report, Dr. Beresford having gone with a convoy of wounded, I started to Shumla for tents and stores, and arrived back at Cherissa on the 18th, when I heard that Dr. Beresford was taken suddenly ill with dysentery, and removed by Dr. Hayes to Varna. On the 20th I moved my ambulance to the camp, thence to Kaselevo on 26th. I worked with Busby up to Sept. 30, when Nedjib Pacha, having expressed a 'wish that one of our ambulances should join him, I moved up and pitched my tent alongside his. On Oct. 2 we moved to Kadikeul, and on the 9th I was joined by Dr. Edmunds. During this time we had but one wounded man. When

Increasing amount of sickness in camp.

at Kaselevo our daily number of sick was about 40, but since that time the number, varying according to the weather, has gradually increased up to 200 per diem. The cases treated have chiefly consisted of diarrhœa, dysentery, intermittent fever, and rheumatism, with cases of scurvy and camp-sores. Unless I am very much mistaken, all the cases of sickness in Nedjib Pacha's division have been treated by us.

Yamboli, Dec. 23, 1877.

Since the date of my report up to Nov. 23, Dr. Edmunds and I remained at Rasgrad, attached to Nedjib Pacha's division, treating an average of 100 sick each morning at the camp. We reached Osman Bazar on the 27th, the last part of the journey being performed in a storm of sleet and snow. On arriving at Osman Bazar we learned that the camp was at Achmetli, at the base of the Balkans. On the morning of Dec. 4 the Turks attacked the Russians, and drove them

Battle of Elena.

from Marian and Elena. Early in the day we stationed our ambulance at a house in the village of Marian, and were engaged until after dark, extracting bullets and dressing the wounds of the men as they were carried off the field. We attended to over 120 cases that day, to 70 cases on the 5th (not seen on the previous day), on the 6th to seventeen cases, and on the 7th to twelve cases which had been brought in from outlying villages, and cases previously treated by Turkish surgeons, but anxious to have their bullets extracted. We thus attended to 219 wounded; these included thirteen Russians. On the day of the battle a number of Russians were taken prisoners. Over 50 of these were placed under our care and protection by Suleiman Pacha, who

Russian wounded prisoners.

also entrusted us with the care and treatment of the Russian wounded, who remained in our house until Dec. 8; one of these, a captain, with a gunshot wound at the upper part of the spine, causing paralysis of both upper and lower extremities, died on evening of the 6th. We also had a Turkish colonel, mortally wounded in the abdomen, in the house under our treatment. The wounded were distributed among the houses in the village, which were deserted by the Bulgarians on the approach of the Turks; and having thirteen Russian wounded in our house, with only a scanty supply of biscuits, we could do but little towards giving them food. We applied to the authorities for bullock arabas, and transported the wounded to Achmetli, about eight or nine miles distant, where a temporary hospital had been formed; from thence they were sent on to hospitals at Kezan, and across the Balkans to Slivno. On the forenoon of the 8th we had all the wounded (258 in number) transported from Marian. On the early morning of Dec. 9 our house took fire, and we had to bundle out our goods and stores and sleep in the yard amongst the snow until daylight. The same day we moved on to the camp at Elena; the weather was now very severe. We remained at Elena until the night of the 13th, when the camp retreated towards

Retreat of ambulance across the Balkans to Slivno.

Achmetli; we travelled all night, and reached Achmetli at daylight. We rested the day, and started the next morning to cross the Balkans at Kezan, to Slivno and Yamboli. Owing to the nature of the roads and the difficulty of getting the artillery along, we travelled slowly, and had to spend the night among the Balkans without any shelter except a good covering of snow. We started on the forenoon of the 19th by a bridle-path across the Balkans to Slivno; the snow had been falling fast since the previous afternoon, and was then over two feet deep and drifting. We slept in the little village of Vetshna, and went on the next day, reaching Slivno after a very difficult, cold, and fatiguing journey. The road went right over the very high Balkans, and in many places the snow was up to the horses' necks. At Slivno we learned that Fuad Pacha had gone by rail from Yamboli to Tutar-Bazardjik, where we now are about to follow him.

SECOND AMBULANCE OF THE LOM.

Tatar-Bazardjik, Jan. 12, 1878.

I started in the morning and got as far as Banya that night. Before setting out the next morning I learned that Samakov had been evacuated by the troops, and most probably by that time burned. Sketchley and Williams soon turned up, having marched since two o'clock that morning. I saw Hasme Pacha, who said it was no use going on; so came back with Sketchley, arriving here last night. Here we found everything in a state of confusion and panic, the town looted by the soldiers, and all the army retreated on this place. We have been unable to learn any definite news here yet, but I keep the arabas and horses loaded ready to start at any moment. I will endeavour to save as much of my stores as possible, but am afraid some of them will have to be left behind. I will follow the army as much as possible so as to be in all the fighting, if there should be any.

Dr. McQueen's reports. Arrival of Mr. Sketchley's ambulance. Panic at Bazardjik.

Constantinople, Feb. 2, 1878.

After my last report I started, on Dec. 27, for Yamboli, where I had left the ambulance. I did not reach it until the night of the 30th, the trains having been blocked up by a heavy fall of snow. The trains were almost stopped running on the Yamboli section of the line, being engaged in carrying fugitives from Tatar-Bazardjik, so that we were unable to leave until Jan. 5. Dr. Edmunds left me at Tirnova-Semenly for Constantinople, to have a few days' rest. I arrived at Tatar-Bazardjik with everything safe on the 6th, and reported myself to Fuad Pacha, who was acting-governor of the place. I expressed to him a desire to go to the front, where I might be of service until his division should have some prospect of fighting; and at his suggestion started for Samakov on the 10th, and arrived at Banya that night, after an eight hours' ride. Next morning early the troops from Samakov marched into Banya, having evacuated the place and being in full retreat on Tatar-Bazardjik, so there was nothing left for me but to return. At Tatar-Bazardjik I attended to several men who had been wounded in skirmishes during the retreat. On the evening of Jan. 13, I started, along with Drs. Sandwith and Sketchley, for Philippopolis, which we reached on the afternoon of the 14th. The same evening we received a message from Suloiman Pacha through the British Consul, expressing a wish that all the Stafford House doctors should remain with the wounded in Philipoppolis. At that time there was not a wounded man in the town. We replied that we were essentially engaged in the work of flying ambulances, with all the requisites for such, and with none of the appliances necessary for an hospital; that there was a Stafford House hospital in the town, the surgeon in charge of which was prepared to remain; and that we did not see the necessity of impairing the future usefulness of the Stafford House by so many surgeons being left. On the 15th, at the station about a mile and a half from the town, we saw Chakir Pacha, who asked us to remain and go along with him. Between ten and eleven o'clock that night we were prepared to start, and had the arabas along the line, when suddenly the Russians, who had crossed the river in the darkness, opened fire at us at a distance of 200 or 300 yards; in the confusion resulting on this surprise one of my arabas containing stores got separated from the rest, and I never saw it again; about ten minutes after the firing commenced the station buildings were in a blaze, including, I believe, the wooden shed containing about 100 wounded awaiting transport. We travelled all night, and arrived at the village of Stanimaka in the morning, and here we attached ourselves to Baker Pacha's brigade. Soon after arrival we learned that an attempt would be made to cross the Rhodope Balkans to the sea, and as there was merely a track and no road available for wheeled vehicles, I had to leave the arabas behind and put the stores on pack-horses.

Fighting at Tatar-Bazardjik. Retreat over the Rhodope Mountains.

Night surprise by Russians.

Arrival at Stanimaka.

[Dr. McQueen in the latter portion of his communication gives an account of the further progress of the retreat, which corresponds with that given by Dr. Sandwith, page 64. The Second Ambulance of the Lom was dissolved after the retreat, and its staff, Drs. McQueen and Edmunds, were detached temporarily to attend refugees in the mosques at Stamboul.]

(C)—ROUMELIA DISTRICT.

FIFTEEN SECTIONS.

SHIPKA AMBULANCE.

The staff of this section, under Surgeon Attwood, was despatched from Constantinople on July 24, 1877, and was soon after actively engaged at Tirnova-Semenly railway station attending to large numbers of wounded being sent to the rear, after Raouf Pacha's defeat at Yenisaghra. It subsequently undertook the charge of 300 wounded in an improvised hospital at Adrianople, until they were handed over to the permanent S. H. Adrianople hospital staff.

The section was attached to Suleiman Pacha's head-quarters in the Balkans on Aug. 19, and was engaged during the grand attack on the Russian positions in the Shipka Pass at the end of that month, and during all the subsequent attacks. On these occasions very large numbers of wounded passed through the hands of the surgeons. When there were no wounded they were employed in treating the sick in camp.

On Dec. 11, the ambulance was withdrawn from Shipka, and early in January proceeded to Ichtiman and thence to Otloukeui.

During the retreat from Otloukeui on Bazardjik (Jan. 11) some of the ambulance wagons broke down. Surgeon Attwood, having at no small risk remained behind to guard the stores, was taken by Cossacks, and, in spite of his formal protest, conducted back to Otloukeui. There he was employed in attending to wounded Turkish prisoners until he was invalided to Philippopolis. Surgeons Hume and Sandwith, with the remainder of the ambulance, succeeded in joining the S. H. Samakov and Second Lom sections near Bazardjik, and thence retreated with Suleiman's army across the Rhodope Balkans.

I wish here to record the gallant conduct of Surgeon Hume, who, at great personal danger, rejoined his ambulance at Philippopolis by means of travelling along the railway line on a trolly at night in close proximity to the enemy. He was carrying instructions and a considerable sum of money from Constantinople.

Period of service: July 24, 1877, *to* Feb. 15, 1878.—Number of sick treated, 756; number of wounded treated, 3,013—total, 3,769. The following served on the staff of this section: Surgeons Attwood, Hume, and Sandwith, with assistants for transport.

The following are extracts from reports to the Chief Commissioner:—

Suleiman Pacha's head-quarters, Oct. 1, 1877.

Drs. ATTWOOD, HUME, and SANDWITH'S reports.

Raouf Pacha's defeat near Yenisaghra.

Messrs. Attwood, Hume, and Sandwith found at Adrianople on July 25 about 400 patients under four doctors in three hospitals. Nine-tenths of the cases were suffering from dysentery, the remainder being wounded from the Turko-Servian war. The treatment of the latter did not appear to be all that could be desired. On July 28 they went to the head quarters of Suleiman Pacha, and on the 30th they established themselves at Tirnova-Semenly, on the line between Adrianople and Yenisaghra. Two days later numerous trains arrived from the latter place, where Raouf Pacha had just sustained two severe defeats. From Aug. 1 to 5 they were occupied in attending upon the graver cases of those who thus passed to the rear. On Aug. 5, learning that but few wounded remained at the front, they returned to Adrianople to determine the nature of the provision there, for the large number of wounded that had passed through their hands. On Mr. Barrington-Kennett's arrival at Adrianople it was determined that they should remain there until the arrival of the other S. H. surgeons from Constantinople. Two buildings were assigned to them, in one of which there were 205, and in the other 101 wounded. The condition of the patients was most pitiable. Most of them were lying on the bare ground, the remainder on bare matting. The stench was sickening; the wounds of many had not been dressed since their infliction, in some cases for as long as nine days. The arrangements for feeding them were extremely inadequate, the supply of food being insufficient and irregular. This was as far as possible remedied by the purchase of food, coffee, and tobacco. During six days Messrs. Attwood, Hume, and Sandwith were engaged, from morning till night, upon work of an unusually trying character.

Drs. ATTWOOD, HUME, and SANDWITH's reports.

Wounded at Adrianople.

On Aug. 13 Nouri Pacha, Inspector-General of Hospitals, proposed that the patients should be transferred to a partially demolished barrack, without and on the opposite side of the town, where it was intended to place 1000 wounded. In the evening Drs. Moore and McIvor, S. H. surgeons, together with Drs. Kirker and Woods (Lord Blantyre), arrived from Constantinople. The following day, Aug. 14, Dr. Bond Moore and Dr. Attwood accompanied Nouri Pacha to the barrack to determine the question of transference. The site was found to be healthy, the accommodation satisfactory. Having regard to the better nature of the conditions under which the patients would find themselves, Dr. Bond Moore and Dr. Attwood concurred as to the advisability of transference of the patients, although on other grounds it had been wished that they should be treated in buildings entirely under the control of English surgeons. This transference was effected on Aug. 16 and 17. On Aug. 16 Drs. Sandwith and Hume left Adrianople to join the army of Suleiman Pacha. They arrived at the camp on the 19th, and two days later the attack on the Russian positions in the Shipka began, lasting six days. The Turkish loss was over 10,000. During this time and the two following days Drs. Sandwith and Hume were incessantly occupied in operating upon and dressing wounded men. With the exception of Dr. Leslie, of the National Aid Society, there were no other operating surgeons present. In more than half the cases in which amputation was deemed necessary the patients withheld their consent, yet in spite of this they performed as many operations as they could well undertake.

Arrival of S.H.C. surgeons.

Wounded after the first attack on the Shipka.

On Aug. 25 Dr. Attwood left Adrianople for Shipka. He reached Kesanlik, five miles from the camp, on Aug. 27. He found the town literally full of wounded, to the number of over 4,000. It is impossible to give an adequate idea of the terrible condition of things. Many badly wounded men were lying in the streets, in the extremity of torture; others were seen at the windows of the houses, imploring assistance for themselves, and the still worse cases within. At the request of Dr. Constantine Carcallis, a Greek gentleman of exceptional skill and energy, Dr. Attwood remained to operate, and to assist in making general arrangements. The transport service coming into full play, nearly 3,000 of the wounded were removed to Philippopolis during the next ten days. The next day a number of Red Crescent surgeons arrived to aid Dr. Carcallis, and Dr. Attwood went on to join his colleagues, whom he found considerably exhausted by their recent labours. No further fighting of a serious character took place till the night of Sept. 16, when 3,000 volunteers made a determined attack upon the Russian batteries. The proportional loss was very great; 1,100 were brought to the Turkish, Stafford House, and National Aid Societies' ambulances; three-fifths of the cases were treated by the English surgeons, by whom were performed all the important operations done upon the field.

Condition of wounded at Kesanlik.

Renewed attack at Shipka.

Owing to the unhealthy condition of Kesanlik, they requested the authorities to send all the cases direct to Philippopolis, with the exception of such as could not possibly bear the journey. From Sept. 19 to the present time (Oct. 1) some of the united party of English surgeons have paid daily visits to Kesanlik, in accordance with an arrangement made with Dr. Carcallis. They have urged the necessity of evacuating the district to the fullest possible extent, and of employing energetic sanitary measures to combat the unhealthy state of the town, where typhus fever and gangrene have made their appearance. At the present moment there remained from 200 to 300 wounded and sick. The camp is in a generally healthy condition, there being but a relatively small number of cases of sickness, chiefly of intermittent fever and diarrhœa, notwithstanding an almost total disregard of the simplest sanitary rules.

Healthy condition of camp.

Dec. 11, 1877.

Since Nov. 1 no wounded have been treated in the ambulance. In spite of occasional heavy artillery fire, there have been very few casualties upon the Turkish side. The few wounded have

General report.

RECORD OF OPERATIONS.

Drs. Attwood, Hume, and Sandwith's reports.

Treatment of sick in camp.

been treated by the Turkish surgeons, with the exception of a case of severe injury to the leg (shell wound), in which amputation was performed by Mr. MacKellar, who was at the time on a visit to Shipka. The health of the camp has been exceptionally good. The prevailing diseases —dysentery, diarrhœa, and intermittent fever—have largely diminished. Forty-seven cases of these disorders—five of the first, twenty-eight of the second, fourteen of the last—have been treated in the ambulance. On Nov. 4, Dr. Sandwith, in accordance with instructions from Constantinople, left for the hospital at Adrianople. Eighteen men, victims of ill-treatment at the hands of the Bulgarians during the retreat of the Russians from Eski-Zaghra, have presented themselves at the ambulance for examination and treatment. Some of these were sent by Mr. Blunt, to whom reports upon the nature of their injuries have been furnished. On Dec. 11 the ambulance left Shipka, its longer continuance there being deemed undesirable, owing to the unlikelihood of further fighting.

Constantinople, Feb. 2, 1878.

Dr. Sandwith's report.

In accordance with your desire I beg to inform you of the proceedings of the Shipka ambulance from Dec. 13 until the present date. The ambulance remained at Philippopolis until Dec. 27, awaiting instructions from Mr. Pratt, but on that day Dr. Attwood proceeded with it to Tatar-Bazardjik, taking Kostoff as interpreter. Dr. Hume was at this time advised to return to the rear for a few days to recruit his strength after a troublesome illness contracted at Philippopolis. I joined the ambulance on Jan. 2 at Bazardjik, and, after buying some horses and making other necessary preparations, started on Jan. 4 with Dr. Attwood for Ichtiman, in order to discover the most useful point for establishing the ambulance. While crossing the Kapudchik Derbend Pass we encountered long trains of refugees from the neighbouring villages, whose oxen and horses were succumbing in great numbers to their prolonged exertions in attempting to traverse the icy roads. On arriving at Ichtiman the following day we learnt from Zabit Pacha that all the troops and population had been evacuated to the rear, and that no fighting was expected. We accordingly left the town, which was already in flames, at daybreak, with the Pacha, it being immediately entered by the enemy. At Kapudchik village we had an interview with Muchir Safvet Pacha, who desired Dr. Attwood to form a small ambulance in the village of Yetrena, to be prepared for the forcing of the Kapudchik Pass by the enemy. Dr. Attwood accordingly obtained possession of some suitable houses for this purpose, and after visiting the sick and wounded soldiers and inhabitants of the village, we returned to Bazardjik on Jan. 7 to procure additional stores. News having arrived in the meantime of the retreat of Chakir Pacha and Baker Pacha's armies on Otloukeui, and of the complete loss of medical stores and of most of the doctors attached to those armies, Dr. Attwood was requested by Fuad Pacha to proceed thither to make any arrangements he thought necessary for the wounded during the (then supposed) armistice. The chief Bulgarian of Bazardjik left the town on Jan. 8, and requested Dr. Attwood to try to protect his house with the Stafford House flag, in return handing over to Dr. Attwood unconditionally horses, carriages, and other necessaries most acceptable in a partly deserted town. Reaching Otloukeui on Jan. 10, Dr. Attwood immediately reported himself to Baker Pacha, and gave medical stores to the English military doctors upon his staff. Very shortly after arrival we learnt that the whole army was in retreat, and that it would be necessary for us to leave that night. A previous thaw of two days' duration was now succeeded by a sharp frost, and the roads became so slippery that the horses were only able to advance very slowly. About one hour from the village the horses of the fourth carriage proved unable to ascend the thick sheet of ice which coated the whole surface of one of the hills. Leaving it in charge of a soldier, we continued our journey until, in another half hour, the wheel of the third carriage came off, and we were obliged to relinquish it also. Soon afterwards the second carriage became fixed in a stream, and the tired horses were unable to drag it out and carry it up a steep hill. It being then about one hour after midnight, Dr. Attwood proceeded with the dragoman to the nearest village to find ox arabas to transport our stores, while I remained with the second carriage. I was fortunately able to make a large fire and warm some of the sick and stragglers who passed me during the night. Of the former many were Arabs, and nearly all were suffering from frost-bitten hands and feet. Eight soldiers and dozens of horses succumbed during the night to the severity of the climate and of the night's march. At daylight I secured the aid of twenty soldiers, and succeeded in getting the third carriage to the top of the hill, and then continued my journey, meeting Kostoff about 11 A.M., returning with three ox arabas to bring on the contents of the abandoned vehicles. In the afternoon I came up to Dr. Attwood, and found him in the Refugees' Barrack erected last

Arrival at Ichtiman.

Retreat of Chakir and Baker Pachas.

Retreat from Otloukeui.

Suffering of Arabs.

year by Mr. Long in a village (Kaliglari) half way between Otloukeui and Bazardjik. He expressed his determination to remain there until the return of Kostoff, but requested me to proceed at once to Bazardjik with all the remaining portion of the ambulance. The road being then fairly level, and no longer blocked by masses of men and pack-horses retreating with the army, I was able to arrive at Bazardjik the same evening, and there learnt for the first time of the non-existence of the armistice. On the morning of Jan. 12 I returned to repair the first carriage, which had broken down and been left by me in a village the previous evening. I also rode for one hour and a half on the Otloukeui road, in the hopes of meeting Dr. Attwood. Bazardjik at this time was in a very excited state; incendiaries were diligently at work; roving Bashi-Bazouks were forcing their way into many of the houses, and the Stafford House flag was able to afford protection for the night to many frightened women and children. I left the town during the night to rejoin the army, which had retreated to an adjacent village, and returned the next morning to find Dr. Attwood and Kostoff still missing, and left word for them in the event of their arrival. [See Dr. Attwood's report following this.] By the advice of Baker Pacha we left for Philippopolis the same afternoon. The telegraph and the railway had then ceased to work, and the environs of the station were crowded with refugees who had been unable to get away by train. As we passed through the town we saw many large buildings on fire, and groups of Christian inhabitants accosted us with every expression of sorrow. After proceeding for one mile outside Bazardjik we were ordered to retreat by Osman Nouri Pacha, who was drawn up with his division on the main Philippopolis road to receive some Cossacks who had been seen in the neighbourhood. The ambulance which had now joined those under charge of Dr. McQueen and Dr. Sketchley therefore accompanied the army along a bye-road towards Philippopolis. Owing to the narrowness of the road and the amount of traffic and the number of cannon, for which we had to wait at every rough piece of ground, we had not advanced very far by two o'clock A.M., and encamped in a village blazing and smoking like the others on our route, in order to rest our horses till daylight. Crossing a rickety and very slippery bridge in the morning light a cannon fell into the river, closely followed by one of our small carriages. We were only enabled with difficulty to save the horses and the stores contained in the vehicle. On arriving at Philippopolis the ambulance was joined by Dr. Hume, who had made extraordinary exertions to do so, having travelled on an engine, and for the last part of the journey on a trolly worked by hand. I had been enabled to bring all the stores with me, and now handed over to Dr. Minassian all the heavy matériel for use in his Stafford House hospital. Suleiman Pacha telegraphed to Mr. Consul Calvert asking which Stafford House doctors would remain in the town to take charge of any wounded who might come in after the fighting at this time going on; and on Dr. Minassian volunteering to do so, assisted by Dr. Langdon and Dr. Heath, of the Turkish service, his Excellency at once ordered all the military and civil hospitals with their personnel to be placed under the control of the Stafford House representative. On Jan. 15 a battle in the plain furnished Dr. Hume and myself with some patients, who, after being dressed, were sent to the Stafford House hospital. We proceeded to the railway station in the afternoon, and placed ourselves under the orders of Safvet Pacha. At midnight we started with the Pacha and troops for Stanimaka, when the enemy, who had advanced to within a distance of 300 yards, opened a very brisk musketry fire as we left the station. Our servants and arabajis on this occasion showed the greatest fortitude, and exhibited no anxiety to leave their posts, in spite of the confusion and flight of the Turkish cavalry around us. Reaching Stanimaka the next morning at 6 A.M., we rested there until the night of the 17th. During our stay we attended the wounded who accompanied us from Philippopolis and those who resulted from the fighting then going on immediately without the town. We now learnt from Captain Burnaby that it would be impossible to take wheeled vehicles further, and accordingly procured pack-saddles, on to which we transferred as many of our stores as it was possible to carry upon horses. The carriages, stretchers, and some stores were of necessity abandoned. Starting with the staff of Baker Pacha at 2 A.M. on the 18th we proceeded, with the exception of four hours' halt, until 8.30 P.M. After five hours' sleep in the snow we proceeded once more, and at daybreak commenced the ascent of the Rhodope Mountains. The hill-side, covered with deep snow, except where its many zigzag paths had their surface beaten into glassy ice, seemed an almost insuperable obstacle to tired men and horses. On every side, upon the ice and in the snow, struggling and falling horses, soldiers and wounded mixed in frightful confusion with women and children flying from their burnt houses, all toiling wearily upwards. During the ascent the explosion of an ammunition box, which had fallen from a mule, added not a little to the general confusion. In the plain below could be seen the Cossacks advancing to the foot of the hill, and as, from there, they fired on the struggling masses, soldiers with pack-horses on all sides cut loose their baggage and so hurried

Dr. SANDWITH'S report.

Protection afforded by S. H. flag.

Meeting of the S. H. C. ambulances at Philippopolis.

Loss of an ambulance carriage.

All hospitals in Philippopolis placed under S. H. staff.

Retreat across the Rhodope Balkans.

Difficulties of retreat.

66   RECORD OF OPERATIONS.

Dr. SANDWITH's report. — to escape. Our servants exerted themselves so well that they made the ascent with the loss of only one box, a somewhat heavy case of provisions. After the climb of three hours we halted on the hill-top and cautiously advanced through the district, where roads from Haskeui offered an opportunity to the enemy to cut off our retreat. We went on through the hills, the bitter cold gradually relenting from day to day as we travelled southwards, until, after spending a night at the small town of Kirikh-Ali, on the banks of the Arda, halting at various hamlets and traversing

Arrival at Gumurgina. — the almost pathless mountain gorges, we reached Gumurgina on the morning of Jan. 23. Here we were very hospitably entertained by the Greek bishop and other inhabitants of the town, who afforded us most welcome food and rest. On the afternoon of the 24th we proceeded four hours

Arrival at the coast. Embarkation of wounded. — to Bumbaya, and on the following day by fording two arms of the sea reached Porto Lagos (Karagatch). On the 26th and 27th we were occupied in dressing the wounded, of whom we had succeeded in bringing some through the hills. During these two days our patients were gradually embarked and placed on board the steamship *Sultanié*, where we joined them on the evening of the 27th, having been specially requested by Suleiman Pacha to accompany them to Constantinople. The decks being covered with between 3,000 and 4,000 troops, the wounded and sick, the former numbering 380 and the latter 120, were crowded together in the state saloon and the after cabins of the vessel. The authorities were unable to provide them with anything but biscuit, and it was with great difficulty that we succeeded in obtaining a very inadequate supply of water for them. By the kindness of Mr. Young, chief commissioner of the National Aid Society, who arrived in the steamship *Osmanié* on the morning of the 28th, we were enabled to supply them with soup, bread, and underclothing. To the same source we are indebted for several hundred bandages, of which our own stock was by this time nearly exhausted. They were assisted on board by a willing staff of Turkish dressers. Eight men succumbed during the voyage, but we had the satisfaction of relieving to a great extent the sufferings of the wounded and of curing a large proportion of the sick. At Gallipoli we were enabled to procure oranges and tobacco, for which our patients

Arrival at Constantinople. — were deeply grateful. We arrived at Constantinople on the evening of Feb. 2, and on the following day the wounded were removed to various hospitals. This report cannot be closed without acknowledging the unfailing kindness of General Baker and Captain Burnaby.

London, Feb. 23, 1879.

Dr. ATTWOOD's report. — Dr. Sandwith and I left Tatar-Bazardjik for Otloukeui on Jan 9, arriving the following afternoon. This was done after consultation with Fuad Pacha, in command at Bazardjik, who said that there was an armistice, and that we should do well to join Chakir Pacha and General Baker Pacha at Otloukeui, where we should probably find wounded for whom there was little surgical provision, while at Bazardjik there was a sufficient number of surgeons. We took four carriages containing surgical stores and provisions, and were accompanied by Kostoff, a Bulgarian inter-

Arrival at Otloukeui. — preter who had been transferred to me at Philippopolis by Dr. Minassian. On reaching Otloukeui, however, we found that the wounded had been sent forward or left at villages on the way. Shortly afterwards word was brought to us that the retreat was to be at once continued, and that General Baker desired us to return with the troops. Much as we might have wished to remain to rest our tired horses, it was clear that we could not do so in the face of the General's recommen-

Retreat. — dation. About nine o'clock at night we set out on the return-journey. It had unfortunately happened that, whereas for two or three days previously the weather had moderated and the roads were soft, just as we reached Otloukeui a sudden severe frost set in, rendering the roads extremely slippery. We had therefore every reason to fear that our journey would be attended with difficulties. The first of our carriages got along well enough, and reached Bazardjik without mis-

Carriages break down. — hap. Of the remaining three, one broke down so completely a short distance outside Otloukeui that I directed it to be abandoned, transferring its contents to the others. These other two we managed to get along with great labour some miles over the frozen bridgeless roads, but at length, about four o'clock in the morning, they came to a complete stand-still. I went forward with Kostoff to the village of Popensy, to procure aid in the shape of men and oxen. This was accomplished between seven and eight o'clock. I instructed Kostoff to return with the men and oxen, and remained at the village in charge of the horses taken from the abandoned carriage, my own horse, papers, and some articles of value. Kostoff was confident that he should be able to bring on the carriages in a few hours with the aid obtained. A little after mid-day Dr. Sandwith arrived at the village with one of the carriages. He had got it along by impressing into his service some soldiers, and had met Kostoff, who had gone on in search of the other carriage. He offered to await Kostoff's return, leaving me free to proceed to Bazardjik with the carriage, but we agreed that he should go on and that I should follow later, allowing three or four hours for Kostoff to return. When it began to get dark, about five o'clock, I considered I had waited long enough, and made towards the road, which was at a distance of 400 or 500 yards from the village. On approaching it I was met by some of the villagers, who told me that the road had been cut some distance ahead, and was occupied by Cossacks and armed Bulgarians. I determined to return to the village and make another attempt at daybreak, hoping that the Cossacks had but made a reconnaissance and would retire to Otloukeui for the night. At early dawn I made for the road, leading the horses, and seeing it apparently clear, thought there was a prospect of getting away, but when within 50 or 60 yards of the road, six or seven Cossacks, riding rapidly round a bend in it some 300 yards off, in the direction of Otloukeui, came up opposite me and fired. The light being dim and the road raised high above the frozen ground I was traversing, they did not pursue me. Returning to the village, I tried to engage some-one to conduct me across country in the direction of Philippopolis. When a man had been found to undertake this, and we were on the point of quitting the village on the side opposite to the road to Bazardjik, it was surrounded by Cossacks. I was detained until the arrival of the General. To him I gave an account of myself, and requested to be allowed to make my way to Philippopolis, making reference to the Geneva Convention, which seemed but to provoke amusement. I was ordered to remain in the village in charge of some officers of the Imperial Guard, who had advanced with the Cossack troops and were to await the coming of the rest of the army. I made an unavailing protest against the seizure of the horses I had with me. Next morning General Krudener arrived. I again claimed to be allowed to betake myself to Philippopolis or Adrianople, but the General told me I must go to Otloukeui and there remain until the arrival of the Grand Duke Nicholas, which would probably be a matter of but two or three days, after which I should no doubt be set at liberty. I was then rejoined by Kostoff. He told me he had met Dr. Sandwith, that he had then proceeded in search of the other carriage, that he found that the men in charge had left it—they having, as was afterwards ascertained, become alarmed for their safety and gone off with the horses to Bazardjik, where they rejoined the rest of the ambulance—that he had then, notwithstanding my express injunction to the contrary, gone on to the carriage abandoned close to Otloukeui, and that while taking it along towards Popensy he was made prisoner. He was allowed to remain with me, and we were directed to set out in charge of a Cossack for Otloukeui. After having gone about a quarter of the way, we halted at a shed, where were collected some 60 or 70 Turkish soldiers—stragglers—many of them sick and frostbitten, under the charge of a dozen armed Bulgarians of the worst type. Our Cossack declared that he should go no further, having been expected to be relieved at this spot, and that we must go on with the others. This was about mid-day. We then continued our journey, which was of a painful character. On the way we met a number of Russian linesmen, and were made to halt that they might inspect us. Here one of the prisoners was by one of the escort wantonly struck to the ground, and then by another shot through the head. Several of the Russian soldiers could have prevented this act by simply stretching out their hands. They did not seem to me to have suggested or encouraged it; their attitude was that of amused indifference. Three times on the way was this repeated, in each case no provocation being given other than inability to march as rapidly as the escort desired. Later on a halt was made, and, from what I could gather at the time and subsequently by questioning Kostoff, a general massacre was proposed, but was negatived by the less savage and excited among the escort. At dusk we reached Otloukeui. The Russian Commandant sent word that he was too busy to see me, and that the police were to find me a lodging for the night. Next morning I was taken before him. On my narrating the occurrences of the previous day, the chief of the police stated that it was impossible to bring the escort to account for their conduct, as they were unknown at Otloukeui, and had gone off in various directions immediately after their arrival. The Commandant told me that if I would pledge my word not to attempt to escape he would allow me to shift for myself in the village, that he knew nothing as to the coming of the Grand Duke, and that I must remain there until further orders in attendance upon the sick and wounded Turkish soldiers there collected to the number of about 300. I was thus engaged until the middle of February, when I fell suddenly ill. A few days later the Commandant received orders to evacuate Otloukeui with his prisoners. I was put into an ox-wagon by Kostoff and carried off to Philippopolis. A fortnight later my colleague, Dr. Hume, hearing of my condition, came from Constantinople to look after me, and tended me through a long and severe illness with the greatest skill and kindness.

[*Note.*—Dr. Attwood returned to England invalided in April, 1878.]

ADRIANOPLE HOSPITAL.

This hospital was first formed in two empty houses, on the great influx of wounded to Adrianople after the battles of Yenisaghra and Eskisaghra, and was subsequently transferred to a wing of the large cavalry barracks. In addition to their hospital work, the Staff were frequently engaged at the railway station in attending to the large numbers of wounded passing through on their way to Constantinople.

The wounded were evacuated the day before the occupation of the town by the Russians, and the Staff retired at the same time, after leaving the valuable part of their stores in the hands of the British Consul.

Period of service: Aug. 12, 1877, to Jan. 19, 1878.—Average number of beds occupied, 200; treated in hospital, sick, 200; wounded, 983; treated at railway station, 3,180; total, 4,363. The following served at different times on the staff of this section : Surgeons Moore, McIvor, Kirker, Woods, Sandwith, Assistant-Surgeons Stuart and Azzopardi, Dispenser Spanopoulos, and Turkish assistants.

The following are extracts from Reports to the Chief Commissioner :—

Adrianople, Aug. 29, 1877.

Dr. Moore's report.

I beg herewith to send you the following report of the wounded men we have had in our charge since our arrival here. Men in old hospital when I took charge, 206; sent to Constantinople convalescent, 87; died before removal to Barrack Hospital, 3; removed to Barrack Hospital, 146. Of these there have been sent to Constantinople, 76; died in Barrack Hospital, 4; men remaining in hospital too seriously wounded to be removed, 66. When next I see you, I will explain the difficulty of giving an accurate report of patients transferred to our wards during our absence in the night-time by the Turkish surgeons. We have not in any single instance objected to attend to these men. They were nearly all suffering from active erysipelas or its results; and, in justice to the Stafford House Committee (without I have your authority), I object on their behalf to be responsible for the high rate of mortality which occurred amongst these men, irrespectively of the instances in which our patients contracted from them the contagion. We have received information that about 600 wounded men are en route for our hospital.

Difficulty of obtaining accurate returns.

Adrianople, Sept. 8, 1877.

Everything is going on now pretty smoothly, quite as well as we ought to expect perhaps, all things considered. I cannot make you a report as to work done very well; for the patients are moved so often that it is next to impossible to keep a list of them. And it is in this way. A batch of weary, wet, but slightly wounded arrive with six or eight days' interval of dressing. We take them in, give good food, warm beds, and clean dressing for two or three days, when they are fit to go on to Constantinople and make room for the most urgent cases. Scudamore and Cowan are of great assistance to us, and to-day a French officer who speaks English fluently has offered his services gratuitously.

Adrianople, Sept. 10, 1877.

At present I want nothing very urgently in the way of stores beyond bandages, marine lint, carbolic acid, &c., all of which I wrote for on Friday. The blankets will be very acceptable. I have not yet received them; but M. Morisot, who is very useful, has gone down now (6 A.M. Monday) to the station to see after them. Yesterday I cleared out every patient able to go, leaving about 59 only; these I have put in the corridor, and thrown the wards open for ventilation and whitewashing, &c. On Tuesday we fill again. My little children patients at the other hospitals are all doing well. The Sultan's aide-de-camp visited us on Saturday, and caught us hard at a 'bullet in the knee-joint,' which luckily we extracted before he left; he expressed much satisfaction.

[Note.—Dr. Moore, with a small transport section, was shortly afterwards attached to the Sultan's Circassian Guard. Dr. McIvor succeeded him as chief of section.]

ADRIANOPLE HOSPITAL. 69

Adrianople, Sept. 28, 1877.

Blankets are required for our patients, as stoves have not yet been fitted up in the hospital. A military inspector from Constantinople visited us on Wednesday; he examined all the wards most accurately, also our operating and store-rooms, and seemed well pleased. Everything is going on well here. We have now 201 patients. — *Dr. McIvor's reports. Increased number of patients.*

Week ending Oct. 13, 1877.—Patients remaining in hospital on Oct. 6, 116; admitted during week, 96—total, 212; patients discharged during week, 1; died, 6; remaining in hospital, 205; minor operations performed, 12; major ditto, 1 (in Turkish hospital). Assisted their surgeons to perform another. — *Weekly reports.*

Week ending Oct. 20, 1877.—Patients remaining in hospital on Oct. 13, 205; admitted during week, 2—total, 207; discharged, 1; died, 4; remaining in hospital, 202; major operations performed, 1; minor ditto, 9; one major operation in Turkish hospital; 300 pair of socks distributed to patients.

Week ending Oct. 27, 1877.—Patients remaining in hospital, Oct. 20, 202; admitted during week, 22—total, 224; discharged, 80; died, 2; remaining in hospital, 142; minor operations performed, 6.

Week ending Nov. 3, 1877.—Patients remaining in hospital on Oct. 27, 162; admitted during week, 81—total, 223; discharged during week, 44; died, 3; remaining in hospital, 176. The 81 patients admitted as above were in a most deplorable condition, many suffering from severe diarrhœa, mostly all complaining of rheumatism, and some stating that their wounds had not been dressed for three days. Although patients have been admitted in such a state, I am happy to say that no case of tetanus, erysipelas, pyæmia, or gangrene have occurred in our wards during the last month.

Week ending Nov. 10, 1877.—Patients remaining in hospital, Nov. 3, 176; admitted during the week, 134—total, 310; discharged during week, cured, 97; died, 5—total, 102; remaining in hospital, 208.

Week ending Nov. 17, 1877.—Patients in hospital, Nov. 10, 208; admitted during week, 49—total, 257; patients discharged during week, *nil*; died, 6; remaining in hospital, 251. I may again report that the wounded who arrived here from Sofia were in a most miserable condition, both as regards their clothing and the state of their wounds. Amongst them were several cases of erysipelas, and many of diarrhœa. I have also to report that during the past week we have increased the number of beds in one hospital by 63. These also contain most severe cases. During the past week we have performed three capital operations. We also operated on a case of fistula in the person of an officer who had twice before been operated on by Turkish doctors, but without any beneficial effect, and during the past fortnight 40 minor operations have been performed in our wards, which include incising abscesses, removing dead bone and parts of fingers and toes, and extraction of bullets. — *Extension of hospital.*

Week ending Nov. 24, 1877.—Patients remaining in hospital, Nov. 17, 251; admitted during week, 3—total, 254; died during week, 2; discharged, 18—total, 20; remaining in hospital, 234; number of empty beds, 40; major operations performed, 2; minor ditto, 10. Received stores, also an ambulance wagon fitted up with necessary appliances for the comfortable carriage of wounded.

Week ending Dec. 1, 1877.—Patients in hospital, Nov. 24, 234; admitted during week, 32—total, 266; discharged, cured, 2; died, 4—total, 6; patients in hospital, Dec. 1, 260. During the past week, six partial resections were performed in hospital—two of both bones of forearm, one of tibia, two of bones of feet, one of part of sacrum. The resection case we received from you has enabled us to perform these operations efficiently; and as those patients on whom we have operated are progressing most satisfactorily, we hope to substitute resection for amputation in certain cases—a matter which is evidently a great boon to the patients, who would otherwise be crippled for life.

Week ending Dec. 8, 1877.—Patients in hospital, Dec. 1, 260; discharged during week, 3; died, 9—total, 12; in hospital, Dec. 8, 248. The following operations were performed during the week, the patients being under the influence of chloroform:—Two patients, resections of humerus; one Chopart's operation of foot on account of gangrene caused by frost-bite; one bullet removed from thigh after an interval of four months (bullet removed on admission); three amputations of fingers and one of thumb; one partial resection of ulna; one partial resection of lower jaw; one partial resection of clavicle; one amputation of five toes on account of gangrene caused by frost-bite. On Dec. 1, sixteen patients were admitted suffering from diarrhœa and dysentery of the

RECORD OF OPERATIONS.

Dr. McIvor's report. most aggravated character, which they had contracted at Plevna and Shipka. On admission, six of them were *in articulo mortis*. The best treatment was of no avail, as they were almost unable to take either medicines or food. Three died on second day, two on third, and one on fourth day; the remainder, who were in a most precarious condition, are now gradually improving.

Week ending Dec. 15, 1877.—Patients in hospital, Dec. 8, 248; admitted during week, 72—total, 320; discharged during week, 73; died, 3; remaining in hospital, 244. Operations: one resection of ulna; one extraction of bullet from arm after two months; sixteen minor operations. The ambulance wagon lent by Baron Mundy is being used to convey our wounded to the bath of the palace, about half-a mile distant; his Majesty, the Sultan, having placed the bath at the disposal of the wounded.

Week ending Dec. 29, 1877.—Patients in hospital, Dec. 22, 243; admitted during week, 71—total, 314; discharged during week, 57; dead, 6; remaining in hospital, 251. Operations performed during the week: two partial resections of humerus, two of tibia, one of fibula, and two of tarsus; one extraction of bullet from calf of leg; one removal of toes; and ten minor operations. During the week Mahmoud Damad Pacha visited the hospital, and on leaving expressed himself highly satisfied with the care we took of the patients, saying he would specially mention the same to his brother-in-law the Sultan.

Inspection by Mahmoud Damad Pacha.

Addition of two wards. *Week ending Jan. 5, 1878.*—Patients in hospital, Dec. 29, 251; admitted during week, 63—total, 314; discharged during week, 90; dead, 11; remaining in hospital, Jan. 5, 213. Operations: one excision of os calcis; six minor operations. I have to report that during the past month, our hospital has been enlarged by the addition of two wards containing seventeen beds each.

Week ending Jan. 12, 1878.—Patients remaining in hospital, Jan. 5, 213; admitted during week, 48—total, 261; discharged during week, 250; died during week, 11—total, 261; patients remaining in hospital, Jan. 12, none. Operations performed during week: one excision of metatarsal bone of right foot; one partial resection of tibia; one partial resection of femur; one partial resection of astragalus; one amputation of toes. On Wednesday, Jan. 9, we received official orders that all patients were to be removed from hospital next day, which orders were accordingly carried out, although we protested against the evacuation of some patients who were unable to undergo the journey. On Friday we received notice that 1,500 wounded were at the station. We proceeded there with all our staff as quickly as possible in our ambulance wagons, and attended to between 400 and 500 men. Owing to the wounded having objected to being dressed with cold water, we have made arrangements that hot water will always be in readiness on their arrival. We have retained our full staff on account of the near approach of the Russians and the likelihood of early fighting; in the meantime I will utilise them as far as possible in attending to the wounded at the railway-station.

Evacuation of hospital.

Evacuation of Adrianople by the Turks. *Week ending Jan. 19, 1878.*—Patients remaining in hospital, Jan. 12, none. 19th: Patients admitted during the week, 130; discharged, 130. On Sunday, Jan 13, a train of 300 wounded at station was dressed by us. On Friday morning we received official information from Djemid Pacha that it would be necessary for us to leave as soon as possible, as no resistance was to be made to the enemy by the garrison. I had scarcely received this information when all our servants left with the regiment of soldiers quartered in another part of the barracks. I proceeded immediately to the Commandant (Ahmet Eyoub Pacha), and asked him for means to transport our wounded to the railway-station, a distance of three miles. He promised to send some if possible. After waiting two hours we sent a second time to him, receiving the same reply. As the day was now far advanced, and still no appearance of arabas, we were obliged to proceed to the surrounding districts to search for them, and after much difficulty succeeded in obtaining twelve; into these we put all those patients who were unable to walk, and conveyed the remainder on foot to the station. After having disposed of our wounded, we removed the greater part of our medical stores to the British Consulate, and it being now night we were unable to remove the remainder. For our ambulance wagon and horses we could not procure transport by rail, and at twelve o'clock at night we sent them by road in care of our personal servants. The medical staff, owing to the kindness of the Vali, were able to obtain places in the same carriage as himself, and after a journey of four days and five nights we arrived at Stamboul safely. At Tchorlou, Dr. Kirker performed a Syme's amputation of foot with instruments contained in a small pocket-case. The doctors went into the fields, caught the oxen, yoked them up, and then carried down the wounded from the wards themselves. All the Turkish staff had fled. Firing from windows on the flying Turkish population was going on, and pillage on all sides, as they left.

PHILIPPOPOLIS HOSPITALS.

(Including general relief in private houses.)

This section, under Surgeon Neylan, was despatched early in September to Philippopolis, where there was a great and sudden influx of wounded from the fighting in the Shipka Pass. Thirty houses in the town were turned into hospitals and crowded with wounded, who were in a most pitiable state, owing to the insufficient number of the Government Medical Staff and want of most ordinary hospital supplies. The supervision of all the Government hospitals in the town was entrusted to Surgeon Neylan by Ibrahim Pacha, the Governor; at the same time two hospitals containing 130 cases were specially handed over to the Stafford House Staff. In October these were established in the Bulgarian Metropolitan's Palace and the Greek School.

Surgeon Neylan returned invalided at the end of September, when Surgeon Eccles was appointed chief of section. This gentleman returned invalided with typhoid fever in November, when Surgeon Minassian was appointed chief. Surgeon Calfoglou, another of the Staff, suffered severely from typhoid.

During the fighting in the neighbourhood, preceding the occupation of the town by the Russians, the S. H. Staff was actively engaged. On abandoning the town, Suleiman Pacha left the greater part of his wounded in the charge of the S. H. surgeons, who volunteered, under Surgeon Minassian, to remain at their posts.

The section was continued for three months after the Russian occupation, during which time, in addition to their work at the hospitals, this section relieved the wants of many hundred wounded who were sent through Philippopolis from Sofia and Kesanlik, on their way to Constantinople.

The hospital was ultimately handed over to the Red Crescent Society.

Period of service: Sept. 1, 1877, to *April* 15, 1878.—Treated in hospital, sick, 322; wounded, 2,084—total, 2,406. Average number of beds occupied, 140. No record was kept of the numbers treated at the railway station or in private houses. The following served at different times on the staff of this section: Surgeons Neylan, Eccles, Wood, Minassian, and Calfoglou, Dispenser Akestorides, and Turkish assistants.

The following are extracts from Reports to the Chief Commissioner:—

Philippopolis, Oct. 1, 1877.

On the receipt of news that Philippopolis was full of wounded, who were without any proper attention, I proceeded there in accordance with your instructions on Aug. 31 with Dr. Minassian and two assistants. On my arrival (Sept. 2), I found 2,000 wounded scattered about the city in 30 private houses. The cases brought from Shipka by the transport service under Dr. Stoker and Weller were well cared for; but the condition of those brought by the authorities was dreadful in the extreme. The journey from the Pass, occupying four days in open oxen-wagons over rough roads, without proper food or attention to their wounds, many of which were full of maggots, lessened considerably their chances of recovery. At a meeting convened by the military commandant (Ibrahim Pacha), I was given supreme control over all the hospitals. As a preliminary to getting affairs into order, I sent 600 of the lighter cases to Constantinople; the remainder were placed in nine large buildings (Bulgarian schools, mosques, &c.) in airy situations. Myself and colleague took charge of three of these and had them filled with the most serious cases. The rest were under the care of the Turkish military surgeons, and were visited daily by me. Gangrene, pyæmia, erysipelas, and

Dr. NEYLAN's report.

State of wounded on arrival of S. H. Staff.

S. H. staff given control over all Philippopolis hospitals.

Dr. NEYLAN's report.	tetanus were rife, but the mortality was not high, as I at once isolated the worst cases in tents removed some distance from the hospitals. The serious nature of the cases will be seen by the fact that, in a hospital containing 45 beds, there were eleven compound fractures of the femur and six penetrative wounds of the knee-joint. Carbolic acid and drainage-tubing worked marvels in wounds of the most foul description. Hypodermic injection of morphia was very much appreciated, all the occupants of an hospital where it had been once or twice used crying out for it. The sick, which at first were not numerous, increased afterwards, and by the end of September, formed about one-fifth of the cases brought from the front. Nearly all were suffering from dysentery and intermittent fever. The authorities provided mattresses and blankets, and, after ten days, 600 bedsteads. I had an operating-room fitted up in a central position, to which all cases were brought. Dr. Woods (Lord Blantyre), Stafford House, and Dr. Manoury, French Society for the Relief of Ottoman Wounded, and Dr. Razis, Croissant Rouge, arrived on the 15th, and immediately took charge of an hospital each. It was extremely difficult to obtain the patients' consent to amputation; in fact, they rarely gave it, except when they thought themselves *in extremis*. All were 'secondary,' and many fifteen days after injury.
Result of operations.	The result of 42 major operations performed by myself and the above-mentioned surgeons from Sept. 2 to Sept. 29, inclusive, was to-day (Oct. 1) as follows:—

Operation	No.	Died	Doing well	Causes of Death
Amputation through upper third thigh	2	1	1	Pyæmia
,, ,, middle ,,	2	0	2	
,, ,, knee-joint	4	2	2	Pyæmia and dysentery
,, ,, middle third leg	4	0	4	
,, ,, 'Syme'	1	0	1	
Disarticulation at shoulder	2	1	1	Pyæmia
Excision of shoulder	4	0	4	
Amputation through upper third arm	4	2	2	Gangrene
,, ,, lower ,,	9	1	8	Intermittent fever
,, ,, forearm	7	1	6	Pyæmia
,, at wrist	2	1	1*	Secondary hæmorrhage

* This man had his other arm amputated at Shipka seventeen days before.

A very large number of minor operations were done which I had no time to make note of. Chloroform was administered 139 times without mishap. Out of 2,000 cases, there were only fifteen cases of sabre and bayonet-wounds, and about 150 shell-wounds, the rest being rifle bulletwounds. In the vast majority of instances, the bullet passed through the arm or leg. I extracted 28 bullets. About 60 per cent. were wounds of the fingers and hand (generally the left). There were many wounds of the knee and elbow-joints; wounds of the head were uncommon. In two instances the inferior maxilla was blown completely away, and the men are recovering. [N.B.— Dr. Neylan returned invalided and was succeeded by Dr. Eccles.]

Philippopolis, Oct. 20, 1877.

Dr. ECCLES' reports.	The residence of the Bulgarian Metropolitan, and the Greek school for boys, have been placed, with three dressers, an apothecary, and a staff of hospital attendants, under the control of the S. H. officers, and we trust in a few days to have arranged for 152 patients. On Thursday 300 patients, whose wounds or diseases were of a slight nature, or best able to travel, were forwarded to Adrianople at the request of the Deputy-Inspector of Hospitals here. Mr. Eccles, with two dragomans, assisted in the transport of patients to the station, where they were confided to the care of Dr. Barker's S. H. railway ambulance. The following evening about 500 sick and wounded arrived from Kesanlik, and were distributed among the hospitals. Thirty-five were received at the Metropolitan's hospital, and 24 into the Greek school; the majority of them are suffering from diarrhœa, dysentery, and miasmatic fever, only one or two cases being wounds. The patients were
Filthy condition of wounded.	literally starving with cold and hunger, and parasites had even carried their attacks into the ears, nostrils and eyelids. Some of the sufferers were so exhausted that it was found impossible to send them to the baths, or even to employ fumigation. There is great need of bed-linen, night-clothes, and mattresses stuffed with a material softer than hay; as it is impossible to avoid bedsores under the present condition of affairs, and any attempt to keep patients at rest for the union

of fractures is frustrated by the unendurable pain occasioned by lying in one position on bags stuffed with hay.   Dr. Eccles' reports.

Philippopolis, Oct. 20, 1877.

The number of patients in the S. H. Greek School hospital on the 18th was 52, of whom two have returned to their regiments and 24 have been sent to Adrianople ; the remaining 26 were all cases of gunshot wounds, one having also an attack of typhoid fever. On 19th inst., 24 patients were received from Shipka, of which five were from gunshot wounds, and nineteen suffering from diarrhœa, &c. ; thus making total of number now in hospital 50, of which there are 30 cases of gunshot wounds, one typhoid fever, one sciatica, ten diarrhœa, one conjunctivitis, five debility, one inguinal hernia, one bronchitis ; total, 50.   Report on Dr. Minassian's hospital.

Philippopolis, Oct. 27, 1877.

At present there are nearly 2,000 sick and wounded in the town, about 300 of which lie in the S. H. hospitals. The majority of the sick are in a fit state for transport to central hospitals, and not a few are convalescent, and await orders to be sent to their homes on sick leave.

Philippopolis, Nov. 3, 1877.

On Friday, Nov. 2, 300 patients were conveyed from Philippopolis to Adrianople. This evacuation has relieved the hospitals of overcrowding, and has enabled us to take measures for cleaning the wards. Every day the want of a central hospital with good arrangements becomes more apparent, and the necessity of a strict observance of hygiene is painfully shown in the high rate of mortality, and in the condition of the sick, who are in many cases suffering from the circumstances in which they are placed, rather than from the disease which originally brought them into their present miserable position.   Evacuation to Adrianople.

Philippopolis, Nov. 10, 1877.

Number of patients in Bulgaric Metropoli, 61 ; Greek school, 45—total, 106. Fourteen are progressing favourably, two of them being cases for operation ; but interference has been delayed that the patients may be brought into a sufficient state of health to sustain the shock. During the past week two patients have succumbed to the fatal effects of overcrowding and neglect.

[*Note*.—Dr. Eccles returned invalided and was succeeded by Dr. Minassian.]

Philippopolis, Dec. 8, 1877.

Owing to the fact that the authorities here have made no transfer of patients to Constantinople since my last report, and no additional wounded have arrived from Shipka, the number in hospital has not much varied. Diarrhœa and dysentery are the usual complaints as yet, which I find difficult to treat from the fact that the cistern in the hospital is almost empty, and we have to wait for a good rain to have a supply of water. The river-water will only keep up the action of the bowels as long as it is used. I try, however, to get cistern water from other places as much as I can. The changes in hospital since my last report are as follows : Remaining at last report, 78 ; admitted during week, 2 ; died (typhoid fever), 1 ; remaining at present, 79 ; and Dr. Calfoglou has this morning reported himself for duty.   Dr. Minassian's reports.

Philippopolis, Dec. 15, 1877.

Our new hospital arrangements are now quite completed. I have placed both the laundry and kitchen in working order. The number in hospital has not yet undergone great change. Some hundreds were sent to Constantinople this week, but only six taken away from our hospital, and those only at my request. There were three cases of diarrhœa admitted, and one died this morning, a case of diarrhœa being of long standing, thus leaving 74 in hospital. Dr. Calfoglou has commenced visiting a second hospital, which of course needs a good deal of metamorphosis before I can say much about it. It contains 75 patients, some still having their beds on the floor. It will take me some days to have bedsteads made, &c.   Organisation of a second hospital.

Philippopolis, Jan. 5, 1877.

Since my last report we have received no new cases in our hospitals, for the reason that none have arrived at the front. Gentlemen passing through the city, who visited Shipka and neighbourhood, report that there is a large number sick in that locality, and many cases of frost-bite,

Dr. Minassian's reports.	yet none have been brought to this place for some little time now. The number in Bulgar Metropole is now 47, and in Karatoprakli 49, so that we have about 60 empty beds in the two hospitals. I am hoping every day, for the sake of the poor sufferers, that new cases would be brought in; but we all know how slow things move here, even in fair weather, and it would be doubly so in the winter-time. I met Rifaat Pacha yesterday, who is second in command in this district, and asked him why the sick from Shipka were not brought here. He replied, in their characteristic way, that 'Thank God, we have very few sick now—very few indeed, almost none; and what few there are could be cared for at Kesanlik;' while gentlemen report here that the hospitals there are full, and medical men are very much driven for work. Additional supplies of medicines having arrived, our patients have everything they need now, while our neighbouring hospitals lack everything, and the chief pharmacien begs of Mr. Akestorides (our dispenser) to lend him medicines. [I have given instructions to give medicines when possible to Turkish hospitals.—W. L. S.]

Philippopolis, Feb. 28, 1878.

Suffering entailed by evacuation of hospital.

On the morning of the 11th ult. all the hospitals in the city were evacuated in accordance with an order from Nouri Pacha, and all the inmates, about 850, were placed in a large barrack near the railway station, together with a portion of the hospital furniture taken from the different hospitals, expecting three trains from Constantinople, as stated in the order, to take patients, furniture, and all medical staff, to the capital. The trains never arrived, and the result was the state of things as will be subsequently described. Matters in the city grew worse from day to day, and two days before the arrival of Suleiman Pacha's troops, Jan. 15, it was almost impossible to go out without some risk. The Circassians and Bashi-Bazouks had commenced their work in earnest; portions of the city were on fire; the local authorities powerless; Turks running away, as it were, to save their lives; and, lastly, a rumour went about that Suleiman Pacha intended to burn the city, which last was not very pleasant news for us, cold as it was in those days. On the day of the skirmish here, Jan. 15, Suleiman Pacha sent a letter to me, through the British Consul, to take charge of the wounded, together with what was left here of the Turkish medical staff, when I immediately had the Bulgar Metropole hospital placed in order to receive the wounded, and Mr. Akestorides, the pharmacien, superintended the removal of the wounded from the hill, where a battery was in action, commanding the bridge of the Maritza river, the soldiers fighting also from rifle-pits all around the hill. The last of the retreating army left the railway station at midnight, and the next morning, Jan. 16, the city was occupied by the Russians.

Wounded placed under S. H. staff.

Panic in the town.

Occupation by Russians.
Terrible condition of wounded.

Early in the morning of the 16th I directed Mr. Akestorides and the storekeeper to have the patients taken to the hospital, as I knew they would have suffered much from hunger and cold, which after proved to have been the case. Of the 850 sick and wounded, only about 120 were taken back to the hospitals; about as many were found dead, and the rest had escaped. Many had their fingers or toes frozen, and it is a wonder that all of them were not frozen to death, since there were no fires kept in the place. We had thus 150 in the two hospitals; and subsequent arrivals of sick and wounded prisoners brought up our number to 250. Of course the buildings were very much crowded, and the medical men of the Turkish staff had a building given them for hospital purposes, to accommodate the new arrivals.

Dr. Attwood's wounded men came from Otloukeui the same day that doctor fell ill with typhoid fever, and the total number in hospital is now 373. I was unable to get any rations for the men until the 9th instant, when they commenced paying 15 kopecks per head, i.e. about 90 paras per day, so that I was able to get along with what Stafford House funds I had on hand. The first few days after the occupation of the city we had great difficulty in finding provisions, wood, coal, &c. I always succeeded, however, in getting wood enough for all purposes. I now draw all the ration money for the 370, and provide for them all, as 15 kopecks per day is not sufficient for the wants of the patients. In the Stafford House hospitals we now have 193, the rest being in another building, attended by the Turkish military doctors. Dr. Calfoglou was taken ill with typhoid fever on the 17th inst., and I was obliged to get Dr. Vlathos, a very good man of this city, to help me. Dr. Calfoglou is now doing very well; Dr. Attwood also is, I think, improving. Dr. Hume will stay until Dr. Attwood is able to be taken away; and I shall forward this with some one intending to leave for Constantinople on Monday next.

Illness of Dr. Calfoglou.

ROUMELIAN RAILWAY TRANSPORT SERVICE.
(*Combined Service with the Imperial Ottoman Railway Company.*)

This section was organised in the middle of August, to supply medical attendance and nourishment to the masses of sick and wounded brought by train from Philippopolis, Adrianople, and the Balkans to Constantinople.

A railway van was fitted up by Surgeon Barker as a dispensary, while the Railway Company furnished four other vans with beds for the worst cases. The five carriages were attached to the trains full of wounded. Surgeon Barker attended to the gravest cases *en route*, and the surgeons from the S. H. hospitals at Philippopolis, Adrianople, and Stamboul met the train at their respective stations whenever their services were required. Where practicable Surgeon Barker had mattresses placed on the bottom of the luggage-vans in which the wounded were transported.

Soup-kitchens were established at the stations of Bazardjik, Tchorlou, Tirnova, and Stamboul terminus. At these rations of soup, bread, cigarettes, and sometimes coffee or milk, were served out to the wounded and sick.

This service continued until the occupation of the entire line by the Russians up to Tchekmedje.

Period of combined service: Aug. 20, 1877, to Jan. 20, 1878.—Total number of sick and wounded transported in trains accompanied by our medical staff, 11,253; total number of rations of soup, &c., 39,904. Surgeon Barker, with Colley and other assistants at the soup-kitchens, were in charge of this section.

The following are extracts from reports to the Chief Commissioner :—

LIST OF JOURNEYS, WITH DATES AND NUMBERS OF MEN TRANSPORTED UP TO JAN. 19, 1878.

Bazardjik—Adrianople	Philibé—Adrianople	Adrianople—Stamboul	Dr. BARKER'S reports.
Dec. 4 . . 271	Sept. 3 . . 850	Sept. 4 . . 580	
„ 14 . . 256	„ 10 . . 421	„ 11 . . 401	
„ 23 . . 488	„ 19 . . 337	Oct. 1 . . 200	
Jan. 3 . . 160	„ 23 . . 850	„ 20 . . 150	
„ 7 . . 482	„ 30 . . 783	Nov. 12 . . 59	
———	Oct. 8 . . 200	„ 18 . . 465	
1657	„ 12 . . 297	„ 23 . . 275	
	„ 19 . . 317	Dec. 5 . . 241	
	Nov. 17 . . 169	„ 17 . . 345	
	„ 28 . . 265	„ 28 . . 629	
	„ 30 . . 226	Jan. 9 . . 510	
	Dec. 9 . . 255	„ 19 . . 250	
	Jan. 12 . . 521	———	
	———	4105	
	5491		
Total of sick and wounded 11253			

N.B.—Between the dates Oct. 29 and Nov. 12, Dr. Woods carried a train of wounded men from Philibé to Stamboul, the number of which I do not know. Of the above number carried, no accident occurred from the transport, and only seven died en route ; the cause of death being in all cases either want of nourishment, rendering them too weak and unfit to be transported— against which I appealed in vain—or else severe exposure to cold. In no case was it from hæmorrhage.

RECORD OF OPERATIONS.

TABLE OF RATIONS GIVEN TO SICK AND WOUNDED OTTOMAN SOLDIERS DURING TRANSPORT.

₊ *A ration consists of a bowl of broth, with meat and rice; half a pound of bread, and (where practicable) a cup of coffee or milk; a packet of tobacco, and cigarette papers.*

Dr. BARKER'S reports.

	Soup-kitchen at Stamboul Turnhuis	Soup-kitchen at Tchorlou, under M. Groteman	Soup-kitchen at Timova-Semenly, under La Guidan	Soup-kitchen at Tokar-Bazardjic, under Gaspar Monté	Remarks
Aug. 25	—	210	—	—	
„ 27	—	200	—	—	
„ 29	406	36	—	—	
Sept. 1	—	437	—	—	
„ 4	—	575	—	—	Received extra bread
„ 5	—	564	—	—	
„ 6	662	—	—	—	
„ 7	700	400	—	—	
„ 8	538	516	—	—	
„ 9	—	11	—	—	
„ 10	—	300	—	—	
„ 11	300	—	—	—	
„ 12	—	411	—	—	
„ 13	401	—	—	—	
„ 14	238	—	—	—	
„ 15	281	250	—	—	
„ 17	—	347	—	—	
„ 20	297	—	—	—	
„ 24	67	—	—	—	
„ 28	7	—	—	—	
Oct. 1	165	—	—	—	
„ 3	37	—	—	—	
„ 4	405	—	—	—	
„ 5	175	—	—	—	
„ 12	48	—	—	—	
„ 15	39	—	—	—	
„ 16	171	—	—	—	
„ 18	119	—	—	—	
„ 20	157	—	—	—	
„ 23	579	—	—	—	
„ 26	32	—	—	—	
„ 27	206	—	—	—	
Nov. 2	339	—	—	—	
„ 5	—	—	300	—	
„ 7	379	—	—	—	
„ 10	—	—	340	—	
„ 11	586	590*	—	—	* 140 received bread and tobacco only
„ 12	110	60*	—	—	* Received tobacco only
„ 18	—	465*	160	—	* 30 received bread and tobacco only
„ 19	423	—	—	—	
„ 23	208	275	—	—	
„ 28	443	410	250	—	
Dec. 1	—	—	226	—	
„ 4	—	—	271	—	
„ 5	258	241	—	—	
„ 9	—	410	—	—	
„ 10	425	—	—	—	
„ 11	—	—	225	—	65 received bread and tobacco only
„ 12	—	—	—	127	With Joseph Görlitz, S. H. C.
„ 14	—	—	341	—	185 Russian prisoners
„ 15	175	190	—	—	

[TABLE OF RATIONS—continued.]

	Soup-kitchen at Stamboul Terminus	Soup-kitchen at Tchorlou, under M. Groieman	Soup-kitchen at Tirnovo-Semenly, under La Guidara	Soup-kitchen at Tatar-Bazardjik, under Gaspar Moulé	Remarks
Dec. 17	345	345	—	67*	* Under care of Dr. Smith, R. C.
,, 19	—	—	—	2,100	Total during transport of 450 men up to the 25th
,, 24	320	150*	—	—	* 73 received bread and tobacco only
,, 27	—	—	431	—	
,, 28	—	—	400	—	
,, 29	634	629	—	—	
Jan. 3	333	—	104	—	
,, 5	—	—	51	—	
,, 7	550	200	482*	—	* 214 received bread and tobacco only
,, 9	250	680	300*	—	* Received bread and tobacco only
,, 10	511	866*	—	—	* 206 received bread and tobacco only
,, 11	792	—	—	—	200 received bread only
,, 12	600	650	—	—	
,, 13	261	2,050	—	—	
,, 14	146	250*	—	—	* Received no tobacco
,, 15	—	500	—	—	250 received no tobacco
,, 16	657	400	—	—	
,, 17	528	270	—	—	
,, 18	250	365	—	—	
,, 19	152	210	—	—	
,, 20	81	—	—	—	
,, 21	78	680	—	—	
,, 22	729	310	—	—	
,, 23	100	—	—	—	
,, 24	200	—	—	—	
,, 25	—	—	—	445	
,, 26	209	—	—	320	
,, 27	45	—	—	315	
Totals . .	17,196	15,453	3,881	3,374	Grand total 39,904

Dr. BARKER's reports.

Stamboul, Sept. 4, 1877.

In accordance with instructions, I proceeded, in conjunction with Mr. Cullen and dragoman Williams, to Adrianople on Aug. 30, our object being to accompany the wounded from station to station, giving any assistance which might be required. At the station in Stamboul, we found awaiting us a van which had been kindly lent to us by the railway company for stores, and a free first-class pass all along the line. On arrival at Adrianople, we met the Stafford House surgeons under Dr. Bond Moore. The following day, on arriving at the station, we met the Pacha, who welcomed us, and told us that he expected a train of wounded to arrive from Philippopolis shortly. We forthwith prepared our stretchers, so that we were quite ready to receive them on their arrival, much to their astonishment, many of them remarking on the interest taken in them by the English surgeons. We were able to render them good service, I myself having dressed 56 and amputated a finger. Messrs. Cullen and Williams were both equally busily engaged, and had not finished dressing them by the time the train moved off out of the station. The next morning we proceeded to Philippopolis, where we found large numbers of wounded continually arriving from the front, most of them in a wretched condition, many of whom had not having had their wounds dressed for twelve or fourteen days. We called on the Pacha, who received us cordially, and entered fully into the spirit of our work. He expressed himself highly pleased with our object, but thought that a road transport from Kesanlik to Philippopolis was absolutely necessary, as they had no means of conveying the badly wounded from the front. Nevertheless, he said he would afford us every assis-

Dr. BARKER's reports.

tance in his power. We started that afternoon with 850 wounded, our van being attached for Adrianople. We dressed the wounded all the way to Tirnova, passing along from carriage to carriage, till darkness put an end to our labours. We were then enabled to procure a little soup for the worst cases. Many of the wounds, though trifling in themselves, were, from want of attention, becoming gangrenous. On arriving at Adrianople, the worst cases were sent to the hospitals; and another train of 580 was made up for Stamboul. We dressed whilst the light lasted, but were unable to get through so much as on the previous day, there being no communication between the carriages. At Tchorlou, we distributed soup, each man receiving a bowl. The following morning, we had a few bad cases of hæmorrhage, doubtless due to oscillation, one of which was so serious that it demanded an operation, which I had to perform under most disadvantageous circumstances, the operating-table being a railway trolly, with a burning sun overhead. The shock, though severe, I am glad to say, was almost recovered from by the time we arrived at Stamboul, the man having been supported by stimulants. With regard to stores, I found the assorted cases most useful for dressing at railway stations, and would propose that one be left at Adrianople under the charge of the station-master. I also gave some of my stores to Lady Strangford.

Tchorlou soup-kitchen.

Stamboul, Sept. 16, 1877.

We started from Stamboul on our second journey to transport the wounded by railway ambulances on Sept. 6. An hour from Stamboul, we passed a train of 600 wounded, most of them slight cases, but thought it better to go on, as they were so near the end of their journey. At Tchorlou we met another train, but they were very slight cases ; and, there being no time to transfer Mr. Sketchley's stores, we went on, arriving at Adrianople at 8 P.M. the same evening, having given tobacco to the wounded in the second train. We slept in the van at Adrianople during the night, going on in the morning by the mail to Philippopolis. The following day (Saturday, the 8th inst.), I accompanied Dr. Neylau to his hospital, where I was struck by the number of bad cases, there being a good many cases of erysipelas and pyæmia, also several cases of incipient gangrene. Cullen, arriving Sunday evening, brought me four ambulance railway-wagons for the transport of the worst cases. Each contains eight beds, and is well fitted up, having all the necessary appliances; these are to be attached to my van wherever it goes. Monday, 10th, we started at 1.30 P.M. with 420 cases, most of whom were only slightly wounded. At Tirnova, we gave them soup. At Adrianople, Drs. Temple, Moore, McIvor, and Kirker assisted me to dress all the wounded, and picked out nineteen of the worst cases to stay behind. At 3 P.M., we resumed our journey. At Tchorlou, each man received a bowl of soup, bread, and tobacco. The following morning, I dressed as many of the worst cases as possible, till we arrived at Stamboul about 2 P.M., on Wednesday, 12th inst., when each received soup, bread, and tobacco. Thus ended my second journey.

Ambulance wagons provided by railway company.
Tirnova soup-kitchen.

Mr. CULLEN's report.

Our transport service arrived at Adrianople at 8.5 P.M., on Aug. 30. The next morning, the 31st, a large train of wounded men arrived from Philippopolis. They were at once removed to a temporary shed which had been erected near the line for their reception. Mr. Barker was the only surgeon on the spot at the time, and removed the first man who left the train on a stretcher of our own. Drs. Moore and McIvor came down soon afterwards, and were at once in full work. During their labours, Djemil Pacha and Mr. Blunt, our consul, several times passed through the building and saw the Stafford House men at work. The Pacha expressed himself in high praise of their labours, and held them up to the native doctors and dressers as an example which they would do well to follow. It did one good to hear the thanks and blessings the wounded so liberally bestowed on our men for the care and attention they had shown them. On Saturday, Sept. 1, we proceeded to Philippopolis, and arrived there at 7 P.M. On Sunday, Sept. 2, I went with Dr. Barker and Mr. Sketchley to Mr. Calvert's, the British Consul, and thence to the Pacha. The latter was exceedingly cordial, and gave me all the information I wanted. He said that were between 4,000 and 5,000 men at Kesanlik, and that every day the number was added to; that there was no properly organised transport service, no competent surgeons, and no stores; and that he should be only too thankful if we would undertake a service of our own between Philippopolis and Kesanlik. The same day at 3 P.M. we started for Adrianople with a train of wounded, and were all of us hard at work dressing the poor fellows. At Tirnova, we procured soup for the worst cases, and saw them safely discharged at Adrianople, where we arrived at 3 A.M. on Monday, Sep. 3. At 3 P.M. the same day, we started for Constantinople with a train of 520 wounded men, who were being sent on from Adrianople hospitals. These we tended on the road to the best and utmost of our abilities,

Gratitude of wounded.

ROUMELIAN RAILWAY TRANSPORT SERVICE. 79

and, having telegraphed from Adrianople, we were able to distribute soup to every one of the poor fellows at Tchorlou at 3 A.M. the next morning. The military officer in charge of the wounded, who journeyed with us from Adrianople to Constantinople, particularly requested me to furnish him with our names, as he wished to report them to the Seraskeriat for the care we had taken of the men under his orders, and expressed his personal gratitude to me for what we had been able to do for them. We arrived at Constantinople at 4 P.M. on Tuesday, and soup was distributed under your orders to all the wounded men before they left the station.

Mr. CULLEN'S report.

Pera, Aug. 31, 1877.

I attended at the terminus of the Adrianople railway to-day to receive a train of wounded soldiers from the front, expected to arrive at 12.30 P.M., and to organise a system for distributing to them quickly, between the time of their arrival and their transhipment for Scutari, certain refreshments supplied to me from the funds of the Stafford House Committee. I brought with me a body of zaptiehs (gendarmes), and these men I told off, so that each should take charge of a carriage immediately on the arrival of the train, count the number of wounded it contained, and when the provisions were properly issued, see that those who were unable to feed themselves were cared for. The station-master, from whom I received every assistance, kindly showed me the exact spot and line of rails on which the train would be brought up, and at a central point were placed two large cauldrons of hot soup, which was ladled into large bowls, each containing sufficient for twenty men; these bowls were then taken up by a fatigue-party of soldiers, who were extended along the line, so that a bowl would rest opposite each carriage on the arrival of the train, and, the instant the train stopped, would be deposited in that carriage; at the same time two gentlemen commenced from each end of the train distributing small loaves of bread, being informed by the zaptieh in charge of each carriage how many men it contained; another gentleman took charge of the tobacco and another of the coffee. Thus, in a very few minutes, 709 wounded soldiers had been served with soup, bread, tobacco, and coffee. This system seemed to me to work thoroughly, and I can recommend its adoption in other places.

Col. COOPE's report.

Establishment of soup-kitchen at Stamboul.

Adrianople, Sept. 25, 1877.

I left Stamboul on Sept. 13, arrived at Adrianople the same night, and delivered Dr. Moore his stores. On the 15th and 16th, I assisted Dr. Neylan in his hospital. Heard that wounded were to go on the 19th, and left with a train of 337 wounded. Gave them tobacco on the road, and 150 bowls of soup at Tirnova. The cases were mostly slight. I find that the ambulance wagons kindly placed in my charge by the railway company are admirably adapted to the severer cases. I have great difficulty in preventing the wounded from appropriating the bedclothes, they having in many cases hardly any clothes of their own.

Dr. BARKER's reports.

On Sept. 23, I found a train of 50 carriages containing 450 wounded from Tatar-Bazardjik, and afterwards we received 400 from here; in dressing I found many to be bad cases. In the night, about 10 P.M., the engine broke down and we were detained four hours. We were told that only the wounded from Philippopolis were to remain in the hospitals of Adrianople, and that the rest were to continue their journey. So we set to work to dress them, but later on we received a telegram from Constantinople to say all were to stay there; so we sent them up to the hospitals.

Stamboul, Nov. 19, 1877.

I left Stamboul by the post train with my wagon and two wagons with beds, and arrived the same evening (Monday, the 12th inst.) at Adrianople. On the road I met Dr. McKellar. On Friday, the 16th inst., having learnt by telegram that there were 160 wounded to start from Philippopolis, the next evening I proceeded there, and found the men ready seated beside the line. I picked up the worst cases, and put them in the beds, many of them being in a very feeble state, the greater part of them being sick, and some seriously so. We were supposed to start in an hour's time after my arrival—viz. at 6 P.M.—but owing to some bridge requiring mending, we were kept at Philippopolis station till 1 o'clock, A.M. At 4.30 A.M. we arrived at Tirnova-Semenly, where soup was ready, and awaiting our arrival. Each man also received bread and tobacco. Between Tirnova and Adrianople, at which place we arrived at 11 A.M., I was able, with the assistance of a Turkish dresser, to attend to all the wounded. On arriving at Adrianople the wounded were placed in the Government barrack erected beside the line, where each received a piece of bread. At 4 P.M. we left Adrianople with 468 wounded, &c. We travelled very slowly, only arriving at Tchorlou the following day at 4 A.M., where soup, tobacco, and bread was again served out. Two men who were in a very exhausted state, died on the way, notwithstanding that every care

RECORD OF OPERATIONS.

Dr. BARKER's reports.

was taken of them. At Kabadjia I was able, owing to a long stoppage, to dress many of the wounded, and during the day I managed to get all dressed by passing from carriage to carriage. In this I was assisted by some Turkish dressers who accompanied the wounded. These men were sick, not wounded, and, like many others, in my opinion ought not to have been moved from Philippopolis or Adrianople, as the case may be, being hardly able to crawl out of their carriages.

Soup-kitchens at Tirnova and Tchorlou.

With regard to the Stafford House soup-kitchens at Tirnova and Tchorlou, I think it is one of the best undertakings we have, and that many Turkish soldiers could say, 'We owe our life to British generosity in feeding us during our return from the front'; those from Philippopolis only having received loaves of bread for rations from the Government during 48 hours. I have to thank the railway officials for kind assistance.

Stamboul, Dec. 1, 1877.

On arriving at Philippopolis I found that the wounded were to leave there the next day. They were placed in their carriages at 6 P.M., but we did not leave till 1 A.M. At Tirnova they were all provided with soup. At 11 P.M we arrived at Adrianople, where the wounded were handed over to the authorities. The following morning we left for Bazardjik, but on arriving at Philippopolis found wounded were again to leave the following day, and on 30th we left with 226 men, mostly sick. At Tirnova they all received soup, bread, and tobacco. We arrived at Adrianople the following morning at six o'clock.

Stamboul, Dec. 8, 1877.

Left Adrianople for Tatar-Bazardjik on 3rd inst., with all the wagons. On arriving there we found a train of 271 wounded, who had been placed in wagons, on their arrival from Sofia, by the kindness of the station-master, there being no place of shelter or baraque for them; and only a small hospital (a private house) of 50 beds to be found in Bazardjik itself; so that the men on their arrival from Sofia—a three days' journey at least in bullock arabas—have to undergo a further fatigue of two days in the railway. None of the societies are represented at Bazardjik, but there are two military Turkish doctors, I believe. We placed the beds in the wagons, which makes them more comfortable and decidedly warmer. At the Stafford House kitchen, Tirnova, they all received soup, bread, and tobacco. On arriving the following morning at Adrianople, the wounded were all transferred to the baraque, where they were all dressed; they were then replaced in their wagons, and the same evening we resumed our journey, and arrived next morning at three o'clock at Tchorlou; here again the men received soup, bread, and tobacco. We arrived at Stamboul the same evening at nine o'clock. Since writing this report I have seen Mr. Pratt, who has authorised me to institute a soup-kitchen at Tatar-Bazardjik station, and it is to be placed under the charge of part of my ambulance. The men can now obtain food on their arrival from Sofia if brought to the station.

Establishment of soup-kitchen at Bazardjik.

[*Note.*—At the Bazardjik soup-kitchen 3,374 rations were served between Dec. 12 and the end of the month.—V. B.-K.]

Stamboul, Dec. 15, 1877.

Hearing there were wounded to leave Philippopolis on the 10th inst., we had our van attached to the post at Bazardjik and went down. The same evening we left with 255 wounded for Adrianople. At Tirnova they were all served with soup, bread, and tobacco, and resuming the journey, we arrived at Adrianople at 7 A.M. on the 11th inst. On the 14th inst. we left Bazardjik with 256 men by the post; these also were served with soup at Tirnova, and at Adrianople on arrival were placed in the station baraque. These last were met by Mr. Pratt on his road to Sofia, who sent back with them the pharmacien from Sofia to provide soup for them on the road to Ichtiman, and to give Monté notice at Bazardjik. Since my last report I made a contract with a man to build a hut at Bazardjik railway station for the soup-kitchen; and before I left it was finished and in working order, Monté having given soup to the men once.

Stamboul, Dec. 23, 1877.

I started from Adrianople on 17th inst. by post train from Stamboul with 345 sick and wounded men, who received soup, bread and tobacco at Tchorlou, and arrived at Stamboul the same evening without any deaths. I took over 480 wounded on 22nd inst. from Dr. King (Red Crescent) at Bazardjik, found them lodged in a khan and two Bulgarian houses without food or fuel; went to the Bey, who promised bread. Monté (Stafford House) supplied the men with soup and charcoal.

They were in a miserable state, being sheltered in some cases on shelves and cupboards, some in the open air in verandahs. I placed all under cover, and on the 21st and 22nd soup was served out in the town. The Government also gave bread the same days.

Dr. BARKER'S reports.

Stamboul, Dec. 29, 1877.

On the 23rd inst. at Bazardjik soup and charcoal were served out to the men (480 in number) and their wounds attended to. On the 24th soup served out, and they received bread for two days from the Government. The morning of the 25th occupied in preparing the carriages for the wounded. At twelve o'clock soup was served out to the men in the carriages, and we left about 3 P.M., arriving by 5 P.M. at Philippopolis. We did not leave Philippopolis till 1 P.M. the next day, during which time the men remained in their carriages. When we started we got to the first station, where we had to wait two hours and a half (why, I know not). After which, at the three succeeding stations, we had a stoppage of two hours each, and arrived at Tirnova at 3 A.M. Here it poured with rain, and as it fell it froze, so that it was only with great difficulty we could distribute the soup, the carriages all being locked by the frost. At Adrianople we had only one man dead. All the men were sent up to the hospital. Next day (27th) another train arrived from Bazardjik, in which there were said to be 700 men. We started in the evening with 629 wounded, the worst cases being left behind at Tchorlou. Received soup, bread, and tobacco. At Stamboul all the men received good soup. We collected all the blankets which we had distributed at Adrianople and placed them in a wagon for our next trip.

Stamboul, Jan. 12, 1878.

On 6th inst. left Adrianople for Philippopolis, on arriving at which place we were informed that a train of sick was coming that night from Bazardjik. We left Philippopolis at 1 A.M. At Tirnova, of the 482, 268 received soup, and the whole either biscuits or bread and tobacco. On the journey, in an open wagon, we found two men frozen to death, and another dying; a fourth had his fingers frozen and had lost his senses—I was able to restore the circulation in his fingers by the application of snow. He was much better after the administration of brandy, which I find the most useful medicine I possess for the chief part of the cases. Another man, who had got out of his wagon, fell down and went to sleep on the snow, but finding him in this state I was able to restore his vitality. At Adrianople they were placed in hospital; we had five deaths—four soldiers and one fugitive—all being from cold, as well as we could make out. On the 9th started from Adrianople at 8.30 P.M. with 510. At Tchorlou 300 obtained soup and all bread or biscuits, time not allowing of tobacco.

Sufferings of wounded from frost.

Stamboul, Jan. 19, 1878.

Left Stamboul for Adrianople on Saturday, the 12th inst., where we arrived the same evening, to find the station filled with refugees, who are to be found in all sorts of conceivable places; all the luggage vans and wagons for merchandise being literally crammed outside and in. On enquiring of the station-master I found that there were some 250 sick and wounded to leave in the morning by the Red Crescent sanitary train, and that these were the last that there were, so I ordered my van to be attached. On the 13th inst. we were engaged placing the men in the wagons and in changing the dressings, in which we were assisted by Drs. Stewart and Azzopardi, of McIvor's section. We started by 8.30 P.M., the men having all been previously fed. At Pavlokeui station we had to stay to let the post from Adrianople to pass, about six hours. We then made another start at 3 P.M.; when we arrived at Baba-Eski station, part of a fugitive train was placed in rear of our carriages. At Baba-Eski we met another train of fugitives which had stayed where it was 24 hours. These fugitives and those attached to our train, thinking it was our fault that they were delayed, threatened to kill the station-master, drivers, and railway officials, as also the doctors, if they were not immediately sent on. Mr. De Castro, of the Red Crescent, taking the responsibility, ordered the train on, but it was only to find at each station several trains of grumbling fugitives. At Siedler station we had to stop for coals to be sent up from Tchorlou, since by our lengthy stoppages we had burnt all we had. After two hours' waiting another engine was sent to our help, and we managed to get to Tchorlou about 9 P.M. Here the soup, which I had ordered by telegram, was given out to the men, and it was fortunate I had done so, for the kitchen stove of the train had set fire to the bottom of the wagon, rendering it unfit for cooking in. The cause of our delay was due to a refugee train that had run off the line at Yarim-Bourgas. Tchorlou presented a more imposing sight than Adrianople, for all its lines were taken up with wagons—filled inside and out with fugitives—and between the lines at night they lit their camp fires. Some of the trains had been

Refugees at Adrianople.

Red Crescent train.

Accident to refugee train. Scene at Tchorlou.

M

Dr. Barker's reports.

there two days. Colonel Blunt was there providing soup and bread for them. On the 16th inst. we had still to wait at Tchorlou; meanwhile the number of fugitives kept increasing, there being two trains in rear of ourselves and we not lying in the station, several of whom died from exposure, I believe, there being continuous frost. I found some more wounded, to the number of 50, scattered about amongst the refugees, so I ordered them soup. On the 17th inst., at 4.30 A.M., we left Tchorlou, having the post attached to our train. At each station en route we passed trains of fugitives. At Tchataldja we were joined by Baron Mundy. At Stamboul the men all received soup, tobacco, and bread.

[*Note.*—On Jan. 18 Adrianople was evacuated by the Turks and all the wounded sent to Constantinople.]

Stamboul, Jan. 26, 1878.

Soup-kitchen at Stamboul at work night and day.

In accordance with your wishes, on Monday (21st) I proceeded to the station at Stamboul to await the arrival of the trains containing wounded. I arranged that Dr. Azzopardi, with Monté as dragoman, should take duty from 8 A.M. to 8 P.M. and I, with Isaac Colley, the night duty. At 9 P.M. a train, which had met with an accident, by three of its carriages running off the line, arrived. It contained 48 soldiers, one of whom had been wounded by the accident, his foot being smashed. They all received soup, and we dressed their wounds. On the night of the 22nd inst. four trains arrived containing in all about 560 wounded; these all received tobacco, but owing to their being transported away so quickly to make room for others, some of them failed to receive soup. We attended to as many of them as possible. The soup supplied was very good in quality. On the 23rd inst. I was informed that our wagon was to be removed to St. Stefano station, so, in accordance with your orders, have had all the contents and stores removed to our store, the cupboards alone being left in.

Stamboul, Feb. 2, 1878.

In accordance with your instructions Dr. McIvor and myself, together with Colley as dragoman, left Constantinople on the 29th ult., and proceeded up the lines as far as possible to gain information as to where the fighting was, and if there were any wounded requiring assistance. On arriving at Tchataldja, the first station beyond the lines—which is the furthest point to which trains run at present—we were fortunate enough to obtain a train through the kindness of the inspector. It consisted of a fourgon, service-carriage, and engine. After frequent stoppages, owing to the line being used as a road by Circassian fugitives, we arrived the same evening at Sinekli; here we

Occupation of line by Russians.

passed the night, the inspector kindly placing his carriage at our disposal. The next morning we returned, it being considered not safe to go to Tcherkesskeni, the next station. As we returned we could see the villages on either side of the line being burnt by the Circassians. On the 31st we again started from Constantinople by boat with stores for San Stefano, where we arrived the same evening. We had the stores placed in my old wagon, and another one which I have obtained of the company. On the morning of the 1st inst. we had our two wagons attached and came up here. We are still here, and shall continue to remain till further orders or fighting.

[Since the withdrawal of the Turkish troops from the lines these sections have been withdrawn. Another under Dr. Sketchley is with the forces at Kutchuk Tchekmedje, where there is much sickness and distress amongst the soldiers.—W. L. S.]

Plevna District Ambulance.

Surgeon Moore and a small staff were attached to the Sultan's Circassian Bodyguard, under Kiazim Pacha, on the occasion of their expedition to Plevna in advance of Chefket Pacha's relieving column. They had with them the matériel for a small 'cacolet' (litter) ambulance transport. This section accompanied the column to Plevna, and subsequently, at the request of Osman Pacha, returned to Sofia with a large convoy of wounded. Chefket Pacha's column was only engaged in a few small skirmishes during this expedition, and in consequence the work of this section was confined to attendance on sick and wounded on the line of march, and no record kept of the exact numbers.

Period of service: Sep. 20 to Oct. 10, 1877.—The staff employed were Surgeon Moore, and Messrs. Morisot, Harvey, and Scudamore.

The following are extracts of reports :—

Adrianople, Sept. 19. 1877.

Dr. MOORE's reports.

Kiazim Pacha was immensely pleased when told last night that Stafford House surgeons were to accompany him and the Sultan's body-guard. He stated that every man in his regiment would die for the Stafford House surgeons. The band played 'God Save the Queen,' the whole of them rising to their feet, both officers and instrumental performers.

Orkhanie, Oct. 2, 1877.

I decided to go to Osman Pacha and volunteer the services of my little staff to work in the Plevna town hospitals. He explained to me that he was very much obliged to England for sending our doctors and stores, but that the former were not required there, and he would be glad if we would take our staff to Sofia. After a consultation I sent Captain Morisot to beg his Excellency to reconsider his decision. The reply received was, 'If you wish to see any fighting or my batteries, you are welcome to remain here as long as you like; but if you want to help my wounded, go to Sofia and help them there.'

[*Note*.—Dr. Ryan informs me that not more than 200 wounded were left in Plevna after the general evacuation of wounded ; Osman Pacha had therefore good reasons for requesting Dr. Moore to follow the great masses of wounded evacuated on Sofia. Moore left all his stores in Plevna, and acted as Osman Pacha wished.—(See Letter to Sir A. H. Layard, p. 22.)—V. B.-K.]

SOFIA HOSPITAL.

In November 1877, in consequence of urgent requests for help from Sofia, an ambulance section under Surgeon Busby was sent to that town, together with a large supply of stores. Surgeon Busby first undertook the charge of 150 wounded men in three private houses, and then established a hospital in the Pavilion. The town was occupied by the Russians on Jan. 3, but the S. H. surgeons continued at their posts until the end of the month, when they evacuated or transferred to the Government hospitals all their wounded, and returned themselves to Constantinople.

Period of service: Nov. 14, 1877, to Feb. 14, 1878.—Treated in hospital, 260 wounded ; average number of beds occupied, 130. The following served on the staff of this section : Surgeons Busby and Wattie, Assistant-Surgeon Boyd, Dispenser Görlitz, and Mr. Cullen.

The following are extracts from Reports to the Chief Commissioner :—

Sofia, Nov. 28, 1877.

Dr. BUSBY's reports.

We arrived here Friday afternoon, and delivered your letter to the médecin-en-chef the next morning. I told him we were prepared either to do work as an ambulance at the front or establish an hospital here. He said that should Mehemet Ali approve of the latter course, he would give us a hospital, but that we must wait for Mehemet Ali's decision as to which of the two we should do. Unfortunately he was away at the front, but his return was expected daily. We set about hiring arabas so as to take us up to Orkhanie. But arabas here are very scarce, and we found we could not organise this in so short a time ; moreover we heard that all that ground was well occupied by the Red Crescent men. Being convinced that we were more likely to do good by remaining here, I went to the médecin-en-chef again and told him we were anxious to get to work at once, and proposed taking an hospital without waiting for Mehemet Ali's return. They promised to see about this, and let me know later, but nothing came of it. We told him we were not willing to remain inactive so long, and proposed that, if he could hand over to us an hospital with its patients, and all the necessary requisites for carrying on the work, we would replace these requisites with our own as soon as we could get them up from Constantinople. On these conditions we are to receive an hospital for 150 beds, and begin work to-morrow.

RECORD OF OPERATIONS.

Sofia, Dec. 15, 1877.

Dr. Busby's reports.

Drs. Wattie, Boyd, and myself began work on Dec. 1, in a house with 87 wounded. On the following day another house, containing 55 more, was handed over to us; and on the 5th we received a third house, full of patients, making the total number of wounded under our care 159. The houses are overcrowded, the patients lying on the floor, the bedding being miserably insufficient and dirty. This is at present unavoidable, owing to the large number of wounded constantly coming in, and the disturbed state of the town, making it impossible to obtain immediately what is necessary; but I hope the next report will show a considerable improvement. The Turkish regular hospitals, however, are good and well found, and are managed by a competent surgical staff. Amongst the more important cases we have as follows :—Thirty-five wounds of thigh; four bullet-wounds of knee-joint (one death), seventeen of leg (one death, three amputations), five of ankle-joint, seven of foot (one frost-bite, loss of toes both feet); ten wounds of arm (two amputations), six of forearm and nineteen of hand, seven of back and loins ten of head (one death); four non-penetrating wounds of chest, and one wound of chest with penetration of lung (death). The remainder are lighter cases—flesh-wounds and wounds of fingers (of which there have been four amputations).

Establishment of S.H. hospital. Turkish hospitals.

Constantinople, Feb. 14, 1878.

Fresh arrivals of wounded from Tashkessen.

I have been unable to send any report since the third week in December, in consequence of the communication being interrupted by the Russians. On Dec. 27, admitted 30 wounded from an engagement near Tashkessen, and on the same evening 25 more; the hospital was already overcrowded, but as their wounds were for the most part confined to the upper extremity, we were able to find shelter for these additional cases. During the next day or two all those cases that were able to bear transport were evacuated in compliance with an order from the Turkish authorities. A very large number of wounded were sent away from Sofia at this time. Most of the hospital employés also left us; indeed there remained but one Timardji (dresser) to assist Dr. Wattie and myself in carrying on the work.

Occupation of Sofia by the Russians. Evacuation of wounded. Panic in town.

On Jan. 1, admitted some 35 fresh wounded from a fight at the covered bridge, Tashkessen road; and on Jan. 2, 20 more from the same engagement. During the night of the 2nd the town was evacuated by the Turkish troops. Early the following morning the patients in hospital were seized with panic; those in any way able to move left of their own accord, notwithstanding all the endeavours we made to induce them to remain. Their fear of falling into Russian hands was very great. Many were very severe cases, and all in a condition quite unfit to bear the exposure to the intense cold. This left us with many empty beds. The Turkish hospitals close by had been deserted by the surgeons and attendants, the wards were in a bad state from the accumulated filth and the dead not having been removed. The patients that by the nature of their injuries were compelled to remain, were in a most miserable condition, without food, and their wounds not dressed for many days. We attended to some of these, and were able to remove a number of them to our hospital, placing them in the beds vacated by those who had left so hurriedly in the early morning. On this same day (the 3rd) the Russians entered the town. Owing to the great disorganisation, the food supply was at this time irregular and insufficient, wood very scarce—some days none—so that the suffering from cold was great. On the second day of the Russian occupation, I requested General Gourko to send us back to the Turkish lines. This he said he was unable to do, but that we were free to return by way of Belgrade. On the day following this interview, many of the Turkish wounded that had tried to get away were brought back as prisoners. I learnt that some had got as far as Samakov, and that others had died on the way frozen; of those brought into the town the greater part were severely frost-bitten. As there seemed to be great need of surgical assistance, I thought it best to remain in Sofia for the present and carry on the hospital. All the patients subsequently admitted were cases of frost-bite. During the following ten days, the number of severe cases became much lessened, and having ascertained that there were quite sufficient surgeons remaining in the town to attend to all the wounded, I applied to the Commandant for permission to leave for Belgrade; but he would not grant it, and said we must go by way of Bucharest; this I declined to do. Some four days later, however, we were provided with the necessary papers to leave by way of Nisch and Alexinatz. We accordingly started on the morning of Jan. 21, on horseback (Dr. Wattie, myself, Görlitz, Colley, and Constantine), with one extra horse to carry provisions and some baggage. The weather was very severe, our journey being much hindered by the slippery state of the roads and the drifting snow. At Pirot we came under Servian control. We reached Alexinatz on the 25th, Belgrade on the 30th. Here Mr.

Gen. Gourko.

Hospital work continued.

Departure of S. H. staff.

SOFIA HOSPITAL. 85

White, the British Consul, arranged matters for us, and on Feb. 1 we crossed over the Save to Semlin, on the Austrian frontier; we were then free to continue our journey as we pleased. Arrived on the opposite side of the Danube, we hired sledges and started for Panchovar, which we reached that night by crossing three other rivers. Left Panchovar the following morning (Feb. 2) for Verschatz, where we arrived that evening. Here there was a railway, so left by train the same night, going by way of Legedin, Vilany and Agram to Trieste, which was reached on Feb. 6. I, together with Görlitz, Constantine, and Colley, left Trieste by the Austrian Lloyd's steamer on Feb. 9, and arrived in Constantinople Feb. 14, all safe. — Dr. Busby's reports.

Dec. 16, 1877.

Ayant accompagné Mr. Pratt de Tatar-Bazardjik pour Sofia, nous avons rencontré un convoi des blessés, en nombre de 130, qui n'avaient ni couvertures ni de médicaments, et dans des voitures ouvertes. J'ai été autorisé par Mr. Pratt d'accompagner les blessés et de faire tout mon possible de leur donner un abri, et s'il y avait possibilité de leur faire préparer de la soupe, &c. &c. Ainsi aussitôt arrivés à Yeni-Khan à neuf heures du soir, je me suis engagé avec le chirurgien de loger les blessés, mais n'ayant pu trouver de la viande, j'ai distribué quelque morceaux de pain à ceux qui n'en avaient pas. Le lendemain nous sommes arrivés à Vettrina, où nous avons fait la même chose. Mardi nous sommes arrivés à Ichtiman, où j'ai trouvé de la viande, et fait de la soupe pour les blessés, et distribué du pain à une 40me d'hommes. Enfin nous sommes arrivés à Tatar-Bazardjic, où Gaspard Monté ayant eu des ordres antérieures à préparer de la soupe pour tous les blessés, qui ont été installés dans trois Khans, et qui sont partis très contents le lendemain pour Adrianople. — Mr. Görlitz's report. Transport of wounded to Bazardjik.

STAMBOUL MUNDY BARRACK HOSPITAL.

This hospital was built at the expense of the Red Crescent Society, from designs by Baron Mundy, and was handed over by that Society to the Imperial Medical School. The Stafford House Committee provided the surgical staff, beds, and medical stores, and undertook the general working of the hospital. Four Saxon Sisters sent by the Queen of Saxony formed the nursing staff. It was intended to receive only very grave cases.

Period of service: Dec. 4, 1877, to June 8, 1878.—Treated in hospital, 77 wounded; average number of beds occupied, 23. Surgeon Neylan, and subsequently Surgeon Lake, assisted by Dr. Maussner (chief surgeon of the Railway Company), acted as surgeons in this section.

The following are extracts from reports to the Chief Commissioner:—

Stamboul, Dec. 4, 1877.

To-day the new model barrack hospital in the Military Medical School, Stamboul, was visited by the Princess Reuss, to introduce there the four sisters of charity sent by the Queen of Saxony as nurses. The Princess, with the Prince and a large suite, were received at the entrance of the hospital by Marco Pacha, Director of the Medical School (Gul-Hané); they were then conducted over the barrack by Dr. Mundy, and the Princess expressed her satisfaction with all the arrangements. The design is an original one of Baron Mundy, M.D., who has also superintended all the steps of the construction, as well as its total internal fittings. It is a rectangular wooden building divided in two, longitudinally, by a partition. These divisions communicate at one end. There are four entrances. Each half contains fourteen beds, which are again separated in the centre between each seven beds by a movable curtain. It is heated by four large porcelain stoves. It is lighted and ventilated by skylights and alternate side windows, which are arranged so as to give complete ventilation without causing an injurious draught. In each compartment are clocks, barometers, thermometers, and calendars, both in European and Turkish styles. At each end of the two divisions four small rooms are curtained off. Of these, one is fitted up as an operating-room, and contains an operating-table (Baron Mundy's design), of ingenious mechanical construction; a second, as a depository for drugs and appliances; a third, as an office, &c.; and the remaining one is for the use of lady nurses. There is a raised platform around the hospital covered — Dr. Neylan's reports. Opening of hospital. Description.

RECORD OF OPERATIONS.

Dr. Neylan's reports. by an awning, which can be used as a promenade by convalescents even in inclement weather. It must be mentioned that both sides of the hospital can be lifted up, thus in summer converting that part of the building into a tent. The closets are erected at about 20 yards' distance (to which a covered way leads), and are constructed according to modern sanitary rules. Each iron bedstead is provided with a straw paliasse, horsehair mattress, two pillows, ditto linen sheets and blankets; by its side is a handsome walnut stand or table for the patient's medicine, drinks, cigarettes, &c. The dressing-tables, fitted with every necessary, are on rollers, and can be easily propelled from bed to bed. Commodes also on the same principle. The ward tables, glass cases for instruments, &c., are of superior manufacture; in fact, the furniture is good enough for a respectable residence. Most modern surgical appliances are employed—amongst many the following may be enumerated: English, French, and German splints; Esmarch's bloodless ligatures; irrigators and triangular bandages; carbolic acid and ether spray-producers; cradles for suspending fractures and keeping off the pressure of the bedclothes; water-beds, air-cushions, and pillows; amputation and resection instruments; urinometers; clinical thermometers; hypodermic syringes; enema apparatus; stomach-pump; Nélaton's and other bullet-probes and forceps; drainage tubing; basins and trough for foul wounds—in fact, nothing which could contribute to the patient's comfort or recovery has been forgotten or neglected. From its admirable hygiene, and the facility it affords for the isolation of the gravest from the less severe cases (and it is to be devoted solely to heavily wounded), it is pre-eminently a model barrack-hospital. That this will be of benefit, not alone to the wounded, but to the country at large, will be at once seen if its situation is considered. It is placed in the centre of the quadrangle of the great military medical school of the empire, where nearly 500 students may become daily familiarised, if they wish, with modern surgical appliances and treatment. The benefit so derived will be, no doubt, disseminated throughout the length and breadth of Turkey. It is essentially an international creation, as the cost of the building (500*l*.) has been borne by the Croissant Rouge. Baron Mundy fitted up the interior with the funds collected by him (through the press) in Germany and Austria. Stafford House supplied the chief surgeon, the beds, surgical instruments, medicines, and stimulants. Mrs. Layard has kindly provided this model barrack hospital with excellent sheets, flannels, shirts,
Saxon nurses. jackets, &c. Finally, the Queen of Saxony gives the four nurses under the patronage of the Princess Reuss; whilst the Ottoman Government, to which the school belongs, will provide food for patients, and other requisites.

First arrival of wounded. On the arrival of a train of wounded at 10 P.M., Dec. 24, 23 cases were selected by me and sent to this hospital. They were attended to there by Dr. Mausner, and four nuns who are skilled and trained nurses. The following morning two more arrived, making the number 25. They were all old or neglected cases of gunshot injuries, several having been wounded at Eski-Zaghra, so far back as July last. On Dec. 30, five of these cases were, by the use of frequent baths, constant irrigation, and antiseptic applications, sufficiently improved to bear removal to a general hospital. The aim of the hospital is to keep grave cases, as long as they remain in a critical state. The hospital is well adapted for carrying out this plan, by reason of its limited extent, and proportionately large trained nursing staff, thorough ventilation, sanitary arrangements, and regulated temperature. All old bandages, poultices, dressings, &c., are on their removal consumed in a furnace especially constructed for that purpose. The patients are well supplied with flannel shirts, dressing gowns, &c.; they all express themselves highly satisfied with their lot; the only drawback is that considerable powers of persuasion are required to persuade them to leave their comfortable quarters. A clinical class of 21 senior students has been attached, for purposes of instruction, to the hospital,
Clinical class of students. by Marco Pacha, director of the school. They are without exception intelligent dressers, devoted to their work, and anxious to improve. During the past week five new cases have been received. I have extracted one bullet (wound three months old); performed three minor operations, and one partial resection of the bones of the forearm. Several cases, at present in an exhausted condition, are receiving liberal diet, stimulants, &c., so as to be in a fit state to bear the shock of an operation at a future period.

Jan. 24, 1878.

Patients in hospital, Jan. 5, 26; discharged, 6; transferred, 5; died, 2—total, 13; received since Jan. 5, 13; now in hospital, 26. One death was from pyæmia, and the other from gangrene of both feet following frost-bite; the patient not consenting to amputation. We have performed ten minor operations and three major, viz., one amputation of the arm, two amputations of the leg. Up to the present, these cases are doing well. This morning, I extracted a bullet which had been lodged in a man's buttock for five months. In addition to the operations performed on occupants of the hospital, I have given the use of an operating room, instruments, assistance, &c., to other surgeons who were attending to the sufferers by the late railway accident on the line. Yesterday, the 23rd, five amputations were performed. Four students who have had a month's training in the hospital are now employed in attending to the wounded refugees at the station.

Dr. Neylan's reports.

Feb. 8, 1878.

Remaining in hospital, Jan. 24, 27; discharged, 10; transferred, 2; died, 2—total, 14; since admitted, 13—total, 26. One death resulted from extensive frost-bite, followed by inflammation of the lungs, and the other from secondary hæmorrhage, occurring in the night eighteen days after amputation. Since last report I have performed two major operations, viz. amputation of thigh, amputation of both feet, and eight minor operations. A filter which has been fitted up after the design of Dr. Macnamara is found to answer well.

[After Dr. Neylan's departure for England the hospital was kept up under Dr. Stiven, until invalided, and subsequently under Dr. Lake.]

SAMAKOV TRANSPORT.

This section was despatched under Assistant-Surgeon Sketchley to assist the wounded in the general retreat of the Ottoman forces from Sofia and the Balkans.

Period of service: Dec. 26, 1877, to Feb. 2, 1878.—Number of wounded attended to during transport, 1,265. The following were the staff of this section: Assistant-Surgeon Sketchley, and Messrs. Banfather and Williams, with assistants.

The following is Mr. Sketchley's general report to the Chief Commissioner:—

Tatar-Bazardjik, Feb. 12, 1878.

I left Stamboul Dec. 30 to proceed to Sofia, according to instructions received from yourself and Mr. Pratt, to transport wounded to Tatar-Bazardjik.

Mr. Sketchley's report.

Dec. 31.—Arrived at Philippopolis, where I was joined by Williams.

Jan. 1.—Went on to Bazardjik, where I was joined by Banfather same day; received telegram from you to the effect that if the road from Sofia was cut to leave Banfather and Williams at Bazardjik and take Barker's van. From information received I found the road *vid* Samakov was open, and decided to go on and, if possible, carry out my instructions.

Jan. 4.—Started for Samakov, and arrived same night, 10.10 P.M.

Jan. 5.—Visited Caimakan, who told us troops were evacuating Sofia *rid* Dubnitza with wounded; decided to start for Dubnitza and render all assistance possible; met troops on road, and returned to Samakov; dressed all men who were wounded retreating from Sofia.

Jan. 7.—Rechid Pacha arrived with fifteen battalions; asked us to stay with troops, as they intended to fight their way to Bazardjik; told us 800 wounded would arrive same night. Sent you telegram for lint, bandages, and L.T.100. Same night Nedjib Pacha arrived with more troops, who told us wounded had gone round by Uskup.

Jan. 8.—Osman Pacha, commander, arrived with remainder of troops, 32 battalions in all; requested us to stay with him and attend to sick and wounded; no doctor with him or any necessaries.

Jan. 9.—Gave us large Jewish house for hospital, and placed in it all sick and wounded; same day informed us of news of armistice; one hour afterwards (3.30 P.M.) heard cannonading, and found fighting had commenced half an hour from town. Williams and I rode out and attended wounded. Osman Nouri Pacha sent out flag of truce, and fighting stopped. Russians knew nothing of armistice. Dressed wounded until 2.30 A.M.

Temporary hospital. Battle near Samakov.

Jan. 11.—Osman Pacha sent and told us that he was sending all wounded and sick down to Bazardjik; wished us to accompany them, as he was going to evacuate troops. Started 2.10 A.M., and arrived here with 110 wounded and 200 sick at 8.30 P.M. At his request we attend Osman Pacha's troops. We met Dr. McQueen and ambulance at Banya on his way to Samakov, who returned with us to Bazardjik.

Evacuation of Samakov by Turks.

Osman Nouri Pacha treated us with every kindness, and gave us all assistance in his power. Williams showed great courage on the field, and acted with his usual energy.

RECORD OF OPERATIONS.

Mr Sketchley's report.

Battle of Stanimaka.

On the 12th we joined Baker Pacha's division at a village near the town, and on the 13th we left with the troops and the wounded for Philippopolis. At night we camped on the snow—a foot deep—and the following day arrived at Philippopolis. At 12 P.M. on the 16th we retreated on Stanimaka, fighting all the way. On the 17th a battle was fought at which Chakir Pacha lost 3,000 killed and 4,000 prisoners. From Stanimaka we retreated across the Balkans towards Gumurgina, taking the wounded with us. The roads were simply mule tracks, and very slippery and dangerous.

TCHIFOUT-BURGAS DISPENSARY.

In Feb. 1878 there was a great amount of sickness among the Ottoman troops occupying the lines of defence of Constantinople. In consequence, Surgeon Hayes was appointed, with a dispenser and assistant, to establish a dispensary in the lines, and assist in forwarding the sick to the Constantinople hospitals. The dispensary was closed on April 5, when the remaining medicines were distributed under the personal supervision of Surgeon Hayes.

Period of service: Feb. 28 to April 5, 1878.—Number of sick treated, 800; average per day, 65. Surgeon Hayes and Dispenser Tamolini, with Turkish assistants, served on this section.

The following are reports to the Chief Commissioner:—

Camp, Vidos and Tchifout-Burgas, March 9, 1878.

Dr. Hayes' reports.

The division of Osman Nouri Pacha is scattered over the four above-mentioned villages or farms. At Vidos, where Osman Pacha himself is, there are four battalions; at Tchifout-Burgas, where Tahjah Pacha is, there are six battalions; at Injir Chiflik there is one battalion; at Chaim Pacha there is one battalion; and at Makrikeui there are five battalions; these latter are under the medical care of a Stafford House surgeon. I have established a kind of dispensary, with a room

Establishment of a dispensary.

wherein are four beds for urgent cases, and I see and prescribe for about 50 or 60 men a day; at Tchifout-Burgas, where I for the present live, I visit the other camps as opportunity offers, and see and prescribe for the men, and send those who are seriously ill to hospitals. These men are chiefly suffering from long exposure and bad food on the retreat from the Balkans, great numbers of them being from the warm parts of Asia, and simply ill from the cold. One half have intermittent fever. It must be understood that the hospitals are at some distance apart, and that owing to the state of the roads no wheeled vehicle can traverse them. At Vidos and Hazenada Chiflik there is a Turkish surgeon, to whom I am going to furnish a few drugs of a simple kind. My staff at present consists of Tamolini, pharmacien; Theodore, general servant, and interpreter, Arslan Chaouch; two soldiers placed at my disposal by Caijah Pacha, who seems inclined to look with favour on our work.

Tchifout-Burgas, March 16, 1878.

Increased sickness in camp.

The week has been most unfavourable to men in camp; constant rain, high wind, and a low temperature. Three hundred and fifty-six patients have been seen and given medicine to; of these 186 were new cases (of which 77 suffered from intermittent fever). The remainder cases seen before and still under treatment, 170; sent to hospital, 10.

Tchifout-Burgas, March 31, 1878.

Though the number of sick has increased owing to the larger number of troops in camp, and the heat of the weather causing a slight increase in the cases of intermittent fever, the results of treatment have been most satisfactory as far as I am able to learn, only six deaths having occurred here since my arrival. The distribution of soup to the more severe cases has proved of the greatest benefit. One hundred and seventy-three rations of soup have been given. Number of new cases, 203; old cases under treatment, 287; total cases seen and supplied with medicines, 490; number of cases sent to hospital, 30.

Tchifout-Burgas, April 5, 1878.

Withdrawal of dispensary.

The sickness in camp has somewhat diminished. The number of deaths during one month is six. The ambulance was removed on April 5. Several drugs, some bedding, and other useful things have been handed over to the military authorities at this and other camps. Lists of these things are enclosed, as is also an acknowledgment in Turkish signed by the Pacha and others for the services rendered to the camps. In an interview I had with Osman Nouri Pacha, when leaving, he expressed himself as more than satisfied and most grateful to the Stafford House Committee for what had been done. Eight hundred soldiers have received medicine and treatment since the ambulance was sent out, at a cost of less than 70 liras Turkish, inclusive of everything. *Dr. Hayes' reports.*

Tchekmedje and Makrikeui Hospitals and Dispensary.

On the retreat of the Turkish army to the lines of Tchekmedje, Mr. Sketchley was sent to that town with the matériel for a small hospital and soup-kitchen. When Tchekmedje was occupied by the Russians, Mr. Sketchley fell back with his staff on Makrikeui, where a hospital was at once established. On the withdrawal of the Stafford House staff, the hospital, with the stores and patients, was transferred to the Government.

Period of service: Feb. 9 to April 25, 1878.—Total number treated, 2,888 sick. Average number under daily treatment, 182. The following served on the staff of this section: Assistant-Surgeons Sketchley and Azzopardi, a Dispenser, and R. Williams.

The following are extracts from reports to the Chief Commissioner:—

Tchekmedje, Feb. 19, 1878.

From instructions received from Mr. Stoney I arrived at Tchekmedjé with staff, the object being to establish a receiving hospital for sick men coming from the lines, to supply them with soup and other nourishing food and medicines, and forward the worst cases to the hospital at Constantinople. I visited the commanding Pacha and explained my plans to him, which he at once entered into. He said it was the very thing he wanted, as the place was full of sick, and nobody to attend to them properly. He at once gave me a large building that would hold about 150 men, which I fitted up with Stafford House stores as an hospital, and which was completely filled by the following night with men suffering chiefly from intermittent fever, dysentery, and diarrhœa. A few days afterwards he gave me another large house that would hold about 100 men, which I turned to the same use, and also fifteen tents at the railway station about 1½ miles from the town. These I had filled with hay, and gave each man three Stafford House blankets. To these tents, which are well warmed and lighted, I draft the worst cases, to be forwarded to the hospitals in Constantinople by the first train that arrives. I have also established a soup-kitchen here, and at the hospitals the patients are supplied with soup, good nourishing food, medicines, and tobacco. Many of the men are able to return to their respective regiments after a few days, as in some cases it is simple exhaustion from long-forced marches and privations, and the effect of a little nourishing food and attention is miraculous. Within the last week I have forwarded to Constantinople upwards of 500 men, and have now in the hospital here about 200 more. They arrive here from the lines in numbers of from 30 to 40 daily, some of them in a most emaciated condition. The pachas here so appreciate our work that there is not a single thing that I have asked them for that they have refused; they have even sent away their own doctors so that we shall not be interfered with in our work. I am also endeavouring to establish a soup-kitchen at San Stefano on the same plan, and hope to get it into working order in a few days.

Mr. Sketchley's reports.

Establishment of hospital.

Tent hospital.

Great amount of sickness.

[Mr. Sketchley's work at Makrikeui was carried out in a similar manner.]

Constantinople, April 17, 1878.

To-day, Wednesday, April 17, I handed over to Nedjih and Assam Pachas, for the Turkish Government, the S. H. Hospital at Makrikeui, of which I had charge, according to the instructions which I received from you at Constantinople. The matériel consisted of 100 beds, bedding, &c., together with the reserve stock, also medicines, utensils, soup-kitchen plant, and all other effects, which are included in the receipts sent in this morning. A Turkish doctor arrived this morning to take charge of the hospital. The Pachas were profuse in their acknowledgments of the services to the Turkish troops rendered by the Stafford House Committee. Last week Osman Pacha (of Plevna) inspected the hospital and expressed himself highly pleased with all the arrangements. Upwards of 400 cases of typhoid have been treated successfully in the hospital, and many cases of dysentery, fever, &c.

Transfer of hospital to Government.

Inspection of hospital by Osman Pacha.

SALONICA HOSPITAL.

Large numbers of the sick and wounded from Suleiman Pacha's retreating army having found their way to Salonica, the hospitals of that town became overcrowded, and great distress prevailed. Accordingly, on March 1, a strong section was dispatched there, and a hospital established in Midhat Pacha's Orphan Asylum, a building chosen by Surgeon Eccles for its elevated position and good sanitary condition. The hospital was fitted up with 150 beds, which were rapidly filled with some of the most severely wounded. To quote Surgeon Eccles's own words :—'The suffering at this time was increased tenfold in comparison to what we had seen during the war; typhus, dysentery, gangrene, and erysipelas swelled the formidable array of difficulties with which we had to contend.'

The work of this section was extended to Thessaly, where, in the middle of March, an outbreak of hostilities occurred. Surgeon Eccles distributed relief at Volo, and rendered great assistance to the wounded men in the engagements which took place between the Ottoman troops and the insurgents on the slopes of Pelion.

Period of service: March 1 to April 15, 1878.—Total number of wounded treated, 248; average number of beds occupied, 123. The following served on this section: Surgeons Eccles, Beresford, Clement, Roe, Dispenser Spanopoulos, with Turkish assistants.

The following is a general report condensed by Surgeon Eccles from his special reports to the Chief Commissioner, from March 1 to April 15, 1878.

Dr. Eccles' report.

Large numbers of sick and wounded.

Outbreak of typhus.

Establishment of S. H. hospital.

Hospital increased.

Advices having reached the S. H. Commissioner from H.B.M. Consul, Salonica, and from Dr. Temple, chief medical officer Imperial Ottoman Service in Salonica, of the great distress prevalent in that town, Mr. Eccles, accompanied by Mr. Beresford and a small staff of assistants, was despatched to Salonica with instructions to take such measures as he thought best for the relief of the sick and wounded. On arrival, over 2,000 patients were found lying in the military hospital, barracks, mosques, and other buildings in the town. An epidemic of typhus had broken out, and large numbers had died, the mortality in some hospitals reaching fifteen per diem; the local government was without either funds or matériel to meet the urgency of the case, and several of the Ottoman medical officers had been attacked by disease, thus leaving an inadequate staff to carry on the work which daily became more arduous. Most of the patients exhibited the appalling effects of the privations they had endured, many of them had been wounded at the battles of Plevna, Tashkessen, Orkhanie, and Sofia, having been subjected to the combined influence of famine, cold, and want of medical care in their flight from Sofia. In the confusion arising out of the sudden influx of these unfortunates, sick and wounded had been crowded together irrespective of the injuries or diseases from which they were suffering, thus inducing the spread of infectious diseases among patients primarily affected with slight disorders. Dr. Temple, who had lately arrived, placed at the disposal of the S. H. C. officers, H.E. Midhat Pacha's Orphan Asylum, a building chosen by Mr. Eccles for its elevated position, and better sanitary condition. This hospital, on the arrival of the S. H. section, was occupied by nearly 300 sick, though barely capable of containing 150 wounded, for whose reception it was speedily prepared, its previous inmates being transferred to the large barracks on the eastern shore of the bay. The building was thoroughly cleansed, whitewashed, and disinfected throughout, a washhouse and store-room were erected, and all the furniture and necessary arrangements made for the reception of 150 patients; the bedsteads, bedding, night-clothes, &c., being made on the premises by the boys of the Orphan Asylum, under Mr. Eccles's supervision. On March 7, 58 patients chosen from among the gravest cases of wounds, were admitted to the S. H. hospital, being conveyed from the barracks to the hospital in ambulance wagons, kindly lent by the Salonica Sub-Committee of the Red Crescent Society. On March 13, Mr. Clement having arrived

SALONICA HOSPITAL.   91

with additional stores, we were enabled to raise the number of patients to 119, reserving the rest of our beds for the isolation of gangrene and other infectious cases. Dr. Eccles' report.

Many of the patients, in addition to the wounds from shot, shell, and sabre, afforded examples of the worst form of frost-bite, while all were in such a low state of vitality that, with the greatest care and attention, restoration to their former physique could hardly be hoped for, but a generous and varied diet supplied from our own kitchen, combined with the extra comfort and the scrupulous cleanliness maintained in our wards, soon produced most gratifying results; indeed, the rapidity with which patients, with apparently fatal symptoms, recovered from the shock their systems had sustained, was a matter of great surprise and congratulation for the medical men under whose care they had come; several operations which had been decided on, so soon as the patients' health would allow, were not performed, the reparative powers exhibited in the majority of cases precluding the necessity of operative interference. Condition of wounded.

Notwithstanding the extraordinary injuries to which our patients were victims, conservative surgery, as our statistics will show, proved eminently successful; very few of the patients left the hospital unable to perform the ordinary duties of life; indeed, many were ready and willing to take the field once more. The suffering at this time was increased tenfold in comparison with what we had seen during the war. Then the sick and wounded came under treatment at a comparatively early date, before Nature, battling against cold, hunger, and neglect, exhausted herself in attempting to heal a wound, or mend a broken limb; but now, added to these, typhus, dysentery, gangrene and erysipelas swelled the formidable array of difficulties with which we had to contend; yet at no period of our career, while succouring our fellow-men, did we see the fruits of our labours in such gratifying results. The moral influence of our work and the physical effects of our treatment as shown, on the one hand, by the interest excited by it among all classes of the inhabitants of Salonica, and on the other, by the quick and established recovery of our patients, stimulated each and all the members of the staff to perform their duties with unrelaxing energy, and, although some of us suffered from the effects of over-work, the retrospect of our short stay in Salonica must be a source of pleasure to all.

The outbreak of hostilities in the province of Thessaly called the attention of the Commissioners to a fresh field of labour, and with a view to ascertaining the necessities of those suffering from the effects of the insurrection, Mr. Eccles, leaving the section at Salonica in charge of Mr. Beresford, went to Volo on March 21, whence, after distributing relief to the refugees in that town, he proceeded to Sarissa, the seat of government, where having made an inspection of the military hospitals in that town and at Tirnova, he handed over a quantity of surgical stores and medical comforts to the authorities, returning to Volo in time to render assistance to those who were wounded in the engagements which took place between the Imperial Ottoman troops and the insurgents on the slopes of Pelion. Unfortunately, our funds would not allow of the establishment of a hospital or ambulance in Thessaly, so Mr. Eccles was recalled to resume his duties as chief of the section in Salonica. On April 1, 25 fresh cases were admitted to the hospital, the lobbies being furnished for their reception, as large numbers of sick and some wounded continued to arrive in the town from Uskup and Metrovitza. On April 8, 76 cases from our hospital, with other convalescents from the hospitals in the town, were evacuated, being removal from their quarters to the place of embarkation being effected by means of the Red Crescent wagons in charge of some of the S. H. officers. Each patient on leaving was given from the S. H. stores one or more articles of warm clothing. The same day 104 fresh cases were admitted to the S. H. hospital. Rising in Thessaly.
Dr. Eccles' expedition to Volo.

Owing to the resignation of Mr. Beresford (who was obliged to return to England on urgent private affairs), and the transfer of Mr. Clement to Gallipoli, the medical staff was reduced to two surgeons, Mr. Roe having been sent to take Mr. Beresford's place; but as the patients, with few exceptions, were in a fair way to recover, we were able with three dressers to continue our work in the wards until April 15, when most of the wounded in the town being convalescent, they were evacuated, with 103 from the S. H. hospital, on Constantinople. Mr. Roe, with a dispenser and two dressers, accompanied them to Constantinople on board the I. O. transport *Medjidieh*, Mr. Eccles remaining in Salonica to transfer the hospital with all stores and furniture to the Red Crescent authorities, the wounded left in the town being under 200 in number. Transfer of hospital to the Red Crescent Society.

The food of all the patients during their stay in the S. H. hospital was prepared under the supervision of one of our officers on the premises; the ordinary rations of bread, rice, and meat, with charcoal and wood for cooking and washing purposes, were provided by the Government; but all the stores, furniture, and drugs for the use of the patients, with the extra articles of diet, *e.g.*, milk, eggs, beef-tea, fresh vegetables, stimulants, and other delicacies, were procured and served at the Committee's expense. Diet arrangements.

RECORD OF OPERATIONS.

Dr. Eccles' report. The following are the statistics of the hospital from the date of its establishment to that of its transfer to the Government.

S. H. HOSPITAL, ISLAHANE, SALONICA.

March 7:—Number in hospital, 58; entered, 190; discharged, 179; died, 2; remaining (April 15), 67: total admitted, 248.

Regions wounded or injured	Admitted	Amputations	Other operations	Died	Discharged	Remaining April 15
Head and face	12	—	—	—	12	—
Chest	7	—	—	1	5	1
Back	2	—	—	—	2	—
Upper extremity	125	5	8	—	95	30
Lower „	86	3	—	—	50	36
Perineum and genitals	3	—	—	—	3	—
Penetrating joints	5	—	—	1	4	—
Frost-bites	8	—	—	—	8	—
Total	248	8	8	2	179	67

GALLIPOLI.

The Stafford House operations at Gallipoli began by taking over the National Aid Society's Hospital on March 11. The patients were transported into a larger and more convenient building on April 13, and this new hospital was kept up until June 1, first under Surgeon Barker and subsequently under Surgeon Eccles. After that date the work assumed much greater proportions, owing to Osman Nouri Pacha, the Military Governor, having handed over to the S. H. staff the medical superintendence of the whole of the troops under his command. The increasing prevalence of fevers and other diseases, and the danger of their spreading to the British fleet anchored off Gallipoli, rendered it most desirable that energetic measures should be taken to improve the sanitary state of the garrison. Accordingly the staff was at once augmented and established in the Sultan redoubt in the Boulair Lines, and a soup-kitchen and transport service between the lines and the town hospital organized. The work of this section could never have been carried out on so large a scale had it not been for the personal support and valuable advice of Rear-Admiral Sir E. Commerell, in command of the fleet at Gallipoli, and a member of the Stafford House Committee. Among those officers of the fleet who took a most active part in the work were Captain Jackson, R.N., Lieutenant Gresley, R.N., Staff-Surgeons M. Trevan, R.N., of H.M.S. *Condor*, and W. Drew, R.N., and also Messrs. Guarracino and Guerriera.

Period of service of hospital: *March* 11 *to June* 1, 1878.—Total sick treated in hospital, 259; average number of beds occupied, 61.

Period of service of operations in Boulair Lines: *June* 1 *to Sep.* 15, 1878.—Number of cases treated, 19,241; average treated per day, 545; total number transported by Stafford House transport service, 2,684. Soup-kitchens: total number of rations, 58,377.

The following served on the staff of this section: Surgeons F. R. Barker, A. S. Eccles, S. F. Clements, Assistant-Surgeon Sketchley, Dispenser Görlitz, Mr. R. Williams in charge of transport, Mr. Aslan, storekeeper.

GALLIPOLI HOSPITAL.

The following is a general report of this section, condensed by Surgeon Eccles from the special reports of Surgeons Barker and himself. This report refers first to the work at the Gallipoli Hospital and afterwards to that in the Boulair Lines.

GALLIPOLI HOSPITAL.

On March 11, 1878, the National Aid Society's hospital at Gallipoli, of forty-six beds, was transferred to the Stafford House Committee, Surgeon Barker being placed in charge as Surgeon-in-Chief.

The distress among the troops stationed in the Lines of Boulair was at this time very great, and much sickness prevailed, while hospital accommodation, the medical staff, and matériel were insufficient for the large numbers of sick daily increasing. The patients were lodged in several of the largest houses of the town of Gallipoli, but none of these buildings were in any way adapted for the purposes to which they were necessarily put. Hospital furniture, of the simplest and most ordinary kind, existed only in a few of the hospitals, while in many houses the patients lay on mats spread on the floors, with no other coverings than their overcoats. Of eight hundred sick, not more than one hundred were provided with the barest necessaries, including those under the care of the Stafford House medical officers; provisions were difficult to obtain; of drugs there were none, save those furnished by the National Aid Society and the Stafford House Committee, and no means of transport existed between the Lines of Boulair and the town.

With a view to increase the aid afforded by the Stafford House Committee, Surgeon Barker endeavoured to obtain, and with much difficulty succeeded in obtaining, a larger building, and opened the new hospital April 13. Surgeon Clement was sent to assist him, and stores of matériel, clothing, and drugs were forwarded. The number of beds in charge of the Stafford House medical men was raised to sixty-five. Surgeons Barker and Clement, in addition to their duties in the Stafford House hospital, also aiding the Turkish medical officers, and distributing stores where the need was greatest. A soup-kitchen was established in Gallipoli by the officers and men of H.M. ships stationed at Gallipoli and in the Gulf of Xeros, at which the sick on arriving from the lines and the convalescents returning were daily provided with wholesome, nutritious soup.

On May 10 the superintendence of the section was transferred from Surgeon Barker (on his return to England) to Surgeon Eccles, who, with an augmented staff, carried on the work of the hospital in Gallipoli till June 1, when the section was transferred to the Lines of Boulair. Attempts were made to obtain another building in Gallipoli, suitable for hospital purposes, in order to enlarge the sphere of our labours, but these were frustrated by the objections raised by the inhabitants or owners to permit their houses to be converted into hospitals. Meanwhile the civil and military local authorities were doing their utmost to hasten the completion of a barrack hospital, capable of receiving five hundred patients, which was in course of construction on a good site just outside the town.

The deficiency in the medical staff was only too apparent; the number of medical officers in the Government service was totally inadequate to the demand made on their time and strength; and the want of officers properly qualified for the superintendence of the sanitary arrangements of the camps, and the inspection of men placing themselves on the sick list, was seriously felt. Over two hundred men arrived daily from Boulair, suffering from diseases more or less serious; but the majority of these cases were originally of too trivial a nature to require admission to a hospital, if they could have been treated as out-patients in the lines, and would have been spared the fatigue of marching nearly ten miles along an open road, affording no shelter from the rays of a scorching sun, or the torrents of rain which occasionally fell, whereas after exposure to such fatigue the diseases from which these men suffered became aggravated, and swelled the number of patients, overcrowding the hospitals and raising the death-rate considerably.

It was impossible to provide room for the enormous number of cases daily presenting themselves for admission to the already crowded hospitals; patients who were not fit to

RECORD OF OPERATIONS.

Dr. Eccles' report.

return to their regiments were necessarily discharged before their convalescence was fairly established, in order to provide accommodation for their more seriously sick comrades. The Stafford House officers were compelled to admit to the hospital a greater number than was due for the maintenance of hygiene so necessary to the well-being of their patients, and recognising the deplorable condition of affairs, they were impressed with the necessity of adopting some means to remedy the existing circumstances.

In accordance with Surgeon Eccles's suggestion, Assistant-Surgeon Sketchley, with a dragoman, was sent to take charge of a dispensary and soup-kitchen established in the Sultan redoubt of the Boulair Lines, and Mr. Williams, with two ambulance wagons and a number of horses, was appointed to transport the sick, fit for admission to hospital, from Boulair to Gallipoli.

On May 20 the work of inspection of sick was in full swing, the men presenting themselves being divided into three classes, viz. :—Out-patients treated on the spot ; In-patients sent to Gallipoli hospitals ; Malingerers sent back to their duties. The first two of these groups received a basin of soup and some bread per head immediately after having been seen by the Stafford House medical officer.

Advantage of the ambulance at Boulair.

Mr. Sketchley's work at the lines soon produced a sensible diminution in the number of cases admitted to hospital, the strain on the medical officers was reduced, and much overcrowding avoided. But, although the cases for admission were reduced, the number of patients claiming attention at the lines increased, as the season of great solar heat advanced, to such an extent that no time remained to Mr. Sketchley for superintending the improvement of sanitary matters in the camp.

The advantages derived from the establishment of this branch at the lines were so marked that it became a matter of consideration as to whether the means at the disposal of the Committee were sufficient to warrant the elaboration of the plans proposed for the sanitary improvement of the camp and the superintendence of the health of the troops stationed in and about the Lines of Boulair.

The importance of the means proposed to be taken for curtailing the sickness so rife at that time among the troops was fully recognised, and the Committee, having made a further appeal to the public for support, was enabled to carry out its work on a more extended scale. To this end the Stafford House Hospital in Gallipoli was handed over with its furniture to the Turkish medical authorities, while the staff, with the necessary material, was transferred to the Lines at Boulair.

The following are the statistics of the Stafford House Hospital at Gallipoli :—

	March 11 to April 13	April 13 to May 10	May 10 to June 1 inclusive.
In hospital	46	59	64
Entered	82	106	25
Discharged	69	81	34
Deaths		6	5
Remaining	59	64	50
Total treated			259

Average number of days spent in hospital by each patient, 12 ; longest time by any one patient, 40 days ; shortest time, 3 days.

BOULAIR LINES DISPENSARY TRANSPORT AND SOUP-KITCHENS.

Boulair ambulance.

On June 1, the hospital at Gallipoli having been given up to the Turkish medical staff, the Stafford House tents were pitched in the Sultan redoubt, which crowns the ridge between the Gulf of Xeros and the Straits of the Dardanelles. Close by was a large barrack, a room in which was devoted to the reception and examination of the sick, who, to the number of about five hundred per diem, presented themselves for inspection.

BOULAIR LINES DISPENSARY.

The room was divided by barriers, the men, according to their brigades, being examined by one or other of the medical men as they passed his table. Each man on his first visit received a card, which was taken from him when he was fit to return to duty. The name, brigade, regiment, &c., and native place of the individual, with the disease and prescriptions, was written by the medical officer, the man passing on to the dispenser, who administered the medicine and passed the patient into a waiting place, either to the right or left, to receive his soup, bread, and tobacco; such cases as were too severe for treatment as out-patients, on having been examined, passed into a waiting place apart, where they also received soup, &c., and whence they were removed to Gallipoli in the Stafford House ambulance wagons. The particulars of each case were entered by a clerk who assisted at each table, into a book, and thus a complete register of the work was kept. *Dr. Eccles' report. System of relief.*

In addition to the examination every morning of all the men on the sick list of the battalions encamped in and around the Lines of Boulair, the sanitary condition of the camp also occupied the attention of the Stafford House officers, and measures were taken to improve the water supply, drainage, and arrangement of tents, while at the same time the diet and clothing of the men were augmented and improved on representation made to the authorities. *General sanitary arrangements of camp improved.*

While the great majority of the cases coming under the notice of the medical men were scorbutic, much of the sickness of the camp was due to an insufficient water-supply, in many instances the water containing decaying organic matter; but sources of good water were eventually discovered, wells were dug, and filters put down. The wells sunk under the superintendence of the Stafford House officers were provided with Atkins's charcoal filters, which were found to fulfil all requirements in effectually destroying the influence of deleterious matters. After the establishment of a better water-supply the number of cases of ague, dysentery, and diarrhœa sensibly diminished. *Advantage of filters.*

Scurvy being very prevalent among the troops, an attempt was made to procure a sufficient quantity of fresh vegetables; but the Chersonese peninsula affording none, all fresh antiscorbutics were necessarily brought from the opposite coast, where the supply would not bear the pressure put on it to provide so large a body of men, so that we were reduced to the inferior means of employing lime-juice, vinegar, garlic, and onions, which proved useful to a certain extent, and after their adoption undoubtedly reduced the number of scurvy cases. *Scurvy.*

Careful regulations were made as to the disposal of camp refuse; but it was found very difficult to contend against the carelessness of the individual soldier, who could not understand the necessity of the slight extra fatigue required to convey decaying matter to a distance, but preferred to throw his scraps just outside his tent, and contented himself with an occasional heaping together of the offal with which he surrounded his encampment. *Camp refuse.*

In the month of July two battalions having produced cases of smallpox, one in the one case and three in the other, those who had not suffered from the disease were vaccinated, the tents in which it broke out were isolated and thoroughly disinfected by fumigation, their inmates being placed in quarantine, while the battalions themselves were also placed in quarantine with regard to others, as far as was possible, until all fear of an epidemic had ceased. *Smallpox.*

Towards the end of the month of June the number of men presenting themselves for inspection was so large that six hours daily did not suffice for the examination and treatment of the patients, and the tax on the physical strength of the members of the Stafford House staff was consequently so great that all of them suffered more or less from the effects of overwork, two—Messrs. Cowan and Williams—being compelled to resign their posts. This reduction entailed so much extra work on the remaining members, that it was feared we should be obliged to abandon our labours; but several of the executive and medical officers of H.M.'s ships stationed at Gallipoli came forward and proffered their services, which were gratefully accepted, and we were thus enabled to continue until September 15 in our attempt to relieve the poor fellows who were suffering from the effects of a disastrous war. Drs. Trevan and Drew, Captain Jackson and Lieutenant Gresley, and Messrs. Guarracino and Guerriera gave us their help at intervals until the closing of the section. *Illness of medical staff. Assistance given by officers of H.M. fleet.*

RECORD OF OPERATIONS.

Dr. Eccles' report. The following statistics will show the work carried out in connection with the dispensary and soup-kitchen in the Sultan redoubt from June 1 till September 15 inclusive, when the work of the Stafford House Committee in Turkey was brought to a close:—

	Number of Cards issued at the Morning Visit, i.e. Number of Individuals treated	Sent to Hospital at Gallipoli by S. H. Transport Service	Relieved, reported for Change of Air or for Discharge from Service	Cured	Numbers remaining on Books
June (30 days) . . .	6,820	935	780	4,563	542
July (31 days) . . .	5,804	871	642	3,764	527
August (31 days) . .	4,232	628	302	2,894	408
September (15 days) .	2,385	250	86	1,682	367
Total	19,241	2,684	1,810	12,903	

In addition to the 19,241 individuals treated at the morning visit, 692 were seen and attended at other hours of the day and night by the Stafford House medical officer of the guard. On reference to the register kept of the numbers seen daily, we learn that the exact number of times patients have been prescribed for and have received relief at the morning visit is as follows:—

June	18,157	Average per diem	605·2
July . . .	17,020	,, ,,	549·3
August . . .	15,767	,, ,,	508·6
September . .	7,433	,, ,,	495·5
Total . .	58,377		

One of the medical men was always on guard, and on several occasions severe injuries, in some cases necessitating immediate operation, were brought to the surgery at different hours of the day and night.

Letter from ADMIRAL COMMERELL.

H.M.S. 'Agincourt,' Gallipoli, March 24.

Admiral Commerell's letter. DEAR KENNETT,—The large garrison here are for the most part composed of Suleiman's army, which, after their heavy winter campaign, have brought with them the seeds of disease. Typhoid and dysentery are very prevalent among these, and chest diseases among the Arabs and Syrians. The poor soldiers are very grateful for the assistance rendered, and if you saw the poor weary sick soldier toiling in from the lines, you would regret as I do the chance of the withdrawal of the hospital. We have just got a Greek house to hold one hundred and twenty men, and to show how the authorities value our assistance, the civil governor has offered his own house for hospital purposes.

You may put my name down for 25l. for Gallipoli hospital.

Yours truly,

(Signed)   J. E. COMMERELL.

STAMBOUL NEW BARRACK HOSPITAL.

This barrack-hospital was built at the expense of the Ottoman Government in the grounds of the Ecole Militaire, and handed over to a Stafford House staff under Surgeon Stiven. The barracks were completely furnished as a hospital for 100 patients at S. H. expense. On Surgeon Stiven being invalided, Surgeon Lake was appointed chief surgeon. The hospital was transferred to Marco Pacha, the Director of the Ecole Militaire, in June 1878.

Period of service: March 15 to June 8, 1878.— Total number treated, 131 wounded; average number of beds occupied, 83. The following served with this section: Surgeons Stiven and Lake, Assistaut-Surgeon Azzopardi, six Turkish medical students, Dispenser Beylikgy, and four Saxon Sisters of Charity sent by the Queen of Saxony.

The following are extracts from reports to the Chief Commissioner:—

Stamboul, Stafford House Barrack, March 23, 1878.

On Thursday, March 21, the Stafford House hospital erected in two large barracks adjacent to the Stamboul railway terminus, having its first two wards fully equipped with their full complement of beds and everything ready and in order for the reception of patients, commenced to perform its functions by receiving within its walls 94 wounded patients. The majority of the wounds are of a severe nature, and will require a large amount of slow, earnest, and careful treatment, principally on account of the low condition (physically) of the patients, produced by their late hardships and privations, and also that the wounds had been greatly neglected during their transportation from place to place. Everything with regard to the hospital is going on in a highly satisfactory manner, the wards being in charge of Dr. Lake and myself, with the assistance of three Sisters supplied by the Queen of Saxony, and six aides-chirurgien from the military medical school. I am not at present able to give a detailed list of the nature of the wounds, but hope I shall be able to supply it in my next report. Every step is being taken to have the other two wards of the hospital made ready for the reception of patients.

Dr. STIVEN'S reports.

Opening of S. H. hospital.

Barrack Hospital, Stamboul, April 13, 1878.

From the date of my last report, written on March 25, up to the present date I am glad to be able to report that everything has gone on in the most satisfactory manner, and still continues to do so, in the new barrack hospital at Stamboul. At the request of Marco Pacha, I undertook a class, with the assistance of Drs. Lake and Azzopardi, to instruct a certain number of students from the military medical school. At the first 35 students came regularly and received instructions on the nature of the wounds, their treatment, &c., along with practical instruction in dressing, bandaging, and prescribing any medicines that might be necessary. At present, however, the zeal of many of its members has died off, and we have only about twelve to fourteen who attend regularly, the others dropping in now and then, as it suits their fancies (after the manner of all students both at home and abroad). There are at present in hospital 91 patients, the majority of which are severe cases and require great attention, which is duly given to them, as all severe cases are dressed twice a day regularly, and the Sisters of Charity are always in constant attendance, giving out milk, soups and wine to those who are in most need of extra support and nourishment. Since the commencement of the hospital 105 patients have been treated within its walls; and of these thirteen have been discharged to their battalions, and one patient has died, the cause of death being typhoid fever, he having been brought into our hospital amongst the first 94 while suffering from the first stage of fever; he had also a severe wound of the upper arm.

Class of Turkish medical students.

Subjoined is a list of the parts of the body wounded, &c.:—

Received in Hospital.				*Died in Hospital.*		
Wounds of the head		2		Wounds of the arm		1
,, ,, face		4		(Cause of death, typhoid fever)		
,, ,, neck		1				
,, ,, chest		8		*Discharged from Hospital cured.*		
,, ,, arm		49		Wounds of the neck		1
,, ,, leg		40		,, ,, arm		7
,, ,, joints		1		,, ,, leg		5
		105				13

Constantinople, April 27, 1878.

Dr. Stiven's reports. Since the date of my last report on the 13th inst. everything in connection with the New Barrack Hospital has proceeded in a most satisfactory manner. During the past fortnight eleven wounded have been discharged cured and fit for duty, while other three wounded have died. Two of the above deaths were due to hospital gangrene imported into our hospital from the other Turkish hospital from whence our wounded were received. The other death was a bayonet wound of the chest. Many of the wounds, when received into our hospital, were suffering from gangrene; but I am thankful to say the result of the treatment used in the hospital has been very successful, and we have but one or two cases only left at present. There are at present in hospital 77 patients, who are all doing well.

KESANLIK RELIEF SECTION.

The following is a report from Mr. R. Williams, who was sent to Kesanlik on March 17 with a large supply of stores to the relief of over 1,000 Turkish wounded prisoners who had been abandoned there in the hasty retreat of the Ottoman army. Mr. Williams distributed the stores, and also assisted in the transport of the wounded Turks to Philippopolis:—

The following is Mr. Williams' report:—

April 9, 1878.

Mr. Williams' report. I have the honour to present the following report:—On March 17 I left Constantinople and, upon arrival at Adrianople, waited upon the Russian inspector of hospitals. He informed me that there were about 900 Turkish sick and wounded in the hospitals of Kesanlik under the care of 24 doctors. March 19, left Adrianople and arrived at Philippopolis. Tried to obtain bullock-arabas, but did not succeed. Waited upon General Stalipin, the Russian Military Commandant, who received me most kindly, and procured for me four arabas. He told me that the roads were too bad to allow of my taking them all the way to Karlova, and advised me to go to Karlova, to the Governor of which place he gave me a letter directing him to assist me in procuring fresh arabas. General Stalipin also furnished me with a Cossack as an escort. March 21, left Philippopolis for Karlova. There I found fifteen wounded and sick Turkish soldiers in a filthy building, the remnant of a party of 120 who had been placed there two months before. They were in a condition of indescribable filth and misery. They had been totally neglected, except that they had each received half an oke of bread daily, but of medical and surgical attendance and of all means of cleanliness they had been deprived. I gave them soup, bread, and tobacco, and informed the Governor of their condition.

Miserable condition of wounded at Karlova and Kesanlik. He immediately gave me wagons in which to convey them to the S. H. hospital at Philippopolis. I also supplied them with provisions for the journey. At Karlova I procured five fresh wagons. March 23, left Karlova for Kesanlik. At Kesanlik I found 1,224 Turks, viz.—587 wounded, 294 convalescent, 15 surgeons, 15 doctors, 22 assistant-surgeons, 12 druggists, 279 refugees. They were housed in eleven buildings, and although not overcrowded, the stench was almost insupportable. The bed linen and bedding had not been changed since the Russian occupation. Cases of typhus

Absence of medical stores. were scattered amongst the wounded. The doctors were without medical stores of any description, not even a bandage. The Russian doctors had given them what medicines they could spare, but that was very little. I at once gave all the medical stores I had with me to the Turkish Government doctors, and distributed blankets, tobacco, Liebig's extract, and wine myself. The Russians supply good rations to the wounded, and pay doctors and officers two francs a day. On March 26

Relief given. the Russian Governor placed 80 Red Cross wagons at the disposal of the Turkish doctors, and sent 330 wounded to Philippopolis. A cook was sent on before to prepare food at the village of Ouba, where the party passed the night. The same precaution was adopted at Thikouv, where the next night was passed. On the afternoon of the third day the party arrived at Philippopolis. On March 28, 170 serious cases were sent on to same place; both parties were escorted by Russian soldiers. I distributed tobacco and blankets to all the sick and wounded, and sent a S. H. man to attend upon them. There now remain 160 wounded and 150 convalescents whom I was unable to bring away, being recalled by your telegram. At the time of the Russian occupation there were

Great mortality. 1,920 sick and wounded Turks at Kesanlik, of whom upwards of 600 have died. On March 31 I

KESANLIK RELIEF SECTION. 99

left Kesanlik for Philippopolis; there I procured ration-money (15 kopecks per man) for the wounded, and handed it over to the Red Crescent doctors, who are now attending them. I cannot conclude without mentioning the courtesy and ready help of the Russian authorities wherever I have been brought into communication with them.

Mr.WILLIAMS' report.

(D)—ASIA.

FOUR SECTIONS.

ERZEROUM STAFFORD HOUSE HOSPITAL.

This hospital was handed over to the S. H. staff by the Turkish medical authorities, and contained 300 beds, which were nearly always occupied by severe cases. For a few days, owing to Surgeon Ryan's severe illness, it was retransferred to Turkish administration, but on his recovery and the arrival of an additional staff of surgeons, it was again worked by S. H. surgeons.

Period of service: Nov. 12, 1877, *to April* 17, 1878.—Treated: sick, 521; wounded, 353; total, 874. Average number of beds occupied, 293. The following served at different times on this section: Surgeons Ryan, Woods, Stoker, Stiven, Messrs. Harvey, Morisot, and native assistants.

The following are extracts from reports to the Chief Commissioner:—

Trebizond, Nov. 16, 1877.

I arrived here at nine this morning, and called immediately on Mr. Biliotti, the English Consul. By his advice and that of Captain McCalmont, one of the military attachés just come from Erzeroum, I am leaving to-morrow morning for Erzeroum, hoping to arrive in three days. It will be a hard ride, but I trust that we can manage it. The Consul thinks it of the utmost importance that we should try to arrive there as soon as possible, as there is a fearful amount of work to be done there.

Dr. RYAN's reports.
Arrival of Staff at Trebizond.

Erzeroum, Nov. 22, 1877.

We arrived here last night at eight o'clock, having taken five days from Trebizond; 190 miles over bad road, snow and frost latter half. Woods suffered considerably, but showed immense pluck. I called at once on Mr. Zohrab, H.M. Consul here, who received me with the greatest kindness. I had a long talk with him, and eventually agreed with him that the best we could do would be to take over from the Turks an hospital, and work it in the same manner as that worked by Dr. Fetherstonhaugh. I called this morning on Mukhtar Pacha, who received me most courteously, and told me he was exceedingly glad that we had come, as there was any amount of work to be done; he also told me that anything he could do for me he would. Later I called on Yussuf Bey with Mr. Zohrab, and have agreed to take a hospital, containing 250 beds, which has hitherto been worked by the Turkish doctors. I am to have sole charge of the hospital, retaining the services of four of the Turkish zairah bashis (otherwise dressers), and paying them half what they receive from the Turkish Government. I am also taking an apothecary on the same terms, and will pay the attendants, as they will work much more satisfactorily. There are at present 3,500 wounded here, but I expect in about four or five days the place will be flowing in blood, as the Turks will make a very determined resistance. Mr. Zohrab takes the greatest interest in the working of the hospitals here; our hospital will be distinguished by the name of the 'Stafford House Hospital,' in distinction from the other, which is called the 'English Hospital.' [Williams arrived with all stores on Dec. 1.]

Arrival at Erzeroum.
Establishment of S. H. hospital.

Erzeroum, Dec. 1, 1877.

Since writing to you we have got fairly to work in our new hospital and everything now is in full swing. We took over from the Turks the hospital just as it was, taking on all the servants

Dr. RYAN's reports.

connected, and agreeing to pay them in Caïme one-half of the salary they ought to receive from the Government. By doing so we get more work out of them, and we have them, so to speak, more under our control, for in case of disobedience we can punish them by stopping their salary. In addition to the actual servants who are necessary in carrying on the work of the hospital, we have taken on a house-surgeon, whose business it is to make the visit in the morning, and who has a room in the hospital itself, so that in cases of hæmorrhage we have always a competent person there to arrest it, until one of us can come up; also an apothecary and two dressers. I think it probable that we shall take on another dresser, as we find our work rather heavy. Our hospital was formerly a large khan, and contains at present 300 beds. It consists chiefly of two large rooms, containing respectively 98 and 62 beds, and several smaller rooms off the largest room. This is 100 feet in length, having a width of 65 and a height of about 30. It is ventilated and lighted by means of three large glass skylights, which are let into the roof, and which can be opened. Three times a day I have this done, so that the heated and foul air can escape. The weather is too cold at present to have them continually open. In addition to these skylights, ventilation is carried on by means of two large stoves placed at the two ends of the room, and which are always lighted, thereby causing a good current of air. Off this room on all sides are smaller rooms each containing about eight beds. These are the worst wards we have, as they are rather small and stuffy. We are doing our best to remedy them. We have, I believe, fourteen in all of them. In addition we have a pharmacy, an amputation-room, a doctors' room, and a store-room. The entrance to the large room is a fine broad passage about 20 feet in width, and as you enter the room has quite a picturesque appearance, with its many coloured beds, as most of the quilts are of various hues. The second ward, containing 62 beds, is like the largest in every respect except that it has no rooms off it. It is 81 feet long by 45 wide, and is, I think, the best ventilated and most healthy room we have in the hospital. We have also, in connection with the hospital, a kitchen and several closets. I hope by next mail to send you a drawing and plan of the hospital, as possibly it may be interesting to you. We have at present 299 wounded in the hospital. During the last week we have had six deaths, and have sent out 30. Most of the cases are lightly wounded, but we are gradually filling our beds with more serious ones, and probably in another week we shall have nothing but grave cases. We have performed two amputations, both at the shoulder-joint. One was performed to-day by Dr. Woods, the other was performed by myself. I regret to say we have found among the wounded several cases of typhoid and typhus fever, all of which we sent out to the Medical Central Hospital, as we took our hospital on the condition of having only surgical cases. I am happy to say we have been so fortunate as to obtain the services of Dr. Pinkerton, one of Lord Blantyre's men, who was with Dr. Fetherstonhaugh, and as he (the latter) has a hospital containing 150 beds, he kindly allowed Dr. Pinkerton to assist us. I have ordered 100 beds, which are now ready, as many of our wounded were lying only on mattresses; and have also ordered 30 soft mattresses and some stores. We give the soldiers tobacco once a week, as they feel the want of it greatly. We have now enough stores to last us some time, and should Erzeroum not fall (which I sincerely hope it will not) during the next fortnight, it will be free, at all events, until next spring. Mr. Zohrab is receiving quantities of stores from Lord Blantyre, as also from Mrs. Layard, but they have not yet arrived. I am happy to say that Williams arrived with stores this afternoon, everything having come on all right; he was delayed on the road in consequence of bad weather. Captains Morisot and Harvey (volunteers) have been making themselves very useful in the hospital, in giving beef-tea, bandaging, &c. We have had a heavy fall of snow, and in consequence the hospitals here have been filled with sick. I believe there are at present about 4,000 sick and wounded here.

Description of hospital.

Ventilation.

Arrival of stores.

Erzeroum, Dec. 7, 1877.

Harvey leaves to-morrow for Constantinople. I am very sorry to lose him, for he has been very valuable and obliging since he came here, and has done all he can to be of service. Now that Williams has arrived, we can get on quite well without him. Morisot makes himself very useful in helping me to bandage, and in giving out beef-tea to the patients, &c. We have only two regular dressers, and I have handed them over to Drs. Woods and Pinkerton. We have to-day in hospital 305 patients. I am most satisfied with the Turkish servants in the hospital; I find that by paying them half of their salary from the Government they work most satisfactorily : this applies especially to the two dressers, who are capital men. We have weeded and sent out most of our light cases, so that we have a great many grave ones in at present. Williams, the dragoman, makes himself very useful in the hospital, and I am very pleased with him. We have had nine cases of typhus fever among our wounded. I have weeded them out from the wards, and have had a room

Efficiency of Turkish dressers.

specially prepared to receive them. I am happy to say all are doing well. I should like to have sent them out to the Turkish medical hospital, but as they had all wounds I was unable. We have performed three amputations since we took over the hospital. The first was an amputation at the shoulder-joint (a gunshot wound, shattering the head of the bone), performed by myself. The poor fellow went on very well for three days, but then got an attack of pleurisy, from which he died last night. The majority of our deaths have been from pyæmia, which was raging when we got the hospital; but by paying the greatest attention to the ventilation of the wards, I am in hopes of diminishing very considerably the number of cases. We have also had six deaths from gunshot wounds penetrating the lungs. Many of our patients complain greatly of the cold, and unfortunately the supply of wood is very limited, and at the present time it is impossible to buy more, so that we can only make up for its deficiency by giving extra blankets to them, which Mr. Zohrab, her Majesty's Consul, has handed over to us, being some of those sent out by Lord Blantyre. I make a point, after finishing my cases, of going round and giving personally beef-tea and mutton-broth to those of our patients who are most in want of it. I enclose you a plan of our hospital, which speaks for itself. I have had occasion several times to call on the head of the hospital here, who has always received me with great courtesy, and who has been only too willing to assist me in every way. I do not know what we should do without Mr. Zohrab, who devotes a large portion of his very valuable time to our hospitals. The cold is intense, the thermometer registering at night 40° below freezing point. Every night five or six soldiers are found frozen to death on outpost duty. There are at present 5,050 sick and wounded in Erzeroum, and I believe that about 150 to 200 sick come in daily, not more than 50 going out.

Dr. RYAN's reports.

Valuable services of Consul Zohrab. Intense cold.

Erzeroum, Dec. 19, 1877.

I am glad to say that our hospital is progressing well. To-day, we have 331 in hospital, 800 men having come in from Kars. All those who were slightly wounded and able to walk, the Russians sent on here, giving each man a small baksheesh; the men say they were well treated. I sent up to Yussuf Bey to say that we could not have our hospital overcrowded, and that we really had not accommodation for more than 300. He sent back word to say that the town was overcrowded with sick and wounded and that there was no place for them; fortunately they are very slightly wounded, and I hope in a few days to be able to send about 30 of them back to their 'Tabours.' The result of overcrowding in the various hospitals is that both typhus and typhoid fevers are rife, and hospital gangrene has broken out. I have had eight cases, but fortunately it does not show a disposition to spread. I have lost three men from it, but the other five of them have thrown it off, and are now progressing favourably. We have still about fifteen cases of typhus and typhoid fevers, notwithstanding that we have done all in our power to keep a free ventilation, but I am happy to say that nearly all are recovered. I greatly fear that, if the same number of sick keep coming into hospital, we shall have an epidemic in the town, which will carry off a great many. Out of five amputations performed, two are at present doing well, the other three having all died from pyæmia. We do not find ourselves overworked. Dr. Pinkerton has charge of 128 beds and I have the rest; he has one dresser and I have two, and we manage to get on very well. Mr. Morisot has been of great assistance in bandaging, giving beef-tea, &c., as has also been Williams, who I regret to say is ill. There are far more sick than wounded at present in the town. Even should we be surrounded by the Russians, I have plenty of money, and do not think it necessary that you should send me more.

Arrival of wounded from Kars. Overcrowding in hospitals.

Prevalence of typhus and typhoid.

Erzeroum, Dec. 22, 1877.

We have in hospital to-day 345, 40 more than we have room for; we have only 305 beds, and the other poor fellows have to lie on the floor. Out of seventeen Hungarian doctors here in the Turkish service, ten are now in bed, most with typhus fever; we buried one of them to-day. Fetherstonhaugh is now, I am glad to say, convalescent. All our new cases are frost-bites; we have not less than 50 patients who have lost all their toes; but they get on very well. Typhus in our hospital is on the decrease, and although we have had a good many cases, we have had very few deaths from it; also hospital gangrene has decreased; we have not more than seven or eight cases now.

Hungarian doctors.

Erzeroum, Dec. 27 and 30, 1877.

I take advantage of Dr. Fetherstonhaugh's leaving to send you a few lines. We have been very busy for the last few days, owing to an influx of wounded sent by the Russians from Kars. Mukhtar Pacha told me that of 2,000 who left, only 317 arrived; but I cannot help fancying that

Dr. Ryan's reports.

Sufferings of Turkish wounded sent from Kars.

such a statement was a little too highly coloured. At the same time, the mortality has been very great. I have about 50 of them in hospital at present; and one told me to-day that he left with a party of 30, and only ten arrived here, the remainder having died on the way. Out of the ten who arrived, seven of them lost all their toes from frost-bites. I am very happy to state that we have very nearly stamped out hospital gangrene from our wards, and both typhus and typhoid fever are on the decrease; but I believe that in the town generally and in the other hospitals the rate of mortality from these diseases is on the increase. Three days ago we sent out from hospital 66, who started to march to Baiburt. They were the slightly wounded, and those whom we considered able and fit to march, chiefly those wounded in the hands or arms. We were able to give the poor fellows warm jerseys, drawers, long stockings, and comforters, thanks to the generosity of

Distribution of Lord Blantyre's warm clothing.
Mortality among Turkish surgeons.

Lord Blantyre. To-day we sent out another 30, and, in addition to giving them clothes, gave each man ten piastres from Lord Blantyre's fund here (British Hospital Fund). The town has been overcrowded, and so these men have been sent out both to lessen the chances of epidemic and to diminish the work of the doctors here. No less than seventeen of the latter are ill in bed (more than 50 per cent.), and four have died during the past month. The number in hospital to-day is 281—four days ago it was 345; but we have sent out a great many since; probably by to-morrow morning all our beds will be filled up. Our mortality is becoming smaller every day. Our new cases are nearly all frost-bites; we have about 60 where the men have lost all their toes, but, as a rule, they do very well. Our Turkish surgeon has been ill in bed for three weeks past, and one of our dressers, so that just at present our hands are very full—not more, however, than we can manage. Williams has been very ill with 'Erzeroum fever' (I know no other name for it)—it appears to be an endemic fever of a malignant type; but I am happy to say he is up and about, and in another week I intend sending him to Constantinople, when he will be strong enough. Mr. Morisot has been ill, but I hope he will soon be all right again. Dr. Denniston tells me that he has a case of small-pox in his wards, the first that has come under our notice in Erzeroum; but, judging from my experience in Plevna, it is not likely to spread rapidly. Dr. Pinkerton is laid up with the same fever that Williams had, but to-night he seems much better; he says as soon as he is well that he thinks he will leave, and probably Morisot will leave with him, so that we shall send Williams, Morisot, and Pinkerton off together. Dr. Denniston is working the English hospital, and I am working the Stafford House. I have a great deal to do, but manage it all right. Nearly everybody is ill here; a surgeon (Turk) was buried yesterday, and great sickness prevails among the poor people, chiefly typhus.

[Early in January Dr. Ryan was taken ill, and for a short time the management of the hospital was transferred to the Turkish authorities. The following is a letter from Vice-Consul Biliotti on the subject.]

Trebizond, Jan. 18, 1878.

Vice-Consul Biliotti's letter.

Dr. Pinkerton's death and Dr. Ryan's illness.

I enclose you a letter which has just arrived from Erzeroum through a private messenger. I grieve to say that it conveys you sad news of your party in that town. Poor Dr. Pinkerton is dead, and Dr. Ryan very ill. I transcribe a paragraph concerning them from a letter from the American missionary now at Erzeroum :—'I was down with poor Pinkerton a little time as he was in the last fearful struggle with the king of terrors. He was delirious for the last four days. Now poor Ryan is sick, and I fear may not live. Only one poor lonely fellow, Dr. Denniston, is not sick. The sick have been so delirious that he had to sit in his chair night after night, and get what sleep he could in that position. The sisters of charity assist him in the daytime. I wished to help him, but he would not consent for my sake; says he has had typhus, so he shall not be in danger. Pinkerton was buried in the Protestant Cemetery at Erzeroum.'

Erzeroum, Feb. 8, 1878.

Dr. Ryan's reports.

Recovery of Dr. Ryan.

Frost-bite.

In a private letter of mine written a few days ago, I informed you that I had written to the head of the hospitals here, giving up the Stafford House hospital, as I was at the time unable to attend to it through illness, and Dr. Denniston, who superintended the working of it during my illness, had so much to do in his own hospital that he could not look after it. At the same time I informed you that as soon as I felt strong enough, it was my intention to help Dr. Denniston in his hospital, as I considered that my own hospital, which contains 300 beds, was too large for one man to work; but circumstances have changed, and I found on visiting the hospital that it had been so miserably neglected that I determined to take it on again, which I have done, having commenced work to-day, assisted by Dr. Stoker. All the beds in the hospital are full, by far the majority with frost-bites. Nearly all the patients wounded have been sent out cured. Many of

ERZEROUM HOSPITAL. 103

the cases of frost-bite are very severe, being far worse than most gunshot wounds; for the latter you can do something, but for the former cases very little. I have more than fifteen cases in which both feet are entirely lost, and I have two in which the frost-bite extended half way to the knee. They are the most pitiable cases, and generally occur in men so weak and thin that they have no vitality, and very little chance of recovery. We have a good many cases of hospital gangrene, but they seem to be on the decline, and *typhus fever is pretty well stamped out*, we having no recent cases, only those convalescent. I performed an amputation of the leg for frost-bite to-day. The man had both feet gangrenous; one of his legs I amputated in the calf, and I cut his other foot off with a pair of scissors. I do not know what your intentions are with regard to Dr. Stoker, but I hope, if possible, he will remain on, as there is a great amount of work in the hospital. We have stores enough to carry us on for another month, and I hope by then that Rennison will be able to come up. We shall only run short of carbolic acid, marine lint and English lint; we have long ago finished all our charpie. The sanitary condition of the town is improving every day, and there is not much typhus at present. [I have approved of Dr. Ryan's keeping up the Stafford hospital at Erzeroum, and shall keep him supplied with stores until the wounded are evacuated elsewhere.—V. B.-K.]

Dr. Ryan's reports.
Resumption of work at S. H. hospital.
Improvement of sanitary condition.

Erzeroum, Feb. 11, 1878.

I have the opportunity of sending you these few lines by Dr. Stiven, who leaves to-morrow morning. Lieut. Morisot also accompanies him. He leaves at our advice, as he has been very ill with typhus fever, and his convalescence is naturally very slow here at present, while the town is full of sickness, and the air far from being pure. He has been of the greatest assistance to me all through, doing all in his power to make himself useful, notwithstanding that the town was rife with disease. He insisted on sticking to me, and working with me, when poor Dr. Pinkerton took ill, and I had the whole 300 patients to look after. He dressed every day 100 of them. He will be a great loss to us here, as he was also very useful in writing letters in French to the commander, &c. We are now fairly settled at work again; the hospital is full of very serious cases of frost-bites. I heard to-day as a positive fact that during the last three months, no less than 9,500 have died in the various hospitals here. As one of the persons concerned, I have to thank you most warmly for sending relief to us, when you heard we were ill.

Illness of Lieut. Morisot.
Mortality in hospitals.

Erzeroum, March 8, 1878.

Our hospital is working well, and is continually kept full, owing to the Turks emptying their hospitals into ours, thereby increasing our work and doing very little themselves. It is only five days ago that I had sent to me a batch of 50 sick, and as my beds were all full, they had to be laid on the floor. The next day, however, I went to the chief of the hospitals, and told him positively that I would not take them, and so had them sent back. There are only six Turkish hospitals here at present, the others having been emptied. The new cases that we are receiving now are all sick—as there are no more wounded or cases of frozen feet, and the majority of them are suffering from chronic diarrhœa, and medicines seem to have no effect upon them, the only treatment would seem to be change of air and nourishing food. Dr. Denniston had eight cases sent to him four days ago; four died the first night, and the remainder the second. They appeared to be suffering from nothing but diarrhœa. The cases that were sent us by the Turkish doctors are much the same, several of them often dying the same night. I must enter the strongest protest against the manner in which poor unfortunate soldiers are sent out of one hospital to die the same or the next day in another. You will see that our mortality during the last 24 days has been great owing to the above causes. It would seem that we have the worst or only dying cases sent in to us, only to increase our mortality list. I have looked up one of the small wards containing nine beds, as it was too unhealthy, and I intend to do the same with regard to three or four more as soon as I have some empty beds. I have been fumigating all the wards with crude carbolic acid, which arrived a few days ago with Rennison. I received last week nine Turkish officers, all of whom had been wounded, but are now nearly well. We have only two cases of typhus fever, and hospital gangrene has almost entirely disappeared. I performed yesterday an amputation at the middle third of the tibia, for gangrene of the foot and ankle. I also excised a tumour situated just over the upper eyelid. We have also had several minor operations for necrosis, and have amputated several fingers. During the last 24 days we have had 111, who have died in hospital, 68 have been sent out cured; 198 have been received in hospital, and we have at present 293; out of these about 40 are sick, the remainder being wounded, or having lost their fingers or toes through intense cold. I believe that several of the Turkish doctors are being sent to join the army at

Prevalence of diarrhœa.
High death rate.

104   RECORD OF OPERATIONS.

Dr. Ryan's reports.	Erzinghian, and I should think that in another month that they would be able to transport those sick and wounded remaining at Erzinghian. I believe I mentioned to you in a former report that according to a calculation which I believe to be quite true, about 18,000 or 20,000 bodies have been buried within the walls of the town—13,000 soldiers, the remainder being civil population. Now, as most of these bodies have only been put about two feet in the ground, when the snow melts and the rain falls, decomposition will go on very rapidly, and the air will be saturated with the most purulent and unhealthy odours. The Russians are fully alive to the danger of a pest which is always liable to break out under such conditions, and accordingly General Melikoff has sent a telegram to Tiflis, and a sanitary commission is to arrive in two or three days, to consider what are the best means to be taken, and he has asked us to attend it, which we shall do. Dr. Roy tells me that ten cases were sent into his hospital last night, and they all died before twelve o'clock.
Danger of pest.	

Constantinople, April 18, 1878.

Transfer of hospital to Turkish Government.	In accordance with your telegram received on March 27, I made arrangements to leave in three days, and handed over to Ismail Bey, chief doctor of the Turkish army in Asia, our hospital, containing at the time 250 sick and wounded. I made out a list of our stores, reserving four large boxes of chloroform which I gave in charge of Mr. Cole, the American missionary. I received a receipt in full from Hakki Bey, the then Civil Governor of Erzeroum, for the articles received, which I enclose. I also received from him his warmest and most grateful thanks for the services rendered to the Turkish soldiers by the Stafford House section in Erzeroum, as also a letter of recommendation to the Chief Pacha of the Seraskeriat. We left Erzeroum on March 31, and I regret to state that Dr. Price, of the Red Crescent ambulance, died of typhus on the 30th. When we left there were in Erzeroum 13,000 sick and seventeen Turkish doctors, besides six doctors of the Red Crescent, and as the sickness prevailing was not of a very grave character, the work of the doctors was far from being heavy. In our hospital, at the time of handing over, we had eight cases of amputations, all doing well, and I am sanguine enough to hope that under careful treatment they may all recover. We left Erzeroum on the 31st, and took eleven days to arrive in Trebizond. We were obliged to travel slowly, as all our baggage was conveyed by a Persian caravan. The road over the Kop-Dagh, which is about 9,000 feet above the level of the sea, was very bad and dangerous, the road being not more than two feet in width, and extending for some miles on the edge of a steep and dangerous precipice. We were unfortunate to lose three of our horses over it. We all suffered very considerably from the glare of the snow, the whole country being covered with it for the first five days of our journey. We arrived safely and without further mishap on April 10 in Trebizond, and were most kindly and hospitably treated by H.M. Consul there (Mr. Biliotti), who, throughout our stay in Erzeroum, has been most kind in forwarding stores, telegrams, letters, &c., to us. I cannot lose this opportunity of expressing our thanks for all that he has done for us during our residence in Erzeroum. We left Trebizond by the French steamer Simois, and after a good passage, delayed only by having to remain for a considerable time in Kerasond, Samsoun, and Sinope, we arrived yesterday. In conclusion, let me, on behalf of our section, thank the representatives of the Stafford House in Constantinople for the prompt and ready measures which they adopted for relieving us as soon as they heard of our illness. I have great pleasure in giving Mr. John Williams, our dragoman, the best character; although for a long time very ill and suffering greatly, he stuck to us like a man, even though he could have left with Dr. Stiven for Constantinople. I feel I am only doing my duty to him in adding the above.
Thanks of authorities.	
Departure of staff.	
Arrival in Constantinople.	

Erzeroum, Feb. 8, 1878.

Dr. Stoker's report.	Owing to stress of weather we did not arrive at Trebizond until Jan. 27, but found all preparations completed for our journey up country, and after two hours' delay we started. [Mr. Stoney had telegraphed to Mr. Biliotti.] We were obliged to stop most of the night at Jevislik to rest the post-horses. We started early the next morning and spent the night on the top of the Zegana pass; the road was excessively difficult, the snowdrifts were in some places twenty feet deep, and what little path there was (about two feet wide) was frozen and slippery, and wound along the edge of a cliff about 900 feet high. At times the baggage horses fell and we were obliged to unpack and reload them—these unfortunate accidents delayed us greatly, and it was two hours after dark before we reached the summit of the pass. The next day we reached Gumush Khané without any difficulty, and here for the first time since leaving Trebizond we got a relay of post-horses.
Description of journey to relief of Erzeroum Staff.	

ERZEROUM HOSPITAL.

On the following morning we left Gumush Khané two hours before daylight, and after a ride of eighteen hours arrived at Baiburt. We spent the next day endeavouring to get horses to go on, and succeeded at last; we were, however, obliged to lodge the value of the horses with General Kemball, lest they should be seized by the Russians. On Feb. 1 we left Baiburt, and passed the night in Kop village, at the foot of the pass. On the morning of the 2nd, the weather was very propitious, so we determined to try the pass Kop-Dagh, and after a great struggle of nine hours succeeded in arriving at Furnagaban. We were informed that the Russian outpost was at Ashkala, a distance of three hours, so we determined to await daylight to approach it. Accordingly the next morning we hoisted the ambulance and English flags, and advanced to Ashkala. The Cossacks let us pass at once, and gave us an escort to Ilidja; there we were most politely received by the Russian General Sistovitch, who telegraphed at once to General Melikoff for permission for us to pass the Russian lines into Erzeroum; he provided us with quarters and supplied all our wants. As no answer arrived, we were obliged to remain all next day at Ilidja. The longed-for permission arrived this morning about 9 o'clock, and we entered Erzeroum about 1 o'clock, P.M. Thank God, all our friends are well, and those we feared to see no more were the first to welcome us. All except Dr. Denniston have been very ill, Dr. Ryan most so of all; but he is now quite recovered. Dr. Denniston has done his duty nobly, and we hear his praises sounded on every side; with his three comrades sick with typhus, and two large hospitals to mind, he never flinched, and has come most successfully out of all his troubles. We hear that there are 8,000 sick and wounded here, and a staff of only about 20 doctors. The sick are dying here at the rate of 200 per diem, but the typhus is on the decline, so we hope the city will soon be entirely free of it. You will see that it took us seven days and a half to come here from Trebizond, inclusive of two days lost, one at Baiburt and one at Ilidja; as far as Baiburt we came with the mails. Considering the bad state of the roads and the lack of post-horses, we hope you will consider that we have not delayed unnecessarily under the present circumstances. I beg to state that we received the greatest kindness and assistance from General Kemball. He mainly helped us in getting horses to come on here from Baiburt.

Dr. STOKER's report.

Arrival at Russian outposts.

Gallant conduct of Dr. Denniston. Great mortality among sick.

Gen. Kemball.

TREBIZOND RELIEF SECTION.

(VICE-CONSUL BILIOTTI.)

During the whole course of the Stafford House operations M. Biliotti acted as representative of the Committee at Trebizond, where he rendered most important aid in arranging the transport of the surgical staff and stores from Trebizond to Erzeroum.

On March 15, 1878, M. Biliotti undertook the distribution of money relief in small sums, varying from ten to forty piastres, to the convalescent soldiers who passed through Trebizond on their way home in a miserably poor and half-starving condition.

Number relieved up to April 5, 1878, 297; number relieved up to May 14, 1878, 1,411—total, 1,708; total amount distributed, 135 L.T.

The following are some of M. Biliotti's letters on the subject:—

Trebizond, March 15, 1878.

DEAR SIR,—Mr. Morisot has handed me yesterday afternoon your letter of the 11th inst., in which you kindly authorise me to spend up to L.T. 200 (about 180*l.*) for the Turkish soldiers passing through this town.

M. BILIOTTI's letters.

I am very grateful for your attention in placing me in a position to take a direct share in the distribution of the funds placed in your hands, and which under your management has alleviated countless cases of misery, and saved many thousands of lives. There is one way of doing real good to the poor, sick wounded soldiers, but I do not know whether what I am about to propose is admitted by the rules by which you are guided. It often happens that, to make room for other patients, sick and wounded are discharged from the hospitals, and sent back to their homes in a very weak state, and with very little money, if any, in their pockets to enable them to travel.

M. BILIOTTI'S letters.	Under these circumstances, many of these poor wretches die on the road from privation, and those who manage to see their houses do so only after great suffering.
Distress among convalescents.	I witnessed yesterday morning the embarkation of a number of these unfortunate people, and was thinking whether it would be possible to do anything on their behalf. The scene was most heartrending; those who could stand on their legs were crawling to the seashore; the others were carried by porters and embarked. They are landed along the coast, and have to find by themselves their way to their native districts, sometimes several hundred miles from the seashore. When I received your letter in the afternoon, I considered it God-sent. There is no doubt that a few piastres may in many cases be the means of saving life, and, at all events, to give some comfort to the last moments of those who are doomed to death. What I propose is, to be authorised to give a small sum, varying according to circumstances, to this category of sick and wounded, keeping a detailed list of the names, country, regiment, and battalion of all those so relieved. This is a moment when an arrangement of this description would be most welcome, the hospitals being emptied as much as possible to make place for the sick and wounded coming from Batoum. If you accept my suggestion, let me know by telegraph on whom I can draw L.T. 50.

I remain, dear sir, yours very truly,

(Signed) ALFRED BILIOTTI.

To V. Barrington-Kennett, Esq.

[*Note.*—Suggestion accepted and credit opened by telegram. On April 5, Mr. Biliotti sent to Mr. Barrington-Kennett a detailed list of 297 relieved.—V. B.-K.]

Trebizond, May 14, 1878.

Relief to convalescents in Asia.	DEAR SIR,—You must pardon my having allowed so long to elapse without informing you of my proceedings with respect to the funds entrusted to me for distribution to Turkish convalescent soldiers. I have had a good deal to do lately, but that has not prevented me from carrying out your good intentions with respect to the relief to be granted to the suffering.

The following are my distributions since the detailed list which I sent to you on the 5th ult.:—

L.T. (Turkish pounds)

277 convalescents who received					27· 2
145	,,	,,	April 26, 2720 at 258		10·54
303	,,	,,	,, 30, 5440 ,, 260		20·92
545	,,	,,	May 9, 10410 ,, 272		39·27
141	,,	,,	,, 14, 1690 ,, 273		6·19
Total 1,411				L.T.	102·94

March 12, for Dr. Schaeps	5·16½
Postages by Erzeroum surgeons	1·24½
Balance in my hands	11·65
Total L.T.	121·00

There seems to be no end of sick from Batoum, and within the last week a number of convalescents have also arrived from the interior. Now that the roads have become practicable, I expect many more of the latter will arrive, and, should more funds be available, much suffering may be relieved. I make the distribution in person just before the men are embarked, which allows them to procure provision for the voyage. The sums given vary according to the length the voyages, and sometimes the condition of the convalescents.

Trusting you will approve of my proceedings, I remain, yours very faithfully,

(Signed) ALFRED BILIOTTI.

To V. Barrington-Kennett, Esq.

Lord Blantyre's English Hospital, Erzeroum.

(Combined Service of Stafford House and Lord Blantyre's Fund.)

This hospital was established under the personal superintendence of Consul Zohrab in a large khan. In addition to their hospital duties, the surgeons formed an ambulance on the field in the engagement of Deve Bouyoun, and in the defence of Erzeroum.

Period of service: July 15, 1877, to April 17, 1878.—Treated in hospital and on the field, sick, 137; wounded, 2,613; total, 2,750; average number of beds occupied in hospital, 172. The following served at different times on the staff of this section: Surgeons Casson, Fetherstonhaugh, Buckby, Guppy, Pinkerton, Denniston, with Turkish assistants. N.B.—All the surgeons were in Lord Blantyre's service. Mr. Reginald Zohrab rendered very valuable assistance during the whole period of service of this section.

Surgeons Guppy and Pinkerton died at Erzeroum of fever contracted during the discharge of their duty, which they fulfilled so nobly. The gallant conduct of Surgeon Denniston should here be recorded. With two of his colleagues dead, and three others lying dangerously ill from the terrible fever raging in the town, he remained at his post almost single-handed, and in addition to his own duties undertook temporarily the direction of the S. H. Hospital. Every spare moment was taken up in nursing his sick colleagues, more than one of whom owes his life to his skill and devotion on this occasion.

The following are extracts from reports to the Chief Commissioner:—

Erzeroum, July 22, 1877

I got your things at Trebizond, and brought them on here. I don't quite know how to distribute them, as the people at the hospital say they have got all the supplies they want, but I have not a doubt that in time they will apply to me for them. However, we are working away to rig up an 'English hospital,' and by perseverance and Consular coercion we have got a khan—well furnished as far as wounded goes—220 poor fellows in the utmost state of misery and neglect! The state of the hospitals here generally I have described in a report which I have given to Mr. Zohrab, and which he is forwarding to Mr. Layard. You will no doubt see it at the Embassy. We want some plaster-of-Paris and some good splints more than anything, carbolised tow (marine lint), English lint, oiled silk. Bandages we shall want, but the stock given by Mrs. Layard and the ladies has helped us wonderfully, as well as the shirts, which are most useful to the soldiers when wounded. The wounds are very serious, and require a great amount of lint and oiled silk. Our stock of sticking-plaster is also getting low already. The Liebig and port-wine which I brought out are very useful, and the application of carbolic acid has wonderfully improved the condition of the wounds. I have had quite a fight to get permission to perform operations. I have, however, amputated two legs and an arm, besides fingers and thumbs, and Fetherstonhaugh yesterday amputated a leg. They were all, however, more or less gangrenous before we were allowed to operate, and I fear the mortality will be great. 300 wounded are expected to-night from Kars. A son of Mr. Zohrab is working well as dresser for us; he is quite a lad, and deserves praise for his work. We are both well. [*Note.*—On Dr. Casson's proceeding to the Kars district, Dr. Fetherstonhaugh succeeded him.]

Dr. Casson's report.

Establishment of the English hospital.

Erzeroum, Nov. 14, 1877.

Denniston and I arrived here on Sunday, Nov. 4, the day of the battle of Deve-Bouyoun. Next day we went to the hospital, and helped Fetherstonhaugh and Guppy to dress their cases; a number of new men had come in from the battle of the day before. We went on quietly dressing

Dr. Pinkerton's report.

RECORD OF OPERATIONS.

Dr. Pinkerton's report.

Wounded after the attack on Erzeroum.

till Friday, when we were awakened about 4.30 A.M. by the sound of guns; the Russians had attacked Erzeroum. We got everything ready, and were at work dressing the wounded in the field at 7 A.M. We remained at this place till 1 A.M., and then, as the number of wounded coming in had diminished very considerably, we elected to go right into the fortifications. Besides we four, there were two Turkish surgeons, and an English surgeon in the Turkish service. We calculate that we four passed pretty nearly 1000 wounded through our hands. At the fortifications we were directed to go to a barrack; there we saw about 150 more wounded, a few more cases were dressed in the trenches, and then about 3 P.M. we left, as there was no more work to do. The transport service from where the wounded were dressed was fairly well done, as they were dressed rapidly and roughly taken to the different hospitals. Next morning to our hospital, where we found about 150 new cases, a great number of whom had to lie on the floor, as their number far exceeded that of our beds; but we did everything we could to make them comfortable, distributing blankets, tobacco, and water; besides, every new case had a hypodermic of morphia. We made enquiries also, and found that they had all had food. Next morning we discharged every patient we could, to give as much room as possible; we have discharged about 70, about 40 have died, and at present we have about 130 in the hospital. We have amputated three legs, four arms, and a large number of fingers, all the result of Friday's fighting; quite as many men remain to be done; and a number have died who refused to submit to operation. As the fighting was at very close quarters, most of the bullets went right through the part of the body struck; consequently, we have not extracted a great many. We have lately adopted a new plan in order to persuade men to submit to operation. A Kurd, whose arm Fetherstonhaugh amputated, is sent to any man who refuses to submit to operation; he argues the point with them, and in many cases is successful.

Russian attack. On Monday night (Nov. 12), about 8 P.M., the Russians attacked again, but we got no fresh cases.

Erzeroum, Nov. 14, 1877.

Dr. Fetherstonhaugh's report.

Illness of Dr. Guppy.

Fighting near Erzeroum.

I am sorry to have to acquaint you with the illness of Dr. Guppy. He was with us at the hospital on Monday morning, when he had to leave, and has been ever since feverish, with a severe headache, and very weak. We have had a busy time since last Friday, when at 4.30 A.M. the Russians attacked the eastern forts, got into one of them, but were driven out at the point of the bayonet, and finally repulsed. We were all at work by daylight at a bridge close to the town, over which most of the wounded should come. In a couple of hours we were joined by two Turkish surgeons, who worked well; and at about 11 A.M. by Dr. Hughes, T. O. Army, and Mr. Cole, American missionary. At 1 P.M., as we saw the wounded were not coming so thickly, we went up to the forts and dressed a number of cases which could not be moved till they were looked to. We had finished there by 3 P.M., when we went to our hospital and found the place crammed full, every available spot having a man in it. We distributed blankets, beef-tea, tobacco, and morphia injections, &c., and had the poor fellows fairly comfortable by 8.30, when, thoroughly worn out, we

Large number of wounded.

came home. At the bridge and forts nearly 1,000 had their wounds attended to, and about 150 were admitted to our hospital; nineteen of those died during the night, some few others next day. On Saturday we discharged every case fit to be moved, and so made room for the new men, most of whose wounds were very severe. We have extracted a number of bullets, amputated three legs, four arms, and a number of fingers since, and have as many more to do. Drs. Pinkerton and Denniston arrived just at the right time, and without their aid I should never have been able to get on. Mr. Zohrab telegraphed to you for lint, charpie, and gutta-percha tissue, as we are sure to have another attack soon, when the calls upon our stores will be very large. The latter, even the largest case, is nearly used up. On Saturday we were at work from before 9 A.M. till 7 P.M., on Sunday from 9 to 6.30, Monday from 9 to 5, yesterday from 8.30, and to-day from before 9 to 4.30. Nothing can exceed the gratefulness of the wounded, and numbers of the townspeople came to the hospital to have their wounds dressed, as they have lately been armed by the Government, and as soon as the firing began went out to fight. The transport from the bridge where the wounds were dressed was fairly good, a number of wagons being told off for the purpose. They were not comfortable, but got the men quickly to the different hospitals. Nothing has yet been heard of Drs. Casson and Buckby, but no doubt, if well, they are kept as busy as ourselves. Reginald Zohrab assists us at the hospital, and Consul Zohrab is always ready to render us aid with his presence and advice, and every day sends us luncheon to the hospital.

ERZEROUM ENGLISH HOSPITAL.   109

Erzeroum, Nov. 18, 1877.

MY DEAR MR. BARRINGTON-KENNETT,—I requested Mr. Layard, by telegraph yesterday, to communicate to you the sad intelligence of Dr. Guppy's death. He was ill for five or six days, but till the night before last we did not believe him in any danger; he had typhoid; perforation of the bowel took place early in the morning, yesterday, and he then sank rapidly, dying at 10 A.M. The very exceptional circumstances we are placed in obliged me to order the funeral for yesterday afternoon. It was attended by the medical body, and a guard of honour consisting of a company of infantry escorted the body to the grave, which is in the cemetery belonging to the American missionaries.

Mr. ZOHRAB'S letter.

Death of Dr. Guppy.

This sad event has cast a deep gloom on our little circle. I received your telegram announcing the departure of surgeons and stores. I want more detailed information to organise a second hospital which the authorities here are very anxious to see opened. Mukhtar Pacha has, at my request, telegraphed to the Vali of Trebizond to send on the surgeons and stores with the least possible delay.

I have written to Dr. Casson to try and return here with Dr. Buckby. My letter was sent by Mukhtar Pacha to the Russian lines. I hope to get an answer in a few days.

We await with deep anxiety a development of the Russian plans. Since the 9th, they have not moved beyond throwing out vedettes in various directions. Whether we are to be bombarded, blockaded, or left alone, remains yet to be seen.

Believe me, my dear Mr. BARRINGTON-KENNETT, yours very faithfully,
(Signed)   ZOHRAB.

Erzeroum, Nov. 22, 1877.

Drs. Ryan and Woods, with Capt. Morisot and Mr. Harvey, arrived last night, and commence work to-morrow at a khan containing 250 beds and patients. I purpose placing Dr. Pinkerton with Drs. Ryan and Woods, as Denniston and I can manage the work at our hospital. We have now about 170 patients, and since Nov. 14 Pinkerton has amputated an arm and a thigh, Denniston two arms, besides extracting a few bullets.

Dr. FETHER-STONHAUGH'S reports.

Arrival of Drs. Ryan and Woods.

Erzeroum, Dec. 7, 1877.

Since I wrote last, twenty wounded have entered our hospital, eight have been discharged and eight died, leaving in to-day 150. Stoves have been kept up by the Government and are a great blessing to us, as the cold is intense. We have six major operation cases doing well—three of Dr. Denniston's—i.e., two forearms and an upper arm, and three of mine, all upper arms; one case operated on died yesterday of pyæmia. We have no epidemic of any kind, and hope to keep free.

Intense cold.

[N.B.—Dr. Fetherstonhaugh being invalided, Dr. Denniston succeeded as chief of section.]

Erzeroum, Dec. 27, 1877.

Dr. Fetherstonhaugh unfortunately having been compelled by illness to give up work and return to England, I am now in charge of the English hospital here, and, in accordance with Mr. Barrington-Kennett's request, intend to report the progress of affairs at regular intervals. The average number of cases is 160, and I have two Turkish dressers, who work very well and are extremely intelligent. Most of the cases were slight, and no freshly-wounded men came in till the arrival of wounded from Kars about a week ago. Their wounds were for the most part slight and confined to the upper extremities, but the hardships of the journey and the intense cold aggravated their condition very much. As you have heard, many of the wounded sent from Kars died on the road, but those who arrived here gave a very favourable account of the way in which they had been treated by the Russians. Each man got bread and thirty piastres from the Russian commander, and they seem to have been treated with great kindness on passing through the lines at Deve-bouyoun. On the 24th inst. I was able to discharge 56 men; they were nearly all well, their wounds being in a healing condition, and confined to their bodies and arms, so that they were able to walk; they were to be sent to Erzinghian, a town about six days' march from this, so I provided each man with a little charpie and a bandage, so that, if required, they could dress their wounds on the way. To each man I gave a thick comforter, a flannel jersey, a pair of drawers, and a large pair of stockings, besides ten piastres. All who left our hospital, or the Stafford House hospital, would in all probability stand the journey well. I happened to see a considerable number who had been sent from the Turkish hospitals, and many of them were in a very miserable state, and seemed

Dr. DENNISTON'S reports.

Illness of Dr. Fetherstonhaugh.

Evacuation of wounded from Kars.

Dr. Denniston's reports.	to suffer terribly. I saw one man die on the road before he had reached the gate of the town. The next day about 50 fresh patients were sent in. By far the greater number of these cases were frost-bites, some very serious, involving the greater part of both feet. Several occurred on the foot here, while others occurred in men coming from Kars. I have had about six cases of typhoid fever and one or two of typhus. There have been also several cases of hospital gangrene, and it has been very fatal. This morning an undoubted case of small-pox turned up in one of the wards; the patient had been in for some days with a wound in his chest, and was doing well; where he got small-pox I cannot say, as, on enquiry, I can hear of no other in Erzeroum. I have taken measures to prevent its spreading by removing all the other wounded from the ward, and allowing no one to go near the ward servant. There is every prospect of our being surrounded, I believe, and I only hope that there will be no epidemic, as it would certainly go very hard with both soldiers and civilians. Williams has been rather ill with fever, but is now quite convalescent. All the others are well, and will, I hope, continue so.
Small-pox.	

Erzeroum, Jan. 2, 1878.

Staff attacked with typhus.	I write a hurried line to let you know the state of matters here. Morisot, Pinkerton, and Williams are all seriously ill with what seems to be typhus fever; all three are very bad indeed, and cause me great anxiety, but I hope the issues in all three cases will be favourable. Last night Ryan took ill with feverish symptoms, and remained at home to-day. To-night he is worse, and the fever has increased, and I very much fear that he is going to have fever of some kind, though the symptoms are mild so far. As you may imagine, I have my hands full. Williams and Pinkerton are delirious, and Morisot is very irritable. Ryan will make a good patient, I think. I shall try and work both hospitals as well as I can. The Stafford House hospital has plenty of good Turkish dressers, so that a general superintendence will be all that is required. I hope to be able to keep both going till Ryan gets well. The others will go off as soon as they are able, but Ryan will, I hope, stay. The Russians are expected to cut us off to-morrow or next day, so that will increase our troubles. Thank God, I am strong and well, and fit for any amount of work—and God knows I have it now.
Dr. Denniston undertakes both hospitals.	

Erzeroum, Jan. 11.

Death of Dr. Pinkerton.	There is just a bare chance of this letter reaching you, but I will risk its escaping the hands of the Russians. I really do not know how to begin to tell you the sad news I have for you. You knew that Williams, Pinkerton, and Morisot were very ill with fever. In all the fever was very severe and dangerous, and in Pinkerton's case I am sorry to say it has proved fatal. He took ill on Dec. 27, and the fever shortly afterwards developed itself into a malignant case of typhus. He died yesterday afternoon, having been unconscious for more than a day, and delirious for five days. I enclose a full report of his illness and death for the benefit of his father and brother-in-law, who, I believe, are both medical men. On Jan. 1, Dr. Ryan took ill also with typhus, and he is now very dangerously ill. I do hope that his strong constitution will be able to hold out, but the fever is also of a very bad type, and it will require all his strength to weather it. He is now raving wildly, and knows nothing of what is going on. Morisot has been very seriously ill, but is now, I trust, out of danger, though very weak. Williams, I am happy to say, is convalescent, and will be up in a day or two. I myself have had typhus, and have seen a good deal of it, so there is no fear of my being knocked over with that fever at any rate. The responsibility of taking care of so many serious cases is very great, and I asked the French Consul to recommend a doctor, and he sent an old gentleman who has seen a great deal of typhus, and who is a very good doctor I hear. He calls every day, and thus the responsibility is divided. Two sisters of charity come every forenoon while I am at the hospitals, and an old Roman Catholic priest sits for four hours every evening while I rest, and then I watch for the rest of the night, so that I think all the patients get every justice. We have plenty of beef-tea and chicken-broth, and that is the diet best for them. The only thing I want is milk, and that we cannot get in sufficient quantity for love or money. Poor Pinkerton was buried this afternoon beside Guppy. The French Consul and his cavass, with all the hospital people and a file of soldiers, were present. Mr. Cole (the American missionary) read the service. The hospitals are of necessity somewhat neglected at present. Of course it is impossible for me to do justice to 500 wounded, but I do all I can in the way of superintending the Turkish surgeon, and distributing stores, &c. The Yeni Khan (Stafford House hospital) is far too large for one man to look after, even though there are a lot of dressers; and when Ryan recovers, as I trust he will, I shall advise him to hand over the hospital to the Turkish doctors, and join me in the English hospital, where there is abundant work for two. Typhoid, and
Critical state of Dr. Ryan.	
Prevalence of typhoid.	

ERZEROUM ENGLISH HOSPITAL. 111

of a very malignant type, is very prevalent at the Stafford House hospital, as it is indeed every- Dr.
where. About 75 or 80 per cent. of the doctors here are ill with fever, and mortality is about 50 DENNISTON'S
per cent. I am going to pay pretty sweetly to get this letter out, I believe, and it may fall into reports.
Russian hands. I hope they will let it go on, though. We daily expect a bombardment. I do wish Great mor-
that the Russians were in, so as to be relieved of all this anxiety. If I have an opportunity I shall tality among
add to this daily till the courier goes off.   doctors.

Jan. 10.—A man will get away either to-morrow morning or next day, so I add a short line or
two. Ryan continues very bad—rather worse, in fact. This is the tenth day of the fever, and in
all probability it will go on for four days yet. He has been delirious for three days. Morisot and
Williams are slowly gaining strength. I do not go to the hospitals at all, but remain constantly
with Ryan.

Jan. 11.—A man leaves in an hour, so I add this in great haste. Ryan remains as yesterday,
very ill; the rest improving. My report on Pinkerton's death is not yet ready. I shall send it
afterwards.

Erzeroum, Feb. 11, 1878.

The English hospital has been quite filled since my last. At present there are 176 cases in Sufferings
hospital; of these about 110 are frost-bites, about seven are fever, and the remainder are wounds. from frost-bite.
The frost-bites are very severe, and the cases are very distressing, as in many both feet are completely gangrenous, and in all the men are very weak and debilitated. I may mention one in
which both feet and ankles are completely mortified almost as far as the knee, and in which amputation is impracticable on account of the low state of the patient's health. In the meantime I am
feeding him up, in the hope of putting him in such a state that I can amputate with some prospect
of success. I have also a Yuz-bachi, in whom both feet as far as the ankle-joints, all the fingers of
the right hand, and the whole left hand are gone, and his ears also were attacked, but not severely.
I amputated the left hand, but have great doubts as to the result. These cases will give an idea
of the severity of the frost. Many old wounds still remain, and, as a rule, are doing well; and in
most cases there has been a large extent of surface wounds, and a long time is required for
recovery. I have sent out two amputations of the arm, and have four remaining, three of whom
are doing well. I am sorry to say that we had quite an epidemic of what seems to be hospital
gangrene. Till a month ago the hospital had been comparatively pure and free from infectious Hospital
disease, but about the beginning of January the authorities began to send down very bad cases of gangrene
infectious gangrene, and since then it has spread considerably and been very fatal, notwithstanding prevalent.
the precautions I took. On Jan. 10, 36 cases were sent in, and of these ten died the first night, and
twelve more during the next 24 hours. Every case was suffering from hospital gangrene, and most
were terribly bad; almost all suffered besides from diarrhœa. The wounds were in a shocking
condition; one especially, a case of frost-bite of the feet, which had been poulticed, and the
poultice not changed for 20 days, and the consequence was that the wound was in a disgusting
state and covered with vermin. The next day eight more were sent down, and of those seven died
the same night, and the eighth the next morning. One died before being admitted into the hospital. These facts will account in some way for the high mortality in the hospital, which has been
excessive. I am sorry that I cannot give accurate figures, but while I was so much occupied in the Difficulty
Stafford House hospital and at home all statistics were neglected. Since those cases have been giving
sent in the hospital has never been free from gangrene, which has attacked cases which were doing statistics
exceedingly well. One case of amputation was healed to almost a point, when gangrene attacked
the stump, and the unfortunate man was dead in five days. This state of matters has made the
work rather disheartening, and I find it excessively difficult to purify the wards.

[*Note.*—Dr. Denniston is the last of the surgeons sent out by Lord Blantyre left in Asia.
Stafford House will supply Dr. Denniston with any money, stores, or other help which he may
require to keep up his hospital.—V. B.-K.]

Erzeroum, March 8, 1868.

Since my last report matters here have changed little, and the English hospital under my charge
continues to work well. During the past month there have never been less than 158 cases in hospital; at times there have been 176; 36 have been discharged cured, and 41 have died. The
most notable feature is the increase of the numbers of sick and diminution of the wounded and
frost-bites. For the past month there has been, of course, no outpost duty for the troops, and
consequently fresh cases of frost-bite are comparatively rare; and now, the Turkish troops being
gone, and the weather being milder, no new cases can possibly occur. The authorities have been

RECORD OF OPERATIONS.

Dr. Denniston's reports.

rapidly emptying the Turkish hospitals in town, with a view, I believe, to their occupation by the Russian sick, and the patients have been distributed among the other hospitals. As soon as any bed in the English hospital was vacant, it was immediately filled up by sick, and now I have at least 70 sick in hospital. The diseases are chiefly diarrhœa, chest complaints, convalescence from typhus, and exhaustion. The diarrhœa continues very obstinate, and has proved very fatal. Pneumonia, bronchitis, and phthisis constitute now a considerable proportion of the sick, and these also prove very fatal, owing to the weak and exhausted state of the patients. For convalescence from typhus, and the extreme state of exhaustion in which many of the men are from hunger and exposure, no active treatment is required, and up till now I have merely fed them on beef-tea and preserved soups; but now our stock is run out, and I am obliged to trust to their own not very nutritious food for their recovery. 100 wounded remain, and all, as a rule, are doing well. No serious operation has lately been performed, but in several cases diseased and dead bone has been removed, and in all with good prospect of success. Hospital gangrene, I am glad to say, is almost completely gone. The Red Crescent ambulance arrived about ten days ago, and the staff is now working a large hospital, so that now, with the rapid diminution in the number of sick, and no fresh cases, there are almost too many doctors; in fact, many of the Turkish doctors from the hospitals lately emptied are going about idle. We do not know what your intentions are as regards our movements, and are waiting daily for instructions. I myself think that there is no necessity for our remaining, as very little active treatment is now required, and all that we now do could be done equally well by the Turkish doctors now without work. The Russians are establishing several hospitals in town, I hear, and their sick are very numerous. The weather is evidently changing, and though there is still comparatively hard frost during the night, it is becoming much milder.

Chest complaints on increase.

Arrival of Red Crescent ambulance.

Erzeroum, March 20, 1878.

Sudden evacuation of hospital.

Sufferings of wounded.

Chief Government surgeon arrested.

I have the honour to report that the English hospital here under my charge has been emptied on the 17th inst. by the Turkish authorities. Up till the 17th everything was working in the most satisfactory way. I had 155 in the hospital, of whom 80 were sick, the remainder being wounded and frost-bitten. Many of them were in a very weak and critical state, and quite unfit for moving. I had no idea that anything of the sort was contemplated by the authorities, and was exceedingly surprised when, on Saturday morning early, I was told that they were rapidly emptying the hospital. I at once went up and found the head surgeon, Hussein Effendi, ordering them to hurry off the patients before I arrived. Everything was being done in the most cruel way. They were dragged from their beds, and those unable to walk were carried to other hospitals, but without other covering than their night-dresses. I endeavoured to make the transport easier by getting stretchers, giving clothing, blankets, &c.; but, notwithstanding, the men suffered terribly, and several, who in all probability would have recovered, have since died from the effects of their treatment. When the evacuation was complete, I at once went to Hakki Bey, Governor of the town, and reported the conduct of Hussein Effend, who was at once sent for and imprisoned. I have since handed in a formal written report, of which I enclose a copy. I am now quite unemployed, but will assist Dr. Ryan in the Stafford House hospital, though there there is almost nothing to do for three doctors. If Drs. Ryan and Stoker are recalled, I shall wait and go with them; if not, I shall start soon, unless I receive instructions to the contrary. All the blankets, bed-clothing, splints, &c., I have handed over to Dr. Roy, of the Red Crescent ambulance, his hospital standing in need of many of these things. The health of the town improves, I believe, and there are now only about 2,000 Turkish sick, and there are plenty of doctors.

April 18, 1878.

Since my last report I have been assisting Dr. Ryan in the Stafford House hospital. Almost all the cases in the hospital were in such a satisfactory state that they could be handed over to the care of the Turkish assistant surgeons. There was neither typhus fever nor hospital gangrene in the hospital when we left. In all I believe that about 1,300 patients remain, and there are a considerable number of Turkish doctors, quite sufficient to manage the cases easily. By far the majority of the sickness in Erzeroum among the Turks consists of general debility and chronic diarrhœa. Among the Russians typhus fever is exceedingly prevalent, both in the city and in the villages round about. We saw in Ilidjeh—the first village on the Trebizond road, and the last occupied by the Russians—great numbers of Russian sick, suffering principally from typhus, lying in the stalls of stables, much overcrowded, and without comforts of any kind. On the authority of a priest, we were told that 21,700 men had died since the Russians entered the plain of Erzeroum in the end of December! The road from Erzeroum to Trebizond is yet utterly impossible for transport of any kind, being in some places exceedingly dangerous. After eleven days' journey we arrived at Trebizond, and were most kindly received by Her Majesty's Consul, Mr. Biliotti, who has all through the winter done much for us in the way of forwarding letters. On April 17 we reported ourselves at the office at Pera. I may add that Williams and Rennison, who have acted as our interpreters, have worked exceedingly well; the conduct of the former especially deserving mention, as, in spite of dangerous illness, he continued at his post till the end.

Dr. DENNISTON'S reports.

KARS DISTRICT AMBULANCE.

(LORD BLANTYRE'S.)

In August 1877 Surgeon Casson organised a field-ambulance to be attached to Mukhtar Pacha's head-quarters in the Kars district. This ambulance served at the battles of Soubatan and Aladjah-Dangh. On the retreat of Mukhtar Pacha, the staff were detained in Kars owing to the illness of Surgeon Buckby. They were subsequently captured by the Russians in endeavouring to rejoin Mukhtar Pacha's head-quarters, and against their will were sent to Tiflis, from which place they returned to England.

Period of service: Aug. 22 to Oct. 31, 1877.—Number of sick treated, 150; wounded, 587; total, 737. Surgeons Casson and Buckby served with this section.

The following are reports from Surgeon Casson to the Chief Commissioner:—

Camp beyond Kars, Sept. 16, 1877.

I left Fetherstonhaugh in charge of the hospital at Erzeroum, which was doing well for 200 patients, constantly changing. Buckby I have taken on with me here. I have a small ambulance, and I go out to all the camps after each skirmish, to look up the wounded. The Muchir has promised all possible assistance in the formation of a good surgical ambulance, and when the things I telegraphed for arrive we shall do well, I hope. The stores I gave to Dr. Flüchs for Olti, Fetherstonhaugh tells me, are still at Erzeroum.

Dr. CASSON's reports.

Erzeroum, Aug. 8.

Since I last wrote, a batch of medical stores have been sent out by the Stafford House Committee. They arrived here on the 7th, in charge of Lieutenant Malcolm Drummond, R.N., who kindly volunteered to escort them from Constantinople on their perilous journey to this outlandish region. I have learned within the last few days the truth, which I had for some time suspected, as to the utter want of medical organisation at the front beyond Kars. It appears that, with an army of 30,000 men, there are actually four doctors—two Germans and two Greeks. There is now one case of surgical instruments; until after the battle of Eshek Kallas, there was not even this case. There is not so much as a single hand-stretcher with the whole army. A field hospital of twenty tents has been formed at head-quarters, in which there were 30 patients at the beginning of the present week. None of these were wounded, but they were principally cases of dysentery and tonsilitis. The patients have nothing in the shape of ground-sheets or beds to lie upon, and their sole covering for the nights, which are now pretty cold, are the great-coats of the men who are fortunate enough to have them. The young German student who is in charge of this hospital writes that he is utterly without drugs or medical stores of any kind, and sends a list of things required. At Kars, about 30 miles from the front, there are ten medicals in all, but I believe of the usual kind met with in this country; for a description of which I refer you to Sandwith's 'History of the Siege of Kars,' twenty years ago, things, however, being rather worse now than then.

Want of medical organisation.

Head-Quarters of Ahmed Mukhtar Pacha, Camp, Senegal, Plain of the Arpachi, Sept. 3, 1877.

The arrival, on August 14, of Messrs. Guppy and Buckby, two junior surgeons despatched on the same mission as myself, and by the same generous individual, enabled me to set about the arrangements for carrying out my proposed plan of proceeding at once to the actual scene of hos-

Departure of Surgeons Casson and Buckby.

Q

114   RECORD OF OPERATIONS.

Dr. Casson's reports.

tilities. Leaving charge of my 'English Hospital' in the hands of my first companion and colleague, Mr. Fetherstonhaugh, accompanied by Mr. Buckby, I left Erzeroum for Kars, which is about twenty miles from this camp, on the 22nd. The taking with us of stores and necessaries involved a somewhat slow journey, as the only vehicles which can be procured are the arabas or native bullock-carts, with which a progress of fifteen to twenty miles a day is very fair indeed. These arabas are made without any attempt at springs, and their jolting and jarring on these apologies for roads is something terrible—terrible indeed to the poor sick and wounded, whose only means of transport from the battle-field to the hospital, 130 miles away, is on these vehicles of torture. Having, after much delay and much trouble, got our caravan fairly on the way, we started—a party of five—zaptieh or mounted policeman, servant and interpreter, syce or groom, and myself and companion. After we had ridden on a few miles, we had the pleasure of seeing one of our arabas completely *hors de combat* by the loss of a wheel. This deficiency was made up presently, however, by the substitution of a pole of pine-wood. Very shortly, we came upon a small camp of the Redifs or second reserve; there were perhaps 300 or 350 men, far too old really for service, encamped here, their time being apparently principally employed in mending the road, which was in a very terrible state. I paid a visit to the Bimbashi in command, and asked him if he had any

Medical relief.

sick. He gave orders for the sick to be paraded for my inspection, and, to my intense astonishment, I found a double rank of men, 120 all told, who reported themselves in need of a doctor. Separating the sheep from the goats, I found about 80 who really were ailing; scurvy, intermittent fever, diarrhœa, and a few cases of rheumatism being the principal maladies. Fortunately I had in my saddle-bags a small but comprehensive 'medicine-chest,' containing, amongst other useful things, pills of quinine, opium, and Dover's powder, in practicable doses. Leaving a little stock of remedies in the hands of one of the captains who could speak a little French, and seemed more intelligent than the generality of his grade, we pushed along and arrived at Hassan-Kali, a town of some little pretensions, shortly before sunset. It was hopeless to expect the arrival of the arabas, with tents and provisions, that night, so we were obliged to avail ourselves of the shelter of a khan, which, we afterwards learnt, had been recently used as a fever hospital. We had to spend most of the next day here, as the wretched arabas had not arrived, and it was of no use to go on

Diseases of natives.

without them; so I devoted myself to studying the diseases of the natives, partly Turks and partly Armenians, the former greatly predominating. I was greatly struck with the number of children, the Armenians in particular, who had strumous ulcers of the cornea; seven children, all identically suffering, were brought to me for inspection, and I saw at least a dozen more similarly affected, many of them being quite blind. Scrofula, in some form or other, seems to be one of the great curses of this country; but the form in which the evil manifests itself varies much in different localities. At Trebizond I noticed many cases of necrosis and affections of the liver and internal organs. At Erzeroum there seems an immense amount of glandular scrofula; and further east, in the town of Hassan-Kali and the villages around, this affection of the eyes seems to prevail. The Circassians, as fine-looking a race of men as you can well imagine, who inhabit some of these villages, suffer to an extent that is quite proverbial from pulmonary phthisis. I cannot but think that the dark, almost underground hovels which the Armenians call houses, and the absence of animal food from their ordinary diet, must have much to do with producing this dire disease. Rising with the sun, we pushed on to Kaprikoui, where there was a large camp of Bashi-Bazouks and infantry. Here I found a doctor, an Armenian educated at the Constantinople Medical

Want of medical stores at Kaprikeui.

School; he informed me that from day to day wounded and sick men passed through and called upon him for treatment on their way from Kars to Erzeroum; but that he had no medicines to give them, or materials for dressing the wounds. I offered to give him a few essentials from my stock, but he declined the offer, as he said he was leaving on the following day, having been recalled to Erzeroum, he believed, in consequence of having sent a telegram to the head doctor there, saying that, as he was not a magician, he could not cure the sick without materials and medicines. I, however, insisted upon his taking a few opium pills for some soldiers of his regiment who were suffering from diarrhœa, and a few other simples for immediate use. Before I left the place, two wounded Circassians rode up from Kars; assuming, as all the natives do, that every Englishman must be a doctor, they came up to me, and I found that, in spite of their riding as if nothing ailed them, one had a compound fracture of the radius of the right arm, a gunshot-wound, which wanted dressing badly enough, and the other had a fractured rib, with a bullet somewhere in his thorax, but *where* it defied him to tell me, or I, after examination, to tell him. The next day, on our way, we met a train of arabas with a load of 150 sick, nearly all cases of fever and scurvy, and five wounded, on their way to the hospitals at Erzeroum. They had been six days on their way from Kars, and I suppose it would take them about four or five days more to reach Erzeroum.

Fortunately none of them seemed very bad; but they complained bitterly of the noise, tedium, and jolting of their most uncomfortable journey. There was not the least attempt at any shade from the burning sun in any of the wagons. One officer had had his hand amputated. I was somewhat surprised to see this; but at last he informed me that it was literally blown to pieces, so that its removal was not a matter involving much deliberation. He said, however, that the stump did not heal, which was not a thing to be wondered at, as the operation was a circular one, *i.e.*, à *la Turque*, an incision made down to the bone, and the bone sawn through, the operator not troubling himself much about the covering of skin or such small matters. A German doctor in Kars the other day told me he had improved upon the 'circular' method, and now always dissected back the skin, so as to leave a 'lambeau' sufficient to cover the bone. He seemed rather astonished that I did not admire the novelty of *his* method.

Dr. CASSON's reports.

Our journey was continued much in the same manner till we arrived at Kars on the ninth day after our departure from Erzeroum, without any incidents calling for special remark. While at Kars, I visited the hospitals there, and found them all more than full, and in a very unsatisfactory state. A more detailed account, however, I must reserve till next week, as the post leaves here in an hour's time, and I have many letters to finish and despatch. On my arrival here, I found that there was indeed plenty to be done. The Russians, however, have retreated on to their own territory, and I hope that something may be done in the way of forming an ambulance, now that the fear of frequent and hurried retreat from station to station with literally no provision for sick transport is removed.

Arrival at Kars.

The camp is healthy in the extreme; but it would be surprising were it otherwise in such a naturally healthy situation on a large open plain, 8,000 feet above sea-level, surrounded completely by snow-capped mountains—among others, the venerable Ararat, which, though 90 miles away, does not appear more than ten. I was most courteously and civilly received by the Muchir Ahmet Mukhtar Pacha, and am receiving the hospitality and most valuable assistance of our worthy English general, Sir Arnold Kemball. Next week, I hope to be able to tell you of some practical work done.

Gen. Kemball.

Head-quarters of Ahmed Mukhtar Pacha, Sept. 15, 1877.

Since my letter of last week, several sharp skirmishes between the Russian Cossacks and our Circassian cavalry have taken place, and each day there has been plenty of work in picking up and attending to the wounded, which generally number ten to seventeen in each engagement. A small body of infantry has occasionally also been engaged, and we have had several very interesting cases from among them. On Monday (10th), a Circassian officer of high rank, named Said Bey, received a bullet-wound in the chest; the ball perforated the sternum a little to the right side, traversed the lung, and found its way out through the left scapula. I found him in his tent, having ridden home about two miles from where he was wounded, in a very exhausted condition. On Thursday, after a very smart affair at Jala, in which ten of ours were killed and seventeen wounded, on passing the Circassian camp on my way home, I was hailed by an orderly of the Pacha, to knowif I would kindly call and see a wounded officer. Of course I went, and found, among several others wounded, a very handsome young officer, with a bullet *somewhere* in the elbow. Attending upon him, I found a wild-looking old Circassian, who was sucking the wound, in the vain hope of thus extracting the bullet—the simplest and safest way, he assured me, of performing this operation. After this interesting experiment had been continued until the operator was thoroughly exhausted, and without, I regret to say, his labours being crowned with success, the mollah or priest was called in consultation; but, by this time, the Pacha, who was present, and who wished me to think him superior to the superstitions of his people, asked me to interfere. I did so, on the condition that I should have the officer removed to our ambulance, which that morning had come into existence, though in a very small way, it is true. To this he consented; and, after his arrival, I put him under chloroform, and found that a good deal of sucking or enchantment would have been required to extract the ball, which had entered the ulna, and carried before it a portion of the olecranon, which was wedged firmly, together with the bullet and fragments of clothing, between the split condyles of the humerus right into the cancellous tissue. Having cleared out all the fragments of bone, I found that a sufficiently complete 'resection' of the joint had been made without my further interference; and, under the nearest approach to antiseptic measures which I have at command, in this fresh healthy air, and with the robust constitution of the patient, I hope to save him a tolerably useful arm.*

Circassian surgery.

---

* This case turned out remarkably well. It is fully recorded in the *Medical Press and Circular* of March 13, 1878.

Dr. Casson's reports.	In camp I found three wounded men to attend to, one of whom was struck on the head by a large fragment of shell, and was insensible, bleeding pretty profusely from a superficial wound of the scalp. I could detect no fracture or actual indications of compression. I ordered his removal to the hospital, where he arrived some hours afterwards, and where the passage of a catheter through a most obstinate urethral stricture was attended with results which soon brought about complete restoration to consciousness.

My colleague rode off to a small camp of Bashi-Bazouks, where he found a poor fellow shot through the abdomen: he died shortly afterwards. At the same camp, the previous evening, I had found a Bashi-Bazouk with a wound which shows how miraculously bullets travel without injuring vital parts. The ball had entered behind in the right shoulder—fortunately, in the supraspinous fossa; penetrating that muscle pretty deeply, it ascended the neck; winding round to the front, it came out just above the pomum Adami, and made a superficial groove right up the angle of the chin. Notwithstanding the dangerous path through which the bullet travelled, the patient had not lost certainly half an ounce of blood. He is doing very well, and I hope to discharge him from hospital in a few days.

We are at present, as I said, in a small way in our 'Ambulance Anglaise'; but we have got eight patients already, who are very happy, and are all doing well. Arrangements take a long time to develope themselves in a complete state here; and up to the present time we have had to find all provisions for our patients, aye, and to cook them too. This morning, however, a *sous-officier* has arrived, and he says other soldier-servants are coming immediately. I have set this 'lieutenant' to dig out a latrine trench—work, I assure you, which he does not consider at all beneath him—and promised him some 'mastick' every night if he behaves himself. Last night we received marks also of our recognition by the authorities in the posting of two sentries—both of them suffering from bronchitis, by the way—to guard my tent. I have had some distinguished patients during the week, including the Muchir himself and Hadji Reschid Pacha. I am glad to say their ailments were not serious, and that they are all quite convalescent by this time. |

Head-quarters of Ahmed Mukhtar Pacha, Oct. 5, 1877.

Engagement at Jala.	On the morning of Oct. 1, after a long intermission of hostilities, very sharp firing in the neighbourhood of Jala, on our right centre, announced the fact that the Russians, whom we knew to have received some considerable reinforcements, to the extent of 12,000 men, we had reason to believe, intended to do at last. For about three hours, the firing was very close and continuous; and we could not quite make out why the enemy had brought out so many men, and a battery of heavy guns, against a handful of our cavalry, most of them Circassian irregulars, who were out probably on one of their ordinary foraging expeditions. I went down at once, with a party of men with stretchers and a tent, thinking to make a small shelter where the wounded might be dressed on the spot. On arriving at the village, however, upon which the Russian shells were pouring fast and thickly, I could only discover one man wounded. I got up to him just in time to find him dead. He was badly shot through the lung, and hæmorrhage had been most profuse. On searching about the field and visiting the Circassian camp, which was in the immediate vicinity, I found seven wounded in all, and there was a report of another man killed. After a time, our batteries opened an answering fire upon the assailants, who immediately retired with considerable expedition. It was evident, however, that they suffered severely. I myself saw three consecutive shells fall right in the midst of the very compact bodies of troops; and in the hand to hand engagement between the opposing cavalry, to judge by the number of Russian coats, in which the Circassians had attired themselves, the number of their original wearers killed must have been considerable. Towards evening, the explanation of this attack became apparent.
Attack on Nachsivan.	At the time that this was going on in the centre, a large force, which had worked their way round under cover of the night, attacked a Turkish position at Nachsivan, on the extreme right; and owing partly to the superiority of the defenders' position, and still more to the indomitable courage with which the Turkish soldiers always engage with greatly superior numbers of the enemy, the Russians—in numbers at least three times greater than our troops—were three times, the last time finally and completely, repulsed, with very great loss. It is said that at least 300 Russians were left dead on the field. The accuracy of this statement I cannot vouch for. Our loss was officially reported to be eight killed and twelve wounded, besides a few scratches that did not put the recipients *hors de combat*. Having got this hint that it was time to set our houses in order, during the night I had all available tents pitched and arrangements for extra supply of

water and other necessary details carried out, and the morning proved that all our preparations were not unwarranted; for with the early dawn commenced the most important battle which has been fought on Asiatic territory since the commencement of hostilities. As soon as an opinion could be formed where one was likely to be of use, I set out, with such necessary things as our horses could carry, in the direction of the Yhanilagh, a large hill between us and Kars, occupied by a few of our troops, against which the brunt of the Russian attack seemed directed. Column after column appeared on the horizon, marching towards this mountain, and for a time it seemed as if nothing we could do could prevent them making good their way to cut off our communication with Kars, and perhaps to turn our left flank.

Dr. CASSON's reports.

But let me say shortly here, that although the position was for a time actually taken and occupied by a small force, the main body of the assailants met with such a reception a little further on at the hands of Mehmet, surnamed 'Captain' Pacha, who occupied the smaller Yhanilagh, opposite to its namesake, that they were glad to make the best of their way back again. I was accompanied by a dragoman-servant, Fortunato, who had only arrived the previous evening from Erzeroum. I had also with me a Turkish soldier who is acting as our scullery-maid in days of peace. Poor Buckby, my junior colleague, had been ailing for a day or two, and that morning undoubted typhoid symptoms showed themselves. Poor fellow, it is a terrible thing for him to go through a smart attack of typhoid in this distant country, without friends or comforts, in a leaky tent, and with only the attention that I can give him in the midst of a pressure of work which has been almost too much for me. Riding out about three miles, we came upon a batch of wounded just by one of our artillery positions. The fire here was hot and furious ; in every direction, fragments of bursting shells whizzed round our heads, and for a moment I doubted whether one ought to stay even to attend to the wants of the poor wretches. However, after a minute or two, one gets used to fire, and carrying, as well as we could, four poor fellows very terribly wounded with shell under the apparent shelter of a ledge of rock, we commenced our work. Just as we had finished bandaging up the wounds, two arabas, which I had despatched a soldier for, came up, and in these jolting carts, the only ambulance conveyances we can get here, we sent the sufferers to our tents. One man, with a severe compound fracture of the thigh, died before his arrival. While we were thus engaged, a shell burst on the summit of the lodge from whence we had carried our patients, and killed an officer and an artilleryman on the spot. A little further on, we found a group of seven wounded, all by musketry fire, and in different places we found and made as comfortable as possible for the time, in all, 21 wounded. After being dressed, the poor fellows had to be told to wait till we could get arabas to transport them to the tents; and as we could find no more wounded in that immediate vicinity, I thought it was time to make our way back to our head-quarters, where, by this time, the wounded must be beginning to arrive from different parts of the battlefield. On the way home, fortunately, I observed at some little distance three arabas, which were evidently being taken away stealthily from a little village adjoining to escape their being used by the military authorities. I rode up, with the soldier Omar, to this train ; there was one man and two lads in charge of them. I told the man I must have them to fetch up some wounded, and that if he would go at once and bring them carefully, on his arrival I would pay him liberally. However, he flatly refused to have anything to do with the matter, and so I told him if he did not at once go with the soldier I would shoot him like a dog as he was. My threat was successful, and very submissively he went off with the trusty Omar, who kept him under judicious terror by the occasional demonstrative manipulation of his Winchester repeating carbine, and presently eleven out of the seventeen we had left found their way on these arabas to our ambulance. Having escaped the fire of the enemy, however, danger was by no means over ; for, after passing on our return by the spot where we had left one of the wounded, in pretended attendance upon whom was a soldier who ought to have been fighting with his comrades, and who had given me a good share of abuse about his friend being left, where he was till the arabas might come up, a bullet which struck the rock we were ascending made us turn round just in time to see the wounded man or his companion, probably the latter, take another deliberate pot at us. This time the bullet fell within five yards of my horse. As we were pretty well out of shot, and just turning the brow of the hill, I did not feel justified in riding back to see the end of the matter, but our loud shouts to stop firing were answered by another shot, which fell short of us. Neither the patient nor his companion turned up at the hospital, or it would have been worse for them if I had seen them. When I arrived, I found about 70 or 80 had come in for attention, and the work to be done—having only the assistance of Fortunato, who worked as well as any dresser—during the whole of the day and most of the night can be better imagined than described. A striking

Attack on the Yhanilagh.

Surgeon Buckby's illness.

Battle of Soubatan.

Want of transport.

118 RECORD OF OPERATIONS.

Dr. Casson's reports.
Prevalence of finger wounds.

feature was the enormous proportion of wounds of the index or trigger finger; the last three days I must have amputated upwards of 40 which were literally smashed to pieces. To describe the wounds would be impossible. Out of the 250, or thereabouts, that have come in for treatment, only six or seven were shell-wounds. Considering the very small amount of damage done by the costly artillery pieces, one wonders that their employment is not discontinued, except for siege purposes, by universal consent. There are several wounds of the lower jaw; in most instances the jaw is smashed to pieces. A large number are wounded in the chest; in several instances the bullet has passed completely through the lung. I have two Russian prisoners, both of whom are shot in the chest; one, I think, will not recover. There are, out of the whole number, some five or six cases which require amputation of one or other extremity, but I have been unable to get the consent of the patient; of course, they will be anxious for it when it is too late, our usual experience in this country. This (Friday) morning, I have got them all comfortably dressed, some sent away to the Kars hospitals, some slight cases sent back to their regiments to attend as out-patients, and the rest, to the number of 86, still remaining in the tents. The battle continued with some severity during yesterday, and a few shots are still to be heard to-day, so we may expect the arrival of still more wounded. This is the first moment I have had to sit down quietly or to rest at all since Tuesday morning. From that time till now, with the exception of a few hours' sleep in my clothes, I have been at work without intermission.

Some more Stafford House stores and a large selection of most useful splints and appliances, as well as 'medical comforts,' which Mr. Young, of the Red Cross Society, is sending out from Erzeroum, are on the road. I hope they may soon arrive, as my splints, such as they were, are used up; my chloroform all but gone; and I certainly have not more than fifty bandages left to meet all emergencies.

I have had no time to make enquiries at the two other Turkish field-hospitals; but I am sure, from their greater proximity to where the thick of the fight has been, that they must each of them have had considerably more patients than ours. On the first day, a great deal of the fighting was on the Kars side, and many wounded would find their way to the hospitals there. Altogether, I should say that we cannot have less than from 2,000 to 3,000 wounded. The number of killed I have no means at present of judging, but the slaughter on the Russian side must have been terrific. Whilst our men were for the most part behind entrenchments, the enemy's troops were exposed to our full fire. The Grand Duke at present appears to be well beaten back to his starting-point, or even further, having sacrificed thousands.

Head-quarters of Mukhtar Pacha, Oct. 13.

Retreat of ambulances to Eolia-Tepe.

State of Dr. Buckby.

As stated in my last letter, I had between two hundred and three hundred wounded upon my hands during the battles of the 2nd and 3rd. On Monday, the 8th, I had left in my tents about twenty patients; the rest had been disposed of; the majority sent to the Kars hospitals, some of the slighter cases back to their regiments, and ten, I think, had died: not a very large proportion considering the circumstances and the severity of the wounds. My greatest anxiety, however, was naturally for my young colleague, who was dragging through the wearisome second week of a very severe attack of typhoid. The day was the coldest we had hitherto had: you may judge what was the state of my feelings to receive a peremptory message late in the afternoon that we must at once move the ambulance and wounded five miles over the mountain to our rear. There was nothing to be done but to ride as quickly as I could, taking a few tents with me on baggage-horses and arabas, to have a place ready to shelter the unfortunate travellers when they should arrive. Having made the necessary arrangements with all haste, I rode back, and found a few more arabas just starting, loaded with my patients, nearly all of whom were thus provided for. It was now quite dark, and the road over the mountain was a terrible one even by day. I was compelled to send off all the patients, including a Russian, who was brought in at the last moment, having just been found on the mountain, where he had fallen wounded six days before, having had from that time, he said, neither food nor drink, but having kept himself alive by eating the grass he could gather. A biscuit was found for him by a wounded Turkish soldier who was on the same araba, and he washed down a few teaspoonfuls of Liebig's extract with some water. [After a most perilous and difficult night's march the party arrived at the camp near Eolia-tepe.] It is not a plan of treatment that I should feel justified in recommending for the future to patients suffering either from typhoid or from chronic diarrhœa; but it is a fact that from that night Buckby has not had one untoward symptom, and I myself have almost got rid of my enemy the diarrhœa, and feel stronger and better than I have done any time for the last three months. Our poor fellows were also exposed through the night, having, like us, lost their way; two of the worst died and

KARS DISTRICT AMBULANCE. 119

were buried on the road; the rest were no worse for their removal. Ronison reported that, almost immediately after our departure, our old position was occupied by a battery of artillery. In the afternoon there was another brisk fight, which went on for the two following days, and provided me with a moderate amount of fresh work to do in my new position near the Eolia-tepe. Yesterday I got a very stringent order to send all the patients into Kars, and I am now left with only a wounded Bimbashi, who, although about twenty years my senior, has adopted me as his 'baba,' and will not leave me; another officer who has come in to-day slightly wounded in the thigh a few days ago; and one of the soldier-servants, who has an attack of acute rheumatism. These, with Buckby, who is progressing slowly but favourably, are my present patients. A consignment of National Aid Society's (Red Cross) stores have this evening arrived; they are selected with admirable judgment, and I feel quite rich and fully equipped for any contingency that may arise.

Dr. Casson's reports.
Continued fighting.

Kars, Oct. 18.

At a quarter to six o'clock on the morning of Monday, Oct. 15, the English ambulance near Eolia-tepe, with a large white flag, having on it the red crescent, flying in a most prominent position on a rocky eminence just above, received definite orders to move its situation, in the shape of a large shell thrown deliberately into the middle of the little encampment. It fell and exploded ten yards in front of the tent in which I and my sick colleague, Dr. Buckby, were, and the fragments, with a shower of earth, fell all around us—thank God! without hurting anyone. In about five minutes' time this shot was succeeded by a second, evidently aimed at the Turkish ambulance about one hundred yards lower down the hill; there was here, too, the ambulance flag flying conspicuously in front. This second shell also exploded, providentially, without inflicting damage. I immediately conveyed poor Buckby and the four other patients to a spot sheltered by the rocks from the direct fire, and gave them each a cupful of warm cocoa with a little brandy in it. Just then, up rode Ahmet, one of the Muchir's aides-de-camp, and he told me that the fighting was going on near the Nalban-tepe, about two miles to our rear. My search for arabas and horses had now been attended with partial success, and, taking a few of the horses, my wretched milazim, contrary to my express orders, which were for all to move together or not at all, packed on them his personal belongings, with a couple of bales of our blankets, and while I was attending to the safety of the patients, taking his guard-soldiers with him, he made off, caring for nothing but his own safety. I mustered among the men I had left and the attendants of the wounded Bimbashi two sets of four men to carry Buckby and that officer on their stretchers, the other three patients being able to ride horses. Having arranged everything in as orderly a manner as possible, we set off in the direction of the Nalban-tepe. When we had arrived at the foot I rode to the summit to consult the Muchir as to the best course to pursue, and he advised a temporary erection of the ambulance anywhere in that neighbourhood for the reception of the wounded, who would soon be beginning to come in, from the very hot fighting going on. I rode down again, and was going to unpack a few things for the dressing of the wounded, when we saw close on our right the whole mass of our skirmishers being driven in in utter confusion. There were Cossacks mixed up with them, fighting hand-to-hand, and a sweeping fire commenced right in our direction. I took out my revolver, and told the bearers of the litters that the first man who attempted to desert from his post or to leave the sufferers I would shoot like a dog, without a moment's hesitation, and they kept manfully and steadily to their arduous toil. We were now in the midst of a crowd of troops of all arms who were all flying in the utmost confusion from the face of the advancing enemy. We were forced into a narrow defile, where the shells from Russian batteries on each side of us, and Congreve rockets, were incessantly pouring down upon the retreating masses. One large fragment of shell actually fell between Buckby's stretcher and Fortunato, who was riding close by his left side; I was on his right, and it passed just over my head. Our greatest danger, however, was perhaps in the fear of the litter-bearers being knocked down and trampled under foot by the mad crowd of men and beasts, or run over by the artillery, battery after battery of which had now joined the general stampede. I saw many of the patients of the Turkish ambulance, who had been deserted by their doctors—a Greek and a Turk—who had ridden off to Kars as fast as their horses could carry them immediately the shell was fired at their ambulance, as well as some poor fellows who had been wounded in that day's fighting, thus trampled down. At last, we passed safely out of this 'valley of the shadow of death,' and, having got out into the open plain, we at length pushed on to the village of Veziwkur. [Here Dr. Casson's staff and their wounded were exposed to great danger from the disorderly retreating mass of the defeated Turkish army, and accordingly proceeded to Kars.]

Ambulance under fire.

Fight at Nalban-tepe.

Narrow escape of ambulance.

RECORD OF OPERATIONS.

Dr. Casson's reports.	Hussein Bey, colonel of artillery, the camp commandant, with a small body of men (who made a most determined attempt to arrest the mad rush onwards of the soldiers), let me pass through with my charge, giving me as I passed by what cheered as much as it astonished me—a few words of encouraging compliment, in the best of English, for what was my simple duty and my high privilege to do. By the time we approached the lines, the mad rush was thicker and more desperate than ever, and, to avoid being actually trampled down, we made a few yards' digression to our right. Fortunately for us we did so; for suddenly a terrible explosion shook the ground, while there was showered all around us a hail of fragments of metal. A limber-waggon full of shells, jolting in its rapid flight over the rough ground, had exploded in the path we had just left, and the amount of destruction and death it dealt out to those immediately around was
Arrival at Kars.	terrific. A few minutes afterwards, I had the intense satisfaction of depositing all my patients, with a few other sick I had picked up on the road, in safety in the consultation-room of the principal hospital of Kars, where, after getting such food as the Greek doctor 'on guard' could procure for us, I was glad to lie down with them and seek repose after the fearful events of the day, and the words of my great Master found their way into the few utterings of thanksgiving I was capable of: 'Of those whom thou hast given me have I lost none.' This is not the place for what might be considered 'religious cant'; but I am not ashamed to record my thanks to the Almighty, who had protected and preserved us unhurt through all.

London, April 7, 1879.

Notes by Dr. Casson.	The day after our arrival at Kars, after the retreat of Mukhtar's army (Oct. 16), I devoted to searching for such remains of our stores and belongings as might have escaped capture by the
Loss of arabas.	enemy or loss during the terrors of the retreat. Two only of the eight arabas arrived in Kars, and these did not unfortunately contain by any means the most useful of our stores. A couple of bales of blankets, jerseys, and comforters were rescued, but beyond these all the newly-arrived stores sent by the Red Cross Society, as well as what was left of our original stock, were lost. These I distributed at once to the patients in the Kars hospital, who seemed most in need of them. On
Departure of Mukhtar Pacha.	the following day Mukhtar Pacha left for the Soghanli-Dagh, on the way to Erzeroum. He wished me to go with him, as he took no surgeon with the remains of his army, but in consideration of the state of Buckby's health (he being very much weaker from the excitement of his dangerous journey on the 15th), acting on the advice of Sir Arnold Kemball, I obtained permission to remain behind until such time as Buckby should be able either to accompany me in rejoining head-quarters or be safely left behind at Kars. For ten days I remained within the fortifications, ready to attend any wounded that might come in. I also volunteered to place my services at the disposal of Ghalit Bey, the principal medical officer of Kars, but the hospital organisation of the city was in such a state that I found I could be of very little use. In one of the hospitals I found a young Englishman, Cowan by name, who was dying of consumption and the effects of typhus, from which he had only recently recovered; he died on the 25th, and I saw him decently buried in the Christian cemetery at Kars. On the 27th Hussein Bey informed me that if we wanted to leave Kars for Erzeroum we must do so that day. Accordingly Buckby, who was now strong enough to
Departure of ambulance from Kars.	sit his horse, elected to go rather than stay behind, and we set out, accompanied by Renison and Fortunato, our groom and a Persian, with two baggage horses. (During his stay in Kars Buckby had been most hospitably entertained and kindly cared for by Dr. Schoepps, a German surgeon in the Turkish service.) Hussein Bey gave me letters to the Russian general in case we should fall into their hands, asking that we might be allowed to pass through on our mission as independent volunteer surgeons unconnected with the Turkish army. Towards evening we fell in with a
Staff taken prisoners.	Cossack outpost, who conveyed us blindfolded to the camp of General Melikoff, who refused to permit us to pass on towards Erzeroum. After two days' detention in camp we were sent on to Alexandropol under escort, and, after a week's further delay, were subsequently sent on to Tiflis, where, through the intervention of Mr. Ricketts, H.B.M.'s Consul, we obtained our freedom. At Tiflis we had to wait some time for the arrival of money from England, and at last we left Tiflis, travelling through Russia to Vienna, thence to Paris and home to England. At Vienna and Paris we received most kind help and attention from Sir Andrew Buchanan and Lord Lyons. Renison
Arrival in England.	and Fortunato were sent home to Constantinople from Vienna, viâ Trieste. We arrived in London on Dec. 8, 1877, Buckby being convalescent, but very much weakened by his terrible illness and privations.

(E)—VARIOUS REPORTS.

SECTIONS WORKED IN CO-OPERATION WITH THE RED CRESCENT SOCIETY.

RED CRESCENT TRANSPORT.

Early in August a large transport service was established by the Red Crescent Society for service in the Balkans. By special arrangement Stafford House provided the surgical staff, medicines, instruments, &c., while the Red Crescent defrayed the cost of the horses, wagons, and all working expenses. On Nov. 1 the Red Crescent took over the whole working of the section, and Surgeon Stoker's services were transferred to that society. Surgeon Weller was invalided to England, in November, after a most dangerous attack of fever contracted in the Balkans.

Period of combined service: Aug. 21 *to Oct.* 31, 1877.—Number of wounded transported during that period, 2,002. The staff of this section consisted of Surgeons Stoker and Weller, and Messrs. Banfather and Smith.

The following are extracts from reports to the Chief Commissioner:—

TABLE SHOWING AMOUNT OF WORK DONE BY DR. STOKER'S AMBULANCE.

(*During Combined Service*).

Date	Stations	No. of Days	No. of Wounded
Aug. 26	Shipka, Kesanlik	1	60
,, 27	ditto	1	60
,, 28–30	Shipka, Kutchukli, Choukourlou, and Philippopolis	3	250
Sept. 4–6	ditto ditto ditto . . .	3	30
,, 13–15	ditto ditto ditto . . .	3	1020
,, 24–26	ditto ditto ditto . . .	3	432
Oct. 16–18	Plevna, Tellich, Yablonitza, Orkhanie . . .	3	55
,, 20–21	Orkhanie and Sofia	2	40
,, 25–26	Sofia, Ichtiman-Bazardjik	2	55
	Total	21	2002

Yamboli, Aug. 23, 1877.

On Monday, Aug. 21, 1877, with twelve ambulance wagons mentioned in Report 1, I left Adrianople for Haïn Boghaz. I thought it best to go all the way by the carriage-road, and not part of the way by railway, because it was necessary to test exactly the capabilities of our transport in crossing a rough country, and this before any sick or wounded had been received. Up to the present, all has gone well. To-morrow early we shall arrive at Yeni-Zaghra, where I will make all enquiries which will influence our further movements.

Dr. STOKER's reports.

Philippopolis, Sept. 2, 1877.

The cacolets are absolutely necessary to get the wounded off the mountains. If you could send some more, or induce the Committee to get some made after your pattern, it would save lots of lives and suffering. I am getting twenty more wagons, and only came here to buy the harness. I have arranged two stopping places for our ambulances, and food will be provided whenever we send on to give two or three hours' notice. I shall want a couple more doctors shortly, as my other duties prevent me from attending to my medical ones.

[*Note.*—These cacolets are litters slun across pack-saddles by means of which a horse or mule can carry two wounded men.—V.B.-K.]

Utility of cacolets.

R

122   RECORD OF OPERATIONS.

Philippopolis, Sept. 3, 1877.

Dr. Stoker's reports.

On Aug. 23 I arrived at Yeni-Zaghra, where I learned from the military commander that Suleiman Pacha had left Hain Boghaz five days before, and was now attacking the enemy in the Shipka Pass, so I determined to go to Eski-Zaghra, and from there to Kesanlik. I rode on in front to secure lodging, &c., for the horses. On entering the town, I was obliged to dismount and lead my horse; the streets were so strewn with wounded, dead, and dying, to whom it seemed not

Miserable state of wounded at Kesanlik.

the slightest attention was being paid. I saw the head of the medical staff, who told me that there were only four doctors and surgeons to attend nearly 6,000 wounded. We set to work at once, and dressed 50 cases before the night closed in. The next day Dr. Weller stayed in Kesanlik, and dressed with his own hands over 100 cases, and went to the camp with ten wagons and brought back 30 serious cases. The horses were very fatigued, so he was obliged to rest them the next day; while Dr. Weller and myself spent all day dressing the wounded. We performed three capital operations and innumerable small ones. I got 50 bullock-wagons from Suleiman Pacha,

Transport of wounded.

and started the next day for Philippopolis with 250 wounded. For the most part, it was impossible that we could change their dressings every day; but we did as many as we could. On the third day we arrived at Philippopolis. There was some difficulty in finding a place to put the wounded in, as no preparations had been made. The Pacha seemed to think it was my duty to find a place for my wounded; but that was clearly beyond my duty, so I requested him to do so. At length a place was found, and the wounded deposited. I telegraphed to Mr. Kennett for twenty pairs of cacolets, and purpose bringing ten or twenty more wagons. [*Note*.—I sent all I could spare, three pairs.—V. B.-Kennett.] I have established two stopping places on the road, and arranged with the head man in each of these villages that, when I send him word, he will have sufficient food ready for the number I name as about to arrive. There is an urgent need of doctors here and at Kesanlik.' I beg to call the attention of the Committee to the excellent manner in which Dr. Weller and Lieutenant Banfather have performed their arduous duties.

Note.—Dr. Weller returned to Constantinople in October dangerously ill from fever, and was nursed with great care and devotion by Mrs. Cullen (wife of Dr. Cullen) in her own house. The following month he was invalided home.

Varna Hospital.

(*Combined Service with Red Crescent.*)

Varna being a terminus of the Rustchuk and Varna railway line, was selected for the establishment of a small hospital. By a special arrangement, the Red Crescent Society took over the building, and supplied the greater part of the matériel, while Stafford House furnished the surgical staff. This arrangement terminated on Nov. 1, 1878, when the Red Crescent Society took over the whole working of the hospital, including the services of the surgeons.

Period of combined service: Aug. 3 to Oct. 31, 1877.—Average number of beds occupied, 36; total number treated during combined service, 96. Surgeons Cullen and Kouvaras served on this section.

The following are extracts from reports to the Chief Commissioner :—

Varna, Sept. 16, 1877.

Dr. Kouvaras' report.

J'ai l'honneur de vous remettre ci-joint copie du tableau que j'ai adressé au Comité Central du Croissant Rouge à Constantinople, comprenant la statistique du mouvement médical de cet hôpital du 21 Août, époque à laquelle nous avons commencé de recevoir des blessés, jusqu'au 31 Août, vieux style. Il résulte de ce tableau que durant ce temps nous avons soigné 49 blessés, juste le nombre de lits que l'hôpital peut disposer. De ces 49 blessés, 1 a guéri, 3 sont morts, 11 devront rester encore sous traitement, et 34 étaient susceptibles d'être évacués.

VARNA HOSPITAL.

État du Mouvement Médical de l'Hôpital du Croissant Rouge à Varna du 21 au 31 Août, 1877, vieux style (2 au 12 Septembre).

Dr. KOUVARAS' report.

Blessures des malades et accidents qui les ont compliquées	Pris en traitement	Aptes à être évacués	Guéries	Morts	Restent	
Blessures dans la tête avec lésion de l'encéphale par coup de baïonnette ou sabre	1	...	...	1	...	
Ecorchure dans le visage par coup de feu	1	...	1	...	...	
Sillon transversal dans le visage par coup de feu	1	1	...	,...	...	
Plaies dans les cuisses par coup de feu	12	8	...	1	3	Dont 3 avec fractures.
Plaies dans les jambes par coup de feu	5	4	...	...	1	1 avec fractures.
Plaies dans les bras	8	8	...	...	...	2 avec fractures.
Plaies dans avant-bras	6	6	...	...	...	
Plaies dans le cou	3	3	...	...	...	
Plaies dans les épaules	2	2	...	...	...	
Ablation de la partie antérieure du maxillaire inférieur par coup de feu	1	1	...	...	...	L'un de ces trois morts, auquel j'ai extrait par une contre-ouverture la balle, est décédé par suite d'une infection purulente; les deux autres par une hémorrhagie intestinale.
Plaies du tronc par coup de feu	1	...	...	1	...	
Plaies dans les pieds par coup de feu	4	...	...	...	3	
Brûlures (second degré)	4	...	...	...	4	
	49	34	1	3	11	

Varna, Sept. 30, 1877.

État du mouvement médical de l'hôpital du premier au 30 Septembre. Blessés restés du mois précédent, 13. Pris en traitement en Septembre, 55. Opérés 2, guéris 8. Aptes d'être évacués 25. Morts, 8. Restent en traitement, 14.

[Drs. Kouvaras and Cullen were transferred to the Red Crescent Society on Nov. 1, 1877; at the same time all the Stafford House stores belonging to the hospital were handed over to that Society.]

OCHUR KOPPULL HOSPITAL, GUL-HANÉ.

Report of Surgeon NEYLAN (*temporarily attached to that hospital*).

Stamboul, Aug. 28, 1877.

Dr. NEYLAN'S report.

On Aug. 20 I was placed in charge of the Ochur Koppull hospital, Stamboul. It is attached to the Medical School, and in ordinary times is a civil one, devoted to the purpose of clinical teaching, but at present is used exclusively for military wounded. In a sanitary point of view it is well adapted for the reception of soldiers with foul and sloughing wounds, as it is a modern building, well ventilated and drained, and is situated on a height overhanging the edge of the Bosphorus, well exposed to the cool breezes from the Black Sea and Sea of Marmora. It contained 80 beds, which were all occupied by cases of shell and gun-shot wounds. Many of the men were suffering from injuries of a serious nature, but 25 were discharged yesterday (19) cured, and the remainder are on a fair road to recovery. This happy result is in a great measure attributable to the hygiene, which for a Turkish hospital is very good, and also to the care and attention bestowed on the dressing of the cases by the senior students. There are eighteen of these young men, who are very active and intelligent in the discharge of their duties.

First Report by Dr. BUCKLE, Staff Surgeon, R.N., to the Chief-Commissioner.

H.M.S. 'Alexandra,' Besika Bay, Oct. 1, 1877.

Dr. BUCKLE'S first report.

Leaving Constantinople by train for Adrianople, I passed some trains of wounded soldiers sent from Sofia and Philippopolis; the larger portion were suffering from comparatively slight wounds of the head and upper extremities, and were in ordinary third-class carriages; the smaller percentage of more severe injuries were accommodated in cots 'fixed' fore and aft in special carriages.

S. H. Roumelian Railway transport.

All appeared to be contented, comfortable, and well looked after. The energetic Dr. Barker was in charge of one of these trains. At Adrianople Station soup, bread, grapes and cigarettes were distributed to all; those going to Constantinople had their wounds re-dressed in the huts erected for that purpose alongside the railway; the rest were sent in arabas to the large military hospital about two miles from the city, one wing of which had been turned over to the Stafford House Committee, and where, at the time of my visit, about two hundred cases were under the care of their surgeons, under Dr. M'Ivor, and about one thousand sick soldiers were under the regular Turkish medical officers.

Adrianople S. H. hospital.

The patients were in moderate-sized wards (generally of about twelve beds) and in the corridors. All had country-made wooden bedsteads (placed, of necessity, too close together) and well-filled chaff beds and pillows, and good, warm, dark-brown blankets. The wards were very clean, and fairly tidy, and the air in them was unusually fresh and free from any unpleasant hospital odour; the corridors (or one-sided verandahs) being open, and the doors and windows of the wards constantly kept open, free circulation of air was insured. The patients generally appeared comfortable, even cheerful, and grateful in the extreme for the care, skill and attention they received, and appeared to have unlimited confidence in the medical officers. Many expressed their anxiety to get well to rejoin their regiments; their rations seemed fair in quality, and suited to their wants. The nurses were soldiers told off for that special duty, and in which they seemed to take interest, and to be very kind and efficient (comparing most favourably with the underpaid and casually employed so-called nurses in naval hospitals). The rations consisted of fresh meat, soup and bouilli, rice, brownish bread, vegetables, and fruit. The cooking was done in the Turkish end of the building, in the manner the men were accustomed to. Cigarettes were issued, and smoking (a necessity, not a luxury, to a Turk) was allowed in bed. The result of the larger operations had been unusually favourable, the Turks, especially the Asiatics, being surprisingly tolerant of surgery and very patient, many preferring not to take chloroform, but bearing painful operations with stolid endurance. The prejudice against amputations [1] was daily becoming less, as the reports of their good results spread amongst the soldiery. Medical officers not on duty were comfortably, though somewhat roughly, lodged in the Hôtel de l'Europe.

Drawers.—That loose flannel drawers instead of knitted drawers be supplied; the Turks being habituated to loose clothing, anything tight is irksome.

Kesanlik.

At Kesanlik we found many of the houses standing, but all the windows, doors, stairs, &c. destroyed, all the former inhabitants either massacred by Bulgarians, Russians, or Turks, or fled. The houses least dilapidated were being used as hospitals for the Turkish sick, of whom some four hundred were under treatment. There were three Italian or Greek surgeons of the Red Crescent who had been taking charge of the wounded, but owing to some change in the Turkish administration they were leaving for Philippopolis. The corpses had been removed from the streets, but remains of those slaughtered in the houses were still mingled with the general ruins or had been eaten by the dogs. The bodies of the Bulgarians who had been hanged on the triumphal arch they themselves had erected on the entrance of the Russians into Kesanlik, had been cut down and buried. The stench of the town was extremely offensive. The Turkish sick and wounded were but poorly attended to by their own people, those who were supposed to look after them being too few in number, and not doing even what might be done had zeal, ability, or ordinary attention been shown. Able English surgeons, with authority to act, would save some hundreds of lives here. [2]

---

[1] Nearly all the major operations are performed by Stafford House surgeons.

[2] Drs. Stoker and Weller served in Kesanlik, also Dr. Attwood, until he left for more urgent work in the front. It was then left to the Red Crescent ambulance, under Golstein and Sebastopoulos.

DR. BUCKLE'S REPORT.

In the plain to the south of the village of Shipka is the head-quarters camp of his Excellency Suleiman Pacha, about three hours' ride from Kesanlik. I found the Turkish hospital and the Stafford House ambulance under the trees to the right of the Turkish position, whilst the Ambulance Sebastopoulos was on the left. The ambulance consisted of three small shingle huts, a ward or hut built of bushes matted over poles, containing twelve good chaff beds, a smaller but similarly bush-built hut for an operating tent, and some tents for stores, in which were a fair supply of cotton, tow, carbolic acid, medical comforts, bales of bandages, &c., with a few necessary medicines. The patients had just started by an araba train for Philippopolis, so that the beds were ready for a fresh detachment of wounded then expected from the batteries opposite Fort St. Nicholas. The air of the camp was very offensive from the number of bodies of men and horses left unburied, though a daily improvement was taking place in this respect, almost all the bodies on the Kesanlik road having been at least covered over with earth. The means of evacuation of the wounded from the front, as far as they went, answered well, but the number of stretchers and bearers was totally inadequate to the demands upon them. All the available *employés* went with the troops to their front positions, but in such hardly contested and deadly struggles, when often from 10 to 20 per cent. of the forces engaged required assistance, their energies and abilities were utterly overtaxed. The system adopted was that the surgeons and stretcher-bearers follow the first line of troops, and on a man falling he was as soon as possible placed on a stretcher, and after the surgeon had attended to his immediate wants (generally under a heavy fire) he was carried to the rear, or on to the ambulance at the camp, where what operations were necessary were performed, and he was detained until an araba train had been organised for the three days' road journey to the railway line at Philippopolis.[1]

Dr. BUCKLE'S first report.

S. H. Shipka ambulance.

The capital operations performed had been unusually successful, for out of thirty there had been but three deaths, and there had been scarcely any gangrene or erysipelas. I am speaking now only of the patients entirely under the Stafford House surgeons' control. The sick, of whom there were considerable numbers (suffering chiefly from dysentery, diarrhœa, rheumatism, and fever), were as anxious as the wounded to be taken to the English ambulances, but that could not be. They were all sent to the Turkish hospital at the north-east of the camp, past the village of Shipka. The accounts from these are very unfavourable, and there is little doubt the charges of want of skill and attention brought against the Turkish medical attendants are too true. Their treatment of the sick and wounded in the araba trains on the three or four days' journey from Shipka to Philippopolis or Yeni-Zaghra, and the neglected, half-fed condition in which the patients arrive at the large hospitals at Philippopolis, Adrianople, and Constantinople, deserve severe censure. Some of the wounded had not been dressed for ten days, and their feeding had been done 'by contract.'

Surgical operations.

The trains of wounded from the Plevna and Orkhanie Sofia district through Philippopolis, and from Shipka through Yeni-Zaghra, all join the main line and pass through Adrianople to Constantinople. It would save much suffering and many weary hours of waiting if the entire control of these trains were handed over to the energetic surgeons of the Transport Department— Drs. Neylan, Stoker, Barker, and Messrs. Cullen and Sketchley—instead of leaving it in the hands of local authorities, who have no interest beyond their own district.

Suggestions for transport.

At the front the belief seemed general that, if it had not been for the assistance rendered by the Stafford House surgeons, many of the seriously wounded would have been dispatched where they fell to prevent their falling into the hands of the Russians and being mutilated.

Good results of S. H. work.

Everywhere the Red Crescent as the ambulance badge seemed to be known and respected by the troops of all the nationalities composing the Ottoman forces.[2] The Turkish authorities promise every assistance, and really, in many cases, try to fulfil their good intentions. The good service the society is doing, and the amount of suffering it relieves, can only be duly appreciated by those who have been through the utterly wasted district and seen the extremity of misery these poor Turkish soldiers, who are fighting so heroically for religion, hearth, and home, are enduring so patiently and pluckily.

---

[1] Dr. Stoker's ambulance transport was regularly engaged on this work from Kesanlik— Hume with cacolets—some stretcher-bearers lent by Suleiman Pacha.

[2] The Stafford House surgeons wear the Red Crescent 'brassard,' with the addition of 'S. H.' stamped on it in black.

Second Report by DR. BUCKLE, R.N.

H.M.S. 'Alexandra,' March 29, 1879.

Dr. BUCKLE'S second report.
I proceeded to inspect the Stafford House hospitals and ambulances in Stamboul, and in the lines between there and the Russian head-quarters camp at San Stefano.

Inspection of Stafford House hospitals.
I found the new buildings near the Government Medical School at Stamboul to consist of two detached, shingle-built, one-story barracks, with red-tile roofs and flat, false ceilings, about 250 feet long, 20 feet broad, and 12 feet high, the floor being of concrete, the sides plastered, and the whole whitewashed. Each was divided by a transverse partition into two large wards, at the outer extremities of which were four small store-rooms—one for the dispensary, one for the officers, and two for stores; each ward was fitted with fifty beds, the four corner ones being screened off for special cases. The closets were separated from the buildings, in Turkish style, well trapped, and drained straight into the sea, and easily flushed. The bedsteads consisted of two iron trestles, across which three thin planks were placed. They were very light, portable, elastic, and cheaply made, and if any parts got broken or lost they could be easily replaced—so they were admirably adapted for field service. The beds were of sacking, filled with well washed and dried seaweed; pillows filled with wool, cotton sheets, and warm, dark Stafford House blankets.

The wards were warmed by stoves, the iron pipes being laid horizontally about one foot below the false ceiling and near the ends of the wards. Sand baths for keeping food and water hot were arranged round the stoves. The ventilation was by the end doors, large central skylights, and opposite windows, the upper half of which, slanting inwards when opened, directed the in-current of air against the flat ceiling. The water supply was plentiful, but, like all in Constantinople, somewhat opaque, though tasteless and odourless. Charcoal filters were in use, and efforts were being made to obtain a supply from a different source. The diets were according to the Turkish military scale—No. 1 being rice water; No. 2, thin broth and bread; No. 3, milk, broth, bread, and rice; No. 4, pillaf, meat, soup, and 1 lb. of bread; No. 5, 1½ lb. of bread, meat stew, and milk; No. 6 (the usual full ration), 1¼ lb. of bread, 1 lb. of meat, rice, flour, vegetables, &c. Extras could be obtained, but were rarely needed. Wines and spirits were issued when necessary. The demands for rations were kept by the captain of orderlies and drawn from the commissariat stores.

The nursing was done by soldiers detached for that duty—one captain, one lieutenant, and 26 men for 200 beds, or, practically, two men to each ward in regular watches, day and night. The kindness and readiness to assist one another, so strongly characteristic of the Turks, makes this a fair allowance. Dressers had been offered from the Turkish Medical School, but I did not see any in the hospital. One of the 'blocks' (100 beds) was still occupied by invalids waiting passage to their homes; they have probably by this time been sent away, and the wards cleansed and filled with some of the thousands of sick and wounded now arriving from Erzeroum. The dispensary was very conveniently though roughly fitted, and well stocked with drugs. The operating room was well lighted from two sides, and provided with instruments, and all that was absolutely necessary.

Mundy model hospital.
Near these buildings, in the square of the Government Medical School, Baron Mundy had erected his model hospital of twenty-six beds in one shingle-built block, divided into two wards by a central longitudinal bulkhead or partition. The beds in a single row faced outwards towards the windows; the fittings were somewhat elaborate; the ventilation, by low movable windows and large skylights in the slanting roof, though scientifically devised, seemed scarcely to answer so well as the through current of air from opposite windows in the Stafford House Hospital. The cases were chiefly amputations, frost-bites, and wounds.

The hospital for female refugees under Dr. Lagondakis, opposite the railway station, had its sixty beds full; the nursing was under the St. Vincent de Paul Society (how clean, bright, and cheery these nurses look in their starched caps!); fever, dysentery, and chest complaints predominated, but the results of exposure and privation were marked in almost every face.

Makrikeui hospital.
Two hours' ride over an irregular stone causeway and marsh brought me to the village of Makrikeui, and in one of the best houses of the principal street I found the welcomed Red Crescent flag over Dr. Sketchley's hospital. It was a two-storied building, the basement being

used as offices. Two upper floors contained four rooms each, and in them were about seventy beds (seven to nine in a ward); the wide landing places being set apart for special cases; in the upper one a suspected case of small-pox had just been placed as I entered. The patients were on thick sea-weed beds, with sheets and blankets as in Stamboul. The cases were chiefly medical. Dysentery, typhoid, ague, and chest complaints (the Turks seem to call all cases of cough, dyspnœa, and fever, by their equivalent to 'engorgement of the lungs'); but the prominent feature in all the cases was intense debility, a playedoutishness, from exposure, cold, overwork, and bad food. Some of the men (and Dr. Sketchley, too) had been from two to three weeks before their arrival marching all day, sleeping in the snow, insufficiently clad, and with rations of either black bread and hard biscuit, or sometimes even without that. Rest, warmth, good diet given cautiously at first, the occasional use of stimulants, wine or brandy, soon relieved these symptoms; many required no other treatment than time to allow nature to restore the balance of supply and demand.

Dr. BUCKLE'S second report.

Before my arrival there had been some difficulty in obtaining bread, as the rations were stopped, and there was nothing to be bought 'in the lines'; but through the persistent energy of Dr. Sketchley, who organised a supply train from Stamboul, all the patients were kept on full rations, though the soldiers had to go without. The hospital rations, when once obtained, were on the same scale as in Stamboul. The water-supply was from a well in the enclosure or garden. It was semi-opaque, but gave no other evidence of impurity to superficial examination. Boiling and charcoal filtration rendered it as little injurious as possible. Little's disinfecting fluid was used in the wards with satisfactory results, and as far as possible the dryearth system was employed in the latrines. The hospital was clean and orderly; the wards were free from close or unpleasant odour (though I was told it was only maintained so by constant supervision, as the Turks, in common with many others, prefer 'fog' to draught, and will close all windows and doors directly they get a chance. The patients, despite their maladies, appeared cheerful and extremely grateful for the treatment they received, and evinced it by the eager readiness to obey any order or to execute any wish of the surgeons; the men were only too eager to get back to military duty. '*If you would fight for us half as well as you care for us, the Muscoves would all be in the Great River (Danube), now,*' said a sergeant I had known at Shipka, as I passed.

From repeatedly confirmed evidence there can be no doubt that hundreds of Turkish sick and wounded were murdered by the Russians during the retreat—Red Cross, Red Crescent, and Geneva Convention notwithstanding.

The whole medical work of Nedjib Pacha's division in the San Stefano lines fell upon the Stafford House hospital; there were about 5,000 troops in that part of the field, and not a single Turkish medical officer. If it had not been for the aid of the English ambulance, hundreds of lives must have been sacrificed. The wretchedness and misery in this district fully justifies the *Graphic's* sketch of the 'Road to Constantinople' (March 9, 1878). Besides the hospital work, some 200 to 300 sick were attended in the tents or the open air daily; and some hundreds of refugees were employed along the causeways to bury the carcases and generally clear the roads; but everywhere was mud, misery, and desolation.

CONSTANTINOPLE MOSQUES.

Report from Surgeon BARKER *(temporarily attached to the Compassionate Fund).*

Constantinople, March 2, 1878.

In accordance with your wishes, I offered my services to the Turkish Compassionate Fund on Feb. 23, until such time as our 'Baraque' hospital should be ready to receive patients. I was appointed to inspect the mosques of St. Sofia and Sultan Achmet, till on 25th inst., being joined by Drs. Clement, Edmunds, and R. Leslie, we were able to divide the work; Dr. Leslie and myself, each taking half of St. Sofia, and the others Sultan Achmet. I found both mosques very much overcrowded, and the people as a rule in a very bad state, in many cases being destitute of covering. In comparing what I have seen of these two mosques, I believe that of St. Sofia, though containing the greater number of fugitives, to be in a better sanitary state, owing to the vast amount of cubic space obtained by its large dome and gallery, and its having three entrances in

Dr. BARKER'S report.

Inspection of refugees in mosques.

Dr. BARKER'S report.
St. Sofia.

constant use. The refugees, however, in St. Sofia belong to a poorer class, and are very much more destitute than those in the Sultan Achmet. In St. Sofia the refugees are all placed on the ground floor, the large gallery being quite free. In the body of the mosque they are placed in transverse rows, squatting in family circles, having under them matting which is spread over the whole floor, and any articles of bedding which they may have been able to preserve in their flight. These last are usually piled in a heap in the daytime, and serve as boundary lines between the various families. In addition to these, a few pots and pans, a handmill and a mangal, and in some instances a cartwheel, which seems to be kept as a souvenir of the old country, as a rule, comprises the inventory of their worldly goods.

State of refugees.

The refugees, who are all Turks, are to be found in every conceivable nook with which the mosque abounds, and, being huddled together, form hotbeds of those diseases which are so painfully making their presence felt. Each family receives daily half a loaf of bread for each individual member, whether adult or infant, from the Turkish Compassionate Fund, which, under the able direction of Mr. Bartlett, is doing a noble work. On no occasion has a case of any family's claim been passed over, and they all seem contented. Although many of the refugees are very poor, they manage somehow to get leeks and halvah, &c., to make their bread more palatable, and I have often seen stout, able-bodied refugees counting considerable sums of caïmé belonging to themselves.

Sickness.

With regard to the kinds of sickness prevalent. We immediately detected the presence of small-pox, the cases of which were scattered variously over the mosque, but were in much greater number in and about the overcrowded nooks. Most of the cases were of a mild type, and the sufferers in all cases children. On the 22nd and 23rd inst., through the kindness of the surgeon in charge of the Turkish Compassionate Fund's women's hospital, and Marco Pacha's, we were enabled to obtain some lymph, and thus we were able to vaccinate a good number. We expected to meet with opposition on the part of the parents, but were agreeably surprised that they flocked around, and contended amongst themselves as to whose child should be vaccinated next. I was very sorry when I found some of those vaccinated a few days afterwards down with small-pox. But this amount of lymph was only like a drop in a bucket, and we could not obtain more unless by paying most exorbitant prices; this I found was due to lymph being a marketable article. I have been informed that medical men sell it at the rate of 10s. per tube. I wrote to London for some to the National Vaccine Establishment, and hope to receive it in a day or two. At first our chief work was to hunt out the small-pox cases, and have them isolated, but we encountered great opposition, owing to want of hospital accommodation and objections of the parents, till Mr. Bartlett, by his unceasing efforts, obtained from Marco Pacha a promise that some baraque hospitals which were in the course of construction for the National Committee should be prepared to receive small-pox cases the following day. We found it impossible to send the children without the mothers. These went very reluctantly, in many cases running out of the mosque and hiding so that they might not be sent. To such an extent was this carried on, that we were obliged to apply again to Marco Pacha, who kindly gave us an officer and men, with full powers to remove any cases we might direct.

Vaccination begun.

Increase of small-pox.

The cases at first discovered on my side of the mosque (since it is of these only I can speak) were all of the discrete form, and as a rule not very severe, but towards the middle of the week their number increased, and several very bad cases of a confluent type appeared. Some of these it was very difficult to discover, owing to their being intentionally concealed by the parents in the folded-up bedding or any available place. Towards the end of the week the cases decreased in number, but I am certain that on my side alone I could not have seen less than 50 separate cases during the week. A curious coincidence in this epidemic is the immunity which adults enjoyed, the most part being children under two years of age. I have only heard of one adult being attacked. I visited as a rule each day the small-pox baraques, and found one containing 30 beds filled on the first day of opening. It was a strange sight to see mothers perfectly healthy, in many cases never having had small-pox, nursing their children. They could not be prevailed on to leave them, although there are Sisters of Charity and special nurses appointed to attend to them. A Turkish doctor was appointed to look after them, but for the first 36 hours I found they had neither had food nor medicines, except a small quantity of milk, and indeed were without disinfectants till I took them some from our store. The sanitary state is reduced to a decided minimum, owing to the latrines being placed between the two adjacent baraques on either side of the communicating closed passage¹. Another formidable evil we have tried to remedy is the bringing back to the mosque, from the hospitals, patients before they have passed through the infectious stage; and since the Turkish surgeons will insist on dismissing them, we have no help but to send them back to the baraques. The other chief diseases which we meet are typhoid

Government hospitals.

and intermittent fevers; scabies, chiefly of the pustular form; rheumatism, frost-bites and sore throats, not to speak of the coughs and colds and petty aches of which nearly everyone complains. To these we give medicines such as we have at our disposal, and send the severest cases to hospitals where there is room. In addition we distribute milk daily, and every alternate day soup, to the cases most requiring better nourishment. On two occasions we have disinfected the mosque, once with Little's Fluid and once with carbolic acid.

Dr. BARKER'S report.

Extract from Report of MR. W. L. STONEY.

(*On Treatment of Russian Prisoners.*)

Pera, Nov. 19, 1877.

A train of Russian prisoners arrived here the other day, taken at Elena. Amongst them were several wounded, and all looked seedy enough. I asked the Minister of War if there would be any objection to our giving soup to the wounded. 'On the contrary,' was the reply, 'we shall feel obliged if you will treat them with the same courtesy and hospitality which you show to our wounded.' Accordingly, I had soup served as usual. The behaviour of the Turks towards their prisoners was excellent; the faintest buzz of curiosity was checked, and the Turkish soldiers helped the wounded Russians from the wagons, and carried them off with every care and attention.

Mr. STONEY'S report.

Russian prisoners.

Extract of a Letter from CAPTAIN BURNABY *on the Stafford House Hospitals in Roumelia.*

Sofia, Dec. 3, 1877.

I arrived at Adrianople last week, and visited the hospital which is under the supervision of the Stafford House Committee surgeons. You will be glad to hear that every attention is being paid to the wounded. The wards are clean, lofty, and well ventilated. The food supplied is of good quality, and there was an expression of pleasure which passed over the poor sufferers' countenances as the English surgeons walked around the wards and enquired after each man's ailment. I conversed with several of the patients, and they expressed their hearty gratitude to the subscribers to the Stafford House fund, the 'Inglis,' as the wounded men termed them, who had sent out such skilful and kind practitioners. I enquired of the medical men if any difficulty was placed in their way with reference to surgical operations, &c., by the Turkish authorities. I was assured that this was not the case. In no instance had any opposition been made to the performance of an operation, provided that the wounded man himself (the most interested individual) was a consenting party. In several instances the Turkish surgeons had called on the Stafford House medical men to amputate in that part of the building which is set aside for the Turkish hospital—thus freely acknowledging that the Englishmen were more skilful operators than the Turks themselves. At Philippopolis there is only one Stafford House surgeon, as Dr. Eccles, the other doctor, has been lately invalided to Constantinople. There are a great many wounded men in this town: 75 of them are looked after by the Stafford House surgeon, to whom I have referred. He has more work to do than he can properly perform, and the sooner he has some more assistance the better. [*Note.* Dr. Calfoglou sent a few days later to replace Dr. Eccles.] I arrived in Sofia yesterday, and visited the Stafford House wards. The wounded men have every attention paid to them; they are well looked after and cared for as they would be in any London hospital. There are altogether 150 patients, who are attended to by the Stafford House medical gentlemen.

Captain BURNABY'S letter.

Adrianople S. H. hospital.

Philippopolis S.H. hospital.

Sofia S. H. hospital

Extract from a Letter to the DUKE OF SUTHERLAND *from* MR. J. W. ZOHRAB, *H.B.M. Consul at Erzeroum.*

(*On the Stafford House Committee and Lord Blantyre's Hospitals in Asia.*)

London : June 24, 1878.

Consul ZOHRAB's letter.

It would, I believe, be very difficult to find any person who could dispute the great services rendered, not alone to humanity, but to the interests of England by the Stafford House Committee and other Societies and persons who devoted their time and money for the relief of suffering among the Turks and administered this relief. This work, as a result, must not be regarded as having been limited to the saving of life and the alleviation of suffering; it went far beyond this. The Ottoman Mahommedans have for generations past regarded England as the faithful and constant ally of their country, and the English people as their firm friends and protectors. The breaking out of the war with Russia was a sore trial to their faith, and, but for the noble efforts of the Stafford House Committee, of Lord Blantyre, whose generous contributions and unwearing attention to the wants of wounded Turkish soldiers resulted in the saving of many lives, and to the contribution of the British National Aid Society, the shock experienced by them at the neutrality of England which they regarded as an abandonment and an entire severance of the old ties of friendship, would have resulted in completely and irretrievably alienating their love and respect from England and the English people—results which would probably have seriously complicated political relations and added very serious, if not insuperable, difficulties to the solution of the Eastern Question. In the aid sent from England to the soldiers who were engaged in a death-struggle for their faith, the Mahommedans felt and learned that the heart of the English people was still turned towards them, and that, however, as a nation, policy might compel England to act as individuals, the English were ready to aid and give them comfort in their hopeless struggle. The Turks went to the war irritated against what they believed to be the duplicity of the English, who, they asserted, encouraged them to resist the Russians and then deserted them. The close of the war saw a mighty change ; though crushed, the Turks no longer bore animosity to the English, they no longer resented the non-interference of England, but they blessed and prayed for the nation which, remembering them in their sufferings, sent them food, clothing, and medicines, and able devoted men to heal their wounded. Thousands of soldiers spread over the empire related how they had been cared for, nursed and saved by the English, and gratitude for England rapidly manifested itself throughout the country. This gratitude is no passing sentiment, but it is so deeply rooted (and I say this from a perfect knowledge of the subject) that the Ottoman Mahommedans would now follow England in any course she chose to steer if she but placed herself at their head. This feeling, now so universally felt by all Ottoman Turks, has resulted from the impulses of those persons, who, putting aside political opinions and leanings, listened alone to the dictates of humanity, and by their noble action not only saved the lives of thousands of men who were worthy of all the aid given to them, but restored to England that influence in Turkey without which her political interests would have been seriously complicated.

The treaty between Turkey and Russia may after all prove but a truce, the questions involved in that treaty are so intricate that the probability, which verges on almost certainty, is that more blood—much more blood—must be shed before the Eastern Question can be finally settled. Guided by this belief, I venture to make a few suggestions as to the organisation and working of hospitals which British philanthropy may again establish in aid of the Turks. The zeal, energy, and devotion shown by the ambulance staff who were employed in Turkey during the late war cannot be too highly eulogised. My long acquaintance with Turkey, the knowledge I gained of the Turkish army during the siege of Kars in 1855 and during the Montenegrin war of 1860-61, and the experience I acquired in hospital organisation and administration at Erzeroum, embolden me to make the following remarks:—

The Turkish soldier in his home seldom eats meat, and his beverage is water. The products of milk and of wheat constitute the staple food of the people. Personal comforts, such as good bedding, nice rooms, solid food, stimulating beverages, are unknown and are unsought for. To give, therefore, to men whose blood may be said to be free from all inflammatory matter such food or drink as a British soldier requires when under surgical treatment would be unnecessary and injurious, and to supply them with comforts to which they are utter strangers is superfluous. Boxes sent to Turkey for field use containing medical comforts should in my opinion contain :—

In the way of nourishment :—
2 Bottles of brandy or rum.
2 Bottles of lime juice.

Several pots of extract of meat.
A small tin of tea, one of sugar, and a little salt.

Of necessaries :—
6 Candles, with a small candlestick.
1 Box of lucifers.
Spirit lamp and bottle of spirits of wine.
A small tin kettle for boiling water.

Medical stores :—
Bandages.
Adhesive plaister.
1 Bottle chlorodyne.
1 Small bottle chloroform.
A few simple splints.

* * * * * * *

The Turkish dressers were found very apt at their work, and with little training they became very efficient, and this can be said of all the attendants. It is to be expected that in whatever town an hospital is established there will be likewise a Turkish military hospital; consequently, as in Erzeroum, the food for the staff and the patients would be supplied from the kitchen of the Turkish hospital where cooks who know how to prepare dietary food are employed. The clothing and blankets sent to Erzeroum were excellent, and proved most useful. I would, however, make the following suggestions :—

Socks.—The native socks being stronger and cheaper than those sent from England, I advise the purchase in the country of those articles, instead of their being sent from England.

Slippers.—I found that list slippers, though warm and comfortable at first, soon ceased to be so. It is impossible to keep the patients from getting them wet, and when once wetted they were soon abandoned. The native leather slipper is much better, and ought to take the place of those sent from England. [*Note.*—All socks and slippers for Stafford House Committee hospitals were bought in Turkey.]

In conclusion, I think I but fulfil a duty in bearing willing and hearty testimony to the great good effected by the hospitals established during the late war in aid of the wounded of the Turkish armies. The number of lives saved through their agency I cannot estimate, but if all the hospitals were as successful as the 'English hospital' at Erzeroum, the results must have been very brilliant, for from that hospital alone from 200 to 300 patients were discharged 'cured' every month. Anything I could say in praise of the volunteer surgeons who worked in Erzeroum would become meaningless before the splendid results of their labour and devotion; they have raised for themselves an enduring monument in the many hundreds of lives they saved, in the loudly-expressed gratitude of the soldiers, and in the respect and love for England which they have received in the heart of the Mussulman peasant.

J. W. ZOHRAB.

Extracts from " WITH THE ARMIES OF THE BALKANS,"

BY LIEUT.-COLONEL FIFE-COOKSON

(*Late Additional Military Attaché, Constantinople*).

From the chapters on Gallipoli :—

After the fleet came hospitals were opened by the Stafford House Committee, under the immediate supervision of Sir E. Commerell, one of its most active members. From the commencement of the war I had been struck by the very efficient organisation of this society; the credit of which must be greatly attributed to Mr. Barrington-Kennett, its Chief Commissioner in Turkey. . . . .

The distribution of relief to the refugees, and all the assistance which was given to the sick and wounded throughout the war by the various charitable societies, almost entirely English, created a strong feeling of gratitude amongst the Turks of all ranks, and had the approbation of the Christian subjects of the Porte who witnessed it.

PART III.

MEDICAL REPORT BY THE SUB-COMMITTEE.

Sir J. FAYRER, K.C.S.I., M.D., F.R.S., *Chairman*.

Sir J. Fayrer's introductory remarks.

WITH the view of preserving some record of the work of the medical officers of the Stafford House Committee, in regard to the medical, surgical, and sanatory aspects of the duties in which they were engaged during the recent Russo-Turkish war; a circular was recently addressed to each, in which he was requested to note his personal experience of certain important questions of a technical nature, that might have come under notice during his period of service in the East.

The large field for observation, of disease and of the injuries incidental to warfare, that was necessarily presented under such exceptionally difficult and trying circumstances as those to which the Turkish army was exposed, naturally offered an opportunity of studying many questions of an interesting character, and warranted the conclusion that, not only would important information be derived from, but that tangible evidence would be afforded by it, that the benefits of medical science had been largely conferred on the sufferers in a campaign that has been unusually fertile in disease and suffering; and this conclusion has been amply justified.

The general report deals with the subjects of administration, distribution of ambulances, the services of the personnel, and expenditure; it is therefore proposed in the medical report merely to supplement that information by such reports of special interest as may have furnished in reply to the circular above referred to.

Of the answers received, three or four contain matter that is of sufficient interest to be recorded as a contribution to the medical history of the campaign. It is to be remembered, however, that the arduous duties and incessant labours incidental to the peculiar character of the services in which these officers were engaged, must have rendered continuous or detailed case-taking and recording of proceedings difficult, and often impossible. It is, therefore, not strange that material for a history of the purely medical and surgical work performed should, under the circumstances, be meagre, or, indeed, in some respects, wanting; especially as many of the medical officers may not have received the circular, some having proceeded abroad, others having entered various departments of the public services, undertaken other duties, or changed their abode, leaving no address; whilst one at least is dead.

Difficulty of preserving detailed surgical reports.

Mr. MacKellar, of St. Thomas' Hospital, who spent some months with the Turkish forces, has submitted a report or rather summary of his observations, which, being that of a metropolitan hospital surgeon, will have the peculiar weight attaching to the opinion of an officer of large and varied experience.

It is to be regretted, however, that so little should remain on permanent record of the experiences of a body of surgeons who had special opportunity of dealing, on a large scale, with matters of prominent interest to military medicine, surgery and hygiene.

Medical lessons of the war.

The great lessons to be derived from such opportunities as those afforded by the Turkish army should be interesting and instructive; and there is no reason to doubt that the medical officers did, as far as their heavy work permitted, avail themselves of such chance as they had of profiting by them; therefore, whilst thoroughly acknowledging the valuable services they performed, we can only accept without comment whatever they had leisure to record and place at our disposal, as it would be obviously unjust, under the circumstances, to be hypercritical, or to expect reports in detail. But it may be hoped that more information will ultimately be contributed by them in relation to the subjects of hygiene, epidemic and endemic disease; injuries from gun-shot and other projectiles; sword and other incised or punctured wounds; tetanus, pyæmia; blood-poisoning; osteo-myelitis, gangrene; amputations, resections and their results, and conservative surgery generally; antiseptic surgery, the use of chloroform, ether, or other anæsthetics; and other subjects which probably have engaged their attention, and on which our knowledge being by no means complete, any further information would be valuable.

The report by Dr. McIvor gives a brief summary of the surgical proceedings of the Stafford House hospitals at Adrianople, and will convey also a good notion of the general character of the work done elsewhere by the same department. The various surgical reports.

The report by Mr. Barker gives some interesting information in regard to the surgical treatment of gun-shot injuries.

Mr. Weller also contributes some interesting memoranda.

The report by Mr. Eccles is an interesting contribution on the subject of the influences of malaria on the troops and especially the wounded. As the result of direct personal observation, it is a valuable addition to the medical history of the campaign.

Mr. Mackellar's report is an interesting summary of his personal experience of the medical and sanitary proceedings that occurred during part of the operations of the Stafford House Committee Medical Service.

Dr. Pinkerton's report is also a valuable summary of his experience in connection with the Stafford House Medical Service, and would have been extended to a greater length had space permitted.

A short Account of four hundred Surgical Cases treated at the Stafford House Military Hospital at Adrianople. By ROBERT McIVOR, M.D.

While in charge of the above-named hospital, I noted the following cases, which are of surgical interest :— Dr. McIvor's surgical report

We occupied a building which was formerly a cavalry barracks. Three-fourths of this building had been destroyed by fire at some distant date, and as the remainder had not been occupied for a very long time, much had to be done to make it suitable for an hospital; and though we had not all we wished, nevertheless, I think those who visited it were not unfavourably impressed with the general arrangements, the cleanliness and cheerful appearance and satisfactory answers of our patients. During our residence at Adrianople we received every kindness and assistance from the Military and Civil Governor, Djaemal Pacha, and most kindly feelings existed at all times between us and the Turkish medical officers. Had it not been for the excellent arrangements of Mr. Kennett and his assistants, in forwarding to us all necessary supplies on the shortest notice, much of our time would have been lost, and consequently much suffering left unrelieved. Barrack hospital at Adrianople.

Let me briefly draw attention to the state of our patients on admission. These soldiers were for the most part wounded at Plevna or Shipka, and had passed through a most severe ordeal in reaching us; in many instances the wounds were of two or three weeks' standing, and being conveyed from the field on arabas, there had been very few opportunities of having them dressed. Suppuration in all cases had done much to weaken the patient, and in some had accomplished irreparable injury. During the summer many of the wounds were alive with maggots, the appearance of which was disgusting. Diarrhœa, dysentery and fever caused many to succumb during this season; when winter set in this state of matters was even worse. Food was to be obtained in neither sufficient quantities nor quality, and in most cases a series of soup-kitchens, established by Stafford House along the route, afforded the only nourishment the men had to subsist on for several days. The depressing influence of the intense cold on men debilitated by severe and suppurating wounds was severely felt. When a number of wounded arrived at Adrianople State of patients on admission.

Dr. McIvor's report.

we picked out all the severe cases for the hospital, so that our time might not be wasted in treating trivial wounds, which could be looked after by the Turks.

Wounds of the upper extremities.

I shall commence with wounds of the upper extremities, and may remark that these accidents are not so dangerous to life as injuries of the lower extremities; that the prognosis is much influenced by the amount of destruction of soft parts, the extent of splintering of the bone, injury to the principal vessels or nerves, or complications such as diarrhœa or dysentery. Fractures of the humerus caused by bullets are always compound; in many instances the bone will be found splintered longitudinally, causing a number of loose spiculæ of the bone to penetrate the soft parts, which, if not carefully removed, cause much irritation. I have collected 44 cases of this accident. Five of these involved the shoulder, and two the elbow joint. Of the 37 cases which did not involve either joint, nineteen required no operative interference except the removal of foreign bodies from the wounds, opening abscesses as they formed, and keeping the broken fragments of bone at rest by well-padded splints. In fourteen cases we had to resect more or less of the humerus, and of these one death followed from diarrhœa, which resisted treatment, the remainder being discharged with useful arms. In four instances it was found necessary to amputate, and three of these cases recovered, leaving hospital with good stumps. Three of the operations were performed at the junction of the upper and middle thirds of the bone by anterior and posterior skin and muscular flaps. The reason why we included the muscles in the flaps was on account of the sloughing which followed if only skin and areolar tissue were included; when the muscles were included no sloughing took place. The fourth patient's arm was amputated at the middle third. The necessity for amputation arose in one case on account of hæmorrhage from the bronchial artery, caused by the separation of a slough, which was probably produced by the bullet at the time of receiving the injury. In the other three cases extensive necrosis of the humerus, with much destruction of the soft parts, accompanied by profuse suppuration, which would have ended in death had the limbs not been amputated. In the case that ended in death everything went on remarkably well for the first fourteen days, when an attack of dysentery set in which soon caused a fatal termination to the already exhausted patient.

In two cases the elbow joint was involved, the bullet having splintered the lower end of the humerus, which was followed by inflammation and suppuration of the joint. In one of these cases the amount of destruction of parts was so extensive that amputation of the arm had to be performed through the lower third, the patient making a good recovery. In the second case excision of the joint was performed, and although the operation was performed with every possible precaution, the wound being well syringed out with a solution of chloride of zinc and carbolised tow applied as a dressing; nevertheless erysipelas set in and caused much delay in the healing process; but in the end he recovered, having a useful arm, being discharged after the lapse of 128 days.

In the five cases which involved the shoulder joint operation, interference was considered to be necessary in three; the other two patients were not in a proper state of health to bear the operation, and in these two death followed from exhaustion. In the other three cases amputation was performed at the shoulder joint, after 'Larrey's' method. One of these patients made a good recovery; the second died on the 14th day, from bronchitis and diarrhœa; the third died on the second day, from collapse.

Fractures of the bones of the forearm.

Fractures of the bones of the forearm are not serious accidents. I have notes of sixteen severe cases of this accident before me, eight of which were treated without operative interference, except the removal of dead spiculæ of bone, opening abscesses or sinuses when such existed, keeping the broken bones at rest by means of anterior and posterior splints, and dressing the wounds daily. In six cases more or less extensive necrosis of one or both bones took place, and had to be resected. In one of these cases so operated on, death followed from gangrene of hand and lower part of forearm; in this case the limb should have been amputated, but at no time after his admission could we get his health into a condition to bear it. In two cases amputation of the forearm was performed on account of extensive destruction of the soft parts, with extensive necrosis of the bones of forearm, and in both cases a good recovery followed. In two cases, which had no operation performed on them, death was caused by gangrene, accompanied by diarrhœa. These two patients were in so debilitated a state on admission that it was thought proper not to interfere.

Bullet wounds of the wrist.

Bullet wounds of the wrist, including all those cases in which the bullet passed through the base of the metacarpal bones, the carpal bones, or the lower end of the bones of forearm, so as to involve the joint at any part, are conveniently treated of together. Twenty cases of this accident were admitted, and although only one death occurred, nevertheless we had a great deal of trouble with these injuries. In all cases their treatment extended over a long period of time, and were always accompanied by profuse suppuration. The hand was removed through the lower part of the forearm in one case, with success, but it was very difficult, and in most cases impossible, to persuade the patients to have an amputation performed for this accident, however severe the injury might be, and we had to be satisfied with removing all dead pieces of bone, maintaining a free exit for all pus as it formed, keeping a splint to the palmar aspect of the hand, maintaining the patient's strength by good food and tonics. When much inflammation existed we kept the hand in a hot bath for a few hours daily, with much relief to the patient and benefit to the wound; many of these patients were discharged from hospital with the parts healed up, but with a stiff wrist joint. In some cases sinuses existed leading down to dead bone, but the recoveries which took place in some of these cases, which should have been removed by amputation, impressed me very much with the reparative powers of the constitution of a Turk. Injuries to the fingers and metacarpal bones only require ordinary treatment. Forty of these accidents were treated by us. In two cases part of one or more metacarpal bones were removed, in thirteen cases one or more fingers were removed, and in no case did death follow. It was remarked that amongst the Arab soldiers the first finger of the right hand was shot off very frequently, but whether or not the soldiers took this means of avoiding service I was not able to satisfy myself.

 Flesh wounds of the upper extremities are not followed by serious consequences except the large vessel of the limb be injured, but such injuries were treated on the field, and consequently did not reach us. Of 50 cases of wounds involving the soft parts only two died, and in both cases the patients were much exhausted by suppuration and diarrhœa. The treatment of superficial wounds is simple. The bullet should be removed, if possible, as much suppuration is caused by its presence, abscesses should be opened in the most dependent position as soon as detected, the wound should be cleansed daily by means of a good stream of carbolic acid lotion, and a dressing of lint wet in some lotion, such as chloride of zinc or carbolic acid, applied, or, what I prefer, a pad of carbolised tow—no dressing, from my experience, being equal to it for suppurating wounds. I shall speak of it more in detail afterwards.

 Bullet wounds of the lower extremities are far more serious than those of the upper extremities. Wounds of the hip-joint are most fatal accidents. I have never seen a patient recover whose hip-joint was injured. Fractures of the femur and injuries to the knee-joint are also very serious on account of the amount of suppuration which is sure to follow. Wounds of the leg and foot are not serious, except complicated. No class of cases are more unsuited than these are for removal from one locality to another, and in no accident received on the field was the result of neglect shown more vividly than in these.

 Bullet wounds of the hip-joint are most serious accidents, and in all cases where the health of the patient will permit, the soft parts not extensively destroyed or the bone much splintered, excision should be performed at once, and the patient kept at the nearest hospital and not removed under any circumstances. If excision is rendered impossible, amputation should then be performed, for neglect of operative interference in these cases is to leave the patient to certain death, when some chance of life, with perhaps a useful limb, if the joint had been excised, might be promised by timely and judicious operative interference. Six cases of this accident were admitted by us, but suppuration of the joint had already put them out of the range of operative interference. The pus had burrowed between the muscles of the gluteal region; hectic fever, diarrhœa, or pyæmia followed after some weeks and caused the death of the patient.

 Fractures of the femur are most difficult accidents to bring to a successful termination, and in no case of gun-shot injuries should more care be given on the field than to these. Every case should be carefully examined as soon after the receipt of the injury as possible, and every possible circumstance brought to bear on the point of operative interference; for now is the time to decide on the future course of procedure, now the patient's life is in the balance, and a step in the wrong direction or neglect in adopting the proper line of treatment is sure in the end to cost your patient his life. If you have a femur extensively splintered, with much injury to the soft parts, a large vessel torn, or the principal nerves of the limb injured, or the bullet lodged in the bone, my advice is to remove the limb at once, for by so doing you give your patient the only chance of recovery, while by adopting an expectant treatment the chance of recovery is very bad. If the bone be very little splintered, the vessels and nerves intact, the bullet having passed out of the limb or so that it can be easily extracted, and a good hospital convenient, with all the necessary appliances for the proper treatment of so grave an accident, then you may have a chance of saving the limb; but even under these favourable circumstances the surgeon should not fail to examine the limb daily, and see himself that the dressings are properly applied, that no pus is burrowing between the

MEDICAL REPORTS.

Dr. McIvor's report. — muscles of the thigh, no sores are forming on the limb owing to improperly padded splints, and also that stimulants and food are administered in proper quantities, for it is only after the utmost care, both from the surgeon and nurse, that these cases are treated successfully. We treated twelve cases of fracture of the femur, and the result was anything but satisfactory. On admission suppuration had established itself, the ends of the broken bones were surrounded by pus, which in some instances had burrowed for a considerable length amongst the muscles of the thigh, necrosis of part of the femur had taken place, or was about to do so, the patient's appetite was failing, diarrhœa, hectic fever, or in some instances a low form of blood-poisoning, gradually caused the patient to succumb, but in many cases death did not take place till after some months. Even under these circumstances four of our patients survived, but it was not till after months that they were able to be discharged from hospital, their constitutions being shaken to the very foundation. In two cases we amputated through the lower third of the thigh, but death followed from tetanus in one case and from exhaustion in the other.

Bullet wounds involving the knee-joint. — Bullet wounds involving the knee-joint are most serious accidents, and require much care and accurate knowledge to bring them to a satisfactory termination. If the joint be at all injured, amputation should be performed at once; for to excise a knee-joint on the field, where no hospital is convenient, with every requisite for their treatment, leaves the patient a poor chance for recovery, and it is only where such exists that excision should be attempted. Six cases of this accident were admitted into our hospital, but neglect at the front had already put them past operative interference, such as excision, and in two cases in which amputation was performed, death followed in one eight days after the operation, from exhaustion; the other case recovered. In two of the cases the joint was very little injured, and anchylosis followed, and in the remaining two cases death took place.

Fractures of the bones of the leg. — Fractures of the bones of the leg are not near so serious accidents as might be imagined on superficial examination, and primary amputation is only called for when there is extensive destruction of the soft parts with injury to the principal vessels. I have notes of nineteen cases of this accident before me, and these were all severe cases, which required much care. In six cases resection of part of the tibia was performed, and five of these made a good recovery, only one dying from dysentery and not from the operation. In one case amputation was performed at the upper third, for extensive destruction of the soft parts, with much splintering of the bone; but death followed on the second day, the patient's strength not being able to withstand the shock of the operation. The remaining twelve cases were treated with much care. Their wounds were dressed daily, all pus being removed by means of carbolic acid lotion, abscesses were carefully watched and opened, Clyne's splints were well padded and carefully applied, all pieces of necrosed bones were removed, and good food, tonics and stimulants administered in some instances. In two of these cases diarrhœa, and in one dysentery, caused death.

Bullet wounds involving ankle-joint, tarsal bones, &c. — Bullet wounds, involving the ankle-joint, tarsal bones, and base of the metatarsal bones, are all conveniently put in the same class, for in most cases an accident to one of these parts involves one or all of the remaining articulations. Excision of the ankle-joint is not looked on with much favour by most military surgeons, and amputation should not be performed unless much destruction of the bones has been produced. I have been led to believe in the expectant treatment in these accidents from watching a number of cases in our hospital at Adrianople which were considered proper cases for amputation, but the patients had refused to submit to the operation; in those cases we removed all dead bones as they became necrosed, removed all sloughs, gave the pus a free exit, in most cases kept the foot in a hot-water bath for a few hours daily, and surrounded the whole foot with carbolised tow, gave the patients plenty of food, and, if necessary, stimulants. Under this treatment, although the amount of suppuration was very great, and exercised a very debilitating influence on the health of the patient, the recoveries which in most cases took place were satisfactory in the extreme, the patient being able to walk out of hospital with a very fair foot. I have notes of 48 cases of these accidents, and nine of these ended in death; we excised one or more of the tarsal bones in eleven cases on account of necrosis, and in one instance Chopart's operation was performed with success. We

Injuries to toes. — treated five cases of injuries to the toes, and in every case one or more toes had to be removed; in no case did death follow. Flesh wounds of the lower extremities are of very frequent occurrence; both legs are injured in a good many instances. I have seen cases where the bullet passed through the posterior part of both thighs without injuring any important structure; these injuries require much care in their treatment; all foreign bodies should be carefully removed; the wound should be dressed with lint saturated in the compound tincture of benzoin, or, what is better, carbolised tow; perfect rest should be insured if possible. When pus has formed, a free exit should be allowed to it ; for, if not, it will be sure to burrow between the muscles of the calf or thigh and put the life of the patient in extreme danger; this was brought very plainly before me by watching a few cases that were admitted into hospital with the whole muscles of the thigh, from the knee to the hip, forming one large abscess ; in these cases many incisions had to be made into the abscess in order to insure the whole of the pus an exit. The abscesses were syringed out daily with carbolic acid lotion ; good food, tonics, and stimulants were freely administered, but in most of these cases a fatal termination followed ; 80 cases were treated in hospitals with a mortality of twelve ; the cause of death in most cases was extensive suppuration, with diarrhœa, dysentery, or pyæmia. *Dr. McIvor's report.*

Gunshot injuries to the skull are most serious and most unsatisfactory in their termination. Unfortunately few of these accidents were admitted into hospital, although I never failed to search for such injuries on the arrival of wounded, and the fact of so few cases reaching us shows very plainly that death soon followed the injuries in most of these accidents. Simple injuries to the scalp are not of serious consequence, and five cases treated ended in recovery, with quiet and simple dressing. In three cases where the external plate of the cranial bones was alone injured, recovery followed, although caries of part of the bones followed, with much suppuration beneath the scalp. In three cases of compound fractures of the skull in which the internal plate was much splintered, and in one of these cases the membranes torn, death followed in two from inflammation of the brain and its membranes, the third patient recovering. *Gunshot injuries to skull.*

Bullet wounds of the face are frequently followed by erysipelas and both primary and secondary hæmorrhage ; much destruction of the soft parts is apt to be produced by the bullet, which often requires some plastic operation to relieve deformity. Ten of these accidents were treated, and all ended in recovery ; in three cases the lower jaw was fractured, and in two instances part of the upper jaw was removed by the bullet. In these cases all loose spiculæ of bone should be removed, and the mouth syringed out daily, the lower jaw being kept in position by a gutta-percha splint carefully moulded to the chin. *Bullet wounds of the face.*

When bullets pass through the neck some important structure is involved in almost every instance. Death frequently is produced instantaneously from wounds of the carotid artery or internal jugular vein. Five cases were treated, in which the bullet had passed through the neck ; in one instance it had injured part of the brachial plexus at its origin, causing partial paralysis of the arm ; in another the bullet had injured the spinal cord, causing partial paralysis of half of the body ; in two cases the trachea was injured, and in one of these the air passed freely through the wound. This patient recovered completely ; only a slight bronchitis complicated the wound until it had completely healed, when several abscesses formed in the cellular tissue of the neck, causing much trouble. *Of the neck.*

Wounds of the chest are best divided into those in which the chest wall is penetrated and those in which it is not so. I have notes of four cases in which the contents of chest were injured, and three of these ended in death from the effects of pneumonia or pleuritis ; in one instance the patient was discharged from hospital after a length of time in a very weak state ; in this case a suppurative pleuritis had discharged for a long time. Ten cases of non-penetrating wounds of the chest were treated, and in all recovery followed. *Of the chest.*

Penetrating wounds of the abdomen were rarely admitted into hospital. In one case the bullet had passed through the bladder, the bullet entering one groin and passing out of the opposite. Urine was freely discharged from the wound, and a catheter was introduced, and the remainder of the urine drawn off daily, but death from peritonitis followed. In four cases of non-penetrating wounds of the abdomen which were treated by us, recovery followed without any serious complication. *Of the abdomen.*

I shall now offer a few remarks on the treatment of wounds produced by bullets and fragments of shell, giving my experience of the value of the different dressings used by us during the war ; and let me urge that all foreign bodies should be carefully removed as soon after the injury is received as possible; for the presence of a bullet, part of the soldier's dress, a button, piece of shell, small stones, or loose spiculæ of bone, will keep up an amount of irritation which will act very injuriously on the progress of the case. It can be very easily imagined how injurious it would be to have a foreign body lodged between the fragments of a broken bone ; yet in one instance a patient was admitted into one of my wards with a fractured femur of two months' duration ; and as no union had taken place, I very carefully examined the wound, when, to my surprise, I removed part of a brass button from between the broken ends of the bone. Having cleared the wound of all foreign bodies, a good stream of carbolic acid lotion should be directed into it, when the force of the current will remove small particles of sand, clots, &c. Should the wound not be large enough to admit a careful examination, it should be moderately enlarged by *Treatment of wounds by bullets and fragments of shell.*

Dr. McIvor's report.	an incision, taking care to avoid any large vessel. If hæmorrhage is going on, it need not excite fear, unless the principal vessel be injured; danger is avoided by position, syringing out the wound with a cold lotion, and if this fail, plugging it with lint saturated in the compound tincture of benzoin. If a large vessel, such as the brachial, be injured, an incision should be made down to it, and both ends of the vessel ligatured; or, if there be much destruction of the soft parts, with the bone splintered extensively, amputation should be performed. Some surgeons prefer amputation in all cases where the principal vessel of the limb is injured. If a large joint is pierced by a bullet, amputation or excision should be decided on, according to the merits of each case, and performed at once, as delay is followed by bad results. I may state that, in general, excision of the joints of the upper extremities is followed by better results than excision of the lower extremities; but I believe that this is caused by the greater difficulty of removing patients with accidents to their lower extremities without causing much disturbance of the parts than in the case of the upper extremities. Primary excision is much better than secondary in all joints; but secondary excision of the joints of the lower extremities should never be attempted. The
Dressings.	dressing which should be applied to gun-shot wounds is of primary importance in most cases; lint wet in carbolic acid lotion, Condy's fluid, spirit lotion, or chloride of zinc lotion, is applied. These dressings soothe an inflamed wound, but I consider them far inferior to a dressing of good carbolised tow kept in position by a few rolls of a bandage. In most cases of primary wounds, whether gun-shot or otherwise, in which I have only used this as a dressing, no suppuration followed; and in those instances in which suppuration occurred, its quantity was small when compared with those in which wet dressings were used. I have also been very favourably impressed with this dressing in those cases of severe suppurating wounds which we received into hospital from the front. Many of these cases were not dressed for days; and, if dressed, were all dressed with wet dressings; large quantities of pus were being secreted daily, and most of the wounds had as unhealthy an appearance as can well be imagined. Nevertheless, these wounds soon ceased to secrete so much pus; healthy granulations soon sprang up; the patients' health consequently improved, and all this was due to the simple dressing of carbolised tow; for in these cases in which we used wet dressings no such marked improvement was noticed. No doubt the power which the tow has of absorbing the pus as it is secreted, and leaving the young granulations unbathed in a decomposing fluid, its stimulating powers, its deodorising and disinfecting
Abscesses.	properties add much to its usefulness. All abscesses should be opened at once, for by so doing all burrowing is prevented; and, although it may seem of little consequence if an abscess should be neglected, nevertheless I have seen the neglect of so doing cost the patient his life. As I have said, it is of the utmost importance that all bullets should be removed. I believe it is also very necessary that the proper precautions should be taken when so doing, as many limbs have been lost by the careless use of bullet forceps. No surgeon should ever introduce a forceps into a wound until he has discovered the exact seat of the bullet, and even then caution is necessary in order not to catch hold of any important vessel or nerve, or, what is often done, pull at a broken bone. The choice of forceps for extracting balls is also a difficult matter, as, unfortunately, not a really good pair is in existence. I could always extract bullets better with an ordinary pair of dressing forceps than with any of the forceps which I had. Their strength and shortness render them valuable, as you always have them under control; but where bullets were seated deeply, I found Weiss' forceps with overlapping long claw points to be useful in many instances.

Pomeroy, Tyrone, *January* 2, 1879.

Surgical Report of Roumelian Railway Transport, August 29, 1877, *to February* 5, 1878. By F. R. BARKER, ESQ., M.R.C.S.

I. SURGICAL.—SECTION A.

I. INJURIES TO HEAD.

α. *Numerical proportion.*—I shall estimate approximately for the whole period; they were about half per cent., but for the first two or three months quite five per cent.; this I attribute to the severe fighting at Skipka which occurred then, and from whence most of the men came. Mr. BARKER'S report. Injuries to head.

β. *Complications.*—The chief and almost only one was erysipelas, and it was not common.

γ. *Treatment.*—The part was covered with cotton wool, and perchloride of iron administered. Trephining never had recourse to, and only in one case were there any symptoms of compression, and these but slight.

δ. *Results.*—These cases bore transport very well, but this can be accounted for by their being selected from hospitals, and lapse of time since receipt of injury. In several cases where the jaw was fractured by a bullet, during the warm weather the sufferers were greatly troubled by maggots, and these I was only able to destroy by means of a solution of carbolic acid 1 in 100. This afforded great relief and was effectual. Carbolic acid for maggots in wounds.

Case I.—Case of shell injury of lower jaw. Omar Mahomet, private soldier of 3rd Regt. Tira Battalion. A native of Anatolia. Wounded at the first attack on Plevna. Had been wounded 34 days when he came under my care. A fragment of shell, which had burst near him, carried away the whole of the body of the inferior maxilla as far as the angle on the left side, and the lower part of the ramus in addition on the right side; carrying away the soft structures as well as leaving a gap or wound, which was bound above by the upper jaw and lip, below by the hyoid bone, and on either side the soft structures of the cheek beyond the angle, the edges being somewhat uneven. The tip and about an inch of the right side of the tongue was carried away. Could speak, though not distinctly, but could make himself understood. He states that it bled very much at the time, but not since; he suffers from the toothache in upper jaw, also in wisdom tooth, which is left on left side with part of angle of jaw; looks well; states that he has lost flesh, and suffers from hunger; his diet consisted of milk and beef-tea, but has also taken meat. Does not suffer much from salivation; no pain about part. Flow of saliva increased after food; great amount of induration about hyoid bone. Tried to bring parts together; would be a good subject for a plastic operation to restore the floor of his mouth. Can smoke a cigarette when his dressings are on. On arriving at Constantinople he was sent to Haidar Pacha Hospital (Florence Nightingale's) at Scutari, where I heard of him three weeks after as doing well. Case of shell injury of lower jaw

Case II.—Ali Mustapha, 2nd Regt. Beyroot Sandjak. Bullet struck him on right temple and passed round skull, passing out at occipital protuberance; temporal artery not wounded; sinus formed in track of bullet in which suppuration occurred; linseed meal poultices applied. Erysipelas occurred, arrested by iron treatment. I removed a sequestrum of frontal bone. Bullet wound of temple.

The first of these cases shows how a vital part may be mutilated and the man recover. The second how a direct shot, though coming with great force, may be diverted from its course by a slight obstacle; the force must have been great, otherwise it would not have passed out, owing to the elasticity of the structures of the scalp.

Case III.—A man wounded at Skipka three days previously was handed over to my care at Philippopolis; the bullet struck him on the cheek, and fracturing the ramus of the jaw just below the condyle, part of which was carried away, together with a part of the petrous portion of the temporal bone, exposing and laying open the middle ear, the small bones of which were visible; in addition it carried away a portion of the helix and the lobe of the external ear. The man was mad with pain, and in his movement had a tendency to tumble towards the wounded side. I should not have taken him had not all the hospitals been full. I put him under the influence of morphia by means of hypodermic injections, and kept him so best part of the journey to Adrianople, where he died in great agony shortly after our arrival. In this case there was hæmorrhage from the internal maxillary artery, and the carotid could be seen pulsating in the wound. He was sensible, but maddened by pain. Bullet wound of jaw.

II. INJURIES TO CHEST.

Mr. Barker's report.

Injuries to chest.

Non-penetrating wounds of chest.

a. *Proportion of Cases.*—These at one time were very numerous, and were usually found in cases where the men had fought behind earthworks, were chiefly among the infantry, and in several cases were accompanied by wounds of the right hand.

β. *Contusions.*—I do not remember to have seen any cases.

γ. *Non-penetrating wounds.*—These mostly occurred in the upper and outer part of chest, and were in very many cases complicated with wounds of shoulder-joint or fracture of clavicle or scapula, more especially the coracoid process. Sometimes the chief force of the ball was met by the elasticity of the ribs, which in some cases were fractured, whilst in others the ball passed round the parietes of the thorax, and was often extracted at the back beside the spines of the dorsal vertebræ.

δ. *Complications.*—In penetrating wounds the chief complication was emphysema. This was in most cases accompanied by pneumonia and pleurisy. In a good number of cases, local emphysema was also present, but in very few cases did I observe general emphysema. I observed hæmoptysis in some cases.

ε. *Treatment.* I.—In non-penetrating wounds of cavities, the bullet was extracted when discoverable, and any loose spiculæ of bone removed; the wound dressed with charpie or water dressing, or else marine lint; and in cases of wound of shoulder-joint, the arm fixed by splint and Esmarch's triangular bandages, which were found to be of great service.

Penetrating wounds of chest.

II. *Penetrating wounds.*—These were mostly treated on the expectant plan, the wound being covered with marine lint, which being a very good absorbent, took up the pus; this dressing required frequent repetition. In many cases I also sprinkled the lint with carbolic acid. Marine lint acted better than charpie, which in most cases had a tendency to hermetically seal the wound. In several cases in which I tried hermetic sealing I found it did not answer, owing to the pent-up secretion causing symptoms of pyrexia; an objection to using the marine lint in three cases was the amount of local irritation it was apt to cause round the edges of the wound, though this was more than counterbalanced by its absorbent and antiseptic properties. In no case was venesection had recourse to by me.

Results.—Non-penetrating wounds bore transport remarkably well, and some were doing well in cases of injury to shoulder-joint where operations had been performed. Amongst the penetrating wounds the results were not so satisfactory, as the motion of the train caused great discomfort, though to this there were exceptions. I have been told that penetrating wounds of chest seldom recovered, but I saw one or two cases which seemed on a fair way towards recovery.

Wound in left triceps.

Case I.—A man was wounded through the upper part of his left triceps, and the ball had passed out, but on examination when he was stripped we discovered a slight curvature of about the fourth or fifth dorsal vertebra to the right, and on the left of this a soft fluctuating tumour, with no inflammatory symptoms, which suggested a chronic abscess from caries of the vertebra; but on close inspection it was found that the ball in passing out from the arm had entered the posterior boundary of the axilla at its junction with the internal, and on following up this track, I thought I could discern a groove running in the direction of the fluctuating tumour. I made an incision into the tumour, letting out pus and extracting the bullet and a large piece of the soldier's jacket; the wound healed, carbolic dressing being used.

In front left chest.

Case II.—A man wounded in the front left chest; the ball entering opposite the second rib passed under the clavicle, which it fractured, but did not injure either the subclavian artery or vein or any of the nerves of the brachial plexus, nor were there any symptoms to lead us to suppose that the pleura had been opened. I discovered and extracted the bullet at the back of the neck about an inch and a half below the external occipital protuberance.

In fifth and ninth ribs.

Case III.—A man struck by a portion of shell had a piece of his fifth and sixth ribs taken away, leaving an aperture about two inches in diameter. The heart could be seen pulsating, but the pericardium was not opened, though the pleura was. I did not discover his case till *en route*. He seemed to bear the journey fairly well considering.

Result not stated.

III. INJURIES TO ABDOMEN.

α. *Proportion of Cases.*—These were by no means numerous, and as a rule slight.   Mr. BARKER'S report.
β. *Contusions.*
γ. *Non-penetrating.*—These were usually grazes with spent bullets, and in several cases the bullet entered the skin, and from the opposition of the recti muscles was deflected round the abdominal walls.   Injuries to abdomen.
δ. *Penetrating.*—I can only remember one case brought under my notice in which the ball had entered the abdominal cavity, and must have become encapsuled, as it caused no local or constitutional symptoms.
ε. *Treatment.*—Non-penetrating, dressed with carbolised tow, or carbolic dressing.

IV. INJURIES TO UPPER EXTREMITY.

α. *Flesh wounds* were very numerous, many being caused by pieces of shell.
β. *Compound Fractures.*—Conspicuous amongst these were fractures just below the shoulder-joint. In one case I amputated, but as a rule I removed any spiculæ and put the arm on splints, owing to difficulty of performing amputation *en route* and having no colleague.   Injuries to upper extremity.
γ. *Treatment.*—Conservatism seemed to be the general practice amongst Turkish surgeons, but with European surgeons amputation was more frequent than excision, if I may judge from the cases that came under my care. No cases of excision that came under my notice seemed to do badly.
δ. *Amputation.*—I amputated in a case of compound fracture of the humerus, of standing—man being worn with suppuration—forming the flaps from wound, which was irregular. The case did well. In another case where there was a wound of the radial artery above wrist, with great œdema of arm as high as elbow, with incipient gangrene of hand, I removed the arm above the elbow by the circular method. I employed Esmarch's tourniquet. The man had lost a good deal of blood. Though the operation was performed under most disadvantageous circumstances, at a railway station, on a trolly beside the line as an amputating table, and myself the only person present who had seen an amputation before, yet with the aid of stimulants, beef-tea and eggs continually administered, the man was able to be conveyed to Constantinople, where he eventually recovered. Amputations with circular division of the muscles as a rule answered best, flaps seeming to take longer to heal. I usually dressed fresh wounds with lint soaked in carbolic acid solution; but for chronic wounds, and where there was much discharge of pus, the marine lint answered very well indeed. Ligature was almost universally resorted to, but several cases of fatal secondary hæmorrhage which came under my notice, I attributed to the Turkish surgeons having tied everything unsafe, in no case separating the artery from its vein. In no case that I saw did an amputation appear to heal by first intention, owing I suppose to the bad state of health of the patients. Finger cases were, I should say, approximately five per cent.; quite as frequently on the right hand as the left. I believe this great percentage to be due to fighting behind earthworks, where the hands would be exposed whilst firing, those struck on the head dying where they fell. In only one case do I remember finding a case which I believed, from the marks of powder and position, was self-inflicted.   Amputation.   Esmarch's tourniquet.

Results.—I was struck by the amount of pain caused by finger injuries, the men—often men who had hardly complained whilst a limb was amputated—if a phalanx of a finger only were removed, complaining bitterly; and even amongst those who had the misfortune to have suffered both these accidents, they often complained more of the tops of their fingers. I am unable to account for this.   Finger injuries.

V. INJURIES TO LOWER EXTREMITY.

α. *Flesh wounds.*—These were not so numerous as those of the upper extremity. This could doubtless be accounted for by the more severe cases having died off, either from hæmorrhage or from hectic, caused by the great drain on the system caused by the profuse suppuration which occurred in these cases as a rule. Most received their wounds below the knee; many through the calf of the leg. Above the knee the chief part of the wounds were either where bullets had   Injuries to lower extremity.

Mr. Barker's report.

grazed the skin or had not penetrated very deeply, also superficial lacerated shell wounds. In some rare cases the bullets had penetrated deeply, and were extracted at a great distance from where they entered, passing between the muscles, and in several cases in close proximity to the main artery, without wounding it. One had a good many cases where the bullet either penetrated the scrotum and passed out, or, penetrating through the hamstring muscles, was found embedded in it; and in two cases the bullet was extracted from the scrotum, which alone it had struck. These scrotal cases as a rule did well, and in no case was castration resorted to.

Compound fractures.

β. *Compound fractures*, except those where the tibia was fractured, bore transport badly; but they were very few.

λ. *Treatment.*—In no case did I amputate the limbs, but had numerous cases where it would have been advantageous to the patient; but with the difficulty of transport, and having no colleagues with me, I considered it better that they should be deferred till the patients were placed in hospitals. In the cases of wounds of the foot, I amputated toes or removed splinters of bones where easily removable. In cases of fracture the wire splints were very useful, and by their aid, with the strong Leslie's plaster, one was able to secure them fairly well. In old wounds I found the marine lint a very useful dressing, providing the wounds were not inflamed; but in fresh wounds it had a tendency to cause inflammation, and a tendency to erysipelas. In many cases charpie was used where there was not a great amount of suppuration, in which case one applied, as a rule, a thin layer of charpie, and over this a thick layer of marine lint. Carbolic acid was used in most dressings, and in many cases with a marvellous effect—wounds which came under one's care in a sloughy state taking on a healthy action very quickly.

Wire splints. Marine lint.

δ. *Amputation.*—In many of the cases where amputation had been performed, the flaps had sloughed, and the bone often protruded from the stump; but these were cases which had as a rule been under the care of Turkish surgeons. In several cases in which circular amputations had been performed (with circular through the muscles), the stumps either had healed or were doing well when they came under my charge. Most amputations were primary; but none, that I can remember, were above the knee.

Case I.—A bullet struck a man just behind the great trochanter on one side, passed through the nates, grazed the posterior surface of the scrotum, and then passed through the other buttock and departed. This man had to lie on his face, having as a complication a large bed-sore.

Case II.—A man was struck with a bullet in the anterior part of the thigh—about its centre in the middle third; the bullet was extracted just above the ankle, lying beside the tendon Achilles.

VI. INJURIES TO JOINTS.

Injuries to joints.

α. *Non-penetrating wounds.*—These were mostly found to be in connection with the shoulder and elbow joints.

β. *Penetrating wounds.*—The most frequent were those of the shoulder and wrist, also in the foot a good many; I can only recall one of the knee, and in that case the bullet struck the patella, and caused a longitudinal fracture. A Stafford House surgeon amputated. The joint was full of pus; and the man died the next day, having well-marked symptoms of pyæmia.

λ. *Complications.*—Paralysis of the limb below the part affected was of not unfrequent occurrence.

δ. *Treatment.*—In no case did I perform excision; but when spiculæ or sequestra of bone could be removed without danger of hæmorrhage, I removed them. In most cases the joints were secured as well as possible, allowing of as little motion as possible. Excision in some of the cases where it had been performed seemed to answer well, but in others there were not such good results.

VIII. INJURIES TO NERVES.

Injuries to nerves.

In many cases limbs were rendered quite useless from the nerves being wounded, but in many cases they might have been ameliorated with proper attention, such as splints, &c. Also many joints became completely anchylosed from want of care.

IX. COMPLICATIONS IN GUNSHOT INJURIES.—INORDINATE INFLAMMATION.

When of a sthenic type I usually administered calomel in the form of blue pill, and if requisite scarified the surface with a lancet, applying cold water dressing. If the part were very painful, I gave Tr. opii, ℞ xxx, in addition to blue pill. In the asthenic type I gave sulphate of quinine in large doses, and brandy.

Mr. BARKER'S report.

Complications in gunshot injuries.

Gangrene (hospital).—An attack broke out in a mosque used as a hospital at Philippopolis, and began to spread very quickly; it was stopped very quickly by placing the patients under canvas, some of whom recovered I believe. In several cases of gangrene of the feet which I had under me it could not be traced to any injury of the main artery of the part, but I think it was produced by the state to which the patients had been brought by the exposure to cold and hunger. It was mostly of the dry description. In these cases I covered over the part with marine lint, and gave Tr. opii where there was severe pain. I had not the cases long enough under my care to see the results. In many cases the gangrene was due to cold, and often then a sequence of frost-bite. This was in nearly every case in the feet. .

Gangrene.

Pyæmia.—Of this I saw very little, and treated it with quinine and brandy. I do not remember having any cases of tetanus under my care, but saw several at our hospital at Philippopolis. Erysipelas was not of frequent occurrence, and when present I treated it with cotton wool locally, and purgatives when admissible.

Pyæmia.

Frost-bite was of frequent occurrence amongst the men in the months of December 1877 and January 1878, most of whom came from Plevna and Kamarli. Some of these were in a frightful state, their feet being gangrenous almost half way up the shin, the feet in many cases having wholly or in part dropped off; either one or both. I cannot account for only the feet being frost-bitten, as they were as a rule better protected than the hands and face, by shoes made of cow's-hide, and inside this sackcloth bound round the leg. I only saw two cases of frost-bite of hands, and these were only incipient; I was able to restore circulation in them by friction with snow. I never saw a case where the frost attacked the head except in my own case, where my nose was touched. I believe there may be some explanation of it in the Turks never taking alcohol.

Frost-bite.

SECTION B.

I could not say what proportion sword wounds formed, but they were more numerous towards the latter part, after the hand-to-hand fighting. The sabre cuts were mostly on the scalp and face, and seemed to do very well, also cuts on the hands. Many of the cases of cuts on the limbs suffered from want of previous attention, in some cases the use of the part being lost; as regards healing, they usually did so very quickly.

Sword wounds.

Treatment the same as ordinary wounds.

In one case a man received six gashes from his neck to half way down his back from a Russian cavalry soldier, but he recovered. Some of the gashes were quite six inches in length, and some of the spines of the vertebræ were partially chopped off.

Bayonet wounds were not so numerous, and mostly in the fleshy parts of the limbs, the worst having died I suppose before reaching me. In one case a man had had a bayonet right through his chest on the right side, and the Russian soldier had to place his foot against the Turk's chest and give three wrenches before he could get it out; and yet the man recovered, and I believe was afterwards raised to the rank of an officer.

Bayonet wounds.

II. MEDICAL.—SECTION C.

Most of the medical cases which came under my notice were either in the mosques of St. Sofia and Sultan Achmet, or at the Stafford House hospital at Gallipoli. The greater part of the sick transported by train were cases of the fever of the country or dysentery.

Acute Rheumatism.—This complaint was rare, and in no case do I remember finding heart complications. As our store of drugs was extremely limited, we gave sulphate of quinine and bicarbonate of potash, the former reducing the temperature well.

Acu rheumatism.

Mr. BARKER'S report.

Pneumonia. Diarrhœa.

Pneumonia.—These cases, though not of very frequent occurrence, were as a rule of a low type, and we followed a stimulating line of treatment as a rule. Carbonate of ammonia and quinine; brandy.

Diarrhœa.—This, as a rule, was a complication, if not a symptom, of all the cases under our charge, and often of a very intractable sort, medicines seeming to have no effect, but diet did wonders in some cases; but the subjects in whom it occurred were, as a rule, in a very bad state of health, broken down with fatigue and want of food, and having had to walk a distance of seven miles from the Lines of Boulair, in a scorching sun. The medicines which in some cases did good were Dover's powder and Tr. opii, but chlorodyne was as a rule useless.

Dysentery.

Dysentery.—This was of very frequent occurrence, and like diarrhœa, it was best treated by diet, though ipecac. in several cases, when the strength was not too much exhausted, answered very well.

Cholera.

Cholera.—Two cases which died very suddenly somewhat resembled cholera in their symptoms, but did not live long enough to allow of a diagnosis. The stools certainly were like rice water, and patients died in a state of collapse.

Ague.

Ague.—Many cases occurred of an intermittent type; some of these quinine would not touch, as a rule it was quotidien, but in other cases of a tertian type; it seemed to answer well, and had most effect when taken whilst the sweating stage lasted. Several cases were of decided remittent type, and these did badly. The miasma was propagated by the men having to obtain most of their water from a well at the lines which was situated in a swampy part, and the ground was impregnated with vegetable matter in a decayed state, and the weather at the time was very warm, there having been heavy rains some time before.

Smallpox.

Smallpox.—We had three cases sent to our hospital, but as soon as diagnosed, we had them transferred to the hospital specially set apart for it, and had all articles worn by the patient thoroughly disinfected. In the Mosque of St. Sofia we had to search for the children—who were the victims for the most part, adults seeming to be exempt—under bedding, or amongst their parents' clothes, and then order zaptiehs (policemen) to see them removed. Parents on seeing us approach would hurry out of the mosque by some side door to avoid their children being sent to the hospital, and would roam about the streets till we had finished our visit; and it was only by combining in ourselves the function of distributing soup tickets and prosecuting our search that we were enabled to capture the truants. Most of the cases were of the confluent type, very bad indeed. The smallpox hospital was under the charge of the International Committee, but owing to mismanagement, what with patients getting no food, or not being properly attended to, it was impossible even by force to keep the patients in hospital; hence the quarantine was only nominal. We obtained a little vaccine, and vaccinated as many as we could with it, and they were very glad to be done, there often being quite a squabble as to who should be vaccinated next.

Typhus.

Typhus.—Of this we had a good number of cases, but not in all was the rash well marked. In three cases there was inflammation, with suppuration in one of the parotid glands; and in two of the cases which lay in adjoining beds, the man who first had it on his right side, and the second who had it, who lay to the right of the former, had it on his left side. One of these cases I know died. I do not know if these cases are sufficient to prove the contagiousness of the affection of the parotid gland in typhus. Diffusible stimulants and diet played a great part in the treatment, the typhus being of a low kind.

Typhoid.

Typhoid.—This was rather common, but the presence of the rash was rare; whether it was due to the patients' skins being so dark or not, I do not remember seeing it in more than one or two cases, and one could consequently only diagnose by the other symptoms, most of which, as a rule, were present. The treatment was expectant, with rest and careful nourishment.

SECTION D.

Railway transport of wounded.

With regard to the railway transport of wounded. It seems to me that it is necessary to have free communication between each carriage, without having to pass from carriage to carriage as the train is in motion; that the best kind of communication is the Pullman description; that the roofs of the carriages might be fitted up for transporting wounded outside in summer; that a certain number of carriages should be fitted up with beds which should not rock with the train—these for worst cases, such as fractures and amputations—but that for the rest, mattresses placed on the floor are the best modes of conveyance; that each carriage should possess a w.c., and that one carriage fitted with dressings, &c., should be attached to the train; that there be a dresser to each 60 patients; that the cooking for the sick be done on board the engine if possible, or that food be provided at various places along the route; no smoking allowed inside the carriages; that the train be supplied with efficient filters for filtering all the water for the patients; that each carriage be well able to be ventilated; that there be a male attendant to each carriage to see after the immediate wants of the patients.

Mr. BARKER'S report.

[NOTE.—These remarks of Mr. Barker are valuable, but it was utterly impossible in Turkey to establish a system of free communication between the carriages, and the other conveniences mentioned, as the carriages in which the wounded were transported were, with few exceptions, the common luggage vans and cattle trucks, which had been used to send troops or provisions to the front, and were filled with the sick and wounded on their return journey. The best that could be done was to make these as comfortable as possible by laying down mattresses or loose hay.

The Red Crescent train consisted of luggage vans, fitted up with slung stretchers on the system proposed by Baron Mundy. One van was fitted up as a dispensary, and another as a kitchen, with cooking apparatus for providing dinners for 300 men. It also included one passenger carriage for the accommodation of the staff, and a few luggage vans fitted up with rough divans stuffed with hay, for the use of patients not seriously ill.

Mr. Barker had at his disposal four luggage vans fitted up by the railway company with wooden beds, and a fifth wagon fitted up by the S. H. Committee as a dispensary. These were attached under Mr. Barker's charge to the trains full of wounded returning to the rear.—V.B.K.]

Two interesting Cases of Gunshot or Shell Wounds. By J. WELLER, ESQ., M.R.C.S.

A young Arab soldier at Kesanlik had a bullet wound in the back, about two inches from the spine on the right side; the wound was fast healing, and had been inflicted eight days previously. A probe was passed, when it was found that the bullet had taken a circuitous course. An examination of the whole chest was then made, and a hard substance detected almost in the middle line of the sternum, about the junction of the gladiolus and ensiform appendix. An incision was made about one inch and a half in length, when the ball readily escaped. The man made a good and speedy recovery. The ball was a small round revolver bullet about half an ounce in weight. This is the only case I have seen of a bullet travelling round the ribs and intercostal muscles. The explanation given by the patient was that his back was turned to the enemy when in the act of loading his rifle, and that he was shot by a Bulgarian with a revolver. Beyond strapping and the application of carbolic solution no further treatment was required.

Mr. WELLER'S report.

Bullet wounds in the back.

An Arab soldier, middle-aged, had received a wound in the back of the middle third of thigh from the bursting of a shell. He had suffered intense pain, the wound was granulating, was about four inches in length and an inch and a half in breadth, of a singular crescent shape. It had been dressed by a Turkish surgeon, and the case had not attracted much attention; having had a similar case with Dr. Wood at Adrianople I examined him carefully. The leg was drawn up and very cold. The man exhibited well-marked Risus sardonicus, but was able to move his jaw perfectly. I passed a probe, but could not find anything for some time; when it suddenly entered a small sinus; an escape of pus followed, and the probe touched something hard. I cut down upon the foreign body, and with some difficulty removed a piece of shell exactly corresponding to the external wound in shape. On introducing the finger I could distinctly feel the sciatic nerve stretched as tight as a harp string. I syringed with a weak solution of carbolic acid, and treated him for tetanus. The next day the leg was better, but the jaw was fixed. However the man expressed himself as 'greatly pleased.'' He had a severe rigor in the afternoon. I then lost sight of the case, to my great disappointment, as I was ordered to convey wounded to Philippopolis. On my return I was informed that the man was able to walk, and that all signs of tetanus had disappeared. I did not, however, see him again.   JOHN WELLER.

In thigh.

On Certain Forms of Malarial Poisoning met with in Turkey, and their local effects on wounds as observed in the Turco-Russian Campaign (1877-78). By A. SYMONS ECCLES, M.R.C.S.E., late Imperial Ottoman Medical Service, and late Chief Surgeon, Stafford House Ambulances at Philippopolis, Salonica, and Gallipoli.

Mr. ECCLES' report.

Malarial poisoning.

At the latter end of August, 1876, I found myself in charge of a battalion of Turkish Redifs in the province of Thessaly, which afforded me opportunities of observing the different forms of malarial poisoning at greater leisure than if I had been appointed immediately to the seat of war in Servia, as some of my more fortunate comrades in the Ottoman medical service.

The men who came under my care during the first three months spent in the city of Larissa were all natives of the province, inhabitants of the villages or hamlets, scattered about in the great plain extending from the slopes of Olympus, Ossa, and Pelion, on the one hand, to the range of mountains forming the frontier of Greece on the other. The hospitals, both of my own regiment and of the other troops in the place, were crowded with cases of intermittent fever, while a large number of out-patients suffering from the milder forms of ague presented themselves every morning; indeed so great was the proportion of malarial fevers over diseases of other nature existing among the soldiery that the first sentence I learnt in the Turkish language was 'Sitmar var' (Anglice, 'I have the fever'), and I was speedily introduced to a class of disease fortunately almost unknown in this country.

The milder cases were for the most part of the tertian type, a smaller number being quotidiens, while those which were admitted into hospital partook of remittent characters, or rather were more appropriately named by my Turkish colleagues stationed in the town *fièvres pernicieuses*, whose existence and differentiation from the bilious remittent, better known to British medical officers, our French brethren recognise more clearly than ourselves. A subsequent intimate acquaintance with the mode of life, habitat, and language of the men under my care enabled me to deduce the following facts bearing on the nature and production of malaria.

It is allowed that malaria may be produced and exist in localities which are not swampy in their nature nor necessarily infected with the miasma arising from vegetable decay, although popular error has always associated the existence of organic putrefaction with the production of malarial poisoning. Striking proofs of ague, attacking subjects who had not been placed under the conditions for imbibing the exhalations from decaying vegetable matter, were noticed; and especially in the case of a battalion of Arabs, who, antecedent to their arrival in Thessaly, had inhabited a region in Syria, accurately described to me as a desert, with no vegetation, except at great intervals; yet the large majority of these men presented all the characteristics of persons who had suffered from ague; the sallow complexions, yellowish sclerotics, wrinkled skin, unnaturally protuberant abdomens, distinctly large spleens, and general look of premature old age, with that peculiar dulness of mental faculties which, I believe, is the outcome of repeated attacks of ague.

Ague.

Yet, while recognising the fact that malaria does exist, and is produced apart from vegetable putrefaction or a swampy soil, one cannot disguise from oneself the very noticeable influence which the peculiar conditions of atmosphere, associated with low-lying marshy districts in high temperatures, exercise over the type of ague produced within such an area, and from personal observations made on the malarial poisoning produced in localities with different soils and atmospheric conditions, I am inclined to believe that the type will vary with the dampness of the soil and the stagnation of the atmosphere. In the plain of Larissa, where the soil is dry and under cultivation, but subject to heavy rains at certain seasons of the year, followed by great solar heat, it will be found that the fever produced is generally of a comparatively mild type, probably quotidien, while 'pernicious fever' or 'remittent' will not occur except as an intensification of the ordinary intermittent from which the patient was previously suffering, and as a result of some excess or of want of proper care, or total neglect to arrest the course of the disease; whereas when a patient not predisposed to ague by a previous attack has been exposed to the effects of malaria arising in a damp marshy locality or in alluvial soils, such as the banks of a river subject to overflow, he will suffer from a more severe form of the disease than if he had been attacked in a cooler and drier region; indeed I have seen a large number of cases of remittent fever occurring *de novo* in a swampy locality where oppressively warm days are followed by cold damp nights, while on the higher grounds and on the plains at a distance from any apparent miasm, the disease has invariably been, in the first instance, mild and beneficent in nature.   *Mr.* Eccles' report.

Towards the end of the autumn of 1876 the battalion to which I was attached was recruited up to full strength, and marched from Larissa to Tricalla—the march was of three days' and two nights' duration through a plain smaller than that of Larissa, hemmed in on all sides by mountains and hills, and traversed by two large rivers which were nearly dry in the summer, but became swollen and overflowed the banks in winter and spring, receiving numberless small tributaries whose banks and beds in autumn were covered with luxurious vegetation; about the centre of the plain is a large tract of marsh rich in vegetable and animal life, and intersected by numerous small sluggish streams; the atmosphere of this locality in late summer and autumn is peculiarly stagnant and the heat very oppressive.   Conditions favourable to malarial poisoning.

Several times during a day's march the men were obliged to ford the shallow rivers, and were constantly slaking their thirst at the various muddy pools along the line of march; but, with the exception of the first night, none were exposed to the night dews; yet before our destination was reached I had three men suffering from pernicious fever, and on our arrival in Tricalla the hospital of 50 beds was immediately filled with cases of malarial poisoning occurring so suddenly that at first they were mistaken for cases of insolation. Six of these terminated fatally before the first exacerbation had ceased; for them the treatment adopted had been that recommended for sunstroke, and I think those of my readers who have met with cases of heat apoplexy and remittent will not hold me greatly blameworthy in having at first failed to differentiate insolation from certain forms of malarial poisoning. The men were brought to me during the night and day following our arrival in quarters at Tricalla, and from notes taken at the time I find that the symptoms in the first 24 hours differed but little in the different cases, the general conditions being the same. The countenance was livid, headache with vertigo was sometimes complained of; while in other cases the patient was comatose, great heat and dryness of the skin, with a temperature ranging from 102° F. to 106° F., a full hard pulse and dry cracked tongue (the pulse reaching 120 at times) were invariable symptoms, while vomiting, dyspnœa, and a tumultuous action of the heart were frequent accompaniments. Those cases which terminated fatally sank very rapidly, the patients never recovering from the state of stupor, into which four of them had fallen before they reached the hospital, the other two cases being distinguished by convulsions.

The treatment employed in the first ten cases, six of which proved fatal, was the following:—   Treatment. With the exception of one in which venesection was practised against my better judgment, but which, contrary to my expectations, did not prove fatal, the patients were placed in a cool ward, with a verandah running round two sides, and were exposed to a current of cool air. The head was shaved, cold affusion supplied, and iced water administered internally. Blisters or mustard leaves were used as counter irritants and derivatives on the nape of the neck and calves, and the body was divested of all superfluous clothing. In those cases in which depression was most marked I administered ammonia.

Six deaths, occurring within thirty-six hours of our arrival in Tricalla, produced great consternation among the troops; and the men of our battalion, with the readiness of Turks to believe in supernatural agency, ascribed the unwonted mortality to the influence of the Devil. Indeed, they loudly complained to their commanding officer that my hospital was *Shaitan ev* ('abode of the Evil One').

While watching at the bedside of one of my patients, I remarked the accession of a slight perspiration, which gradually increased and was attended by a remission of the graver symptoms; the temperature fell, the pulse became more soft and less frequent, and the patient regained consciousness, taking nourishment with apparent appetite.   Typical case

A warm bath was ordered, and immediately after it he fell asleep. My hopes were raised, and I looked upon his state as indicative of recovery; but two hours later my attention was called to a new feature in the case. On finding the bedside I found the sufferer in a state of rigor, the countenance was pallid and drawn, the whole surface of the body presenting the condition known as 'goose skin'; the pulse was frequent, thready, and irregular; the respirations were shallow and weak, the temperature sensibly decreased, and the extremities cold. A little urine was passed, but instead of being thick and high-coloured as in the early stage of the disease, it was now pale and watery; indeed the symptoms, though utterly opposed in character to those which had gone before, were sufficiently serious make us fear impending dissolution; but

Mr. Eccles' report.

before all the arrangements for applying artificial heat to the body were completed, I noticed a change in the symptoms; the shivering, which had been very violent, was subdued; the face became flushed, and in less time than I can write down these facts the patient had relapsed into the state which I have briefly described above as marking the early stage of the attack.

It was this case, the first in which I had the opportunity of seeing a remission of the symptoms, that led me to recognise the true nature of the disease; and I was afterwards able to confirm my suspicions that it was not due to exposure to great solar heat alone, but rather to a malarious condition of atmosphere, the ill effects of which were augmented by the excessive heat, bodily fatigue, and want of proper food and water, to which the men had been unavoidably subjected on the march from Larissa to Tricalla.

The treatment subsequently pursued in all cases of a like nature was attended with the happiest results, and I have had under my care some thousands of individuals suffering from the effects of malaria in different forms, and opportunities of trying various methods of treatment have been afforded. Salicin, bromide of potassium, arsenic, opium, chamomile, and oxide of zinc I have employed in the way recommended by those who have extolled their effects and asserted their efficacy; but I cannot recall one case in which I have seen decided improvement following the exhibition of any of these drugs, except where one or other of the salts of cinchona has been administered in addition. Of the *Eucalyptus globulus* I cannot speak, as I have never had the opportunity of employing it; but of the other remedies mentioned I have had but one experience, viz., that when used in cases of intermittent, they proved useful only in quelling the severity of certain symptoms, while *quinine* rarely failed to produce not only an amelioration, but a cessation of the disease. In the severer forms where the remission was slight, short, and sometimes barely noticeable, I did not hesitate to give large doses of quinine during the attacks, a practice attended by the best results.

Beneficial use of quinine.

General mode of treatment.

The plan of treatment adopted was generally the following, with such slight modifications as the symptoms demanded: An aperient, or in some cases an emetic, was given at first, followed two or three hours later by a full dose of the sulphate of quinine; as many as twenty grains at once have been given without any ill effect. If the stomach was too irritable to retain the first dose, I have repeated it, giving ice, and applying sinapisms to the epigastrium; and when these measures failed, the quinine was administered per rectum. Half a drachm of the sulphate with twenty minims of the Liquor opii sedativus, in two ounces of a weak mucilage of gum arabic, was found to be the most sure and convenient method of exhibiting the specific as an enema; and in very few cases did it fail to produce a decided abatement of the symptoms, while almost always the effect produced was the best that could be desired. If the first dose has failed to modify the symptoms decidedly, I have repeated it after three hours; indeed in some cases, almost despaired of, the patient has taken as much as forty grains of quinine in twelve hours before any effect was produced. In ordinary cases the first dose has been followed by ten grains every four hours; and if an intermission occurred, a dose of twenty grains of quinine with ten minims of the Liquor opii was given. As the patient's condition improved, the quantity of quinine was reduced and administered with Fowler's solution of arsenic in five-minim doses twice daily. During convalescence, the citrate of iron and quinine, or a combination of the mineral acids with one or other of the preparations of bark, was found useful. It is needless to say that measures were taken to avoid the exposure of the patient to any malarious influence as far as possible; and in all cases where it was expedient, change of air was ordered.

The good physique and great powers of endurance of the Turkish soldier have been recognised by all those who have seen him under the many and varied hardships to which he was exposed during the late campaign; and not a few have been compelled to admire his capability of withstanding the effects of cold, hunger, and fatigue under the depressing influences to which he was subjected, whether on the march, in the field, or lastly, but not least, when stricken down by the fire of the enemy, he lay wounded and helpless to defend himself against the attacks of disease more fatal than his original injury.

Rate of mortality during the war.

The rate of mortality during the late war was undoubtedly high; but, when we remember the deficiencies of the medical department both in personnel and matériel, and the length of time which elapsed between the reception of an injury and the subsequent admission of the patient into a hospital or even field ambulance, one must allow that the number of fatal cases was comparatively small. While we may justifiably account for the high rate of mortality in laying it down to circumstances inducing erysipelas, gangrene, and pyæmia on the one hand, and typhoid, dysentery, and diarrhœa on the other, there yet remain two causes, apart from these, sufficient in themselves to influence considerably the termination of cases which, without them, would have commanded a favourable prognosis. I refer to scurvy and malarial poisoning, from which the great majority of the sick and wounded who came under our care during and after the war were found to be suffering. Of scurvy and its influence on the health of the troops I do not intend to treat; so much has been written on the disease, and the subject has been so thoroughly well ventilated, that it would be unnecessary and presumptuous on my part to trouble my readers with observations which could only boast of being reiterations of those already made by many who are authorities on the nature and history of this terrible scourge. But I have not been able, in any of the treatises on Malaria which I have read, to discover more than a casual notice of its effects on wounds. That there is a decided and noticeable local effect produced on wounds has been mentioned by Dr. MacCulloch in his 'Essay on Intermittent, &c.,' where, in speaking of the symptoms in the cold stage of an intermittent fever, he says: 'Pains of the limbs, and chiefly of the back also accompany, with shrinking of the skin and extremities, often attended by the drying up of ulcers and the subsidence of tumours, should these be present.'*

The following cases, selected from a collection of notes hastily made at a time when great pressure of work precluded the possibility of more detailed and accurate case-taking, will serve to illustrate the local effects of malarious poisoning on wounds.

Mr. Eccles' report.

Scurvy.

Case I.—Ali Suleiman, corporal Regular Infantry. Admitted into S. H. Hospital (Bulgar Metropole) at Philippopolis, Oct. 15. Suffering from gunshot wound of right leg, with compound fracture of fibula. Patient was a tall, powerfully built man, a native of the province of Broussa. On admission was suffering from the effects of exposure to cold; had been wounded six days, three of which had been passed on the road between Kesanlik and Philippopolis. The patient was placed in bed between blankets and artificial heat applied to the extremities; a basin of warm soup was taken. On examination a small wound was found on the outer surface of the leg, two inches below the head of the fibula, the bone being fractured in the same place; the probe passed downwards, backwards, and inwards to a large lacerated wound on the inner aspect of the calf. The wounds were exceedingly foul, the edges of the lower wound sloughing. On syringing with a solution of carbolic acid (1–100) a large quantity of discharge with slough and pus came away. The wounds after having been cleansed were plugged with carbolised oiled tow, and the limb at and around the seat of injury was enveloped in the antiseptic marine lint, a splint being applied to the outer side of the limb, which was swung by means of a hook splint on a cradle. There was no great pain complained of, but a sensation of numbness was referred to both lower extremities. On visiting the hospital during the night I found the patient restless and complaining of thirst, with pain in the head and in the seat of the injury of a throbbing nature; had not slept and said he had fever. The face was flushed, the skin hot and dry, the tongue slightly furred, with a temperature of 100·2° Fah., and pulse 105. The dressings were changed, as the discharge had been profuse from the lower wound, about which was some swelling and redness. Injection of morphia gr. ¼ was administered.

Gunshot wound of right leg, &c.

Oct. 16. Patient had slept well. T. 99°. P. 75. Bowels open once. The wound was dressed, discharge offensive, but edges of inferior opening were healthier. Full diet, consisting of meat, bread, rice (pilaf) with beef tea, was ordered. ℞ Decocti cinchonæ, ʒ.; Ammon. carb. gr. v. was prescribed three times daily. A 3.30 P.M. I was told that the patient was worse, and I found him with all the ordinary symptoms of the cold stage of ague, and complaining of severe aching pain down the back of the right thigh and leg. The dressings were changed, the limb being cold to the touch and the parts round the wounds looking blue and dull, the surrounding skin presenting the peculiar puckered appearance generally observed in the cold stage of ague. Warm brandy and water was given. Two hours later, on visiting the ward, the patient begged that the splint should be removed, as it seemed that the leg was becoming too big for it. He was very restless, tossing about, much flushed, the conjunctivæ were injected and some little sordes was noticeable on the lips. Great headache and heat about the seat of injury were complained of. The splint was readjusted and dressings changed. The upper wound looked inflamed with much redness and tumefaction extending over the anterior surface of the leg, which was tender and hot to the touch. A large slough occupied the cavity of the lower wound. The syringe was used with carbolic acid as before, the surfaces of the lower wound bleeding freely on the detachment of the slough; the dressings were applied as described above. P. 106. T. 101·3°. ℞. Pil. quin. sulph. gr. x., to be taken as soon as perspiration sets in, and another after four hours.

Daily progress of case towards restoration.

Oct. 17. Passed a restless night; began to perspire about 3 A.M.; one pill taken. T. 99°. P. 80.

* MacCulloch, 'Essay on Remittent and Intermittent Diseases, including Marsh Fever and Neuralgia.' London: 1828. Vol. i. p. 255.

Mr. Eccles' report.

Not so much pain in leg, which was less swollen. The discharge was very copious and offensive. Wounds not so angry looking as last night; syringing with solution of carbolic acid (1-40), and dressings as before. Diet as yesterday; repeat mixture and pill. 5 P.M. Has had a slighter attack of cold stage, which still continues. The whole surface of the body is in the condition known as 'goose skin.' The edges of the wounds are flabby and purple in colour, the surrounding parts being dull in hue, little discharge from wound; on removing the dressings a thin ichorous fluid trickled from the inferior opening; the bandages supporting the splint were found to be slack. Beef-tea ordered in place of ordinary meal of solid food. 10 P.M. Hot stage, subjective symptoms slighter, pain about seat of injury comparatively less; but on changing the dressings the edges of the wounds were found to be hot, red and puffy, the surfaces when exposed appeared raw, the discharge being profuse, tinged with blood and having a very disagreeable odour. Morphia injection, ¼ gr. T. 102°. P. 110.

Oct. 18. Hot stage ceased about the same time as yesterday; patient was sleeping on my arrival in the ward. Wounds presented no special symptoms; the features were drawn and the patient complained of feeling exhausted. T. 98·2°. P. 75. Bowels open. Brandy and egg mixture, milk and beef-tea ordered. Prescriptions: repeat mixture. Pill to be taken immediately. 5 P.M. No return of fever; dressings changed.

Oct. 19. Slight attack of ague during the night, commencing about 8 P.M. Had taken a morphia pill at 7 P.M.; bowels not open. T. 99·4°. P. 90. Wounds look rather inflamed, discharge very copious, dressings changed. ℞ Magnes sulph. ʒss., Aquæ menth. pip. ʒij. 5 P.M. Patient has been easier during the day, takes food well; bowels open once. Dressings changed; quantity of discharge smaller, wounds looking quiet. Quinine pill to be taken immediately; morphia injection at night when fever had not returned.

Oct. 20. No fever during night; upper wound looks healthier, lower wound discharging thick purulent matter; no slough about the edges, which appear firmer and less irregular; dressings as before. T. and P. normal. Full diet; repeat mixture of Oct. 16. 5 P.M. Dressings changed; bowels open once; tongue slightly furred. Morphia injection at night.

Oct. 21. No fever since 18th inst. T. normal. P. 80. No discharge from upper wound, from which granulations appear to be springing; lower wound still discharging, but swelling of surrounding parts decreased; dressings as before. ℞ Decocti cinchonæ ʒj, vin. rubri ʒss., ammon. carb. gr. v., three times daily.

On November 10, this patient was still in the hospital, the upper wound was cicatrised, and the lower one rapidly filling up with healthy granulations. The patient's general condition was improved, and the size of the spleen (which had been much enlarged during the attack of ague, from which he suffered in the early days of his stay in hospital) was much reduced.

Case II.—Riza Hamid, private, Regular Infantry, æt. 26. Date of admission to hospital unknown. This patient, a spare, dark-complexioned man, born near Sulina, was admitted to the hospital soon after the general assault by Suleiman Pacha on the Russian positions at Shipka, and was in the hospital before it passed into the hands of the S. H. medical officers.

Compound comminuted fracture of humerus.

Oct. 10. This patient was suffering from compound comminuted fracture of the humerus, with much laceration of the left arm. There was no attempt at union of the fragments which were not in apposition, and the surrounding tissues were unhealthy and sloughing. The countenance was anxious, the conjunctivæ suffused much, sordes of the lip, and a dry brown cracked tongue, with a rapid jerky pulse, high temperature and low muttering delirium indicated the presence of a low type of fever. The body was much emaciated and the spleen enlarged, so that it could be felt extending into the left iliac region. The wound was cleansed as far as possible and the arm placed in an angular perforated zinc splint. Brandy, beef-tea, milk, and eggs, were ordered to be given in small quantities at frequent intervals; and the following mixture prescribed:—℞ Quin. sulp. gr. v.; Tinct. opii. mij.; Sp. ammon. aromat. ʒss.; Aquæ camphor. ʒj.; to be taken thrice daily. In the evening the condition of the patient had not improved, but nourishment had been taken.

Progress of case; resulting in death.

Oct. 11. Patient is sensible and has slept. T. 100°. P. 96. Discharge from wound very offensive; stringy sloughs were removed, and the parts well bathed with carbolic lotion; the wound was plugged with carbolised oiled lint in narrow strips, and a poultice applied. At 2 P.M. the patient had a distinct rigor, which was followed by a sensation of great cold, tremor of the limbs and a contraction of the features were noticed, the lips and conjunctivæ were bloodless apparently, the pulse was very feeble, sometimes scarcely perceptible, and the general condition of the patient was akin to the state of collapse. The wound was examined, and its appearance was aptly described by the dresser as 'dry.' The discharge had ceased, and on the removal of the sloughs there was no tendency to bleeding. Stimulants, such as ammonia and warm brandy and water, were freely exhibited. After about an hour and a half the pulse became somewhat fuller and assumed a bounding character, the breathing was quick and the heart's action plainly discernible to the eye. The countenance relaxed, but was dull, with the eyes injected, the veins of the forehead swollen, and the temporal pulse could be felt distinctly throbbing; the patient became delirious and very restless, throwing his limbs about and crying out. T. 103·2°. P. 120. Ten grains of quinine had been taken during the day in the mixture prescribed, but the severity of the disease and condition of my patient induced me to give twenty grains in the form of a pill immediately. About midnight I again visited this patient, whom I found in the same condition in which I had seen him on the 10th inst. The dressings were saturated with discharge, which had soaked through them and stained the bed clothes. The wound was found to be much inflamed, there was great heat and redness of the surrounding parts, spreading up and down the arm, which appeared swollen and glistening; the appearances had altered so completely within the few hours that had elapsed since I last saw the wound that I could scarcely believe it was the same. Towards morning the feverish symptoms remitted somewhat, but about midday of the 12th inst. rigors again set in with such severity that I did not expect my patient to survive them; in the afternoon I was sent for, and on reaching the bedside discovered that the dressings were saturated with discharge, mixed with some little blood; fearing hæmorrhage the subclavian was controlled, while the dressings were removed. Sloughing was spreading, and the edges of the wound were thickened and dusky; coagula of blood were mixed with *débris* in the discharge, indeed the wound had all the appearances of gangrenous phagedæna; the wound was plugged, but during the night I was again called; the patient was in high delirium and trying to remove the bandages; it was impossible to count the pulsations; the temperature was 105°, and I believe if the thermometer had remained longer in the axilla the degree registered might have been higher, for the restlessness of the patient would not permit of its remaining sufficiently long in contact with his body. The urine and motions had been passed involuntarily.

Oct. 13. During the remittance of the symptoms of fever a full dose of quinine was given, beef-tea and brandy were frequently taken during the day, but about three o'clock the patient was seized with rigors which lasted only half-an-hour, and were followed by the hot stage at 5 P.M. I saw the case in consultation with one of my colleagues, but it was decided that nothing could be done during the exacerbation; about midnight I was sent for but did not reach the bedside early enough to control the hæmorrhage which had burst out before it had proved fatal.

Case III.—Osman Mustafa, private Reserves, æt. 22, a native of Monastir, was admitted into the Stafford House Hospital at Salonica, March 6th, 1878, suffering from shell-wound in the buttock. This patient was wounded at Orkhanie, and had been an inmate of one of the Government hospitals at Sofia until the evacuation of the town by the Turks, when he, with a large number of other sick and wounded, was conveyed to Metrovitza, whence he was transported by rail to Salonica, and was received into the hospital immediately on arrival. The wounds were healing in Sofia, but the subsequent hardships endured by the patient had brought on an attack of ague and caused the wounds to enlarge. In addition to the shell-wounds which were situated one on the left buttock and the other on the external aspect of the left thigh, there was a large sore over the sacrum. All the wounds were foul and sloughing; the patient was fearfully emaciated, and sores were threatening over all the bony prominences of the back and thighs. He was placed on a water-bed, and the wounds, after having been thoroughly cleansed, were dressed with carbolised oiled lint packed under the overhanging edges of the sores, the whole being covered with pads of antiseptic marine lint. Milk, eggs, beef-tea, chicken broth, and rum were given in small quantities frequently. So great was the pain and tenderness in and around the wounds that the patient was obliged to maintain one position lying on the right side constantly. After a fortnight's rest and treatment the wounds, which at the time of the patient's admission were foul sloughing sores, presented all the appearances of healing ulcers. The general health improved, and after an absence of some days from Salonica, during which time this and others of my patients had been under the care of my colleague, Dr. Beresford, I returned to find my patient fairly on the road to discovery. But owing to the carelessness of an attendant, the patient was exposed to cold while having his bed arranged, and on April 2 was attacked by ague. Quinine in five-grain doses thrice daily was ordered.

April 3, 7 A.M. Had slept well after 10 P.M. when perspiration set in. T. 98°. P. 70. All three wounds looking well. 1.30 P.M. Cold stage set in, shivering, very severe sensation of numbness in wounds. Granulations pale; on removal of dressings no bleeding as usual was the case; the edges were smooth and adherent, but the surrounding skin was so pale, that the scar

Mr. ECCLES' report.

Shell-wound in buttock.

MEDICAL REPORTS.

Mr. ECCLES' report.

tissue already formed at the edge of the ulcer could not be distinguished from it. Discharge thin and small in quantity. T. 97·6°. P. 65. 4 P.M. The hot stage had supervened, the patient was very restless, complaining of great pain of a burning character in the wounds. The dressings were covered with thick purulent discharge slightly streaked with blood. The edges were swollen and glistening, the surrounding skin being hot and red. The base of the ulcer looked raw and angry; the granulations were very tender, and bled on being touched. An injection of morphia was given. T. 101·4°. P. 100.

April 4. The patient had slept from 7 P.M. till early morning. Slight headache but no feverish symptoms; no pain in wounds except when the dressings were changed; there were no signs of inflammation, an area of slight redness about the sore over the sacrum, all three wounds looked healthy; the amount of discharge during the night had been great. T. normal. P. 80.

April 5. Slight attack of ague; hot stage lasted only three hours yesterday; wounds healing.

April 15. Has had no return of fever; original wounds cicatrised; sore over sacrum about the size of half-a-crown. This patient was convalescent when the hospital was handed over to the Government authorities.

The cases cited above are three out of many which came under my notice, all presenting more or less the same characteristic symptoms, under the conditions of ague attacking individuals already suffering from wounds in different parts of the body, and of varying severity.

I much regret that more detailed notes were not taken when the cases were under observation, but the large number of patients coming under our care precluded the possibility of keeping a register of all; still, from observations made on 60 cases of wounds, I find that 36 presented symptoms such as have been described above, the patients suffering from one form or another of intermittent fever. During their stay in hospital, ten were suffering from malarial cachexia, while fourteen showed no signs of having suffered from malarial poisoning. Of the 36 who suffered from remittent or intermittent fever, nineteen died, while of the 24 who had no attack of ague while in hospital, three only died, one of them having the appearance of a patient suffering from malarial cachexia. I quote these statistics, not as evidence that the existence of malarial poisoning necessarily increases the fatality among patients severely wounded, because I cannot show the cause of death, nor how far the symptoms of the cases were modified by the existence of the fever; but I believe that the nervous exhaustion induced by repeated attacks of ague, and the inflammatory condition of the blood during the attack, are sufficient to influence very seriously the prognosis in cases otherwise doing well, and undoubtedly recovery is retarded, and it is not until the patient has got rid of an attack of ague that one can hope to see a wound take on or resume healthy action.

Local effects of malarial poisoning.

The local effects of malarial poison on wounds may be recognised from the notes of the three cases I have taken as examples, differing, as has been shown, according to the stage of the attack. In the cold stage the discharge decreases in quantity, and sometimes, if the stage has been prolonged in duration, ceases altogether; the surfaces of the wound will look bloodless or will appear congested, and change in colour from a bright red to a dull purple or grey hue; the granulations, if there be any, are pale and bloodless. In this stage pain is rarely complained of, a sensation of numbness being often referred to the wound. In the hot stage all the local symptoms undergo a decided change, the discharge becomes thick, copious, and sometimes fœtid, sloughing occurs in many cases, the surface of the wound looks angry and inflamed; the granulations are florid, sensitive, and bleed on being touched; sometimes on removal of dressings the whole surface of the wound becomes bathed with blood; the edges are puffy, swollen, glistening and painful, an area of redness extending some distance around the wound. The patient often complains of burning or throbbing in the seat of injury. During the intermission, the wound generally resumes its ordinary appearance, but not unfrequently the inflammatory action set up during the hot stage continues, and the local effects remain after the cause has ceased to exist.

Surgical Experiences and Observations as an Ambulance Surgeon in Bulgaria during the Russo-Turkish War of 1877–78. By ROBERT PINKERTON, M.B. and C.M., *Member of the Order of the Medjidie.*

During the late Russo-Turkish war, I was sent out by Lord Blantyre, as a surgeon, to assist the Turkish wounded, and in that capacity acted both independently, and attached to Ottoman Red Crescent ambulances, and also, for a short time, took charge for Stafford House Society of their hospitals at Philippopolis.

<small>Dr. PINKERTON'S report.</small>

In this work I travelled from Constantinople to within a few miles of Plevna, when I was stopped by the advance of the Russians.

I saw some of the active fighting on the Plevna road, and had considerable experience of the wounded from the fighting at Shipka, the hospitals at Philippopolis being the first place to which the Shipka wounded were removed, after treatment by the ambulances stationed there.

My time was so much broken up by being hurried about from place to place, and the amount of work, both surgical and medical, was so overpowering, not only from the large numbers of sick and wounded, but also from the very small number of medical men, together with most inadequate assistance for dressing the wounded, that any definite or detailed record of my work is rendered quite impossible. Yet I venture to hope, the simple statement of some of my experiences and observations may not be devoid of interest.

The first point I would call attention to is the fact that only very few of the wounded, in modern wars, are wounded by cuts and stabs, so few, indeed, that to one who reads in newspaper accounts of battles, of desperate charges with the bayonet, of fearful hand to hand fights at the taking of redoubts, and so forth, where the imagination pictures the wounded from bayonet stabs at hundreds or more, the real number must appear absurdly, even incredibly, small.

<small>Few wounded by sword or bayonet.</small>

In the late Russo-Turkish war, where I had the opportunity of seeing thousands of wounded men, I am sure I did not see more than half a dozen suffering from sword, or sabre, or lance, or bayonet wounds. And all the enquiries I could make did not enable me to come across any one whose experience differed much from my own. Why is this? I suppose it is due to the recent improvements in the firearms with which troops are armed, especially the introduction of breech-loading, by which the rapidity of fire can be so very much increased. In consequence of the ease and rapidity with which a soldier can load and fire his rifle now-a-days, the firing of shot takes place even at close quarters. Even in a regular charge, I believe, it is in great measure only those who fall wounded who are bayonetted—the attacking party and the attacked both trusting more to a rapid fire of small arms than to the bayonet. In the case of an assault, for example, on an earthwork, the holders of the earthwork, if moderately cool and steady, pour in a close and murderous fire up to the very moment the enemy enter the defences, and although there then may be some little hand to hand fighting, it is comparatively trifling, as the defenders of the earthwork if beaten, either retire precipitately, in which case they are fired upon, and only those who fall wounded are bayonetted by the pursuing enemy, or they retire slowly, showing a steady front and keeping up fire, so that the enemy prefer to answer them in like manner. There is another reason why we see so few wounded by either cuts or stabs, besides the fact that in recent wars cuts or stabs are comparatively rarely given or received. And that is because, I believe, the great majority of cases of cuts or stabs prove fatal on the field, and are, therefore, to be numbered among the killed. If one thinks for a moment of the circumstances of a close hand to hand conflict with the bayonet, a scene where the wildest passions reign, and a tiger-like ferocity seems to characterise the combatants, where an enemy is not only overthrown, but trampled upon, one will see the reasonableness of allowing that few of those wounded under such circumstances, and with such a weapon, survive the final thrust, and hardly one lives to be taken off the field. Then there is the fact that the bayonet is, after all, a clumsy and inefficient weapon for close quarters. In fact, it not unfrequently acts as a sort of trap for its unfortunate employer. It may become fixed in an enemy's body beyond power of withdrawal, in time at least to be a defence; or it may be rendered useless by having a body hurled upon it, as was done with so much success by the Zulus at the recent battle of Isandula. Soldiers, at least Turkish ones, don't like the bayonet as a weapon; they distrust it; and, as a rule, prefer firing their rifle to using the bayonet. A weapon

<small>Cuts or stabs generally fatal on the field.</small>

<small>The bayonet an inefficient weapon</small>

x

Dr. Pinkerton's report.

Lance wounds.

such as the short heavy knife with which our Indian Gurko regiments are armed, or the regulation bowie knife of the Americans, is the deadliest instrument in hand to hand fighting.

In a cavalry charge, especially when the weapon of the attacking party is the lance, you can understand many a man laid low by a comparatively slight flesh wound. Indeed, more than one, of the half-dozen I saw wounded by cuts or stabs, were wounded by the lance of a Cossack.

The number of wounded in modern wars, from any other and from all other causes than gunshot, is so insignificant, and the injuries of war which the modern military surgeon has brought under his notice, and is called upon to treat are, therefore, so almost exclusively those resulting from gunshot, that practically the entire scope of modern military surgical teaching comes to be the proper treatment of gunshot injuries.

The nature of the ground on which fighting takes place greatly determining the situation and appearance of bullet-wounds.

The nature of the ground over which fighting has taken place will modify the appearance of bullet wounds, as also it will affect the proportion of wounds in the different parts of the body. If, in inspecting wounded in an hospital in Philippopolis or Adrianople, you found a large number of them suffering from wounds of the upper part of the body, especially of the hands, face, and neck; if you found, moreover, that the wounds of entrance, in most of them, presented a peculiar appearance, being large in size and oblique in direction,—and, further, on looking more closely you found that this large size of these wounds of entrance was caused by a superficial furrow or planing off of the integuments leading up to the point where the bullet began to penetrate the deeper structures,—that, in fact, the wound was a combination of 'a razing shot' and a penetrating shot, then you might be perfectly certain they were men who had been wounded in the fighting at Shipka. The wounded from Shipka were easily distinguishable by the nature and position of their wounds, which were nearly all in the upper parts of the body, and in most of them, the bullet appeared to have struck the body in an oblique direction. This is, I think, satisfactorily accounted for by the nature of the ground over which the fighting took place. The ground was steep and rough, being the entrance of one of the Balkan passes; and, while climbing up the slopes, and over the rough and broken ground, the Turkish soldiers had often to do so on hands and knees, all the while exposed to the fire of the enemy above. Under such circumstances the upper parts of the soldier's body were very much more liable to injury from the bullets of the enemy, and especially was this the case with his hands and face. And this same formation of the ground readily accounts for the oblique direction with which many of the bullets would strike; and for the same bullet, especially in the neck, causing first of all a 'razing wound' and then

Bul et wounds.

penetrating deeply. Generally speaking, you may expect to find in cases of bullet wounds, where the bullet has passed out, that the wound of exit is larger, and with its edges more ragged and torn than the wound of entrance. Of course, besides this, in the wound of entrance the edges are inverted, while in the wound of exit, they are everted. But in these Shipka wounds, the wound of entrance was much larger than the wound of exit, owing to the oblique direction in which the bullets must have struck. But this largeness of the wound of entrance, as Mr. Longmore remarks, 'is only in seeming, and is owing to the projectile having struck the surface slantingly, so that parts of the skin and subcutaneous areolar tissues have been shaved away, as it were, before the projectile had passed inwards through the superficial fascia.' 'There is here,' Mr. Longmore continues, 'strictly speaking, a razing wound on one side of the true wound of entrance; for the true entrance wound is, of course, the commencement of the track of the projectile through the deeper structures.'

A great deal of fighting in this war took place under cover of earthworks, and here the protection, afforded to the lower parts of the body by the earthwork, made it almost impossible for the men to be wounded in any other than the upper parts of the body, and also made it very difficult for them to be hit at all. For example, the farthest point I reached, before being met by the Russians, was a small village called Telis, about six miles from Plevna. Here a camp had been fixed by the Turks, and earthworks thrown up for the protection of the road into Plevna. On one of the attacks by the Russians on this earthwork, although they vastly outnumbered the Turks, they were driven off, leaving behind them on the field many hundreds of dead and wounded, while the Turkish loss only amounted to some 21 killed and about 50 wounded. Here the earthwork gave complete protection to all but the heads, shoulders, and upper part of the chests of the Turks, hence the remarkably small number of their men hit, and likewise the reason why nearly one-third of those hit were killed. Those killed were nearly all shot through the brain or chest, and died instantly. An enormous proportion of the bullets fired here by the Russians lodged in the soft breastwork of earth and did no damage. As an example of the same thing—viz., of the effect which protection or cover to the men fighting has on the proportion of hits to shots fired, Mr. Longmore, in his recent work on 'Gunshot Injuries,' mentions how, on one occasion, during the war in New Zealand, the Maories attacked a British force from cover of thick bush, and both killed and wounded some of our men, and yet it is not supposed that our men succeeded in killing or wounding one of the enemy, although they fired off more than 20,000 rounds of ball cartridge in the attempt.

<small>Dr. FINKERTON'S report.</small>

I have got notes of only about 100 cases, and these are mostly cases from Shipka, or cases seen by me on the Plevna road. <small>Notes of surgical cases.</small>

I find that of these—

> 52 are wounds of the upper extremities,
> 26 of the head and neck,
> 13 of the lower extremities,
> 6 of the chest,
> 3 of the abdomen.

The very marked preponderance shown here of wounds of the upper parts of the body should certainly be attributed to the fact that they are mostly cases from Shipka and Tolis, where the circumstances, as noted by me above, under which the men fought, modified the regional distribution of the wounds. Still the fact remains that the general impression I have left on my mind on reviewing the wounded as a whole is that, dividing the body into an upper part (embracing the head and neck, upper extremities, and all the thorax above the level of the nipples), and a lower part (including all the chest below the line of the nipples, the abdomen, and the lower extremities), wounds of the upper part were quite as numerous as those of the lower part. But here, again, comes in the modifying fact that, in a great deal of the fighting, the Turks fought from cover of one kind or another, not from any fear of meeting the enemy in the open field, but simply because, when it could be done, it was most advantageous for the Turks, who were often in inferior force, and the attacked and not the attacking party.

Again, the 52 cases which I have lumped together as wounds of the upper extremities, I find may be divided into:— <small>Wounds of the upper extremities.</small>

> 27 wounds of the arms,
> 19 of the fingers,
> 6 of the hands,

showing that half of the entire number of wounds of the upper extremities are embraced under wounds of the hands and fingers—this representing one-fourth of the whole number of wounded. This is a very large proportion, and from the very partial statistics on which it is founded, I would certainly not think of building upon it in any way. At the same time the large number of wounds of hands and fingers has been noticed and remarked upon in many previous wars. In the Italian war of 1859 more than one-seventh of the whole wounds received during the war were returned as wounds of the hands and fingers. This frequency of wounds of the hands and fingers has been rightly attributed, I think, to the nature of the fighting. Wherever the hands have to be much used and exposed, as in climbing slopes, or in firing from cover of any sort, as houses, walls, earthworks, or rifle pits, there you must have a large proportion of wounds of the hands and fingers. This certainly was the nature of a great deal of the fighting in Bulgaria, and the large number of wounds of hands and fingers was a constant subject of remark amongst the surgeons.

One day three wounded soldiers were brought into the camp at Orkbanie. They said they had been wounded three or four days before in a skirmish with the Russians, but as there were a number of suspicious elements in their story, they were sent along to the hospital to be examined as to whether their wounds were possibly self-inflicted. On examination I found one suffering from a very severe wound of the right elbow—the bones composing the joint being completely shattered, and the soft parts immediately round it carried away or destroyed. Another had a severe wound of the right hand—the bullet having passed through the hand, entering on the palmar surface and fracturing the 3rd and 4th metacarpal bones about half an inch from their carpal extremities. The third had the index finger of his right hand nearly blown off—the finger remaining attached to the hand by a few shrods of skin and muscle only. From a surgical point of view the most suspicious circumstances in all of them was that the firearms, which produced the wounds, must have been discharged close to the body, so close, indeed, as to scorch the surrounding parts; and on careful examination grains of gunpowder could be detected embedded in the skin and surrounding tissues. Of course I had to return an answer that any of the wounds might have been self-inflicted. The two men, with wounds of elbow joint and hand, were in a remarkably depressed state, their wounds being exceedingly unhealthy and dangerous looking. They had evidently

<small>Self-inflicted wounds.</small>

Dr. PINKERTON'S report. *(continued)*

been much reduced by over-fatigue and exposure, so I was allowed to take them into the hospital under a guard, where, fortunately for the poor wretches, they both succumbed to pyæmia. The third man was marched off to execution. These were the only cases I saw of self-inflicted wounds.

Cases of curious bullet-wounds.

There are many curious wounds seen in military practice. In the Shipka wounded I was often struck by the fact, that bullets entered the neck and lodged three or four inches from their point of entrance, the wound produced being very small. I looked upon such as wounds produced by bullets striking with very much diminished velocity. It was certainly wonderful how often you would get bullets lodged in that dangerous region known as the anterior triangle of the neck, which had produced no serious mischief, and often caused little inconvenience. The most curious case I had of this sort was one where I removed a bullet which was actually jammed in the fork formed by the bifurcation of the common carotid artery. It was so tightly fixed between the two carotids that I hesitated, at first, to remove it for fear of bleeding. The man recovered without a bad symptom.

Wounds in the neck.

Eight wounds by one bullet.

I had a strong muscular young fellow under my care for a short time, who had eight wounds caused by one bullet. The bullet struck him on the outside of the middle of the right arm, and passed through the arm, causing a simple flesh wound; then it passed through the fleshy part of the right breast, below the nipple; then through a corresponding part of the left breast; and last of all passed through the left arm, fracturing the humerus about its middle. The man informed me he received the wound as he was leaning forward, and just about to bring his rifle to the shoulder to fire, which position explains perfectly the course of the bullet.

Another man had a bullet lodged in the left orbital fossa, from which it was extracted. It entered through the left temporal fossa, and caused protrusion of the eyeball, which had to be extirpated. This man was under my care for several days, during which time he was progressing favourably, but I had to leave and, so lost sight of him.

Loss of the entire lower jaw.

Another man had the entire body of the lower jaw, together with the soft parts around and forming the floor of the mouth, carried away by a fragment of shell. Although a hideous-looking object, he recovered so rapidly that he was able to be utilised as an hospital attendant in a few weeks. Generally speaking, however, wounds of the face, no matter how dangerous looking, healed up wonderfully quickly, and well.

I saw very few wounds of the head, but those I did see, impressed me with the importance of non-interference on the surgeon's part, unless for the relief of urgent symptoms. Even in cases of depressed fracture with external wound, if there are no urgent symptoms, the less the surgeon interferes the better. I had one case under my care illustrating this. This man was wounded, in an attack on the Russian positions at Shipka, by a bullet over the vertex. The bullet had passed across the head, at a right angle to the direction of the sagittal suture, causing a wound in the scalp of about two inches long, leading down to a depressed fracture fully a quarter of an inch in depth. The patient, at the moment he received the wound, was running forward firing his rifle, and he fell over the trunk of a tree, and lay stunned for a short time. When I saw him he was quite sensible, and complained of nothing but the blow he had received on his chest in falling. He did not think the wound of his head had caused him to fall; in fact, he would not admit that at all, but believed he had accidentally tripped over the fallen tree. There were absolutely no symptoms demanding interference, so cold water dressing was applied to the wound, he was kept quiet in bed, and special care taken of his stomach and bowels. He recovered perfectly.

Wound in head.

Bullets in brain.

I have several times had men brought from the field in a comatose state, with a bullet deeply lodged in the brain, or having had one driven right through the brain. I have seen men in that state live for several hours, but I mention them, merely to remark, that they are cases which, however harsh it may seem to say so, had better never be removed from the field at all. Hopeless cases like that, which must die, and that generally within a few hours, should only be attended to after you are certain there are no more poor fellows to whom your services and attention may be of some avail. It is here our new Army Hospital Corps of trained bearers, for gathering up the wounded during a battle, and removing them to the dressing stations, will most conspicuously show the advantage of organised method in such work. Instead of spending their time (as has to so great an extent been the case in similar circumstances hitherto) in removing the wounded promiscuously, often taking up a man who dies before they reach the surgeon, they will be taught to distinguish between the wounded, and to carry off only those to whom the surgeon's skill can be of some use. Without this picking out process, in a big battle, a large part of the time and strength of the bearers will be spent in carrying off hopelessly wounded men, to the lasting detri-

Advantage of trained hospital bearers in selecting proper cases to remove from the field.

ment of many others whom they leave behind, and to whom their early assistance would have meant life and home again.

The best way in which to administer chloroform to patients, about to undergo operation, I have found a subject of great dispute, and one associated with wide differences of opinion. Generally speaking, I found that, our Scotch style of giving it on a folded towel was looked upon with great distrust and aversion. I found, however, that, for military practice at any rate, in dispensing with a special apparatus, and in the saving of time, the Scotch style had important advantages over the cone of lint or linen, or one of the German apparatus, such as Esmarch's (formed by stretching a bit of flannel on a wire frame), which were the methods commonly made use of. Wherever you have a towel, or handkerchief, or bit of cloth, there you may give chloroform according to the Scotch style ; it is, therefore, always ready to hand. Thus given, as I shall detail below, the patient falls into the condition of complete anæsthesia in very much less time, remains in such a state more readily, and comes out of the influence of the drug more rapidly than in any other mode of administration.

The conclusion to which I have come in regard to the administration of chloroform is that the giving of it should be entirely in the hands of one individual, with, at most, a single assistant, chiefly to take charge of the chloroform bottle, and to hold the forceps when applied to the tongue. The person intrusted with the giving of chloroform should see that the patient is lying comfortably on the operating table, taking care that his head is low, having it raised but slightly above the general level of the body. He should see that all constriction caused by tightness of clothing is relieved by loosening the dress, which should also be thrown open so as to expose, fully and freely, the front of the chest, as far as the pit of the stomach. He then takes his stand at the head of the patient, with a pair of ordinary bull-dog artery forceps hanging from the front of his coat, and, having folded an ordinary towel once or twice, till it forms a square of about a foot, he should pour about a couple of drachms of chloroform in the centre of the towel, and, telling the patient to shut his eyes and breathe quietly, should with one hand hold it down, in a somewhat arched form, over his mouth and nose. He notes the pulse by keeping his other hand over the temporal artery, and the respiration, both by attentively listening to it, and by keeping his eye on the movements of the diaphragm at the pit of the stomach. He should take an occasional look at the eyes ; and here, Bryant's rule for complete anæsthesia is a good and safe one to follow—viz. ' when the upper eyelid can be raised without muscular resistance, and no muscular contraction is caused by touching the cornea, the patient is, as a rule, sufficiently under the influence of anæsthetic for surgical purposes.' Until this condition is reached, the chloroform should continue to be given freely. And it is of the very highest importance, when this state is reached, not to allow the patient to come out of it for a moment, but by careful regulation of the chloroform to maintain him in it until the operation is so far completed that, by then stopping the administration, he should be restored to complete consciousness about the same time that he is ready to be removed from the operating table. If, during the administration, the patient's breathing shows signs of becoming arrested, assuming a convulsive character, while the abdomen and chest retract and become hard like a board, the chloroform cloth should be removed for an instant, at the same time giving a smart slap or two with the open hand over the chest, and it will usually go on all right. Whenever the breathing becomes snoring, as it generally does in the state of most profound tolerance, the bull-dog forceps should be introduced into the mouth, and, getting a good hold of the tongue, it should be pulled well out of the mouth and held there.

Patients treated in this way, getting chloroform in large quantity from the first, so as to be brought quickly and thoroughly under its influence, stood the administration of chloroform better, came out of it sooner, and suffered less from shock than did those who had it given to them in the usual slow and gradual fashion. The giving it in this way saved both time and assistants, and the quantity of chloroform used was often actually less than in the gradual system. The patient also passed through no stage of excitement hurtful to himself, nor requiring the attendance often of several men to control his struggles. Out of the number of cases in which I have given chloroform in this way, I have not seen one exhibit really dangerous symptoms. I have come to regard the first five minutes as the dangerous period in administration in this way, and if you get safely over that interval, the patient is likely to behave well all through any ordinary operation. At the same time, I never give chloroform but I feel impressed with the seriousness of the situation, and that the patient's life or death may depend on the vigilance and care of the administrator. This sense of grave responsibility, which will deter any one occupying the position of administering chloroform from removing his attention for a single instant from his patient, even to look at an interesting point in an operation, is, I think, a safeguard not unfre-

Dr. PINKERTON'S report.

Administration of chloroform. The Scotch style.

Duties of a person administering chloroform.

Bryant's rule.

The due sense of responsibility when administering chloroform.

MEDICAL REPORTS.

Dr. Pinkerton's report.

quently overlooked; for familiarity is apt to breed contempt, and we are often tempted, after seeing numbers of successful cases of the administration of chloroform, to fall into the mistake of imagining that because the danger attending its use may have been exaggerated, the great vigilance and care taught to be observed in its administration are also exaggerated and unnecessary.

Skin flaps.

Generally speaking, skin flaps, with a circular cut through the muscles, will be found the most useful method of operating in cases of gunshot injury; for this reason chiefly, that you will often get good skin flaps much lower than you can get muscular flaps, bullets injuring the deeper tissues for considerable distances around their track. But here, as in civil practice, he is the best surgeon who is least trammelled by either special methods or special instruments, and who, working on some sound general principles, can improvise both methods and instruments if required, and treats each case on its individual merits.

Generally unfavourable result of surgical work.

The general result of surgical work in this war was unfavourable, owing principally to the bad hygienic surroundings of the wounded, especially in the matter of overcrowding. The wounded were in great part transported from the field in native arabas or bullock carts, vehicles quite devoid of springs, the jolting of which over the rough roads made conveyance in them be looked upon, even by a strong healthy individual, as a kind of horrid torture which was simply intolerable for any length of time, so you can fancy what it must have been in the case of helpless wounded. And, as they do not travel above two miles an hour, you can imagine the length of time the wounded must have been subjected to this torture before getting sufficiently to the rear of the fighting, much less to hospitals 30 and 40 miles off.

Dreadful condition of wounded during transport.

The consequence was that the condition of the wounded, received at a place like Philippopolis, little more than 30 miles from Shipka, was really dreadful. With their wounds in a state of the most profuse and unhealthy suppuration, and often alive with maggots—with nothing but some hard biscuit or black bread for their nourishment by the way, there is little wonder that the fatigue and torment of this awful journey, made as it was too at a time of the year when the heat was perfectly tropical, landed them at Philippopolis far more dead than alive. And yet such splendid and unbroken constitutions had these men that, after a few days' rest at Philipoppolis, they were incessant in their desire to be taken on to Stamboul, which they regarded as their haven of rest.

Antiseptic condition of wounds.

And here it is I should like to say something in regard to the antiseptic treatment of wounds. If antiseptic surgery had done nothing more for us than introduced to our notice carbolic acid, I should say that for that alone it deserves our very best thanks—at least, of those of us who have been in similar positions to those referred to here. With a 1 to 20 watery solution of the acid we attacked those foul suppurating wounds, and after a thorough syringing out with it, we washed them out once a day, oftener if possible, with a 1 to 40 solution, and in a few days the wounds were comparatively fresh and clean, and the patients were neither a source of danger and discomfort to themselves nor to others—the sickening smell of the putrid wounds having given place to what, by way of contrast, might well be termed the fragrant odour of carbolic acid.

Mr. Lister's method.

It is, I think, absolutely impossible in military practice to expect ever to be able to carry out the antiseptic treatment of wounds with all the regard to detail required by Mr. Lister. Even Mr. Lister, in some directions he published for use during the late Franco-German war, entitled 'A Method of Antiseptic Treatment Applicable to Wounded Soldiers,' although he is evidently striving to reduce to a minimum the necessary details of such a treatment, yet most signally fails to solve the military surgeon's difficulty in this matter, and show a possible way of getting some, at least, of the benefits of the antiseptic treatment in active military practice. The method he proposes is cumbersome to a degree, both in regard to the material and the time necessary; and I agree most fully with Mr. Longmore in his adverse criticism of it, especially when he concludes—

Mr. Longmore's criticism.

'from the nature of gunshot wounds, and from the circumstances under which they are inflicted in warfare, it is scarcely credible that any plan of treatment, the success of which must depend on the rigid exclusion of such germs, can ever possibly be carried into practice in the field.' At the same time, I do not see why this system, the fundamental principles of which are now so generally admitted to be true, should not be carried out in military practice so far as possible. It is a mistake often made, to suppose that you must throw the whole thing overboard because you cannot carry it out in its entirety. I think in military practice a great step will have been made in this direction, from which we may expect no small amount of benefit to follow, if the Listerian ideas were only carried out so far as to make it possible to dress each wound with carbolic acid dressings, and wash it out thoroughly and regularly with a carbolic solution of definite strength. This is the length to which we may reasonably expect to be able to carry out the antiseptic treatment in military practice—the only requisites being a good supply of the acid, with means of making up the solution as near as possible, at least, to a standard strength, and, above all, an ample supply of suitable syringes. If this were carried out fairly well, we might reasonably expect a large diminution of unhealthy stinking suppuration among the wounded, which, besides the general comfort resulting therefrom to the patients themselves, and to those about them and working with them, would mean vastly lessened chances of pyæmia and septicæmia, and therefore a proportionately larger roll of saved lives among the wounded.

Dr. Pinkerton's report.

My first operation in Turkey so far illustrates this point. At Philippopolis I performed excision of the shoulder joint on a young Turkish soldier about 25 years of age. He had been wounded some days before at Shipka, the bullet—having entered the joint at its outer and posterior aspect just below the acromion, and fracturing the humerus, both head and shaft—passed out about 2 inches below the joint on its inner aspect. The soft parts were lacerated and contused, but not more than was usual in such wounds, and pretty free suppuration had commenced. The young fellow was much delighted when told that his arm would be saved—that we only intended removing a bit of the bone—so he readily consented to the operation. In this case, as in all others, I used one of Dr. Foulis' bands for controlling hæmorrhage, having taken several out with me—and I would like to mention here, that I found them exceedingly useful in the exigencies of military practice, being preferable in my opinion to either Esmarch's india-rubber tube apparatus or Nicaise's compression belt. They were easily applied, and just as easily taken off, and often enabled you to dispense with an assistant.

Dr. Pinkerton's first operation.

Foulis' bands for controlling hæmorrhage.

Knowing the great shattering power of the modern conical bullet, I determined to make my incision large, and also, for another reason, I decided to have it quite apart and distinct from the bullet wounds. Entering the knife a little to the outside of the coracoid process, I carried it downwards and outwards for about 6 inches, making one clean cut right down to the bone. The joint was easily entered, and the muscles attached to the humerus cleared away—the long head of the biceps, being fortunately uninjured, was carefully preserved. I did not require to remove more than about 2 inches of the shaft of the bone besides the head. Washing the wound thoroughly with a 1 to 20 watery solution of carbolic acid and inserting a drainage tube, I stitched it up with silver wire, putting in a large number of stitches, and putting them unusually close together. With a simple pad in the axilla, and his arm in a broad sling, the man was put to bed, where he got a hypodermic injection of morphia. Next morning I found the patient had slept well—he felt very well, and had taken his breakfast with an appetite. I carefully syringed the wound with a carbolic solution (strength 1 to 40) through the drainage tube and applied fresh dressings, which consisted simply of a couple of thicknesses of lint, saturated with the carbolic solution, sufficiently large to envelop the whole aspect of the joint embraced by the wounds both of knife and bullet, which in turn was covered in by a piece of gutta percha tissue, and the whole bound loosely by a few turns of roller bandage. The wound was only dressed once a day from the first. On the third day the wound looked so well that I removed every second suture, and on the fourth day the drainage tube was removed. By the ninth day the wound was completely healed, all the sutures removed, and the bullet wounds were granulating up from the bottom. I had to leave Philippopolis that day, but instructed the man before leaving how to carry out passive movements in his arm himself. I never saw him again, but believe, after serving as an hospital attendant for some time, he left for his home in a distant part of Asia perfectly well, and with a remarkably useful arm.

I suppose it will be freely admitted that those wounds heal most readily which are the result of a single clean cut, and that being so, it is a matter of much surprise that the sound practical principle embodied in such an admission is so seldom kept prominently in view in actual practice. In the case just quoted (excision of the shoulder joint), it was a very simple matter to cut right down to the bone in a single clean cut, and yet I have noticed not unfrequently in similar cases—for what reason did not appear—a decided failure to do so, and rather a tendency to make several cuts in places where one would have sufficed. I merely refer to this point, but—as I believe one of the most important lessons to be learnt in practical surgery is, that, having made up your mind to operate, and knowing exactly what you have got to do, you should accomplish it in the fewest number of cuts of the knife possible—I trust the reference may not be considered out of place.

Modes of operating

Then, again, I have observed that one of the best means possible of getting a fistulous opening, of moderately recent standing, to close up, is by making a counter opening, and on this principle I made my incision for the excision (contrary to the usual directions), quite apart from

Dr. Pinkerton's report.

Sutures.

the bullet wounds. The result, I think, justified the method, both wounds beginning to heal up together and doing so quickly.

Again, I employed a large number of sutures, for the purpose of keeping the tension as equal as possible along the whole length of the wound. My attention was first directed to this point by my friend, Dr. Macewen, and my experience with him as house surgeon, and since then, has confirmed me in looking upon this as a very necessary precaution to take, when you wish to secure healing by first intention.

Carbolic acid as an antiseptic precaution.

Then the washing out the wound thoroughly and carefully with a 1 to 20 carbolic acid solution, the dressing with a simple carbolic acid water dressing, and the careful syringing with a carbolic solution so long as there seemed to be the slightest fear of discharge lodging in the interior, were all the antiseptic precautions adopted. And I leave it to you, gentlemen, to say whether, with the above mentioned simple precautions, which are capable of being adopted by any one, and which, so far as I am aware, formed the only difference between my case and other similar cases, in the same hospital, which died, you do not think that some part, at least, of the success in this case is to be attributed to the antiseptic part of the treatment, even partial and imperfect as it may appear.

Teale's amputation.

The only other operation to which I shall specially refer is that known as Teale's amputation. Teale amputated by a long and a short rectangular flap, the long flap being cut from that side of the limb where the parts are generally devoid of large blood-vessels and nerves, these structures being included in the short flap. The advantages claimed by Teale, for this method, are a good covering, a dependent opening for discharges, and a cicatrix free from pressure from the end of the bone—and all this may readily be granted, and against it put the disadvantage of having to saw the bone at a higher point than when you use two short flaps. I have already referred to the wedge-like power of the conical bullet, used in modern warfare, by which it splits and destroys a bone far beyond the point where it actually strikes. In this very fact I thought I saw a reason why Teale's operation should be a good one in military practice. The bone is often injured badly a good way above the point of injury to the soft structures, so, by adopting Teale, I thought I would get all his advantages without any drawback at all. I soon came across a first-rate case for the purpose. At Orkhanie I performed this operation on a soldier under 30 years of age, who had received a bullet through the left tibia. The bullet had entered the leg on its outer and anterior aspect, just above the ankle joint, and, missing the fibula, smashed through the tibia, emerging behind about an inch above the inner malleolus. It had evidently passed through at a high velocity, judging by the large and irregularly torn appearance of the wound of exit, and from the great shattering of the bone, which could be made out by inserting a finger into the wound. The man was in remarkably good condition, not much pulled down by his sufferings, and seemed a strong healthy fellow. No case certainly could have appeared more favourable for a Teale. The limb was amputated between the middle and the lower thirds of the leg, the situation considered most suitable for a Teale. The force of the bullet having fallen in great measure upon the bone, left the soft structures comparatively uninjured. The nature and extent of the injury to the bone necessitated its division high up, operate by whatever method we chose, and yet it was possible to get good flaps a considerable way below the point, where the bone required to be sawn, especially on the anterior aspect just where Teale's long flap comes from. I measured and marked out the flaps, with ink, most accurately, according to the rule laid down by Teale himself. The man stood the operation well. Unfortunately I had to leave next morning for duty further along the Plevna road, and when I returned, some days after, I found the flaps had sloughed, and the leg had been re-amputated higher up. This sloughing of the flaps, especially the long one, is the constant experience of all military surgeons who have tried Teale's operation, so that I am afraid we must look upon it as a most unsuitable method. I certainly would never think of trying it again, not because one unsuccessful case is sufficient of itself to condemn a surgical method, but because there was everything possible associated with this particular case to make me distrust this style of operation. Mr. MacCormac, of St. Thomas' Hospital, in his 'Notes of an Ambulance Surgeon during the Campaign of 1870,' states that the only fatal case of amputation in the middle third of the leg was one where Teale's operation had been performed. He significantly adds, 'it was the only instance in which recourse was had to this form of operation.'

Although not a military case, the following, as a rare and what some may even consider an obsolete surgical operation, may be interesting:—While I was acting at Philippopolis as chief medical officer for the Stafford House Hospitals there, I came a good deal in contact with Dr. Vlathos, the chief civil practitioner of the town and district, and who was, besides, one of the

Dr. Vlathos.

DR. PINKERTON'S REPORT.

surgeons in connection with the Government hospitals. Dr. Vlathos was of Greek nationality, about 52 years of age, and had studied and taken his diploma from the Vienna School of Medicine. He was a most intelligent and agreeable gentleman, and a very good surgeon, and took no little trouble in showing me those cases in his private practice which he thought would be interesting to me. One day he asked me if I would assist him at a private operation for stone, to which I most readily assented, never thinking of anything but lateral lithotomy. Accordingly, late in the afternoon, we proceeded to the house of a Greek merchant, where Dr. Vlathos operated on his little boy, nine years of age, by the suprapubic method, and succeeded in extracting an encysted mulberry calculus, about the size and shape of a pigeon's egg, and weighing nine grammes. The wound healed by first intention, and five days after the operation the boy was running about quite well. The operation was performed as follows:—After preliminary sounding, in which there was considerable difficulty in detecting the stone, the sound was withdrawn, and the point of the penis compressed by an assistant to prevent the escape of urine. An incision was then made about two inches long, carried from the pubis directly upwards in the mesial line, and the tissues carefully dissected downwards, till the external coat of the bladder was fairly exposed. During this dissection, the peritoneum was wounded, and the bowels had to be prevented from protruding through the wound. Dr. Vlathos remarked on this incident that, in his experience, he had never seen any great harm come from simple wounds of the peritoneum, if properly attended to. He thought surgeons were too much afraid of wounding the peritoneum. He then thrust the knife right through the coats of the bladder, at the same time causing the point of the penis to be let go, when at once the urine passed out freely by the urethra. He then enlarged the opening into the bladder by cutting downwards towards the neck, and, introducing his finger, found that the stone was entirely enclosed in a long deep cyst, somewhat like the finger of a glove, the top of which was covered in by a thin membranous substance. To get at the stone he had to introduce the knife, and cut through this top covering, after which, by means of his finger and a scoop, he extracted the stone. After the extraction of the stone, I introduced my index finger, which I could easily insert into the cyst, right up to the webbing at the top of the finger. The cyst felt thick and fleshy, and stood out into the cavity of the bladder. A single stitch of silver wire sufficed to bring the edges of the wound closely together, and after a simple water-dressing a sponge was put over all, and firmly bound down. The little fellow was put to bed, and strict injunctions given to keep him on his back. The urine came away readily by the urethra, without the use of a catheter, and there was never the slightest suspicion of urinary infiltration, the wound having healed by first intention. The experience of Dr. Vlathos, of Philippopolis, was entirely in favour of the high operation for stone, especially in the case of children. The case I mention here was the ninth of a series of successful cases. In nearly all these cases, the wound healed by first intention, and the urine came away by the urethra from the first, without requiring to use a catheter, and in all of them the patient was going about very much sooner than he could otherwise have done had he been treated by the lateral method. Again, in the case which I have described, the extraction of the stone, though completely enclosed in a deep and fleshy cyst, was easily accomplished, which, I am sure, by the lateral or any other method would have been not only difficult but impossible. I was much impressed by this operation, and the more I have studied the subject and its literature, the less am I able to understand why an operation, with a history so successful and encouraging as that of the suprapubic operation for stone—one so easy to perform, with so little risk attending it, either of danger to the patient or of failure on the surgeon's part, an operation, moreover, from which the recovery is generally so rapid and complete —should be so entirely ignored by modern surgeons.

I have already incidentally referred to the loathsome presence of maggots in the wounds of soldiers during the hot weather. Fortunately we found the ordinary strength (1 to 40) of carbolic acid solution, which we used for dressing the wounds, a perfect protection from this plague. When we got a case of a deep wound filled with maggots, and where they had probably burrowed, our usual plan was to inject a 1 to 20 solution of carbolic acid, which effectually killed them, and allowed of our picking them out of the wound. After cleansing out the wound thoroughly, we dressed it with lint or charpie soaked in the weaker (1 to 40) solution, which we found proved a complete safeguard from the attacks of the flies. Mr. Longmore, in speaking on this point, says 'that the weak solutions of 1 part in 100, such as are usually employed in direct dressings, are of no avail in warding off flies.' This I can easily believe; but I certainly never saw such weak solutions employed in direct dressings, having always used myself one of, at least, the strength of 1 part in 40.

Marginalia: Dr. Pinkerton's report. Dr. Vlathos' operation for stone. Dr. Vlathos in favour of the high operation for stone, especially for children. Maggots in wounds.

MEDICAL REPORTS.

Dr. Pinkerton's report.

Danger of all forms of tourniquet which unduly constrict the limb.

I have already mentioned as a most useful instrument Dr. Foulis' improved elastic tourniquet. But when I speak of it in this way, I do so simply in connection with its employment by a surgeon at an operation where it is used under professional direction, and where the time it is allowed to constrict the limb is limited. For I consider it, as well as all other forms of tourniquet which act by firmly constricting a limb in its entire circumference at the point to which they are applied and completely arresting its circulation, as most dangerous, and, unless in exceptional circumstances, most unwarrantable contrivances for the arrest of hæmorrhage on the field. On the battlefield a surgeon never knows how long a tourniquet, once applied to a wounded limb, may be allowed to remain without the patient receiving the necessary aid and attention. In a wounded limb left for any length of time thus tightly compressed and strangulated, you cannot expect to find anything else than a gangrenous state of the parts thus unnaturally dealt with—and the more complete this constriction, and the longer it is continued, the greater will be the extent of the parts involved, and the more thorough will be the action of the gangrene. To avoid the great risk run by complete constriction of the limb, tourniquets have been devised with projecting wings for the purpose of relieving the limb from compression, unless just over the main artery, and on the opposite part of the limb where counter-pressure is exerted. This is certainly a step in the right direction, and provided the idea can be efficiently carried out in a practical instrument for field use (as it appears to be in Moffitt's winged screw tourniquet), it is certainly the only form which should be allowed for use on the field. Tourniquets are comparatively seldom required on the field, primary hæmorrhage being an infrequent cause of death on the field. When we consider this, therefore, and look at the risk run by unlimited application of tourniquets, the conclusion, come to by so many army surgeons of experience, and which is said to have been resorted to with much success in the Russian army in the Crimea, that tourniquets should be dispensed with, and the practice taught of stopping hæmorrhage by inserting a finger into the wound, seems a most practical one, and one thoroughly deserving a fair trial.

Moffitt's winged screw tourniquet.

Gooch's splints.

Splints were a source of much trouble to us in Turkey. We had a large supply of ordinary wooden splints, but the difficulty of finding one to fit each particular case, and the trouble entailed in making them fit was a constant source of annoyance. How I have wished for a good supply of Gooch's splints, to which I had been accustomed in the Glasgow Royal Infirmary! I am quite convinced there could not be a more suitable splint for military practice than this flexible splint of Gooch's. It is firm and light, and easily cut to any shape or size you require, and from its perfect flexibility cross-ways admits of considerable moulding to the limb. There are two other varieties of splint formed on this model—viz., Schnyder's cloth splint and Esmarch's splint material, and although I have never used either, I am satisfied, from my experience with Gooch's splint, that this is the proper idea for splints for use in military practice, where lightness, combined with firmness, and the rapidity with which a splint can be fitted to any particular case, are of the utmost importance. Prepared splints, whether of wood, or pasteboard, or wire, or tin, are of comparatively little use, as you seldom get among a stock of prepared splints one which will exactly fit the particular case; and the trouble of moulding and fitting a prepared splint to a particular case is greater and more annoying than any one would believe who has not tried it. With splint material, like Gooch's, on the other hand, you cut out in a few minutes with a pocket knife the sort of splint most suited to each case, and splints moreover exactly to your own mind.

Stromeyer's triangular cushion in compound fracture.

In speaking of excision of the shoulder, I mentioned that after the operation the arm was put up with a pad in the axilla, and supported by a broad sling. Now this pad was roughly and quickly fashioned after the manner of Stromeyer's triangular cushion, the idea and purposes of which I have always, since it first came under my notice, accepted as correct, and endeavoured to carry out in the treatment of injuries of the upper arm and shoulder-joint. And after considerable experience of the sort of cases to which it is applicable, I can well understand the high value Stromeyer places on this invention of his, than which nothing could be more naturally fitted for treatment of compound fractures of the upper arm and cases of injury to the shoulder-joint. It gives a position of most perfect support, stability, and comfort to the wounded limb, while at the same time it entirely removes any risk of the occurrence of gangrene, which is so much to be dreaded in such a part when anything is applied likely to constrict the limb and interfere with its circulation, such as splints and bandages. I think a most valuable addition to army surgical stores would be a supply of such cushions made of india-rubber, and arranged so as to be fitted for use by being filled with air, or they could be stuffed with any soft material, such as wool or charpie, if their air-holding capabilities were in any way interfered with or destroyed. In such a skeleton form, made of either india-rubber or light canvas, of various sizes (from 12 to

15 inches a side), a large supply of Stromeyer's invaluable cushion could be carried with little addition to either bulk or weight of stores.

Plaster of Paris was used a good deal for splints, but my experience of it is not very favourable. I chiefly object to it on account of its weight and liability to crack, and especially in the case of men who had to be conveyed for long distances over rough roads in springless machines, did these objections show themselves and prove most troublesome. I think paraffin, as suggested by Dr. Macewen in a paper published in the 'Lancet,' August 31, 1878, would form a much more desirable and useful material for splints. It has the very great advantages, from an army surgeon's point of view, of being light to carry, not being easily injured—water especially being quite harmless to it—and it may be used many times, old splints being melted down to make new ones. Any one who has had the opportunity of seeing, side by side, two cases of fractured leg, one done up in plaster of Paris and the other in paraffin, will never forget the incomparable look of comfort produced by the lightness of the paraffin splint; and when you come to speak of transporting the two, the enormous advantages of the light paraffin splint will become more and more apparent. The only seeming disadvantage attached to paraffin, as compared with plaster of Paris, is that of its requiring heat for its application; but that is a small matter to put against its very great advantages; besides, fire could readily be got at the first line of hospitals, where the application of such splints is most likely to take place.

The Turks are notoriously a tobacco-smoking people, using however, as a rule, the mildest varieties of the fragrant weed, and chiefly in the form of cigarettes. Nothing, therefore, was more acceptable to us in our work among the wounded than the large supplies we received of tobacco. I really do not know what we would have done without it. As Mr. Longmore most truly and appreciatively says, 'No one can doubt its soothing effect on men suffering from the pain of wounds, or that it allays nervous excitement, and produces a state of calm which helps to secure the rest which is so beneficial to them in every way. The contentment it affords to the patient helps the surgeon in his work, and enables a man to submit cheerfully to many deprivations unavoidable from the circumstances of his position, the absence of which, without it, would fret and worry him,' I have seen the aspect of a whole ward of wounded men changed, as by a miracle, from a silent, sombre wretchedness to one of light and glad contentment by the opportune distribution of a few packets of tobacco and cigarette papers. To have seen such a sight was, in itself, enough to make one for ever thankful that there is such a plant as tobacco, the use of which is capable of affording so much comfort in distress, alike mitigating the tortures of a pain-racked body, and soothing the misery of a troubled mind. There does not appear to be any good reason why such a powerful aid to the doctor should be so thoroughly excluded from our civil hospitals. Its allowance, under definite regulations as to time and place, there is little doubt, would benefit many, and that, too, without interfering in any way with the comfort of non-smokers; while the fact of its being allowed would prevent its use in a surreptitious manner, with its attendant risk of fire. However this may be, there are no two opinions regarding its usefulness and almost necessity as part of army hospital stores.

There are still many interesting points which I should like to have touched upon, had space permitted; but I will conclude by referring briefly to the noble work of aid to the wounded, conducted by Lady Strangford during this war. One of the greatest difficulties we had to contend with, in our treatment of the wounded, was the almost entire absence of nursing. There were soldiers, no doubt, to attend and watch the wounded, but you could not call their care of the wounded, well intentioned and kindly though it always was, nursing, unless by a most vague and general use of that term. How Lady Strangford, in her private hospitals, assisted by her staff of female nurses, succeeded in showing a result, in the comfort of her patients and their chances of recovery, that was utterly unapproachable in the best and most carefully conducted hospitals, where there was only the usual male nursing, any one of the many who have had the pleasure of visiting her hospitals can abundantly testify. Women are incomparably better adapted, both physically and morally, for the duties of nursing the sick than men, and trained female nurses are simply invaluable to the surgeon. Their aid cannot well be rendered available on the battle-field, but there is no reason why it should not be ready to hand immediately in the rear of the fighting, and after the battle.

Report by A. O. MACKELLAR, Esq.

INJURIES OF THE HEAD.

Mr. Mackellar's report.

Proportion of head injuries large.

Mode of fighting.

The number of head injuries was undoubtedly large in proportion to the whole number of wounded; variously and approximately estimated from 10 to 15 per cent. This large proportion is readily accounted for by the Turkish mode of fighting from behind entrenchments, so that the head, neck, upper extremities, and upper part of chest, form the target offered to the fire of the enemy. The battle of Teliche is a good instance of this. I can vouch for the facts. A Russian force, composed principally of regiments of the Guards, numerically more than double, if not actually treble, the strength of their opponents, stormed the strong earthworks of Teliche. They came up the glacis in more or less solid formation, only breaking into loose order for a final assault when within 400 yards of the parapet. The Turks, acting purely on the defensive, had reserved their fire until this moment, only showing sufficiently above the breastwork to enable them to fire; they then poured in such murderous volleys that the Russian attack completely failed, and the stormers retired precipitately, in most complete disorder, and leaving some hundreds of dead on the ground. The loss of the Turks, sheltered behind their breastworks, was 21 killed and 50 wounded. Of the 50 wounded the majority were struck in the hand, fingers, or shoulder; a few received grazing injuries of neck or scalp. Of the 21 killed, two or three were shot through the chest, the remainder through the head. Many died instantaneously. The others, allowed to remain where they fell, were removed by the English surgeons. In all cases there was extensive fracture of the skull, with protrusion of brain substance. They lingered periods varying from 24 to 36 hours from receipt of the injury; but, with one exception, all the cases terminated fatally. The reason that, although the proportion of such injuries was large, comparatively very few of the cases came under surgical observation, was probably due to the fact that in the Ottoman army there is no systematically organised and properly trained corps of Kranken-traeger, or sick bearers, to remove those so severely wounded as to be incapacitated from escaping from the line of fire, so that, unless they attract the attention of a passing surgeon, or charitable comrade, they perish where they fall.

Proportion of cases coming under observation of surgeon small. Sick bearers.

Serious injuries involving fracture rarely came under the observation of the surgeon.

Dr. Macpherson reports two such cases under his care in the hospital of Orkhanie. (1.) A gunshot fracture in occipital region, with protrusion of brain substance. The man died 24 hours after admission. (2.) Compound fracture of the frontal bone from fragment of shell received eight weeks before at Plevna. Had been treated expectantly in Plevna with wet compresses. Suffered from hernia cerebri and dementia; general health good.

The consensus of opinion of Stafford House surgeons was unanimous in favour of strict observance of the rule of surgical non-intervention. I cannot better express this opinion than by quoting from Dr. Pinkerton. Dr. Pinkerton says:—'I saw very few wounds of head, but those I did see impressed me with the importance of non-interference on the surgeon's part, unless for the relief of urgent symptoms. Even in depressed fracture with external wound, the general principle of non-interference should be the rule of practice.' In these judicious remarks, all surgeons having practical experience of warfare will concur.

Case of trephining successful.

Grazing injuries of the skull were comparatively rarely followed by pyæmia, unless the patient was placed in a hospital already attacked by pyæmia. Dr. Casson reports a case of a patient whom he trephined for depressed fracture, and removed some fragments of bone and a quantity of hair that had been driven into the brain substance. The man made a good recovery.

Treatment usually adopted.—Cold applications, absolute quiet and rest when possible, free purgation and low diet.

I do not know of any case where either local or general bleeding was resorted to. Pieces of necrosed bone were never rashly removed. The Turks, thanks to their temperate and abstemious habits, frequently made marvellous recoveries from grave injuries, even when placed under the most unfavourable circumstances.

Dr. Sandwith reports that among the wounded at Adrianople in July 1877 was a Turkish soldier, who was shot through the head from the anterior part of the right temporal fossa to a similar point on the left side. Both his eyes were thoroughly disorganised, and the bridge of his nose was entirely smashed. Dr. Sandwith removed the contents of each orbit, and also several splinters of bone. His wounds were treated with ordinary carbolic dressings, and he made a good recovery, the only symptom referable to the brain being severe pain in the frontal region for a time. His face was permanently much less disfigured than was originally anticipated.   *Mr. MACKELLAR'S report.*

Several extensive shell wounds of head were seen at Shipka, and at other places where mountain fighting was carried on. In some cases the whole of the skull-cap was removed, with the dura mater stripped off, and the pulsating, irregular surface of brain matter fully exposed. The victims of these disastrous injuries remained in a state of complete coma for periods varying from two hours to two days, and, as a matter of course, died. The treatment was absolutely nil, and the men were usually allowed to remain in some quiet place in the immediate neighbourhood of the battle-field until their inevitable end approached.   *Shell wounds of the head.*

Once, while engaged in choosing cases for transport to the rear in a superior form of ambulance wagon, the attention of Dr. Sandwith was directed to a man who was sitting on a form with a number of others badly wounded, in a very crowded room. His face was covered with blood and with a yellow, pulpy matter, which had run down over his forehead, almost blinding him, and matting together the hair on his face. Upon removing the clothes which were bound round his head, Dr. Sandwith discovered a large shell wound of the frontal region. The bone was removed over a space of two inches square, and the brain over this area was disintegrated, and had partly escaped. Yet this man, though suffering from complete aphasia, retained some consciousness, and could move his left arm when told to do so. He rapidly became comatose, and died on the following day in the hospital to which he had been immediately removed.

Dr. Kirker reports the case of Yeinel Suleiman, aged 30, wounded at Shipka on August 12. He had been hit by a bullet fired from a considerable height above him. On examination there was found a compound comminuted fracture of skull at the upper end of right occipito-parietal suture. His wound, not dressed for several days, was swarming with maggots. There was no other wound. The man did not know whether the bullet had dropped out or not. Dr. Kirker made a careful digital examination, but failed to find it. He removed several smashed fragments of bone, but left one large splinter, which was firmly attached. The patient was dull and listless, moaned, and turned often in bed. Light dressing was applied, and aperients given. The man remained in same condition for a fortnight and then gradually improved. On Oct. 4 Dr. Kirker notes: 'Constitutional symptoms disappeared; wound granulating healthily, pulsation of brain communicated to it.' He was shortly afterwards discharged nearly well.   *Compound comminuted fracture of skull.*

Dr. Kirker had under his care a man wounded in right frontal region. The bullet had evidently struck him obliquely, for the integument had to be raised, and the finger passed in some distance to reach the point of fracture. His injury had previously been regarded as a simple scalp wound, and treated as such. There was considerable comminution of bone; the splinters lay loose in a thin puriform fluid; no action about the external wound. The man was dull, stupid, and foeble, and suffered much from diarrhœa. Dr. Kirker removed the loose splinters, and saw brain pulsating beneath. A few days later, his skin and conjunctivæ became yellow; a large abscess formed beneath the scalp, at a point remote from the seat of injury; the diarrhœa increased, the motions being passed involuntarily, and he rapidly sank. Although no distinct rigor was observed, there is little doubt but that his death was due to pyæmia. There was no post-mortem.

GUNSHOT INJURIES OF CHEST.

Wounds of the upper part of chest were frequent, as this, in intrenchment fighting, was a region peculiarly exposed above the breastwork to the Russian fire. The opinions of the surgeons as to the proportion of these injuries vary, those at the front giving a large percentage, and especially if their experience has been of fighting behind earthworks and in shelter trenches. On the other hand, those in the hospitals of the rear—*i.e.*, Philippopolis and Adrianople—estimate chest injuries at a low figure, the worst cases having died during the tedious transport, or the crowded pestilential hospitals on the route, the convalescing cases having been kept near the battlefield where they received the wound. Many die on the battlefield instantaneously from penetrating wound of the heart, or more or less rapidly from hæmorrhage or suffocation.   *Wounds of upper chest.*

Contusion, and non-penetrating injuries from spent bullets, at long ranges, were common. Frequently the injured Turk thought the injury too slight to require surgical assistance or to warrant his reporting himself wounded. If later he came under treatment, it was probably for spitting of blood, with some dyspnœa, due to the congestion or ecchymosis of lung. There were   *Injuries from spent bullets.*

Mr. Mackellar's report.   instances where bullets had been deflected, and gliding round a rib had passed completely round one side of the chest without entering. Such cases were occasionally followed by necrosis of rib.

PENETRATING WOUNDS OF CHEST.

Dr. Macpherson reports six cases coming under his care; three, treated to termination, died. In one case, a patient arrived at the Orkhanie hospital, having been wounded at Plevna three weeks previously. A fragment of shell had passed through the upper right scapular region, fracturing scapula and clavicle. The wounds of entrance and exit were literally alive with maggots. The man was much exhausted. The fragment, a piece of the stud of a shell, measuring 3½ inches by one, was removed from wound, where it had lain for nearly three weeks. Patient died suddenly three days later, apparently from internal hæmorrhage.

Dr. Stiven reports two deaths in the Rustchuk hospital from penetrating wounds of lung.

Dr. Ryan reports six deaths from similar injuries at Erzeroum.

Seven wounds in one patient.   Dr. Neylan reports the case of a Turkish colonel who had seven wounds, five flesh wounds of extremities, a penetrating wound of thorax, and a penetrating wound of abdomen. In the chest the ball had entered to the inner side of the right nipple, traversed the right lung, and was lying beneath skin just below inferior angle of scapula, from which situation Dr. Neylan extracted it by incision. In the abdominal wound the bullet had entered almost midway between umbilicus and anterior superior spinous process of ilium, and emerged posteriorly near end of last rib. Dr. Neylan says: 'Dyspnœa was urgent, and death seemed imminent.'

Hernia of lung   Notwithstanding the gravity and number of his wounds, the colonel returned to his regiment three weeks later. The rare and most interesting feature of this case was the development of consecutive pneumocele, or hernia of lung, posteriorly at the site of the cicatrix of the incision for the removal of the bullet. The patient had had occasional convulsive fits of coughing for some days previously; when Dr. Neylan discovered the hernia the tumour was of the size of a small orange, crepitant, and varied in size with the movements of inspiration and expiration; it gave the man no inconvenience; a simple pad was applied to protect, and the colonel left the hospital well, and returned to duty.

The results of treatment of penetrating wounds of the region of lung seem to have been directly influenced by the locality, character, and quality of the building in which the suffering were treated.

Cases treated in the immediate vicinity of the battle-fie'd, in small buildings such as Bulgarian cottages, with plenty of cubic space, isolated from suppurating and foul wounds, gave a fair percentage of good recoveries. The Turk, from his temperate and abstemious habits, and by his splendid constitution and physique, is predisposed to make a good recovery from severe injuries if he has only a fair chance. The simplest forms of dressing were adopted; opium was found an invaluable adjunct in the treatment. On the other hand, cases sent to the rear, often transported long distances without dressing, without food, exposed to all weather, finally admitted into buildings totally unfitted for use as hospitals—*e.g.* mosques, where the air was always stagnant, never changed, no ventilation, and no drains, filled to overflowing with suppurating and often gangrenous wounds—the poor invalids, breathing a pestilential atmosphere, rapidly became poisoned, and almost invariably died from a low form of pleuro pneumonia or sank exhausted from constant, long-continued profuse suppuration.

No instances of hermetic sealing of chest wounds nor of venesection in the treatment of inflammatory complications came under my notice.

WOUNDS OF UPPER EXTREMITY.

Left hand and left shoulder.   Wounds of upper extremity were extremely numerous, occurring with especial frequency in the hands, elbow, and neighbourhood of shoulder. The left hand and left shoulder seem to suffer more than the right. In the case of the hand, the entrance wound was usually found about the middle of the dorsal surface, or at the metacarpoiphalangeal articulation, the exit wound in the palm being large and rugged from bone being driven out, many spicules remaining in the wound. The position of these wounds is readily explained by the frequency of the soldier receiving his wound whilst in the firing position, as also by the hilly and rugged character of the ground on which many of the engagements were fought.

Obliquity of Wound.—Messrs. Attwood, Hume, and Sandwith, who formed the S.H. Ambulance at Shipka, had been struck with the great obliquity and large size of entrance of wounds received in the heavy fighting there, especially after the severe and determined attack upon Fort St. Nicholas on September 17, when a forlorn hope, composed of 3,000 volunteers, issued from the Russian advanced trenches, distant about 150 yards, and stormed the impregnable crag above them, being during the period of their advance exposed to an almost vertical fire.

Mr. MACKELLAR'S report.

Obliquity of wounds.

So characteristic was this peculiarity that Dr. Pinkerton, who was never at the Shipka, but who had considerable experience of the wounded in Philippopolis and Adrianople, was able at once to distinguish those wounded at Shipka. I quote from Dr. Pinkerton's very able and very interesting paper, read before the Medico-Chirurgical Society of Glasgow, and which happily forms part of the present report:—

'If, in inspecting wounded in a hospital in Philippopolis or Adrianople, you found a large number of them suffering from wounds of the upper part of the body, especially of the hands, face or neck—if you found, moreover, that the wounds of entrance in most of them presented a peculiar appearance, being large in size and oblique in direction; and further, on looking more closely, you found this large size of entrance wound was caused by a superficial furrow, a planing off of the integuments leading up to the point where the bullet began to penetrate the deeper structures; that, in fact, the wound was a combination of a rasing shot and a penetrating shot—then you might be perfectly certain that they were men wounded at Shipka.'

The wounded from Shipka were easily distinguished by the nature and position of their wounds, which were nearly all in the upper parts of the body, and in most the bullet appeared to have struck the body in an oblique direction. This was especially the case with the wounds occurring amongst the troops occupying the Turkish centre, and having for their objective point the Fort Nicholas, situated on the bluff above them. This steep formation of the ground fully accounts for the oblique direction and peculiar rasing character of the wounds.

Dr. Pinkerton quotes Professor Longmore's explanation, that this largeness of wound of entrance, obliquity of direction, and rasing character of wound 'is only in seeming, and is owing to the projectile having struck the surface slantingly, so that parts of the skin and areolar tissues have been shaved away, as it were, before the projectile had passed inwards through the superficial fascia.'

Mr. Longmore continues that this is strictly speaking a rasing wound on one side of the true entrance wound, for the true entrance wound is of course the commencement of the track of the projectile through the deeper structures.

A similar condition of wounds was met with by other surgeons having exceptional experience of fighting in hilly districts.

FINGER WOUNDS.

The proportion of finger injuries was very large, in some engagements constituting 80 per cent. of wounded, the fingers of the left hand being more frequently wounded than those of the right hand. The phalangeal articulations of the left index finger suffered most. Many of the surgeons in Turkey had served with the Servians in the war of the previous year, and had observed the unusually large percentage of finger injuries, and the increase in numbers of this class of wounds aroused their suspicions as to the frequency of self-mutilation for the purpose of claiming exemption from military service. The fact that the finger injured was usually the 'trigger finger,' wounded on its palmar aspect, induced a more careful examination, and more extended observation, fully confirmed their early suspicions.

Injuries to fingers.

Self-mutilation

The Servians guilty of these dastardly acts were generally men of puling, whining aspect, and of poor physique, without any previous military knowledge or training, suddenly transplanted from their normal occupations of agriculture and commerce to the uncongenial arena of warfare. Self-mutilation accounts for a very small proportion of such injuries amongst the Turks in the Russo-Turkish war; the few exceptions being limited to the Egyptian and Nubian contingent.

During the severe weather at Kamarli, when the degree of cold was so intense that the Turkish sentries had to be changed every quarter of an hour, in order to avoid their being frozen to death at their posts (and even with these frequent changes men were occasionally found dead), the Egyptians, to whom cold, frost, ice, and snow, were alike alien and unfamiliar, endured great sufferings, and at times yielded to the temptation of blowing away a finger to escape further hardships and further danger. The Mustafiz, or third reserve, mostly elderly men, afflicted with

MEDICAL REPORTS.

Mr. MACKELLAR'S report — hernia, and with no stomach for fighting, could not resist following the example set them by the Egyptians. But the greater number of finger injuries is readily and at once explained by the Turkish methods of fighting from behind cover, be that cover tree, inequality of ground, shelter-trench, or parapet of redoubt. It is not always easy to determine as to whether the finger wound has been received in legitimate warfare, or has been self-inflicted. Although in the latter class the finger and hand is plentifully begrimed with powder, this charred appearance, considered by itself, is by no means absolute proof of guilt, for a similar condition obtains in the case of a soldier firing many consecutive rounds of ammunition with a rifle heated by repeated and rapid discharges. Then, again, a man receiving his wound at close quarters will very probably have some powder driven in with the bullet. As we have before indicated, more trustworthy guides are the particular fingers wounded, whether the dorsal or palmar aspect be injured, and the characteristic shattered appearance furnished by a wound received by placing a finger over the muzzle of a gun.

Flesh wounds. — Field dressing most generally adopted in the treatment of flesh wounds consisted of lint or charpie soaked in carbolised water, with bandage very lightly applied. A pad of carbolised oakum was found very serviceable placed over the dressing in anticipation of the liability of the patient going several days without a second dressing; its loose porous texture causing it to rapidly absorb the discharges from the wound. The tar which it contains renders it a valuable antiseptic and deodoriser, and facilitates its combustion when quantities of it have to be got rid of after having been used in hospital practice. As a pad, it also protects the part during rough transport, and diminishes the tendency to hæmorrhage. In wounds of large size, accompanied by great contusion and laceration of soft parts as in shell injuries, where the pain is often extremely severe in character, the carbolised oil is a grateful application. Subsequently, in the hospitals, the dressings will vary with the extent and character of the wound, the constitution and habits of the patient, and the sanitary conditions by which he is surrounded. In uncomplicated cases, the patient being a healthy man, and the building in a satisfactory hygienic condition, warm water dressing will be all that will be required. Under conditions less favourable, free use of disinfectants, notably carbolic and Condy, frequent change of dressing, generous diet, combined with tonics, will be required.

Here may be noted in the case of the Turk the great difficulty of persuading a wounded man to take medicine. He invariably replied, 'I am wounded, not sick; I therefore need no medicine.' The religious scruples of the Turk with regard to wine or stimulants had also to be overcome; and, in addition, many were unwilling to lose caste among their fellows by tasting the forbidden liquor.

Ventilation. — Too much stress cannot be laid upon the importance of thorough free ventilation, and the prompt destruction of used dressings.

Where burrowing of pus threatens, early incisions, use of drainage tube, thorough emptying of sinuses, and frequent irrigation must be employed.

An early examination of wound by finger, and extraction of the bullet, fragments of clothes, buttons, or other foreign bodies must be made. When the bullet is beyond reach of the finger, a long bullet probe must be introduced to ascertain direction of channel. It is desirable that a Nélaton's probe be provided, but it cannot be implicitly relied upon. By far the best forceps for the extraction of the ball are the 'rat-toothed' forceps of Tieman, commonly known as the American bullet forceps. Ordinary forceps dilate in the wound too much and prove useless if the bullet is beyond the reach of the finger. The forceps should be so constructed that the expansion of the handles is very slightly greater than at the teeth. The catch ordinarily found on these forceps is useless and objectionable.

Probes and forceps

Plague of maggots. — During the late war, a loathsome but frequent complication of all wounds was the presence of maggots in great numbers. They may be best got rid of by irrigation with very strong carbolic solution, repeated every few hours. A strong solution of common salt also readily destroys them. Weak solutions are useless.

Flesh wounds of shoulder were especially frequent, explained, as before mentioned, by the firing position and the mode of fighting.

Compound fractures were more frequent in the upper arm than the forearm, and as a rule situated in the upper third of the humerus. They were always treated conservatively, unless in cases of great comminution of bone, injury of artery, extensive splintering into neighbouring articulation, profuse suppuration, and colliquative diarrhœa, or the reduced and weakened condition of patient urgently demanded amputation.

Complicated splints are a large and expensive mistake. Plain pieces of wood, ¼ inch thick, with a saw, so that the surgeon can adapt the splint to the patient with pads to correspond, attached by pieces of tape, together with Stromeyer's cushions and bandages, might all be packed in one box for field service, and will prove sufficient for most purposes.

Mr. Mackellar's report.

I can warmly endorse Dr. Pinkerton's recommendation of Gooch's splints.

Stromeyer's cushions were largely used by all the flying ambulances, and were found a boon of unspeakable value to the wounded in the arm.

Stromeyer's cushions.

Angular wooden splints and those made of light French wires were the splints very generally used; a small gutta-percha saddle splint formed a useful adjunct.

Plaster of Paris splints, with fenestra corresponding to site of wound, are well adapted for fixed hospitals when employed by surgeons accustomed to their use and application, but are dangerous at front, or on transport, and when applied by inexperienced individuals. Disastrous results have followed the indiscriminate use of plaster of Paris, by inexperienced surgeons using them for the first time, and applying them so tightly as to cause a degree of constriction resulting even in gangrene of the limb.

Plaster of Paris splints.

Compound fractures of forearm were common, and were always treated conservatively when possible, usually with good results; straight wooden and French wire splints were generally applied.

The reparative power of the hand is, if possible, more marked in military than civil practice: in many neglected cases of severe shell wounds, with great comminution of bone and laceration and bruising of soft parts, profuse suppuration had taken place, and extensive sinuses with necrosis of bone; where there had been no previous surgical attention and no dressing in many cases had been applied to the wound, good results were obtained by means of a hand splint, and thorough cleanliness and patience on the part of the surgeon. The least possible sacrifice of parts ought to be the golden rule of practice.

Amputations of the shoulder-joint were performed by the flap and by the oval methods. They were usually necessitated by severe shell injuries, causing complete destruction of the articulation, with extensive loss of soft parts, often requiring the exercise of all the surgeon's ingenuity as well as considerable tailoring skill to provide sufficient covering for the stump; in some instances it was absolutely impossible to do so, and the huge wound had to be left to granulate.

Amputations of shoulder-joint.

As an illustration of the frequency of such cases, I may mention that during one afternoon of artillery duel in Plevna, in which the Gravitza redoubt was engaged, Osman Effendi, one of the ablest surgeons I had the good fortune to meet in Turkey, and I were compelled to disarticulate at the shoulder-joint in four cases. In a fifth case a soldier, aged 25, had sustained a compound fracture of upper arm from rifle bullet; he declined amputation, and gangrene rapidly supervened. Eventually he agreed to submit to amputation at the shoulder-joint, and made a rapid recovery. So far as it was practicable to follow up the cases, I understood that all these men recovered; but I only saw three of them afterwards, and they were making a satisfactory convalescence.

Amputations of arm and forearm were generally made by the circular method or by the combination of skin flaps with circular division of muscle. I instance a few of the Plevna cases:—

Amputations of arms.

Salim, age 30 years, compound fracture of both bones of left forearm by bullet, amputated in the upper third of forearm. Recovered.

Mustapha, age 22 years, compound fracture of right upper arm by bullet. Amputation. Recovery.

Tahir, age 35 years, compound fracture of right upper arm by bullet. Amputation. Recovery.

Béker, Lieutenant, age 29 years. Left forearm carried away by a shell. Amputation through the arm. Recovery.

Hahl, age 36 years, total destruction of right elbow-joint by ball. Amputation of arm. Recovery.

Mustapha, age 35 years, gunshot fracture of right arm by bullet. Amputation. Recovery.

Hussein, age 24 years, gunshot fracture of left arm. Amputation. Recovery.

Saül, Lieutenant, lower third of forearm torn off by shell. Amputation in upper third. Recovery.

Ahmed, age 27 years, gunshot fracture of elbow-joint, with extensive comminution and splintering of lower part of humerus. Amputation of arm. Recovery.

Ali Baba, age 60 years, right hand and thumb of left hand carried away by shell. Amputation through right forearm, disarticulation of left thumb. Recovery.

Redjib, age 31 years, gunshot fracture of right arm. Amputation. Recovery.

As illustrations of 'least possible sacrifice of parts,' in extensive damage from shell injuries, I may mention two cases of amputation at the wrist-joint by Drs. Leslie and Sandwith, in

MEDICAL REPORTS.

Mr. MACKELLAR'S report.

Excisions of shoulder.

the Shipka Pass. In one case (Dr. Sandwith's) the wound healed almost entirely by first intention.

Excisions of shoulder were numerous, and the results exceedingly good. When possible, they should be primary; they should be performed as early after the reception of the wound as circumstances will permit; when this is not possible, the operation should be deferred until the reactionary inflammation has subsided. Langenbeck's operation was the one usually selected. It was the one that I invariably performed on my own patients. A straight incision is made from the anterior border of the acromion process, for three to four inches down the bicipital groove, the biceps tendon being carefully dissected out of its groove, and the periosteum carefully preserved.

By the conservation of the periosteum and the attachments of the various muscular insertions around the head of the bone, a greater range of motion and degree of power was secured to the patient than could have been obtained by any other mode of operation. A chain saw is of the greatest service in removing the head of the bone. The after treatment consisted in the use of drainage-tubes for the first few days, free and careful syringing, the arm supported on a Stromeyer's cushion, and a gutta-percha splint so moulded to the shoulder as to give support without pressing on or in any way interfering with the incision. Passive motion was and always should be commenced early, or from the 12th to the 18th day. Of course under the circumstances of the constant evacuation of the wounded and daily change of patients in hospital, it was absolutely impossible to follow up the cases as satisfactorily as could have been desired; but, so far as I know, the cases all did well. I know of no death; and those patients which I saw some time after the healing of the wound had a very fair and useful amount of motion and of power in the limb. The weak point in the after treatment was the absence of a course of electricity similar to the one enjoyed by patients whose joints had been excised in the Franco-German war. Cannstatt and Wiesbaden proved most successful physicians in cases of this kind.

A few cases of gunshot injuries of shoulder-joint, treated expectantly, were successful. A man under my own care, wounded in Plevna, had his right shoulder pierced by a bullet, which entered close to the greater tuberosity of the humerus; rather more than half the sphere of the caput humeri was comminuted; there was no wound of exit. I slightly enlarged the entrance wound, and removed three large bone splinters, and several small pieces, together with the bullet, and a piece of the man's coat. The wound was kept thoroughly syringed with carbolic lotion. The patient had no untoward symptom, and recovered completely, with good motion and so useful an arm that he was able to return to duty.

Excision of elbow-joint

Excision of elbow-joint.—Primary, *complete* excisions of elbow gave good results, especially where the patient remained stationary for some weeks after, and had therefore good and continuous treatment at the hands of the same medical officer. In all my own cases I excised by the straight linear incision. I believe this was the operation generally selected and adopted. The beau-ideal of a good excision-splint is undoubtedly the one recommended by Professor Esmarch. The splints used under these circumstances were generally extemporised from any materials to hand; and in default of these an ordinary cushion was resorted to.

In all cases there was abundant suppuration, treated by constant irrigation with carbolic solutions, use of drainage-tubes, and counter-openings when necessary. Passive motion, when possible, was commenced early, and the earlier this was done the more successful the case and greater the utility of limb.

Secondary excisions.

Secondary excisions, as a rule, did badly. In most of these, the injuries were inflicted by shell, with great comminution of bone and laceration of soft parts; in many cases the excision was done as the alternative of amputation. This latter, having been refused by the patient, he arrived at the station hospital after a tedious transport in bullock-wagons of some days' duration, with his wound in a foetid and semi-gangrenous condition, and devoured with maggots, his health broken by long-continued hardship and privation, and still further reduced by want of food and an exhausting diarrhoea or dysentery; excision was adopted by the surgeon under these circumstances from sheer necessity, and the wonder is not that many died, but that any survived.

Of three such cases in the hospital at Orkhanie, two died, and one recovered only when the patient, worn out by severe suffering, consented and submitted to amputation. Partial excisions were as unsatisfactory as they were injudicious; as a rule they were only attempted by inexperienced surgeons. There were some rare instances of gunshot injury of elbow-joint treated expectantly; in some cases fairly good motion was obtained, others terminating in anchylosis. No instance of excision of wrist came under my observation.

There was but little difficulty experienced in persuading Turkish patients to submit to the operation of excision; on its being explained that it was only for the purpose of removing a piece of damaged bone, in order to give them a good chance, not only of saving the limb, but of making it useful to them, they readily consented. Resections in continuity of shaft of bones were extensively practised; further reference will be made to them in the section on injuries of lower extremity.

Mr. MACKELLAR'S report.

INJURIES OF ABDOMEN.

Injuries of Abdomen.—Injuries of the abdomen were comparatively very rare, probably owing to the protection afforded to this region by the Turkish predilection for entrenchment fighting. The non-penetrating wounds were much more frequently met with than the penetrating. Presumably many of the penetrating wounds involving injury to important organs never came under the observation of the surgeon. Owing to the absence of an organised corps of stretcher-bearers, they were left to die where they fell. This statement was to some extent supported and confirmed by examination of the field of battle after an engagement.

Injuries of abdomen.

Oblique wounds of abdominal wall were common, especially among the men wounded at Shipka; wounded as they invariably were by bullets fired from a considerable height above them. In these oblique wounds the bullet usually entered at the upper part of the abdomen above the umbilicus, and burrowed often for long distances between skin and muscles, amongst these or between them and the peritoneum, its velocity becoming so lowered that not sufficient force remained for it to enter the peritoneal cavity. Not the least striking peculiarity of these oblique, non-penetrating wounds was their erratic course, the ball having been deflected by some tense tendon, aponeurosis or muscle.

Such injuries, with their concomitant symptoms of great collapse, vomiting, pain and abdominal distension, often closely simulated the graver lesion of penetration, and required a careful examination, assisted by experience, to distinguish them from cases of visceral injury.

In these cases the superiority of English methods of treatment was most marked; early discovery of 'bagging,' collections of pus, counter-openings, thorough drainage, syringing of wounds, opium to control muscular movement, and suitable diet, gave good results; whilst, on the other hand, cases treated on the *laissez-aller* system, pus allowed to accumulate and burrow, sloughing of muscle, and the cellular and fascial planes, abscess bursting into peritoneal cavity, with consequent acute peritonitis, &c., were followed by death.

Extensive lacerations of abdominal wall, as also sloughs from contusion by shell splinters, were frequently seen. In the rare cases of wounds involving the peritoneal cavity, the principle of non-interference was the absolute rule of practice; no digital examination, or examination by means of sound or probe, was permitted; all protruded parts if not damaged were returned, and simple dressings applied. Opium was regarded as the sheet-anchor in treatment, assisted by a liquid diet.

I am not aware of venesection having been resorted to in any instance.

Dr. Macpherson reports four cases of penetrating wounds of abdomen. One was doing well when last seen. One with a fæcal fistula in groin died exhausted. Two, involving injury of bladder, died.

Cases.

Dr. Goodridge reports the case of a private who was wounded by a bullet entering just above the pubes; there was no wound of exit; a catheter was passed, and some bloody urine drawn off; the catheter was then retained; the following day urine passed by the wound. Sloughing of the tissues around the wound took place, rapidly followed by peritonitis and death. Bullet could not be felt by catheter in bladder. Circumstances did not permit of the making of a post-mortem examination.

Dr. MacQueen records the case of a Turkish colonel, mortally wounded in abdomen (Elena).

Dr. Casson reports three cases of recovery from penetrating wounds of the abdomen in the Erzeroum hospital; in two of the cases the bullet remained in the abdominal cavity.

Dr. Neylan reports some interesting cases. 1. A regular had a rifle bullet wound of stomach, with gastric fistula, through which food escaped a few seconds after eating. A plastic operation was not possible, as tetanus with severe opisthotonos supervened. The tetanus ceased, and the patient made a good recovery. 2. A colonel had seven wounds, five in the extremities, one penetrating wound of thorax, and one penetrating of abdomen. When first seen dyspnœa was urgent, and death seemed imminent. Three weeks after the injury he returned to his regiment. 3. A bullet in one case entered the right buttock and emerged from the left, passing in front of the

Mr. MACKELLAR'S report.

sacrum. Fæces and flatus escaped by aperture of exit and none by anus. A digital exploration of the rectum revealed occlusion three inches above the anus. There was no injury to the sacrum. The man recovered. 4. A soldier during an attack on a mill was fired at almost vertically from the roof, the bullet entering the fourth right intercostal space, emerged through the left rectus with 'two spans of bowels.' Both wounds healed rapidly. There was no peritonitis. He returned to his regiment.

Dr. Stiven had a case under his care in the Rustchuk hospital of a young Turk shot through the abdomen from front to back in the left lumbar region. The bullet had entered almost undiverging between anterior superior spinous process of left ilium and umbilicus, and emerged below last rib just at outer edge of quadratus lumborum; there was no protrusion of viscera. A careful examination of the abdominal wall was made, which proved that the ball had traversed the abdominal cavity, and not merely travelled round under the skin. There was no peritonitis, no vomiting, but some troublesome constipation. Simple carbolised dressings were applied to the wounds, and the patient put upon a liquid diet. He left perfectly well in seventeen days. He had been wounded close to his own home, and during his stay in hospital he was most tenderly and devotedly nursed by his brother, a Bashi-Bazouk, a young lad of seventeen years of age, whom nothing could induce to leave for a single moment the bedside of his wounded brother.

Dr. Stiven reports another gunshot injury of abdomen, where the bullet had entered from behind in the lumbar region; no wound of exit, nor could bullet be felt, nor was there any evidence of its lodgment. After severe constitutional symptoms of some days' duration, a hard mass was felt in the epigastric region, a poultice was applied, and the mass became soft and fluctuating, the abscess was opened, fœtid pus escaped, and the bullet was found in the abscess cavity. The man made a good recovery.

Wind contusion.

Mr. Baird Douglas, whose fate it was to fall into the hands of General Gourko's troops at the capture of Teliche, reports a case of 'wind contusion' among the Russian wounded at Bogot. A Cossack of the Don, on the morning of General Skobeleff's attack and capture of the 'Green Hill,' at Plevna, was seen to fall in the ranks. He was picked up and carried to the rear. He stated that he had been hit by a shell, or piece of shell, in the abdomen, and was knocked down insensible by it. On examination no sign of laceration or contusion could be found, but the man still persisted that he had been hit. He was brought into hospital that night, and on the following morning another careful examination was made of him. This also failed to elicit any evidence of injury. He was kept in bed, and in a few days his stiffness having worn off, he was found covered with bruises about the abdomen. He distinctly said that it was no hallucination on his part, but that the shell buried itself in the ground a few feet from him, luckily *without exploding.*

INJURIES OF LOWER EXTREMITY.—GUNSHOT FRACTURES OF THIGH.

Gunshot fractures of thigh.

The experience of recent wars with regard to the great penetrative power of the cylindroconoidal or modern rifle bullet, and its terrific comminuting effect on the part of bone struck, was amply confirmed. Never perhaps in the surgical history of war was the condition and treatment of gunshot injuries of the femur more hopeless than in the recent campaign; the surgeons, disheartened by the gravity of the injury, and by the insuperable difficulties with which its treatment was beset, were still further baffled by the obstinate refusal of the patient to submit to amputation. They had reluctantly to admit the impotence of their art, and passively to await the advent of that inevitable death which seemed only too long in coming. Even those whom previous experience of war had in some measure prepared for this state of things stood appalled at the ghastly spectacle and fearful mortality. Much has been said in the English journals about the objections of the Turks to amputation. The objections may be thus stated. The Turk, aware of the promise of the Prophet that the soldier falling gloriously in battle against the enemies of his religion, his Padishah, and his country, should be at once and without intervening purgatory translated to the Paradise furnished with the most beautiful of houris for his special enjoyment and delectation, has a very natural horror to enter such an abode of bliss with any physical defect tending to disqualify him in the minds of the fair ones. Again, mutilation by loss of limb is one of the old Mohammedan forms of punishment; therefore the Mussulman soldier is loth to be despised as a criminal when he ought rather to be admired as a hero. Further, this repugnance to amputation is intensified by the fact that the Ottoman Government makes no provision and awards no

Objections of the Turks to amputation.

pension to its cripples and invalids. Anyone acquainted with the character of the Turkish soldier will not be surprised at his natural aversion to add to the legion of maimed beggars who horrify the Western traveller as he crosses on the Galata bridge. Perhaps the most potent reason of all was embodied in the fact that in the early part of this war amputations, and indeed operations of all kinds, in the hands of unskilled surgeons, without adequate appliances, and never performed until the last moment, had proved so invariably fatal, that the Turk had come to regard operation as practically synonymous with death, and preferred to die with a whole rather than a mutilated body. As the last remark may appear to reflect somewhat harshly upon our Turkish colleagues, from whom we received at all times kindness and courtesy, and our relations with whom were characterised by perfect harmony and good feeling, I may explain that, without any wish or intention to disparage their surgical skill, inasmuch as only a limited number of bodies per annum is supplied by the Imperial Academy of Medicine of Constantinople for the instruction in anatomy and surgery of their large numbers of students, the majority can only have been spectators and not actual performers of operations; and they can neither be expected to have the anatomical knowledge, the manual dexterity, nor the surgical experience (only acquired by long practice) to conduct an amputation to a successful issue.

Mr. MACKELLAR'S report.

Turkish surgeons.

The most brilliant exception, I know, was found in the person of Osman Effendi, a Turkish gentleman who had studied for three years in Paris, an able surgeon and an expert operator; fortunately the accident of war has placed him where his services were most required; in Plevna he was emphatically the right man in the right place. When the patient could be induced to submit to operation, amputation was the almost invariable rule of practice. It would have been a criminal procedure to have attempted conservative surgery under the adverse circumstances by which the surgeon frequently found himself surrounded. Even if the surgeon had the rare good fortune to see his patient immediately after the receipt of his wound, the necessity for prompt evacuation of the field hospitals, despatch to the reserve hospital, usually at a long distance in the rear, the arduous and weary transport in open bullock wagons of ten days in duration, exposed to inclemency of weather, the vague uncertainty as to dressing of his wound, and even supply of food during the transit, perhaps in the end for the patient only to arrive at a hospital crowded with wounded, decimated by pyæmia, and to fall into the hands of unskilled surgeons—surely these were circumstances, combined with the frequent absence of splints and necessary appliances, sufficient to deter the most conservatively-minded surgeon. But when, as was more frequently the case, the soldiers, with constitutions broken down, and worn out by long-continued exposure, hardship, and privation, still further reduced by an exhausting dysentery, which treatment seemed powerless to relieve, with wounds stinking with decomposing sloughs and fœtid pus swarming with maggots, came under notice only some days after the injury, the only chance was immediate amputation, if the patient could be prevailed upon to submit to it. Could there have been a more emphatic endorsement of the terse axiom of Dupuytren that he who attempted to save limbs lost lives? Post-mortem examinations generally disclosed very great comminution of bone, with extensive splintering of the diaphysis to some distance from point struck; large sloughs which burrowed in all directions, bathed in fœtid pus; and no attempt at union. The best marked instances of conservative surgery, remarkable to say, occurred in Plevna, and form a striking corroboration of the experience of Stromeyer at Floing near Sedan.

Osman Effendi.

The sufferer had to be carried into the nearest building, and there treated on a *laissez-aller* system; no splints were applied from sheer lack of them, although one is disposed to regret that the thousands of rifles captured from the Russians, and useless as weapons for want of corresponding ammunition, had not been utilised as provisional substitutes; the limbs remained passive (the patients were on the board of straw) from utter inability to move them. In several instances firm union had taken place, with production of enormous masses of callus, great thickening and shortening, together with an infinite variety of mal-position; some cases, from the amount of curvature and distortion, quite justifying the epithet of 'ramshorn' applied to them by a S. H. surgeon. These men had been brought from the scene of action hard by, had been subjected to no arduous transport, had been well housed and well fed. This striking corroboration of Stromeyer's experience should suggest the expediency of treating this class of injuries when possible on the spot; in the event of retreat in civilised warfare, let the surgeons avail themselves more fully of the privileges and provisions of the Geneva Convention, and allow themselves with their wounded to fall into the hands of the enemy. It appeared to me that the deformity in the cases above referred to could have been readily remedied by subsequent refracture or by subcutaneous osteotomy.

In the cases where conservatism may be attempted, and immobility, rest and food can be ensured, let the surgeon keep the limb straight, and not be over-anxious about extension. Let

Conservatism.

174   MEDICAL REPORTS.

Mr. MACKELLAR'S report.

him scrupulously preserve all splinters lying in the axis of the limb—they will assist materially in the consolidation of the fracture—and let him promptly remove completely detached transversely placed splinters; this is a point of the highest practical importance, and when efficiently carried out will go far to diminish the tendency to osteomyelitis. Subsequent deformity, if it occurs, is unimportant compared with the increased safety to life ensured by such treatment, and can be easily rectified by refracture or osteotomy.

Dr. Kirker reports an interesting case of gunshot fracture of the thigh healing almost without suppuration—a young man twenty-five years of age, wounded at Eski-Zaghra. The fracture was treated first by posterior wire splint, with foot-piece; later by a McIntyre, and finally by a Liston, for the purpose of correcting an outward bend at the seat of fracture. When the patient left Dr. Kirker's hands, there was a little deformity of thigh, some eversion of foot, and an inch and a half shortening of the limb.

Gunshot fractures of upper third of the femur were treated conservatively; and when stationary, with fairly good results; when transported long distances, they were almost uniformly fatal.

Dr. Kirker reports the case of a man shot through the hip, who recovered. I know of but one case of excision of hip—the head and neck of femur, and upper part of the great trochanter, having been smashed by a ball. Operation was performed by Dr. Ruddock. Death occurred some days later from pyæmia, which was at that time rife in that hospital. No case occurred of amputation of hip-joint. Penetrating injuries of knee-joint with fracture were generally treated by amputation. Some cases treated conservatively made remarkable and unexpected recoveries; some cases having refused amputation, with anchylosis, but with a useful limb. Only one case of excision is recorded which ought never to have been attempted.

Injuries of the knee-joint.

Gunshot injuries of leg were frequently treated conservatively, with good results; owing to his abstemious habits, wounds do not appear to suppurate so abundantly in the Turk.

When so treated the splinters were removed, and the limb put up in fenestrated plaster of Paris, or wire and box splints were employed.

Circassian surgical treatment.

We may learn a lesson in osteoplastic surgery from the Circassians, who practise in no mean degree the art of surgery. A Circassian may consent to part with an upper extremity, but never with his lower; he rather prefers death than a mutilation that will prevent him from mounting a horse; a Circassian not able to ride would consider himself degraded in the eyes of his people. In gunshot injuries of leg, all splinters are carefully removed by them; if difficulty in reduction is experienced, protruding fragments are sawn off; if a hiatus remains, a piece of bone of a size and form calculated to fill the gap is taken from a foal, or, failing this, from a young bullock—this is put into the interspace, and allowed to remain there. The limb is then put up in bandages, soaked in a paste made of ground Indian corn and water, thickened with white of egg. I have never seen this actually done, but I know many people of authority and position who can vouch for the fact. I have seen old fractures said to have been so treated, and certainly their condition left nothing to be desired.

I have attended a Circassian for a gunshot fracture of leg, who had the fracture put up in the way I describe, and who showed me an old fracture of other leg; the injury had been received many years previously, and had been treated osteoplastically, in the way I have mentioned.

Of injuries of ankle-joint treated conservatively by removal of splinters, immobilisation, &c., I saw many cases, some of which appeared admirably suited for excision later.

Resections.

Owing to the unwillingness of the Turk to submit to amputation, resections in the continuity of the shafts of long bones were more extensively resorted to than under other and different circumstances would have been justifiable. The results on the whole, however, were not encouraging. Excisions of portions of the bones of the fore-arm were most successful; next in order, excision of parts of the shaft of the tibia. Excision of the diaphyses of the humerus and femur were almost universally followed by a fatal result, osteo-myelitis being the tangible cause of death. Amputations were always primarily performed when circumstances would admit, and when the sanction of the patients could be obtained.

Results of amputation.

Plevna, where the amputations were performed within 24 hours of the receipt of injury, gave a uniformly good percentage of recoveries. A few such cases may be cited:—

Achmet, aged 30 years. Compound comminuted fracture of upper third of right leg. Amputation of thigh. Recovery.

Mehmet, aged 30 years. Compound comminuted fracture of upper third of left leg. Amputation of thigh. Recovery.

Ismail, aged 32 years. Compound comminuted fracture of upper third of right leg. Amputation of thigh. Recovery.

Malil, aged 34 years. Right leg carried away by shell. Amputation of thigh. Recovery.   Mr.
Osman, aged 35 years. Compound comminuted fracture of upper part of right leg, involving   MACKELLAR'S
knee-joint. Amputation of thigh. Recovery.   report.
Achmet, aged 24 years. Complete destruction of left foot and lower third of left leg, by shell. Amputation of upper third of leg. Recovery.

Operations selected.—The circular method, or the combination of skin-flaps with circular   Operations
division of muscle, were the forms of operation usually preferred and selected. In the case of   selected.
amputation of the leg, Teale's amputation by rectangular flaps was in some instances performed, but with unsatisfactory results, the flaps generally sloughing away within the first few days. In one case Dr. Pinkerton was compelled to re-amputate higher up. The arteries were more frequently tied than twisted. In my own cases I generally practised torsion, and with the best results. Second hæmorrhage rarely occurred.

LANCE, BAYONET, AND SABRE WOUNDS.

The number of bayonet wounds coming under observation was exceedingly small. The few   Bayonet
opportunities that were afforded and utilised of examining the dead on fields where bayonet con-   wounds.
flicts had taken place would tend to show that the majority of those receiving bayonet injuries expire on the field, for the simple reason that the assailants do not cease their strife until one, frequently both, falls dead. They were not so numerous as sabre cuts. The rarity of bayonet wounds received in recent wars may be accounted for in various ways, but principally by the introduction of breech-loading rifles, which, by giving increased rapidity and accuracy of fire, and at long ranges, have greatly lessened the opportunity of using the bayonet with effect. They became more numerous in later part of war, in consequence of the greater frequency of hand-to-hand conflicts. Chiefly met with in fleshy parts of limbs, more rarely piercing the thoracic and abdominal cavities.

A Turk had a bayonet driven completely through the right side of his chest by a Russian soldier. Such was the degree of force used, and so completely gripped was the bayonet, that the Russian, to withdraw it, had to place his foot on the Turk's chest and forcibly wrench it out. No outward symptom occurred. The man made a complete recovery, and was afterwards raised to the grade of officer.

Dr. Sandwith reports five bayonet wounds in a small Bulgar child in fleshy parts of limbs.
Sabre cuts were more numerous than bayonet injuries. Usually of the scalp and face. Healed   Sabre wounds.
rapidly. Most frequently met with among Circassians.

A Turk received six gashes, from his neck to half way down his back, from a Russian cavalry soldier. Some of the gashes were quite six inches in length. Some vertebral spines were chopped off. Man made a good recovery.

Sabre wounds were only too common amongst the wounded women and children in the female hospitals of Adrianople. The neck and upper back seemed to have been the main points of attack. In the case of Bulgarian (and in some instances, Turkish) women, the Circassians and Bashi Bazouks had literally gashed the back to ribands, in a manner analogous to the 'crimping' of codfish. Generally the poor sufferers sank rapidly, from the combined effects of shock, exhaustion, and hæmorrhage; but I saw several cases where, in spite of the severity of the injury, the patients had made good recoveries.

This 'crimping' seemed to be a favourite amusement of Circassians; we saw it later among the mutilated Russian dead of Teliche.

Circassians were frequently the recipients of sabre cuts, chiefly on head, face, neck, or sword arm. All did well.

Lance wounds were very rare. In the hospitals of Shumla were Turkish women and children,   Lance wounds.
recipients of these injuries, inflicted, as they said, by Cossacks. A few also in the hospitals of Adrianople, which Turkish women and children had received at the hands of the 'Bulgarian avengers.'

INJURIES OF ARTERIES.—HÆMORRHAGE.

Mr. Mackellar's report.

Hæmorrhage. My own experience of warfare leads me to believe that death from primary hæmorrhage on the battle-field occurs much more frequently than has generally been supposed. The tardiness of the Ottoman authorities in the interment of the slain afforded unusual facilities of examining the dead. At Teliche, where I had the opportunity of examining nearly 400 dead, with special reference to cause of death, I found that the injuries, followed by rapid death, were wounds of head involving brain, penetrating wounds of chest, and wounds of large arteries. I saw several bodies where wounding of the axillary and femoral arteries had undoubtedly been the cause of death; probably the tension and stretching of the axillary artery during the act of firing, and of the femoral in certain positions of the lower limb, specially predispose these arteries to injury. Between Plevna and Dubnik I was requested by a Turkish officer to examine the body of a Turkish soldier said to have been the subject of atrocities at the hands of the Cossacks. The story was that a convoy of wounded, numbering amongst them the private referred to, had been surprised and attacked by a band of Cossacks. The man was said to have been shot as he lay wounded in the wagon; when I saw him he lay upon his back in a large pool of blood, his tunic, underclothing, and upper half of trunk being completely saturated, the body blanched and of tallowy whiteness, his right arm was outstretched, and in the axilla was readily seen the hole in his coat made by the bullet. On slitting up the sleeve of the tunic one saw in the middle third of the axilla the wound of entrance. On dissecting up this wound and dislodging a quantity of clot, one came readily upon a large lacerated rent in the coats of the artery, involving nearly three-fourths of its circumference; he had no other wound nor sign of other injury. His fingers were blackened and grimed with powder as if from recent firing. Near him were the bodies of other soldiers also recently killed.

After a skirmish between Circassians and Cossacks in riding over the scene of conflict, we came across the body of a Cossack shot through the femoral artery; the loss of blood had been enormous.

Dr Edmunds reports a case under his care in the Rustchuk hospital of a man wounded in the upper part of thigh; there was only a wound of entrance, none of exit. Examination showed that the bullet had lodged on the outer side of the femoral artery and in immediate contact with it. As the bullet was being removed the artery was distinctly seen and recognised; it had ceased to pulsate; 36 hours later the whole upper part of the thigh became gangrenous, the patient dying 48 hours later. In Plevna one frequently saw cases where a limb had been completely carried away by shell, and the large arteries were seen plugged and pulsating; the amount of hæmorrhage had been comparatively trifling. Very few cases of primary ligature of a large artery came under my observation.

Barrack hospitals. The want of barrack hospitals was severely felt; wood was in abundance; skilled labour could be procured and at a trifling cost; but the authorities could not be induced to erect them. I am strongly of opinion that their employment would have been the means of saving many lives; as it was, the wounded were crowded into mosques, konaks, Bulgarian churches and schools, cavalry barracks, and other buildings utterly unsuited for hospital purposes. The consequences were only too disastrous.

Nursing. Much has been said against the nursing of Turkish wounded by women. It was argued that female nurses would be constantly exposed to insult in their dealings with their patients. Lady Strangford and the nurses with her were unanimous in affirming that quite the contrary was the case; they found that Turkish patients were far more delicate in their relations with females than the average of male patients in an English hospital. In a conversation which I had with Djemil Pacha, the military commandant in Adrianople, he assured me that, even if Lady Strangford had done no greater work, she had broken down the barrier of Turkish prejudice against the employment of females in male hospitals, and that he was perfectly charmed with the result, and that he hoped that in the future, in military and civil hospitals alike, women nurses would be the rule and not the exception. The nurses sent by the Queen of Saxony to Turkey and employed in the Red Crescent hospital at Beylerbey and the Stafford House hospitals at Stamboul were equally loud-spoken in their praises of the Mussulman as a patient. Similar testimony is given by the French Sisters in Adrianople.

Lady Strangford.

MR. A. SYMONS ECCLES' REPORT *of Hospitals at Constantinople.*

May 2, 1878.

In accordance with your instructions I have ascertained the following facts relative to the sick and wounded at present lying in the hospitals of Constantinople. The information is derived from official sources and from personal observation. On Wednesday, May 1, there were in the hospitals in and about Constantinople nearly 22,000 patients, of whom 4,000 are suffering from wounds received on the field of battle, between 2,000 and 3,000 from wounds due to exposure to climate and other influences—i.e. frostbite, &c.—while the remainder are the subjects of fevers, either of a typhoid or intermittent type, dysentery, diarrhœa, and in a few cases of small-pox. Among these patients there are about 2,000 who are convalescents, chiefly those whose wounds are cicatrised; but the great majority are individuals who should not be inmates of an hospital, exposed to the influences of hospitalism, than which no other better example has been afforded of late years than as one sees it to-day in the overcrowded, ill-adapted buildings, necessarily converted into hospitals for the reception of the many sick and wounded still needing care and attention, and the large number of patients daily arriving from the encampments in the environs of this city.

There are at present 27 buildings in Constantinople and its suburbs occupied as hospitals for the Turkish military sick and wounded. The list, as follows, is arranged in accordance with the size of the hospitals:— *Turkish hospitals.*

1. Haidar Pacha.
2. Maltepé.
3. Couleli.
4. Coumberhané.
5. Selimié.
6. Medjidié.
7. Gumush Souyon.
8. Baba-Mushiri.
9. Daoud Pacha.
10. Iplikhané.
11. Seraskeriat.
12. Misafir-hané.
13. Tchatladji-Capon.
14. Tunisse Pacha.
15. Kiamil Pacha.
16. Bulbul-deré.
17. Gulhané.
18. The Marine.
19. Red Crescent.
20. Tchiragan.
21. Zeitun Bournon.
22. Sari-Guzel.
23. Peiki-Zafer.
24. Chadié.
25. Mustapha Pacha.

And two others whose names I could not ascertain.

Of these Haidar Pacha, Maltepé, Coumberhané, Selimié, Medjidié, Daoud Pacha, Iplikhané, and Couleli are large buildings containing over 2,000 patients, and, with the exception of Daoud Pacha and Iplikhané, were built especially for hospitals, the sanitary arrangements of which, although not as good as could be wished, are yet vastly superior to the other buildings more recently appropriated to the use of the sick and wounded. *Condition of hospitals.*

Many of these are barracks which, perhaps, were well enough constructed to meet the requirements of a dwelling-place for men in good health whose life was spent in the open air; but they served only as foyers for disease, as they are now occupied by patients who have suffered terribly both morally and physically, and who are perforce crowded together in ill-ventilated and badly-drained buildings, where isolation and attention to the rules of military hygiene are out of the question. A visit to three of the hospitals in Constantinople, selected as types of the majority, combined with one's previous experience during the campaign, and the knowledge of the conditions under which the Turkish soldier has fought and suffered either at the hands of the foe or from exposure to hardships, has enabled me to judge of the general state of the sick and wounded in the Constantinople hospitals, of the causes of the condition of affairs, and what appears to me the most feasible way of remedying the existing evils.

The patients in the hospitals of Constantinople may be divided into those who are wounded and those who are diseased, but many who originally became inmates of an hospital as wounded, have since been attacked by one or other of the prevalent diseases. Of the wounded 1,000 odd are convalescent, their wounds being healed; but of these not a few are maimed for life, while others have fallen into such a deplorable state of ill-health that they are unfit either for active service or *Condition of patients.*

A A

Mr. Eccles' report.	for the ordinary duties of life in their own homes. Of those who are not yet sufficiently recovered to be discharged, a large number are still suffering from the effects of serious injuries, or are the victims of one or more of the diseases which have played havoc with the patients in this city. Some of them are suffering from erysipelas, gangrene, and hectic fever, others have been attacked by fever of a typhoid type, or are exhausted by dysentery and diarrhœa, and many are retarded in their recovery by falling into a scorbutic state, their wounds, instead of healing, taking on the characteristic action of scorbutic ulceration. Of those who are diseased, one can only say that they have been exposed to the predisposing and exciting causes of these diseases; the majority of them display great loss of flesh, nervous exhaustion, a peculiar muddy tint of the skin; their eyes are sunken, and the depression of spirits, from which they all suffer, renders them liable to contract the prevalent fevers. Many of them are scorbutic, and I believe it would be difficult to find any among them who had not the spleen enlarged, and who had not at some time suffered from one or other form of ague; indeed many of them present marked symptoms of malarial cachexy. In the hospitals I visited, the majority of patients, suffering from diseases of different organs and natures, exhibited intermittent symptoms.
Causes of tardy recovery.	We have seen that the patients are anæmic, scorbutic, subject to ague, and generally ill in mind as well as in body. What are the causes for this condition of affairs?
	Of those wounded who are not yet convalescent, the causes of their tardy recovery are obvious enough. All have been exposed, in the early days of their injuries, to the most fearful suffering and hardship. Many have sustained injuries at first sight almost incompatible with life. Numbers have passed through the miseries of a long siege, without even the necessities of life; others have sustained the hardships of a prolonged retreat; while all have passed days and weeks without the care and attention which might have curtailed their sufferings, if it could have been bestowed in the first instance. Nature has been exhausted in the attempt to sustain life against the odds of physical injury, want of nourishment, and exposure to cold and wet. These remarks are in a great measure applicable to the sick also. These men have passed through the same hardships as their wounded comrades, and, excepting that they have received no actual wound, they have been equally injured. Want of nourishment, clothing, and habitation, added to the moral depression following defeats, has brought men, who were in the first place but ill-adapted for the hardships of a winter campaign, into their present condition of health.
	It must be remembered that most of the patients in the hospitals belong to the reserves, who were called out after the youngest and most vigorous men had been drafted into the army. Many of them have contracted diseases since their arrival in hospital. Admitted originally for diarrhœa or ague, their low condition of health has predisposed them for the attacks of typhoid and other forms of blood-poisoning, from which they are suffering; and it is to their temperate and regular habits of life that the majority owe their lives to-day.
Causes of imperfect treatment.	It is impossible for the medical men under whose care these men come to treat the cases as they should and would do. They have neither the time nor the means at their disposal which should be allotted to each case. Many of the medical men in the hospitals of Constantinople are foreigners, whose services have been engaged for a short term, who have not had the opportunity of acquiring the language of their patients, or learning the rules of the service so as to enforce their directions and orders. There are, at present, only 200 medical men in the Constantinople hospitals. The Government has been taxed in its resources to the uttermost; every available native medical man has been engaged; others have been brought from the Continental medical centres. But what can the most skilful medical men do if they have not the means of treating their patients? The Imperial Ottoman Government, in addition to the thousand and one other claims on it to-day, has to provide places, furniture, food, clothing, medicines, and attendants, for more than 50,000 sick and wounded soldiers. It is impossible, under existing circumstances, that more can be done on the part of the Government; but, if it were possible to alleviate the sufferings of the primary victims of this war, the means must be adapted to the needs which one sees every day.
Recommendations.	The first step to be taken towards remedying existing evils is to avoid overcrowding, and to isolate infectious diseases. This can only be done by establishing convalescent hospitals, where all who are no longer suffering acutely should be received. Special buildings must be reserved for fevers. Then those sick who swell the number of patients daily, from the encampments, should be received and cared for in barrack or tent hospitals, within easy reach of their regiments; this would curtail the length of their illnesses, avoid over-crowding, and prevent the spread of infectious disease. The next great necessity is *food*, sufficient in quantity and quality. Already one

has seen the effects of a wholesome, well-cooked, and varied diet among patients whose lives were almost despaired of. Many who cannot take the fairly liberal diets prescribed in the Government scale would rapidly improve on a more delicate and varied diet. But the Government resources are already subject to heavy pressure in order to provide the seven ordinary diets; delicacies and extras are in consequence only prescribed in cases of absolute necessity, and sometimes not even then.

Mr. ECCLES' report.

If *convalescent hospitals* could be established, *isolation* carried out, the present *diets supplemented*, and *barrack hospitals* attached to the camps around Constantinople, the present number of sick and wounded would rapidly diminish, their sufferings would be curtailed, the spread of disease would be arrested, and the present high rate of mortality would be sensibly decreased.

To the Chief Commissioner, Constantinople.

DR. STIVEN *on the Rustchuk and Stamboul New Barrack Hospital.*

The Rustchuk hospital was first started on July 9, for 100 beds. It received its first 100 wounded on Sept. 3. It was then enlarged to an extra 110 beds—10 beds being set apart for officers. The building was the engine workshops of the Rustchuk and Varna Railway. The wards were large and airy; so ventilation did not enter into the arrangements, as it was already well ventilated. The *personnel* consisted after its extension of three English surgeons, and an assistant Turkish surgeon. The nursing was done by Turkish soldiers, about 30 in number. Six other men, paid by the Society, were instructed how to make poultices, and dress simple cases: their further duties consisted in each taking his turn of watching in the wards two hours every night, and they were made responsible if they did not report at once on cases requiring qualified assistance, as in hæmorrhage, &c. A dispenser was also procured from the Turkish Government. The other subordinates were three washerwomen, constantly at work; one woman for mending and general needlework; and one store-keeper in charge of linen, whose duty it was to see that all soiled sheets were removed at once from the beds every morning and clean ones supplied, also to check the giving and taking of the washing. The rations were supplied by the Government, over the giving out of which a captain of the Turkish army presided. There were two cooks, two water-carriers, and four infirmiers, who had to make themselves generally useful; there were also two barbers.

Dr. STIVEN'S report.

Description of Rustchuk hospital.

The beds were made of wood—two supports with three planks laid across; the head support being carried up, and a tray of wood jutting out behind to support the medicine bottles, spittoons, &c., thus obviating the necessity of little tables alongside the beds. They were supplied with a straw mattress and pillow, and a soft sheep's wool mattress and pillow, with sheets, blankets, and coverlet stuffed with sheep's wool.

The principal difficulties to be incurred were in the forming of kitchen, washing-house, and closets. The kitchen was a wooden shed erected outside the hospital. The waste of fuel was enormous at first; this I obviated by making a ditch of about two feet deep, tunnelling it over with brick, leaving three apertures for the cauldrons, which were supported on iron girders; the one end of the tunnel was patent, where the wood was pushed in; the other was closed, and connected with a flue projecting outside the shed; a good draught was always present, and the smoke did not annoy the cooks. The same plan was followed in the washing-house, for the boiling of soiled linen and bandages. The closet was a movable shed, placed over a deep ditch dug out, about six feet deep, and those patients who were able to move about had to use them. The closets were constantly supplied with chloride of lime thrown down, and the shed removed every month, the ditch being filled up with mud and chloride of lime. The bed-pans used in the hospital were always emptied down these closets and washed with carbolic acid, before being returned to the ward.

The sanitary condition of the hospital was good, as we did not have any epidemic of erysipelas, and hospital gangrene was unknown to us. The precautions taken were as follows: constant supervision as to the patients having clean sheets, shirts, and drawers, whenever soiled by excretory matters, blood, pus, or otherwise; the washing of the patients, especially the feet, by the servants, and for those who were more or less convalescent I had two baths erected, which simply consisted of a concrete floor, with waste-pipe and a boarding run round. These were situated in the shed erected for the servants, and they were supplied with warm water and soap; they could thus cleanse the whole of their bodies as often as they pleased. Sulphur was burnt in the wards,

Sanitary condition of the hospital.

180   MEDICAL REPORTS.

Dr. STIVEN's report. — but more frequently carbolic acid. Before suppurating wounds were opened, a shovel with red-hot cinders was brought in, and some strong carbolic acid was poured on the top; this was placed under the bed, and the wound opened under the fumes; the fumes were not disagreeable to the patient or patients on either side, and it acted admirably in destroying all noxious odour. After dressings were finished the wards were carefully swept, and carbolic acid sprinkled on the floor; and also the fumes were made to purvey the whole ward by men carrying a shovel of hot cinders up and down, and pouring a little carbolic acid from time to time on them. All cases showing any inordinate inflammation were dressed last, and erysipelas cases were at once isolated; these were never dressed till all the other cases were finished, and then under the fumes of carbolic acid, and never by any other hands but our own. The general routine followed was an early morning visit to all our patients, examining them as to their state of health medically, prescribing any medicines necessary, and writing up their rations; we then adjourned to breakfast, and after that was discussed, dressed the patients, each personally.

The closets in many particulars were inconvenient; but, I believe, being quite apart from the building, added to its sanitary state. All bandages thoroughly soiled with pus were never used again, but burnt. The heating of the wards was accomplished with the aid of large brick stoves.

Description of Stamboul hospital. — The Stamboul New Barrack Hospital was constructed in two long, low barracks. The beds were supported on a couple of iron supports with planking. It was fitted up with 98 beds. The closets were attached to the building between the two wards, being approached by a short passage. Large apertures were made through the walls of passage, to allow a through cross current of air, and carry away any smells that may have reached that length, without which it would have entered into the wards. The closets were connected with a drain, and were fitted up with syphon-shaped tubes. These latter acted well, being constantly sluiced out with water; a man was there for the purpose every time they were used. Strong carbolic acid was always poured down and sprinkled about them. Ventilation of the wards was carried on by a centre shaft, and every second window was made to fall inwards, the sides being protected by boarding to stop all draught at the sides; these were always kept open, and thus fresh air was constantly coming in, impinging on the roof first, and then falling downwards, as all cold air will. Sanitary arrangements, as to the free use of carbolic acid, were here also carried out. The *personnel* included a dispenser, three doctors, and a few soldiers as general servants. The nursing was done by German sisters sent by the Queen of Saxony.

MR. E. R. PRATT, *Assistant-Commissioner, on the Organisation of Field Ambulance and Transport in Oriental Countries.*

Mr. PRATT on organisation. — Since the existence of the Geneva Convention, and the establishment of societies for rendering aid to the sick and wounded in war, but little experience had been gained as to the conduct of such aid in Oriental countries until the recent Russo-Turkish war.

After the Prussian campaign in France, elaborate treatises were written, and the fullest information may be obtained as to ambulance organisation, where railways, sound roads, &c., are found, and where troops are well equipped and supplied with good food, as well as models of the wagons, hospitals, stretchers, &c., of the best construction. But in an Asiatic campaign circumstances are very different, both as to the nature of the country, roads, &c., and the habits and mental condition of the inhabitants, and thus ambulance organisation must be conducted under very different rules; the main difference being that, instead of doubts as to the best form of relief, the difficulty would be that of combating time and distance, and prejudices in supplying relief of the simplest description.

In the late war the distress was often so great that the difficulty was not how the wounded should be dressed, but that they should be attended to at all; not how they should be carried, but that they should not die on the road; not how fed, but that they should not starve.

FIELD AMBULANCES.

If field ambulances are not in future confined to the second line, it seems that the amount of good they could do at the front would be measured to a great extent by the liberty of action they are allowed by the military authorities or the society employing them. The movements of the ambulance should be left to the surgeon-in-chief as much as possible; he is generally best aware where the greatest necessity for aid exists, and he should therefore be allowed to move to any overstrained point at a moment's notice, without having to ask for instructions from the central authority, which might not arrive for days, and until all such necessity was past.

STAFF FOR FIELD AMBULANCE.

When communications are bad, an ambulance should consist of three surgeons—*i.e.* the smallest number; this would be, at intervals, reduced to two by sickness or otherwise—one chemist, a dresser, cook, agent, interpreter, and two native servants—all acting, when necessary, as dressers, or to carry water, &c. The latter in Turkey were generally non-commissioned officers and convalescent patients.

Their transport should consist of six or eight wagons, sufficient to carry in the worst weather all the medical stores and provisions; these may be daily employed in carrying sick to the rear, fetching provisions, and occasionally wounded, if not transporting the stores when advancing or retreating.

FIELD AMBULANCE EQUIPMENT.

(1) Tent for surgeons; (2) Servants and cooking; (3) Hospital marquée. The latter should be as large as possible, and supplied with stretchers, blankets, &c. No stove is required, a hole in the ground filled with ashes answering as well. Horse for each surgeon; army saddle, saddle-bags for food, splints, bandages, instruments, &c., when riding to the front. Wagons should be supplied with blankets, stretchers, and spare rope or *raw* hide for repairs, and a bucket or water-jar. All boxes should average about 2 feet by 2 feet by 3 feet, and 60 lbs. in weight, made with rope handles; all contents labelled *outside*; if this is not done it always causes the greatest inconvenience, loss of time, &c. Boxes of this size will go into any wagon, and pack most conveniently on horses or mules.

Assorted cases (surgical) were very useful, and the fact that they locked was also an advantage, except when the key was lost.

Medicine chests, *i.e.* boxes with about eight or twelve half-pint bottles, were useful for medicines when mixed and ready for immediate use.

GENERAL DEMEANOUR (AMONG ASIATICS).

It is advisable amongst Orientals (and Mussulmans especially) to respect and yield to, as far as possible, all religious prejudices. They feel strongly on certain subjects which we are quite indifferent about. A reverse policy can only cause ill-will and obstruction, and is easily avoided. At the same time Orientals are more impressed with a quiet demeanour and politeness, and have often better taste in some matters. They cannot understand noisy singing, nor any, apparently, except through the nose. It is better to meet equivocation and deceit with candour and truth than try your opponent's weapons; at the same time a judicious mixture of kindness and physical force is very advantageous.

TRANSPORT.

In an uncivilised, roadless country, the ordinary patterns of Red Cross wagons are quite useless; they are far too heavy even for strong horses, and quite beyond those obtainable in Eastern countries. They cannot be mended on an emergency by the driver; harness cannot be supplied when deficient. During the retreat of the Russians from the Lom Valley they were able to save everything but their ambulance wagons; these were offered to the S. H. C. by the Turks. In the middle of a long train of arabas, full of wounded from Orkhanie, was one Red Cross wagon, empty, because it could only just be dragged along, and could not carry additional weight. This same wagon had slung stretchers, but wounded put into them would have been frozen to death.

Ottomans have a dislike to lying out straight on stretchers or beds; the latter they are quite unaccustomed to, and sometimes refuse to enter, preferring the floor. They would generally be far more comfortable coiled up in the straw at the bottom of an araba.

In Turkey the best vehicle for transport was the country araba. 1. It could be easily mended

Mr. PRATT on organisation.	by the driver. 2. Being drawn by oxen, its motion was slow and less painful for the wounded. 3. It was less expensive to buy or hire. 4. It was capable of improvement by cross ropes and a mattress or slung stretcher.

In summer the great objection to it is the impossibility of fixing up any awning or covering, so that it will stand the straining and jolting, owing to the sloping sides and round timbers.

In winter this would not be so necessary, as a waterproof sheet over and round the wounded men would be *warmer*, drier, and better in every way, and would need no fixing.

In a country where the roads are bad, light spring wagons would be serviceable for moving rapidly surgeons and their stores from one point to another. The harness should be very light, and the wheels should track and allow of the carriages turning sharply. For transport of wounded the slow heavy wagons of the peasantry are better adapted, and would probably be the only means of evacuating large numbers after a severe engagement; aid should therefore be given in the shape of shelter and food, by improving these carts by awnings, mattresses, and slung stretchers; by supplying surgical assistance and medical comforts at depôts and *en route*. It may be considered wrong to add to the belligerent power of either army by superseding the medical staff in ordinary routine of campaign work. The great object of a Voluntary Aid Society would therefore be to organise its staff so as to meet emergencies at a moment's notice. Its chief representative |
| Inspectors. | should therefore have in different districts responsible agents, with as great discretionary latitude as possible, under whose control the different ambulances should be placed. These inspectors* should be always riding about in the neighbourhood of the combatants, preparing for probable battles, searching for places where help is needed, and in giving relief in money where advantageous. It is quite possible for surgeons to be in close proximity to a great battle and yet quite unaware of it, especially if away from a high road, or at all occupied, until the urgent need for their services has passed. |
| The checking of stores. | On a quantity of stores being despatched for distribution, the simplest system of recording their destination is to have the boxes *numbered* and entered *separately* with contents on the separate left-hand pages of a book; as received, or surgeon receiving one, or taking one from store signs for it on the right page, or for whatever medicines or clothing he may take from them. A book thus kept comprises a list of stores, a delivery register with vouchers, and is also useful for reference; in such a form that they cannot be lost or mixed, *and can be tested and audited without trouble.*

It seems to be almost necessary to the practical utility of volunteer societies that their staff should work independently of and untrammelled by the military regulation of army surgeons. Should volunteer surgeons be under any control of other than the higher authorities, difficulties would be sure to arise, owing to the obviously not unnatural jealousy with which they would be regarded. |

---

* Inspectors should be chosen for their personal character, energy, and practical good sense, and should be as little fettered as possible by stereotyped rules. They should have money and stores at their disposal, for which they should be strictly responsible. If medical men, they should be of somewhat senior standing to those serving in the ambulance sections.

PART IV.

Abstract of Receipts and Payments on account of the Stafford House Fund for the relief of Sick and Wounded Turkish Soldiers, by Sir Henry Green.

RECEIPTS.	£	s.	d.	PAYMENTS.	£	s.	d.	£	s.	d.
Subscriptions paid to Bankers to Dec. 31, 1876	3,212	17	9	Remitted to Constantinople—						
Subscriptions paid to Bankers to Dec. 31, 1877	28,432	2	4	To Ahmed Vefyk Pacha	3,000	0	0			
Subscriptions paid to Bankers to Dec. 31, 1878	7,571	0	4	,, Mr. Barrington-Kennett *	22,394	9	0	25,394	9	0
Subscriptions paid to Bankers to March 13, 1879	15	11	0	Blankets and warm clothing				1,338	8	9
Amount received from Insurance Company for loss of goods shipped by the 'Ganges'	61	17	6	Medicines, &c.	4,292	13	5			
				Surgical instruments, &c.	2,634	9	5	6,927	2	10
				Advertisements in India, Banker's Commission, Postages, &c.				243	16	6
				Salaries of Surgeons, Expenses, &c. (paid in London)				1,097	17	0
				Freightage of goods to Constantinople, Advertising, Printing, Stationery				3,383	1	0
								38,384	15	1
				Balance at credit of Fund				908	13	10
Vouchers examined and correct	£39,293	8	11					£39,293	8	11

(Signed) J. CULVERWELL, *Accountant*, March 14, 1879.

(Signed) HENRY GREEN, Major-Gen., *Hon. Treasurer.*

* See Mr. Barrington-Kennett's Abstract of Expenditure Sheet (*next page*).

Abstract of Expenditure of Funds remitted to the Chief Commissioner, Constantinople.*

	£	s.	d.		£	s.	d.	£	s.	d.
Received from the Hon. Treasurer of the S. H. C. (see Abstract of Receipts and Expenditure, by Sir H. Green)	23,394	9	0	**Working Expenses of Hospitals.**						
Received from private subscription	38	11	0	Bustchuk Hospital	922	6	2			
Received on transfer of Lord Blantyre's Surgeons	90	0	0	Varna "	140	18	7			
				Adrianople "	736	4	7			
				Phillippopolis "	393	8	2			
				Sofia "	709	15	2			
				Mundy Barrack Hospital	177	1	10			
				Tchekmedje and Makrikeui Hospitals and Dispensary	450	12	0			
				Salonica Hospital	453	4	5			
				Gallipoli Hospital and Dispensary (up to Aug. 1, 1878)	671	10	2			
				New Barracks, Stamboul	531	14	0			
				Erzeroum S. H. Hospital	844	10	0			
				Erzeroum British Hospital and Kars District Ambulance; subsidy to Lord Blantyre's British Hospital Fund	776	8	7			
					6,797	13	3	6,797	13	3
				Working Expenses of Field Ambulances.						
				First Lom Ambulance	387	10	4			
				Second "	506	6	2			
				Shipka Ambulance	842	1	10			
				Plevna District Ambulance	450	13	0			
				Sarnakov Ambulance	229	2	0			
				Tchifout-Burgas Dispensary	64	12	5			
					2,473	5	9	2,473	5	9
				Working Expenses of Railway Transport Ambulances.						
				Rustchuk-Varna Railway Service	573	2	9			
				Roumelian Railway Service	93	1	9			
				Soup-kitchens at Railway Stations	875	11	10			
					1,541	15	9	1,541	15	9
				Salaries				6,806	0	5
				Purchase of medical stores, ambulance matériel, &c.				2,398	3	8
				Transport of personnel and matériel				732	8	7
				Chief Commissioner's account				463	14	0
				Rent and fittings for store-depôt and offices. Office expenses, telegrams, translations, printing, and stationery				284	17	2
				Miscellaneous				269	13	0
				Expenses of the Boulair Lines Dispensary under Admiral Commerell, and of the Constantinople depôt, from Aug. 1 to the close of operations				121	4	7
				Difference of exchange in transfer from Turkish to English currency				346	12	9
								281	11	1
£23,517	0	0						£23,517	0	0

(Signed) V. B. BARRINGTON-KENNETT, *Chief Commissioner*, April 24, 1879.
Examined, with Auditor's Statement, and found correct.   (Signed) J. CULVERWELL, *Accountant*, May 30, 1879.

* The items on the right-hand side of this sheet have been extracted from the Chief Commissioner's General Account, and converted into English money

Cash Statement, Extracted from the General Account.

Dr.			£	LT.			Cr.		LT.
1877.					1877.				
June 29	To Cash from Sir Henry Green		1000	1100	Aug. 31	By expenditure to date during month			3012 24
July 16	" "		1000	1090	Sept. 30	" "			1666 02
Aug. 23	" "		2100	2283 75	Oct. 31	" "			1580 32
Sept. 12	" Ramsden		5	5 40	Nov. 30	" "			2561 97
" 24	" Sir Henry Green		1000	1080	Dec. 31	" "			3467 68
Oct. 26	" "		1000	1082 50	1878.				
Nov. 8	" Captain McCalmont			6	Jan. 31	" "			2367 43
" "	" Bill on Coutts			22 77	Feb. 28	" "			2937 37
" 10	" Sir Henry Green		2000	2160	Mar. 31	" "			2666 65
" 19	" Lord Blantyre's Surgeons				April 30	" "			1862 10
	(£22 10 0)			24 30	May 31	" "			1366 52
" 24	" Colonel James Baker			1	June 30	" "			1757 40
" 30	" Sir Henry Green		2000	2170	July 31	" "			327 05
Dec. 15	" Lord Blantyre's Surgeons				" "	" "			64 41
	(£67 10 0)								
1878.						Balance transferred to Supplementary Account.			
Jan. 8	" Sir Henry Green		2000	72 90					
Feb. 11	" "		1000	2165					
Mar. 20	" "		1000	1090					
April 2	" "		2000	2180					
May 10	" "		2000	2160					
June 3	" "		1000	2180					
July 8	" "		1000	1090					
				1090					
				1087 50					
" 31	" Amount Sums returned to Office from the Sections			24141 12					
				1386 24					
				LT. 25527 36					LT. 25527 36

(Signed) V. B. BARRINGTON-KENNETT, *Chief Commissioner S. H. C.*
London, *May* 19, 1879.
W. L. STONEX, *Assistant Commissioner S. H. C.*
Constantinople, *Nov.* 23, 1878.

Certified as correct. (Signed) A. H. SCAIFE, *Auditor.*
Constantinople, *Nov.* 23, 1878.

Supplementary Cash Statement, Extracted from the General Account.

Dr.		£ s. d.	LT.			Cr.	£ s. d.	LT.
1878.				1878.				
Aug. 1	To Balance from Cash Statement		64 41	Aug. 31	By expenditure to date			94 39
Aug. 1 to Oct. 2	To various sums paid into office on account of sales of horses, fittings, &c. (see General Account).		114 95	Sept. 17	Remitted to Hansons for the credit of the Gallipoli section [Admiral Commerell]	200 0 0		218 00
Sept. 17	To bill from Sir H. Green (for Admiral Commerell, per Hansons and Co.)	200 0 0	218 00	Sept. 30	By expenditure to date			42 90
Dec. 29	To cheque from Sir H. Green, to Mr. Stoney	63 9 0	68 47	Oct. 12	" "			11 05
1879.				Nov. 30	" "			99 49
Feb. 12	To cheque from Sir H. Green, to Mr. Stoney	31 9 0	34 28	1879.				
				Feb. 28	" "	31 9 0		34 28
			LT. 600 11					LT. 600 11

(Signed) V. B. BARRINGTON-KENNETT, *Chief Commissioner S. H. C.,* April 24, 1879.

Examined and found correct, } J. CULVERWELL, *Accountant.*
May 30, 1879.

TABLE OF MONTHLY EXPENDITURE.

	Pending Aug. 1877	During Sept. 1877	During October 1877	During Novem. 1877	During Decem. 1877	During Jan. 1878	During Feb. 1878	During March 1878	During April 1878	During May 1878	During June 1878	During July 1878	Total	Balances Returned	Actual Expenditure Piastres	Actual Expenditure £ s. d.
	Piast.	Piast.	Piast.	Piast.	Piast.	Piast.	Piast.	Piast.	Piast.	Piast.	Piast.	Piast.	Piastres	Piast.	Piastres	£ s. d.
Rustchuk Hospital	32646	167	449	34412	42298	440	...	...	...	...	...	...	111532	10078	101454	922 6 2
Varna Hospital	6500	1500	7600	...	...	...	1120	...	...	...	...	...	15500	...	15500	140 18 4
Adrianople Hospital	800	17379	10000	8732	21152	26056	500	9495	5701	1666	...	...	86285	6400	79885	726 6 7
Philippopolis Hospital	200	4442	10000	1432	2958	10000	10000	985	2557	1475	2500	...	44033	758	43275	393 8 2
Sofia Hospital	...	...	...	20667	36570	...	5100	...	1751	2546	1230	...	78264	191	78073	709 15 2
Constantinople Mundy Barrack Hospital	...	...	...	8160	785	2949	1133	22676	19413	9428	4592	...	63069	4582	58487	531 14 6
Constantinople New Barrack Hospital	...	...	...	...	...	...	6960	33614	1935	400	3779	...	50041	187	49854	453 4 5
Salonica Hospital	...	...	...	...	...	...	10813	13900	1545	26005	20650	13760	85220	1354	73866	671 10 2
Gallipoli Hospital	...	...	...	...	...	...	...	23718	14038	3605	2200	...	55216	5650	49566	450 12 0
Makrikeui Hospital	...	...	...	...	...	11655	...	6074	2746	...	...	...	7830	712	7108	64 12 5
Tchifout-Burgas Dispensary	2900	...	5000	6383	10000	558	175	...	...	...	...	...	68433	5391	63042	573 2 9
Rustchuk-Varna Railway Transport	...	2779	620	3339	4980	40	660	...	...	825	...	...	14705	8466	10239	93 1 5
Roumelian Railway Transport	7950	120	...	18900	21300	700	300	...	...	488	1000	...	58094	400	55694	506 6 2
Second Lom Ambulance	22861	...	730	21842	...	...	700	...	...	...	...	...	46133	3500	42633	387 10 4
First Lom Ambulance	21500	90	2434	15000	10000	11691	22364	18230	685	1165	...	...	103149	10619	92630	843 13 0
Shipka Ambulance	10000	31164	7632	3915	100	4701	1000	...	...	...	200	...	58712	9140	49572	450 13 8
Plevna District Ambulance	73058	...	10000	400	1867	3816	...	665	980	10300	...	...	90786	5378	85408	776 8 7
Kars District (Lord Blantyre's) Ambulance	...	...	...	36302	5088	16924	3617	32550	4487	1848	2043	...	111310	18415	92895	844 10 0
Erzeroum Hospital	...	...	...	...	13071	18603	5600	370	2947	934	...	...	39392	14961	24431	222 2 0
Samakov Ambulance	...	7961	...	20480	19028	24188	15891	500	679	373	...	...	96737	422	96315	875 11 10
Soap-kitchens	18831	...	4808	4306	1656	...	400	5544	...	...	...	...	30883	...	30883	280 15 0
Clothing	18395	...	4295	...	23163	41780	9175	11246	636	10300	...	...	104861	4128	100733	915 15 0
Blankets and bedding	33653	...	11162	7691	8234	22957	3681	2135	229	847	2371	1615	23542	3102	20440	185 16 6
Hospital fittings	2900	6179	5871	1315	530	...	1103	3971	3323	5186	86	...	13335	...	13335	121 4 7
Horses and stabling	4000	...	873	1311	620	...	1838	289	933	621	1993	422	8275	...	8275	82 11 10
Miscellaneous	610	400	900	350	8650	468	541	289	933	6275	8150	...	31735	400	31335	284 17 5
Salaries—Office and depôt	...	227	239	3220	2350	4325	2625	3842	6075	2300	9350	1425	84284	3717	80567	732 8 7
Rent and furniture—Office and depôt	1664	900	3300	1085	632	2229	800	3672	2677	5550	2428	1602	598677	7676	591001	5372 14 7
Forwarding charges	16345	1952	2654	24494	10817	2699	2573	36336	94213	43583	43487	...	39035	...	39025	354 15 0
Salaries—Doctors	6050	8716	21694	29571	36774	36924	164641	2131	1656	1044	1368	1316	6512	...	6512	59 4 0
Ditto—Dragomans	4425	10404	6825	7916	856	3618	1408	1157	203	667	939	419	7832	1320	3686	33 10 2
Telegrams and translations	110	6462	266	2097	566	540	246	410	245	581	124	160	3686	...	3686	33 10 2
Postage	33	622	354	442	374	373	407	4189	3705	978	874	201	19464	...	19464	176 18 10
Printing and stationery	452	183	360	1216	4593	1494	460	6462	2074	4495	19402	...	53654	2647	51007	463 14 0
Chief-Commissioner's account	970	2036	3075	12878	1485	80	707	11880	6000	396	26604	3300	69300	...	69300	630 0 0
Assist.-Com. Stoney's account	...	...	...	19800	...	...	1320	...	...	...	...	...	...	...	...	...
Assist.-Com. Pratt's distribution	...	...	...	...	4030	...	...	...	...	...	...	...	4030	4030	...	...
Hayes's (for Pratt) distribution	...	...	...	...	5100	...	...	...	...	...	...	...	5100	5100	...	...
													2546406	138624	2407781	21888 16 2

Certified as correct,
Constantinople, *November 23, 1878.* } A. H. SCAIFE, *Auditor.*

(Signed) V. B. BARRINGTON-KENNETT, *Chief-Commissioner S. H. C.*
W. L. STONEY, *Assistant-Commissioner S. H. C.*
Constantinople, November 23, 1878.

APPENDIX.

LETTERS OF THANKS, ETC.

FROM H.I.M. THE SULTAN.

(*Extract from* Mr. BARRINGTON-KENNETT'S *Report of May* 8, 1878).

Last Sunday, the 5th inst., I was invited to call on Sadyk Pacha, prime minister. After expressing his sincere thanks for the services rendered by our hospitals and ambulances during the war, he informed me that H.I.M. the Sultan had invited me to attend at the Yildiz-Kiosk Palace, the following morning. In the course of my audience with the Sultan which followed, His Majesty referred in most grateful terms to the generous exertions of the Stafford House Committee in aid of his wounded soldiers. He thanked me warmly for my management of the affairs of the Committee at the seat of war, and desired me to convey to every member of our staff his feelings of appreciation and gratitude for the efficient results of their work. He said that he was touched by the good feeling and charitable efforts of the British nation, which had come forward so nobly to help his suffering soldiers and people.

FROM THE MINISTER OF WAR.

Constantinople, le 17-29 Juin 1878.

Monsieur,—Ayant pris connaissance de votre lettre du 2 de ce mois, adressée à la Sublime Porte sur votre prochain retour en Angleterre, il m'incombe le devoir de vous exprimer, d'une manière toute spéciale, mes vifs remerciments pour vos services que vous n'avez cessé de rendre personnellement pour le soulagement de nos malades et blessés militaires, et accomplir ainsi l'œuvre philanthropique de l'honorable comité dont vous êtes membre et commissaire en chef. Je saisis cette occasion pour vous prier, monsieur, d'agréer l'assurance de ma considération distinguée.

MOUSTAPHA,
Ministre de la Guerre.

Monsieur V. Barrington-Kennett,
Commissaire en chef et membre du Comité de Stafford House.

FROM THE PRESIDENT OF THE RED CRESCENT SOCIETY TO THE DUKE OF SUTHERLAND.

Constantinople, le 4 Juin 1878.

Monseigneur,—Monsieur Barrington-Kennett, Commissaire Général du Comité du Stafford House, et son représentant parmi nous, quitte aujourd'hui Constantinople, sa mission philanthropique ayant pris fin en Turquie. Nous ne saurions laisser échapper cette occasion sans remplir un devoir qui nous est imposé, autant par la reconnaissance que par la grandeur et l'efficacité de l'aide confraternelle dont le Comité que préside Votre Seigneurie a comblé la Société Ottomane de secours aux blessés et malades militaires, durant la période douleureuse que vient de traverser notre pays.

Dès l'ouverture des hostilités, en effet, le comité puissant, institué sous votre haute initiative, est accouru le premier apporter sa collaboration généreuse, incessante, au Croissant Rouge, et, partout où l'humanité avait des droits à réclamer, le drapeau anglais, noblement porté par les agents du Stafford House, est venu fraternellement mêler ses couleurs à celles de l'œuvre ottomane de secours sur les champs de bataille. Il nous est impossible de nous dissimuler que, sans ce concours efficace au début de notre œuvre, celle-ci aurait eu à surmonter des difficultés que la prévoyance généreuse de la société anglaise est venue écarter, en affermissant ses premiers pas. Qu'il nous soit permis de rendre à Votre Seigneurie et à la société que vous présidez cet hommage de gratitude, hommage qui sera ratifié par l'armée impériale ottomane et par le pays tout entier, dont nous sommes ici les faibles interprètes. Mais il est un point spécial sur lequel le comité central du Croissant Rouge tient à exprimer ses remerciements au comité du Stafford House : c'est celui d'avoir choisi, pour le représenter parmi nous, un personnage du caractère de Mr. Barrington-Kennett.

Le noble commissaire général du Stafford House a su remplir sa mission avec un tact, une élévation de sentiments et une courtoisie cordiale qui lui ont acquis, dès son arrivée en Turquie, l'estime universelle. Sa tâche, grande déjà par elle-même, a été encore rehaussée par le prestige sympathique de ses qualités personnelles. Nous ne pourrions rendre une meilleure justice à Mr. Barrington-Kennett, qu'en assurant à Votre Seigneurie que, en se séparant de lui, chaque membre du comité du Croissant Rouge ne perd pas seulement un collaborateur actif et dévoué, mais encore un ami cher et dont le souvenir laissera des traces ineffaçables. Puisse cette expression bien sincère des sentiments de toute notre société être pour Monsieur Barrington-Kennett un dédommagement aux fatigues et aux peines qu'il s'est imposées dans l'accomplissement de sa noble et grande mission !

Chargé de vous transmettre, Monseigneur, l'hommage de dévouement et de reconnaissance du comité central du Croissant Rouge, je m'estime personnellement heureux d'avoir à accomplir ce devoir, et je prie Votre Seigneurie de vouloir bien agréer, avec l'assurance de notre inaltérable gratitude, l'expression de notre haute et respectueuse considération.

Le Président, Dr. ARIF.

A Sa Seigneurie le Duc de Sutherland,
    Président du Comité du Stafford House, Londres.

FROM BARON MUNDY.

Constantinople, Nov. 30, 1877.

DEAR BARRINGTON-KENNETT,—Before you leave for your short trip to England, you will permit me to impress on you, in regard to a very important assistance which you have already afforded to thousands and thousands, in reality, of starving soldiers, coming from the front sick or wounded, by railway or other means of transport—I mean, of course, your admirably organised service of soup-kitchens. Having had, so often, opportunities of witnessing the arrival of the wounded and sick at all hours of the day and night at the railway stations, and seeing at the same time the moral and physical result of the nourishment and refreshment (pillaf, coffee, tobacco, and cognac) on these poor fellows, which, if forgotten by the Stafford House Committee, would not have had any chance to keep their sinking bodies and souls together, I must confess that no money was certainly better spent, or in a more deserving way, than by these equally humane as hygienic correct work. Knowing that more than 20,000 sick and wounded soldiers have enjoyed these benefits by Stafford House help, by this charitable organisation of your soup-kitchens, I compliment you highly on it. Allow me to add that in my belief this institution could be more practically developed by buying moveable kitchen-carts, and fitting up kitchens in railway carriages, of which designs and samples are very well known to you. I am sure that your Committee would not object in spending for such a work a certain amount of money, if it would be proposed by you and carried out energetically and economically, qualities which you possess both.

I cannot finish this letter without giving myself the pleasure to express to you and your Committee the highest consideration which I feel in remembering the method in which your ambulance work was carried out in this war, under the most difficult circumstances which I ever met before. Your detached sections at the front, your permanent hospitals, have been of the greatest value to the victims of war. Your transport work, although too limited in matériel and personnel, by want of funds, for this most important branch of the military sanitary service, has nevertheless done great good. You will not, I hope, call me presumptuous if I advise you again and again to develope more and more the transport service, for the success of conservative surgery.

Everybody of your staff and your fellow-labourers, beginning from the chief commissioner to the last hamal who has been by you engaged, merits both praise and acknowledgment, and certainly, above all, your brave and skilful surgeons working in the front, to the benefit of the Turkish army and the honour and repute of their own country.

I hope your health will be improved by your short trip to England, and that you will be able to return soon amongst us here to continue the noble work which you so splendidly have carried out, not only on this occasion, but always in war time, when you have been called for by charitable societies.

Yours faithfully,
T. MUNDY.

FROM TEMPLE BEY.

Salonica, April 15, 1878.

Permit me to thank you for the great assistance you have rendered to the wounded of the Ottoman army at Salonica, during a period of extreme need. As soon as I was informed that you had an intention to send an ambulance, I reserved for you a large school building, which Dr. Eccles and his colleagues in a few days transferred into an effective hospital. Here the wounded were cared for most kindly and treated most skilfully, and results obtained which earned the warm admiration of all the medical military authorities at Salonica, who testified their appreciation of the medical services of the Stafford House corps of surgeons by the presentation of an address, unanimously adopted in a medical council. The valuable stores which you placed at our disposal have been handed over to the Sisters of Charity, who nurse the wounded with rare devotion and extreme care, and who have kindly consented to superintend their daily distribution, and thus to ensure that the stores may be employed to the utmost possible advantage. I am anxious to congratulate you on the happy selection of the surgeons of the Salonica ambulance, for they one and all displayed enthusiasm and intelligence in their arduous work.

I take this opportunity to express warm sympathy with the efforts of the Stafford House Committee to lessen some of the horrors of war. Both in Europe and Asia, during my official tours, I have had intimate personal and official relations with various members of your surgical corps, and I desire to bear my testimony to the untiring energy and indomitable perseverance exhibited by all attached to the Stafford House ambulances. As in the past, so in the future, I shall be ever ready to support, to the utmost of my power, a society which has worthily earned for itself a world-wide reputation for active charity towards the sick and wounded.

(Signed)   WILLIAM H. TEMPLE, M.D.
Colonel, Principal Medical Officer.

To V. Barrington-Kennett, Esq.
Chief-Commissioner.

FROM THE GOVERNOR OF GALLIPOLI.

Gallipoli, 9-21 Mai 1878.

Monsieur le Commissaire,—J'ai l'honneur d'accuser réception de votre lettre du 18 Mai, et de vous remercier pour la bonté que vous avez eue d'offrir aux malades du Stafford House pour les militaires ottomans. Je vous remercie pour les sentiments et les actes de généreuse philanthropie, et pour les nouvelles opérations que vous venez de commencer à Gallipoli, afin d'améliorer la condition sanitaire de nos troupes. Les médecins, les chevaux, des substances pour les secours aux malades, et les voitures pour le transport sont arrivés.

Veuillez agréer, Monsieur le Commissaire, l'assurance de ma parfaite considération,

(signé)   MEHEMET RECHID,
Gouverneur de Gallipoli.

A Monsieur Barrington-Kennett,
Commissaire en chef représentant le Comité du Stafford House.

FROM YAYA PACHA AND THE MILITARY AUTHORITIES OF THE CONSTANTINOPLE LINES OF DEFENCE.

24 Mars (v.s.).

Nous, soussignés, attestons, à l'occasion de son départ pour Londres, que Mr. le Dr. Hayes, médecin en chef de l'hôpital du Stafford House, établi depuis quelques mois à Tchifout-Burgas, n'a cessé, depuis le commencement jusqu'à la fin de sa philanthropique mission, de rendre des services incontestables pour améliorer le sort des malades et blessés de l'armée impériale ottomane, et qu'il a su obtenir, par le zèle et le dévouement qu'il a développés dans cet espace de temps, l'entière reconnaissance de tout le monde: en foi de quoi nous avons rédigé et signé le présent acte.

Chef de bataillon TEVFIK ARIH.
Chef de bataillon MEHMED-ULSAÏD.
Capitaine DJÉMAL.
Capitaine CHAKIR.
Lieutenant-major ISMAÏL HAKKI.

Lieutenant-major AHMED NOURI.
Lieutenant-général MOUSTAFA-UL-RÉCHID.
Lieutenant-général MOUSTAFI.
Lieutenant-colonel REFIK.
Général de brigade YAYA NADJI.

A Monsieur le Dr. Hayes, &c.

FROM THE GOVERNOR-GENERAL OF THE PROVINCE OF SALONICA.

Salonique, Mars 26 1878, V.S.

MONSIEUR,—Tous les médecins de l'armée impériale ottomane apprécient à leur juste valeur les services incontestables dont vous, Monsieur, ainsi que tout le personnel sous vos ordres, ont fait montre à l'égard des malades et blessés de l'armée ottomane.

Quant à moi, j'aurais manqué à un devoir des plus sacrés, non-seulement envers vous, mais envers l'humanité tout entière, si je négligeais les louanges que vous avez si bien méritées ; je m'empresse donc, au nom du gouvernement et de la nation ottomane, de vous témoigner les sentiments de ma parfaite reconnaissance et vous présenter mes hommages les plus respectueux.

J'ai l'honneur d'être, votre tout dévoué,
(Signé)   IBRAHIM.

Monsieur le Dr. Eccles, médecin en chef de l'hôpital
du Comité du Stafford House à Salonique.

FROM THE GRAND COUNCIL, GALLIPOLI.

Gallipoli le 27/9 Avril 1878 (N.S.),
le 6 Tzemadzit Evell, 1295.

Nous, soussignés, déclarons par la présente que Monsieur Barker, médecin en chef de l'hôpital établi ici par le Comité du Stafford House, et par ses soins, a très-bien traité les militaires malades des troupes impériales ottomanes, soignés dans le susdit hôpital, où il a servi avec dévouement, et qu'il a accompli tous les devoirs dus envers l'humanité.

En foi de quoi, pour rendre hommage à la vérité et pour l'apprécier, nous tous, satisfaits de sa conduite et pleins de reconnaissance, lui offrons ce Masbata (certificat officiel), en témoignage de nos remercîments.

MEHMED RÉCHID, le Gouverneur de Gallipoli.
HUSSEIN, le Juge.
MUSTAPHA SIDKI, le Mufti.
NAIM, le Chef de la Comptabilité.

GRÉGOIRE, l'Evêque de Gallipoli.
ABDULLAH HIHNI NETSIA, le Chef de la Correspondance.
MUSTAPHA DANIAH, Membre du Grand Conseil.

A Monsieur le Dr. Barker.

OBITUARY.

F. L. ATTWOOD.

Frederick Lyndon Attwood was educated partly in England and partly upon the Continent, and from his early years possessed and diligently cultivated a taste for letters. He received his medical education at St. Mary's Hospital, London, and, subsequently to his qualification, held the posts of Resident Medical Officer at the Lock Hospital, and of House Surgeon at the Royal Free Hospital. His career as a military surgeon commenced in the Franco-German war of 1870, but was cut short by ill-health, which obliged him to retire before the conclusion of the campaign.

In the summer of 1876 the accounts of suffering among the Servian soldiery, engaged in the Turco-Servian war, aroused in England a feeling of deep sympathy. Attwood, with a small number of English surgeons, left England in July under the auspices of the Knights of St. John of Jerusalem, and formed an ambulance, afterwards taken over by the National Aid Society: with them he travelled to Belgrade, and soon afterwards proceeded to the front. The Turks had driven back the Servians to their southern frontier, and were about to commence an attack upon Alexinatz. This town was reached by the English surgeons on Aug. 19, the day on which the series of battles that took place around Alexinatz commenced. The English ambulance was at once engaged in very heavy work, that had to be undertaken under circumstances of exceptional danger and difficulty. Attwood proved himself of special service. His untiring energy, his conscientious performance of work that lay upon him—to cope with which his delicate physique was so little fitted—formed an example of encouragement, as his skill and kindly help formed a valuable assistance to all those associated with him. Mr. Attwood was afterwards appointed to take charge of the National Aid Society hospital at Belgrade. On the withdrawal of the National Aid Society on Dec. 1, 1876, Attwood determined to keep the English hospital open, and if necessary to supply the funds for its maintenance from his own purse. The hospital was maintained in this way until April 1, 1877, and although some subscriptions were collected, this act of charity was performed by Mr. Attwood at a cost to himself of several hundred pounds.

In the spring of 1877, when the declaration of war between Russia and Turkey appeared imminent, Mr. Attwood returned to England to ascertain in what direction his services might be again applied, and was appointed on the staff of the Stafford House Committee. He arrived in Constantinople in July, 1877, and was appointed chief surgeon of the Stafford House ambulance section attached to the headquarters of Suleiman Pacha, then operating near Yenisaghra. He was subsequently engaged on very heavy work at Adrianople, where he superintended the formation of the Stafford House hospital. In August he returned to the front at Shipka, and rejoined his section, which did such good work during the severe fighting in the Balkans. In December the Shipka ambulance was withdrawn, and Mr. Attwood and his staff were appointed to join the Turkish army retreating from Tashkessen towards Bazardjik and Philippopolis. On Jan. 11, while waiting to recover some ambulance stores, which, in the hurried march of the preceding night, had been left in the wagons broken down in their attempts to traverse the precipitious and ice-bound roads, Attwood was taken prisoner by the Russians, under circumstances described in his letter. Mr. Attwood did his duty nobly. He immediately took charge of 150 sick and wounded Turkish soldiers, who had been abandoned in the hasty retreat of the army; but, cut off from his ambulance and colleagues, without European companions on whom he could rely, without supplies in a country stripped bare of provisions, in a district whose air was saturated and whose water was poisoned with pestilence, the position was, to one more fitted for hardship, hazardous ; to Mr. Attwood we may say that it was fatal. Already exhausted by hunger and fatigue, he could no longer resist the poisonous influences which surrounded him, and was soon prostrated by the fever. Ten days later the order arrived for the evacuation of the village, and Mr. Attwood was transported, by a journey occupying two days and nights, to Philippopolis. He was here found in a condition of unconsciousness by Mr. Hume, who had been sent to his assistance, when it was known that Mr. Attwood had been taken prisoner. Mr. Hume scarcely left his side until his apparent convalescence, and with Baron Mundy nursed him through a long illness. His subsequent prostration was so intense that three or four weeks, during which his life was in continual and imminent danger, elapsed before he was in a condition to be removed, even at great risk, to Constantinople. His improvement was so gradual that it was not until June that he reached England ; he was then apparently convalescent, but in a short time he was attacked with a condition, attributed to the malarious poison with which he was infected, so painful as to render him entirely helpless, and almost incapable of any movement for nearly three months ; the improvement that then occurred never proceeded to complete recovery ; the constitution had been too profoundly shaken to ever be really restored. Although unfit for hard work, he went up to Cambridge for the Lent term, with the intention of taking his degree. He had, however, overrated his strength, and soon after returning to London he was evidently under a melancholy impression that his mental power was permanently weakened. His physical exhaustion and the melancholy arising from it, acting and reacting, resulted in a condition of despondency which terminated only in his death, which occurred upon Friday, April 11, 1879. Aged 35.

JOHN PINKERTON, M.B.C.M.

It is with deep regret that we have to record the death, on January 7, 1878, of Dr. John Pinkerton, of typhus fever, at Erzeroum, in Armenia. He was born at Rutherglen in 1853, and was thus in the 25th year of his age. He graduated at Glasgow University in July 1876, and in November of the same year entered the Royal Infirmary, as resident assistant to the surgical wards under the care of Dr. Hector Cameron. Six months later he passed to the medical side of the House, as assistant to Dr. M'Laren.

In the autumn of 1877, Lord Blantyre, a member of the Stafford House Committee, sent out several surgeons to the seat of war in Turkey, and among these was Dr. Pinkerton, who set out in October, in company with Dr. Denniston of Greenock. They were delayed a short time at Constantinople, but ultimately set off for Erzeroum, which they reached early in November. On approaching that town, a skirmish was in progress between the belligerents, and Pinkerton and his companions narrowly escaped falling into the hands of the Russians, all their personal baggage being lost. The town was soon beleaguered, but letters came at intervals through the Russian lines, written with all Dr. Pinkerton's hopeful spirit, but abounding in details of the misery and death that were rampant within the walls. The surgeons had indeed work enough to do. Owing to the fearful overcrowding of the city, and the great privations to which the besieged were exposed, typhus fever of a virulent type soon broke out, and assumed all the proportions of a plague. A letter received from Dr. Pinkerton, dated Christmas-day, reported him as well, and one dated December 28 bore a similar report. No more was heard of him till in a letter from Dr. Denniston, of January 2, he was reported as dangerously ill of typhus, and a telegram of a subsequent date, from the same writer, brought the sad news of his death. He seems to have sickened about December 28 ; delirium supervened at an early stage of the disease, and he died on January 7, the tenth day of the fever, having been comatose for some time. He was buried within the walls. Nearly all the other surgeons were lying prostrate with the same disease ; but it is consoling to think that all that care and solicitude could do for him was done by his friend and countryman, Dr. Denniston, who seems to have tended him with the care and affection of a brother.

Dr. Pinkerton was well known and much esteemed in college circles. His professional acquirements were varied and sound. His death has been deeply regretted in Glasgow ; and in the circle of his more immediate friends, to whom his kind disposition and frank and manly spirit had much endeared him, it has evoked expressions of the deepest personal sorrow. Much sympathy is felt for his parents in the loss of their only son.

C C

The Sultan, wishing to confer on the memory of Mr. Pinkerton the same honour as on that of Mr. Guppy, presented to his family the Turkish war medal in recognition of his great services and noble self-sacrifice.

W. G. GUPPY, L.R.C.S., EDIN.

William Good Guppy, son of Dr. Stokes Guppy, of Falmouth, was born in 1855, and in 1877 became a Licentiate of the Royal College of Surgeons, Edinburgh, with a view of entering the medical service of the Royal Navy, in which his twin brother is now serving. In July, 1877, Mr. Guppy was engaged by Lord Blantyre, of the Stafford House Committee, to join his staff of surgeons who had established the British Hospital at Erzeroum. He at once proceeded to the seat of war, and immediately on his arrival at Erzeroum was engaged in hospital work of a most trying nature In the following November Mr. Guppy rendered most valuable services on the field at the battle of Devi-Boyoun and the attack on Fort Assizi, being at times exposed to a heavy fire while attending to the wounded. His friend and colleague, Dr. James Denniston, who was with him in his last illness, writes as follows:—

'Guppy died on Nov. 17, 1877, after about six days' illness. His illness we at the time took to be an acute form of enteric fever, but from our later experience we agreed that it was a fever peculiar to the district and well known by the inhabitants, among whom it was very prevalent and fatal. I believe it was from the same fever that both Fetherstonhaugh and Woods suffered. Guppy was a fine, plucky fellow, and did his work like a man. I have no doubt that the excitement and hard work we all experienced in the beginning of November [at the battle of Devi-Boyoun and attack on Fort Assizi] told a good deal on him and affected his health, which never seemed particularly robust. He and Pinkerton are buried alongside each other in a little enclosed cemetery where lie the few Europeans who have died in Erzeroum.'

The Sultan ordered the Turkish war medal to be forwarded to the family of Mr. Guppy 'in recognition of his services at Erzeroum in aid of the Ottoman sick and wounded for whom he so nobly sacrificed his life.'

GENERAL INDEX.

(See also 'Analysis of Medical Reports,' p. 205.)

ABL

ABLAVA, 43
Abstract of expenditure of S. H. funds remitted to Chief Commissioner, 184
Abstract of receipts and payments of S. H. fund, by Sir Henry Green, Hon. Treasurer, 183
Accounts in Turkey, 13
Adrianople Hospital, 68 (and see under 'Hospitals')
Adrianople, pitiable condition of the wounded at, 63
Ahmed Vefyk Pacha, 1, 2, 46
Ahmet Eyoub Pacha, 70
Ahmet Kaïsserli Pacha, his visit to S. H. hospital at Rustchuk, 47
— 50
Akestorides, dispenser, 71, 74
Ali Bey, 16
Ambulance.
— *First Lom*, concise account of, 57
— — 8
— *Kars District* (Lord Blantyre's), concise account of, 113
— — staff fired upon, 117
— — retreat to Eulla-Tepe, 118, 119
— — departure from Kars, 120
— — staff taken prisoners, 120
— *Plevna District*, concise account of, 82
— — 20, 22
— *Red Crescent Transport*, 121
— — table of amount of work done by, 121
— *Samakov Transport*, concise account of, 87
— — formation of, 8, 28
— *Second Lom*, concise account of, 59
— — 8, 28, 44
— — at Elena, 60
— — retreat across the Balkans, 60, 61
— — fired at by the Russians, 61
— *Shipka*, concise account of, 62
— — 8, 125

BAR

Ambulance sections, reorganisation of, 29
— sent to Sofia, 21
— carts, duty done by S. H. at Varna, 56
Ambulances, distribution of, 24
— S. H. C.'s, broken up, 26
— routes of, during retreat of Turkish armies, 8, 26, 28, 65
American Mission, 32
Animals, dead, burial of, round Constantinople, 8, 35
Arif, Dr., President of R.C.S., letter to the Duke of Sutherland, 187
Asia, relief to, 10, 16, 20, 21, 130
— invalided staff in, 25, 99, 101
Assaf Pacha, 58
Attwood, Surgeon, 17, 24, 27, 28, 35, 36, 62, 64, 67
— illness of, 30, 67
— reports of, 62, 66
— taken prisoner by the Russians, 67
— obituary of, 102
Azzopardi, Dr., 68, 81, 82, 97

BAKER PACHA, General, 40, 64, 65, 66, 88
Balkans, retreat across, 60, 61, 64, 65
Banfather, Lieut., 87, 121, 122
Barker, Surgeon, 18, 23, 28, 29, 37, 72, 92
— reports of, 75, 79, 127
— surgical report of, with Roumelian Railway Transport, 139
Barrington-Kennett, V. B., his appointment as Chief Commissioner by S. H. Committee, 2
— his record of the S.H. operations at the seat of war, PART II., 5
— returns of sick and wounded treated, 10
— report on distribution of stores, 12
— accounts in Turkey, 13, 184, 185, 186

GENERAL INDEX.

BAR

Barrington-Kennett, V. B., reports of, 14, 18, 26, 34
— letter of, to Sir A. H. Layard, 22
— previsional preparations of, at Constantinople, in case of war between Russia and England, 35
— 131, 133, 187
Bartlett, Mr., Commissioner of Turkish Compassionate Fund, 34, 128
— his thanks for aid received from S. H. C., 34
— attacked with typhoid fever, 37
Bartoletti, Dr., 18
Batoum, relief to, 21
Beresford, Surgeon, 21, 47, 59, 90
— illness of, 19, 60
Beylikgy, dispenser, 97
Biliotti, Vice-Consul, his distribution of money relief at Trebizond, 10, 34, 38, 105
— 99
— report of, 105
Blantyre, Lord, his contribution to S. H. fund, 4
— expenditure of, 14
— surgeons of, vi., 17
— distribution of warm clothing at Erzeroum, 102
— English hospital at Erzeroum, 107
Blunt, Colonel, 82
Blunt, Consul, 26, 64, 78
Bombardment of Rustchuk Hospital by the Russians, 49, 50
Borthwick, Colonel, 16, 59
Boulair Lines Dispensary, 94 (and see under 'Dispensaries')
Boyd, Surgeon, 21, 58, 83
Bowles, Mr. T. Gibson, appointed Hon. Sec., 1
Brassard, S. H. staff adopt Red Crescent badge with "S. H." stamped on it, 125
British Hospital Fund, 102
Bryant's rule for complete anæsthesia, 157
Buckby, Surgeon, 107, 113
— illness of, 117
Buckle, Dr., R.N., 35
— reports of, 124, 126
Bulgaria, general report on S. H. relief in, 24
— reports concerning district, 43
Bulgarians, ill-treatment of Turks by, 64, 67
Burnaby, Captain, 21, 65, 66
— letter of, 129
Busby, Surgeon, 21, 57, 83
— reports of, 58, 83

CACOLETS, utility of, 121
Caijah Pacha, 88
Calfoglou, Surgeon, 23, 71, 73
— illness of, 74

DIS

Calvert, Mr., British Consul, 78
Carbolic acid, in the treatment of wounds, 72, 160
Carbolised tow, 168
Carcallis, Dr. Constantine, 63
Cash statement of S. H. fund, 185
Casson, Surgeon, 14, 107, 11
— reports of, 107, 113
— taken prisoner, 120
Chakir Pacha, 88
Chart showing total numbers treated by every section every month, *facing title*
Chefvet Pacha, 20, 82
Chloroform, 72, 157
Circassian surgery, 115
Clements, Surgeon, 34, 42, 90, 92, 93
Cole, Mr., American missionary, 104, 108, 110
Colley, Mr., 82
Commerell, Rear-Admiral Sir Edmund, V.C., K.C.B., 3, 7, 33, 35, 39, 42, 92, 131
— letter of, 96
Compassionate Fund, Turkish, co-operation with, 25, 31, 127
— — S. H. surgeons attached to, 31
Conservative surgery, 91
Constantinople, two new barrack hospitals at, 30
— epidemic imminent at, 31
— state of Turkish hospitals at, 39
Convalescents relieved by money donations from S. H. Fund, 12, 34, 105
Coope, Colonel, report of, 79
Co-operation of voluntary societies, 7, 17
Coslowski, Surgeon, vi.
Court, M., 44
Cowan, Mr., 68, 95
Crookshank, Surgeon, 16
Cullen, Mr., C.E., 77
— report of, 78
Cullen, Surgeon, 21, 122, 123
Currency, Turkish, general account kept in, 13
— fluctuations in value of, 14

DAOUD PACHA section, 33
Della Sudda, 16
Denniston, Surgeon, 107
— gallant conduct of, 38, 105, 107
— reports of, 109
De Winton, Major, 30
Diseases of natives, 114
Dispensaries.
— *Boulair Lines*, concise account of, 94
— — 11, 93, 94
— — mode of administration, 41
— — inspection of, 41

DIS

Dispensaries (*continued*).
— *Boulair Lines*, assistance given by officers of H.M. fleet to, 95
— — the illness of S. H. staff at, 95
— — scurvy and small-pox at, 95
— — sanitary arrangements at, 95
— — system of relief, 95
— — statistics of treatment, 96
— *Tchekmedje* and *Makrikeui*, concise account of, 89
— *Tchifout-Burgas*, concise account of, 88
— — 9, 34
Djaemal Pacha, 78, 133
Dressers, Turkish, efficiency of, 100
Dressings for gunshot wounds, 138
Drew, Surgeon, R.N., 92
Drummond, Lieut., R.N., 16, 17, 113
Dysentery (see 'Medical Reports,' PART III.)

ECCLES, Surgeon, 32, 34, 71, 90, 92, 93
— illness of, 71
— reports of, 72, 90, 93, 177
Edmunds, Surgeon, 28, 29, 47, 59
Egyptian wounded, 47
Elena, battle of, S. H. staff at, 60
Embarkation of wounded at Karagatch, 66
Erzeroum English Hospital (Lord Blantyre's), 107 (and see under 'Hospitals')
— Stafford House hospital, 99 (and see under 'Hospitals')
— supplies sent to, 15
— critical position of staff at, 25
— relief to S. H. section at, 26
— intense cold at, 101
— great mortality in the hospitals at, 103
— Red Crescent staff at, 104
— number of burials within the walls of the town, 104
Erzinghian, evacuation to, 109
Eskreff Pacha, 16
Esmarch's tourniquet, 141

FAYRER, Sir J., Chairman of Medical Sub-Committee, introductory remarks of, to Medical Report, 132
Fetherstonhaugh, Surgeon, 14, 90, 101, 107
— illness of, 26, 109
— reports of, 108, 109
Fife-Cookson, Lieut.-Col., extract from his work 'With the Armies in the Balkans,' 131
Finger, enormous proportion of wounds of, 118
Fleet, Turkish, relief to, 21
Foulis' bands, 159

HOS

Frost-bite, 111, 143 (and see 'Medical Reports,' PART III.)
Fund Pacha, 64

GALLIPOLI Hospital, 92 (and see under 'Hospitals')
Gallipoli, 30
— bad condition of hospitals at, 39
— Transport Service, 92
— Grand Council's thanks to S. H. C., 191
General Accounts, 13
Giovan-Tchiflik, battle of, 46
— — wounded from, 48
Gooch's splints, 162
Görlitz, J., dispenser, 24, 76
— report of, 85
Gourko, General, 27, 84
Green, Sir H., Hon. Treasurer of S. H. C., 1
Gresley, Lieut., R.N., 92
Groissman, M., 76
Guarracino, M., 92, 95
Guerriera, M., 92, 95
Gumurgina, the Greek Bishop's hospitality to S. H. staff at, 66
Guppy, Surgeon, 107, 113
— illness of, 108
— death of, 109
— obituary of, 194

HADEMKEUI, as a base of operations for two ambulances, 26
Hakki Bey, 38, 104, 112
Hanson, Messrs. C. & Co., Bankers of Constantinople, 1
Harvey, Mr. (engineer), commissioned to raise a corps of refugees to bury carcases of animals, 9
— 21, 30, 33, 35, 36, 38, 100
Hayes, Surgeon, 28, 29, 36, 53, 88
— reports of, 54, 88
Hayreddin Bey, Surgeon, 55
Heath, Surgeon, 65
Hirsch, Baron, his Committee in co-operation with S. H. C., 25
Hobart Pacha, 21
Hospital-bearers, advantage of trained, 156
Hospitals.
— *Adrianople*, concise account of, 68
— — increased number of patients, 69
— — weekly progress of, 69
— — addition of two wards, 70
— — Railway Station, relief of wounded at, 70
— — evacuation of, 9, 27, 70
— — account of four hundred surgical cases at, 123

HOS

Hospitals (*continued*).
— *Adrianople*, description of, 124
— — Captain Burnaby's visit to, 129
— *Erzeroum English* (*Lord Blantyre's*), concise account of, 107
— — wounded at, after the attack on Erzeroum, 108
— — small-pox at, 110
— — staff attacked by typhus, 110
— — prevalence of frost-bite, 111
— — gangrene at, 111
— — chest complaints, 112
— — sudden evacuation of, 112
— — Consul Zohrab's remarks on, 131
— *Erzeroum Stafford House*, concise account of, 99
— — formation of, 10
— — desertion of Turkish employés, 31
— — determination to close, 32
— — 36, 99
— — description of, 100
— — arrival of stores, 100
— — arrival of wounded from Kars, 101
— — typhus and typhoid in, 101
— — small-pox at, 102
— — prevalence of diarrhœa, 103
— — sufferings of Turkish wounded sent from Kars, 102
— — improvement of sanitary condition, 103
— — Surgeon Stoker sent to relief of staff, 29 104
— — transfer to Turkish Government, 33, 104
— *Gallipoli*, concise account of, 92
— — new hospital chosen, 33, 34, 92
— — condition of sick at, 93
— — enlargement of hospital, 93
— — want of surgeons in the lines, 93
— — statistics of, 94
— — transfer to Turkish Government, 41, 94
— *Makrikeui*, concise account of, 89
— — 32, 35, 36
— — transfer to Turkish Government, 89
— — Dr. Buckle's description of, 126
— *Mundy Barrack*, concise account of, 85
— — 8, 126
— *Ochur Koppull*, *Gul-hané*, 123
— *Philippopolis*, concise account of, 71
— — 8, 28, 32
— — closing operations at, 36
— — all sick and wounded given over to S. H. staff, 71, 74
— — evacuation of wounded to Adrianople, 73
— — terrible condition of wounded after retreat of the Turks, 74
— — returns of serious cases under Surgeon Neylan, 78
— — Captain Burnaby's visit to, 129

HYD

Hospitals (*continued*).
— *Rustchuk*, concise account of, 46
— — formation of, 15
— — bombardment and destruction of, by Russians, 9, 26, 49
— — excellent situation of, 43
— — enlargement of, 45
— — 46, 48
— — gallant rescue of wounded by S. H. surgeons, 47, 49
— — aid to wounded from battle at Pyrgos and Kadikeui, 47, 49
— — narrow escape of S. H. medical staff, 49
— — removal of patients to Varna, 51
— — denial of Russian official statement that hospital was used as a barrack for troops, 51
— — returns, 52, 53
— *Salonica*, concise account of, 90
— — formation of, 9
— — 34, 36, 91
— — transfer of, to Turkish authorities, 38
— — condition of wounded, 91
— — transfer to Red Crescent Society, 91
— — statistics of treatment, 92
— *Sofia*, concise account of, 83
— — occupation by the Russians, Dr. Busby and staff remain in care of wounded, 27, 84
— — Captain Burnaby's visit to, 129
— *Stamboul Mundy Barrack*, concise account of, 85
— — clinical class of students formed at, 86
— — description of, 85, 86, 126
— *Stamboul New Barrack*, concise account of, 96
— — 34, 38, 39, 40, 86, 97
— — Dr. Stiven's class of Turkish medical students, 97
— — table of wounded, 97
— — for French refugees, under Dr. Lagondakis, 126
— *Tchchmedje*, concise account of, 89
— — establishment of, 9
— — great amount of sickness at, 89
— *Varna*, concise account of, 122
— — establishment of, 15, 16
— — transfer of staff to Red Crescent Society, 20
— — combined service with Red Crescent Society, 122
— — table of wounded, 123
Hume, Surgeon, 28, 62, 65, 67
Hungarian doctors in Turkish service at Erzeroum, mortality among, 101
Hussein Effendi, head Turkish surgeon at Erzeroum, complaint against, 36
— his arrest, 112
Hyderabad, inhabitants of, their subscription to S. H. fund, 2

GENERAL INDEX. 199

IBR

IBRAHIM PACHA, 71
— thanks to S. H. C., 190
Isidore, Stamboul depôt, vi.
Ismail Bey, chief army doctor in Asia, 101

JACKSON, Captain, R.N., 92
Jala, Kars district ambulance engaged on field at, 116
Johnson, Mr., 15, 17

KADIKEUI, battle of, 21, 47
Kaprikeui, want of medical stores at, 114
Karagatch, wounded at, 66
Karahassan-keui, battle of, S. H. staff at, 58
Karlova, condition of wounded at, 98
Kars, evacuation of wounded from, 109
— want of medical organisation at, 113, 115
— District Ambulance, 113 (see under 'Ambulance')
Kaselevo, S. H. staff attending wounded at battle of, 44, 58, 59
Kemball, General Sir A., 7, 14, 105, 115
Kesanlik, Turkish wounded at, 33, 63, 98, 121, 122, 124
— stores sent to, 36
— defective hospital accommodation at, 78
— relief given by S. H. C. to Turkish wounded at, 33, 98
— Relief Section under Mr. Williams, 98
Kiazim Pacha, S. H. surgeons attached to his command, 22, 83
Kirker, Surgeon, 68, 70, 163
Kirkor Bey, 24
Kouvaras, Dr., 44, 122
— report of, 122

LADIES' Committee on the Bosphorus, 16
La Guidara, M., 76
Lake, Surgeon, 21, 47, 49, 56, 58, 85, 96
— illness of, 19, 45
Langdon, Surgeon, 65
Layard, Sir H. A., 4, 7, 22
Leslie, Surgeon, of the National Aid Society, 63
Lister, Mr., his antiseptic treatment for wounded soldiers, 158
Lom ambulances, First and Second, formation of, 8
— — First, 57 (see also under 'Ambulance')
— — Second, 59 (see also under 'Ambulance')

MOO

McCALMONT, Captain, 99
MacCormac, Mr., 2
McIvor, Surgeon, 23, 68, 82
— reports of, 69
— his account of four hundred surgical cases treated at the S. H. Military hospital at Adrianople, 33
Mackellar, Surgeon, 22, 23, 79
— at the Shipka Pass, 64
— report of, 164
Macpherson, Surgeon, 166, 171
McQueen, Surgeon, 24, 56, 59, 87
— reports of, 59
Mahir Bey (Colonel Borthwick), 16, 59
Mails intercepted by Russians, 29
Makrikeui, explosion at, 20
Makrikeui Hospital, 89 (and see under 'Hospitals')
Manoury, Dr., of the French Society for Relief of Wounded, 72
Maps showing operations in European and Asiatic Turkey, at beginning
Marco Pacha, 85, 97, 128
Marian, S. H. ambulance at, 60
Marine lint, 142
Masters, Mr., burial of, 42
Matianer, Dr., 85
Medical chests, 131
Medical lessons of the war, 132
Medical Report by the Sub-Committee, Sir J. Fayrer, Chairman, PART III., 132 (and see Analysis of Medical Reports, following Index).
Medical staff, statistics of mortality and sickness among, 40
Mehemet Ali Pacha, 44, 58
— S. H. ambulances with hisarmy, 45
Mehemet Effendi, 49
Mehemet Rechid, governor of Gallipoli, thanks to S. H. C., 190
Melgund, Viscount, 15, 16
Melikoff, General, 104, 120
Metschersky, Prince Vladimir, President of the Russian Red Cross Society, 29
Michaelides, Dr. Aristides, 32
Midhat Pacha's orphan asylum, 90
Milk supplied by S. H. C. to Turkish hospitals, 29
Milligan, Surgeon, 21
Minassian, Surgeon, 23, 32, 65
— recognised by the Russian authorities at Philippopolis as head of the Turkish hospitals, 32
— reports of, 71, 73
Moffitt's winged screw tourniquet, 162
Monte, Gaspar, 76, 82
Monthly expenditure, table of, 186
Moore, Surgeon, 20, 22, 63, 77

MOO

Moore, Surgeon, reports of, 68, 83
Morisot, Lieutenant, 21, 68, 83, 99, 100, 101
— illness of, 103, 110
Mosques, refugees in, 81, 127
Mount Pelion, Surgeon Eccles' services at an action on, 37
Moustapha Pacha, Turkish Minister of War, thanks to S. H. C., 187
Mukhtar Pacha Ghazi, 99, 101, 109, 113, 115, 120
Mundy, Baron, 7, 19, 20, 37, 82
— establishes barrack hospital at Stamboul, 85
— organises Red Crescent Ambulance train, 146
— letter to S. H. C., 188

NACHSIVAN, Russian attack on, Kars district ambulance in attendance, 116
Nalban-Tepe, fight at, Kars district ambulance in attendance, 119
— narrow escape of ambulance, 119
Namyk Pacha, 17
National Aid Society, 7, 17, 28, 37, 43, 63, 66, 92, 93
Natives, peculiar diseases of, 114
Nedjib Pacha, 16, 57, 59, 60
— great amount of sickness in his division, treated by S. H. staff, 60
Neylan, Surgeon, illness of, 19
— reports of, 71, 85, 123
— surgical note by, 166
— result of forty-two major operations, 72
Niamara, Dr., 20
Nouri Pacha, President of the Medical Council of the War Office, 18, 63

OBITUARY, Attwood, F. L., 102
— Guppy, W. G., 194
— Pinkerton, J., 193
Ohannes Bey, 16, 45
Osman Bazar, relief afforded by S. H. staff to wounded at, 16
Osman Effendi, Surgeon, 173
Osman Nouri Pacha, 42, 65, 87, 88, 92
Osman Pacha Ghazi, 22, 36, 47, 89
— his evacuation of wounded from Plevna, 22
— thanks to S. H. C., 41
Otloukeui, retreat of S. H. ambulance from, 64

PEST, danger of, at Erzeroum, 104
Philippopolis Hospitals, 71 (and see under 'Hospitals')

RED

Philippopolis, all the hospitals at, placed under S. H. staff, 32, 65, 74
— meeting of S. H. ambulances at, 65
— occupation by the Russians, 74
— panic in town, 74
— Suleiman Pacha requests S. H. hospital aid at, 27
— Surgeon Minassian volunteers to remain with wounded, 27
Pinkerton, Surgeon J., 100, 101, 107
— illness of, 102
— death of, 102, 110
— obituary of, 196
Pinkerton, Surgeon R., 'Surgical experiences and observations as an ambulance surgeon in Bulgaria during the Russo-Turkish war,' 153
Plevna District Ambulance, 82 (and see under 'Ambulance')
Political effects of such aid as S. H. C. rendered in Russo-Turkish war (see Consul Zohrab's letter), 130
Portland, Duke of, his donation to S. H. fund, 8
Pratt, E. R., Assistant Commissioner of S. H. C. at the seat of war, 2, 59, 80
— reports of, 18, 23, 43
— on the organisation of field ambulance and transport in Oriental countries, 180
Price, Surgeon, Red Crescent Society, death of, 104
Prisoners, number of Turkish and Russian, 37
— Russian wounded, under S. H. protection, 60
— Turkish wounded, under S. H. protection, 82
Pyrgos, battle of, S. H. assistance at, 49

RAOUF PACHA, Turkish Minister of War, 30, 44
— defeat near Yenisaghra, wounded attended by S. H. staff, 62
Rasgrad, S. H. sub-depôt at, 53, 56
Ration, a, what it consists of, 12
Razis, Dr., of the Red Crescent, 72
Reade, Consul at Rustchuk, 15
Rechid Pacha, his thanks to S. H. staff, 39
— 87
Red Crescent Society, 7, 15, 36, 40, 43, 46, 59, 81, 85, 90, 91
— large supplies of S. H. stores given to, 12, 19
— transfer of S. H. surgeons to, 19, 20
— sanitary train, 81
— thanks to S. H. C., 41
— surgeons, 63
— Stafford House sections in co-operation with, 17, 121, 122
— Asia ambulance, 112

RED

Red Crescent Society, respect paid to ambulance badge, 125
— transport returns, 121
Red Cross (see 'National Aid Society')
Refugees, 29, 31, 57, 81, 127
— employment of, 9
Rennison, Mr., 103
Reports from the seat of war, general arrangement of, 5
— 14
Returns of sick and wounded treated, 10
Reuss, Princess, opens Stamboul Mundy Barrack Hospital, 85
Rhodope Balkans, retreat across, 28, 65
Ricketts, Consul, 120
Rifaat Pacha, 74
Roe, Surgeon, 32, 90, 91
Roumelia district, 62
Roumelian Railway Transport service, concise account of, 75
— 18, 28
— list of numbers transported, 75
— table of rations given to sick and wounded soldiers during transport, 76
— treatment of wounded by S. H. staff during transport, 78, 79, 81, 124
— surgical report, 139
Roy, Surgeon, 14, 45, 104, 112
Russian wounded prisoners in care of S. H. staff, 60
— kind treatment of, by the Turks, 129
Russians, great mortality among, 104
Rustchuk Hospital, 46 (and see under 'Hospitals')
Rustchuk, action near, wounded attended by S. H. staff, 47
— bombardment of, 46, 48
— Ohannes Bey's military hospital at, 55
Rustchuk-Varna Railway Transport, concise account of, 53
— 8, 28, 36
— reports to the Chief Commissioner, 53
— arrival of sick at Varna, 55
— tabulated return, 54
— occupation of line by Russians, 57
— distribution of stores to Turkish hospitals, 57
Rutledge, Surgeon, 38
Ryan, Surgeon, 21, 22
— in charge of Erzeroum section, 26
— illness of, 29, 102, 110
— reports of, 99, 102

SAFVET PACHA, 15, 28, 64, 65
St. Vincent de Paul Society, 126
Salar Jung, support of, 2

SOU

Salonica Hospital, 90 (and see under 'Hospitals')
Salonica, poverty and typhus at, 30, 32, 90
— satisfactory results of the aid afforded by the S. H. and National Aid Societies at, 37
Samakov Ambulance Transport, 8, 87 (and see under 'Ambulance')
Samakov, battle near, wounded attended by S. H. staff, 28, 87
— evacuation of, by Turks, 87
Sandwith, Surgeon, 28, 62, 66, 68
— report of, 64
Sarell, Dr., 16, 18, 20, 25
Saxon Sisters of Charity, 34, 86
Saxony, Queen of, sends Sisters of Charity as nurses to Stamboul, 85
Scaife, Mr., Auditor, his report, 14
Schoepps, Dr., 120
Scutari, Lady Strangford's hospital at, 37, 38
Scudamore, Mr., 68, 83
Sebastopoulos, Dr., Red Crescent, 125
Sections, the transmission of sick and wounded through, typical case, 11
Self-inflicted wounds, 155, 167
Senankeui, battle of, S. H. staff at, 58
Servians, self-mutilation by, 167
Services, list of, of staff, v.
Sheitanjik Soup-kitchen, 56
Ship, S. H. hospital, chartered, 10, 40
Shipka Ambulance, 62 (and see under 'Ambulance')
Shipka Pass, wounded after first attack, 63, 71
— S. H. ambulances ordered to the front, 27
Shumla, first convoy of sick from, 17
— seizure of stolen S. H. stores at, 46
— military hospital at, 55
Shumla Road Depôt, 46, 53, 56
Silistria, relief to, 20
Sketchley, Surgeon, formation of his ambulance, 24
— reports of, 87, 89
— 92, 94
Small-pox, 95, 102, 110, 128, 144 (and see ' Medical Reports,' PART III.)
Smith, Surgeon, Red Crescent Society, 77
Smoking a necessity to a Turk, 124, 163
Sofia Hospital, 83 (and see under ' Hospitals ')
Sofia, 21, 24
— evacuation of wounded from, 84
— panic in town, 27, 84
— desertion of Turkish hospitals by their own staff, 84
— attendance on sufferers by S. H. staff, 84
— departure of S. H. staff, 84
— good Turkish hospitals at, 84
Soubatan, battle of, Kars District ambulance in attendance, 113, 117
Soup, contractor's price of, 18, 56

GENERAL INDEX.

SOU

Soup-kitchens, Boulair Lines, 94
— Sheitanjik, 53, 56
— Stamboul, 18, 25, 75, 76, 78, 82
— — at work night and day, 82
— Tatar-Bazardjik, 76, 80, 85
— Tchervenavoda, 53, 56
— Tchorlou, 18, 75, 76, 78, 81
— Tirnova, 18, 75, 76, 78, 80
Soup-kitchens, S. H., number of rations issued at, 12
— S. H., Turkish soldiers' gratitude for, 80
Spanopoulos, dispenser, 68
Splints, 142, 163
Stafford House Committee, list of members of, iii.
— list of staff of, with services, v.
— origin of, 1
— first appeal for subscriptions, 2
— final report of, PART I., 1
— thanks to, APPENDIX, 189
Stamboul, Surgeon Neylan's clinical class at, 27, 86
— Surgeon Stiven's clinical class at, 97
— soup-kitchen, 75, 76 (and see 'Soup-kitchens')
— Mundy Barrack Hospital, 85 (and see under 'Hospitals')
— New Barrack Hospital, 96 (and see under 'Hospitals')
Stanimaka, battle of, 28, 88
Stanley of Alderley, Lord, co-operation of his committee with S. H. C., 1, 4
Statistics, difficulty of giving, 6, 111, 132
Stewart, Assistant-Surgeon, 68, 81
Stiven, Surgeon, 16, 21, 25, 31, 46, 87, 96, 103
— his class of native medical students, 38
— severe illness of, 40
— reports of, 47, 97, 179
Stoker, Surgeon, 20, 25, 102, 121
— reports of, 104, 121
Stolipin, General, Russian military commandant at Philippopolis, 98
Stoney, W. L., C.E., appointed Assistant-Commissioner to S. H. C., 2
— 12, 26
— reports of, 25, 41, 129
Stores, general report on distribution of, 12
— furnished to Red Crescent Society, 12, 19
— — Turkish fleet, 21
— — Turkish hospitals, 29
Strangford, Viscountess, 31, 37, 38, 163, 176
Stromeyer's triangular cushion, 162
Suleiman Pacha, his generals wish for aid of S. H. surgeons, 26
— 60, 61
Sultan, the, his thanks for help rendered by S. H. C., 2, 4, 187

TOU

Surgeons, S. H. C.'s, transfer of, 19
— — list of, with services, v.
— — sickness among, 20, 25, 32, 38, 40, 111
— sufferings of those taken prisoners by the Russians, 26
— statistics of mortality among Relief Societies,' 40
— mortality among Turkish, 102
Surgery, eccentricities of, 115
Surgical reports, PART III., 132
— difficulty of recording details, 132
Sutherland, Duke of, 1
— initiates Stafford House Committee, 1
— letter from Consul Zohrab to, on political effect of S. H. work, 130
— thanks of Sultan to, 2
— thanks of Red Crescent to, 187

TABULATED summary of sick and wounded treated, *facing* PART II., 5
Tahir Bey, chief of the gendarmerie, 22
— deputed by Turkish authorities to express thanks to S. H. C., 38
Tamolini, dispenser, 88
Tashkessen, 84
Tatar-Bazardjik, fighting at, S. H. staff in attendance, 61
— protection afforded by S. H. flag to women and children at, 65
— soup-kitchen at, 75, 76, 80
Tchekmedje and Makrikeui Hospitals and Dispensary, 89 (and see under 'Hospitals')
Tchervenavoda depôt, service after the fight on the Lom, 57
Tchifout-Burgas Dispensary, 88 (and see under 'Dispensaries')
Tchorlou, panic at, 70
Tchorlou soup-kitchen, 18, 75, 76, 81
Teale's amputation, 160
Temple, Dr., 90, 189
Thanks from Turkish authorities, 38, 41, 104
— letters of, 187
— from the Sultan, 2, 4, 187
— — Minister of War, Moustapha Pacha, 187
— — Dr. Arif, President of the Red Crescent Society, 187
— — Baron Mundy, 188
— — Temple Bey, 189
— — Governor of Gallipoli, 190
— — Yaya Pacha, 190
— — Governor-General of Salonica, 190
— — Grand Council, Gallipoli, 191
Thessaly, rising in, 91
Tirnova-Semenly, 62 (and see 'Soup-kitchens')
Tourniquets, 162

TRA

Train, accident to, 81
Transport, Gallipoli, 92
— notes by Mr. Pratt on, 181
— Roumelian Railway, 75
— Rustchuk-Varna Railway, 53
— Samakov, 87 (and see under ' Ambulance ')
— Varna Wagon, 55, 56
Trebizond, convalescents in, aided by a grant of money from S. H. fund, 34
— relief section, under Vice-Consul Biliotti, 105
— list of convalescents assisted by S. H. at, 106
Trevan, Surgeon, R.N., 92
Tricalla, malarial poisoning at, 147
Turkish doctors, mortality among, at Erzeroum, 102
Turkish fleet, S.H. hospital supplies to, 21
Turkish Government Hospitals aided by S. H. C., 29
Turkish soldiers, gratitude of, 35
— — dislike to amputation, 72, 108
— — Consul Zohrab's advice as to medical comforts suitable for, 131
Typhoid, 101, 110 (and see ' Medical Reports,' PART III.)
Typhus, outbreak of, 90, 101, 105 (and see ' Medical Reports,' PART III.)
— S. H. staff attacked with, 110

VACCINATION, 128
Varna Hospital, 122 (and see under ' Hospitals ')
Varna, depôt of stores at, 53
— table of men evacuated to, from the Lom army, and attended to by S. H. staff, 54
— staff and matériel at, 56
Vitales, agent at Shumla Road, 56

ZOH

Viathos, Dr., 74
— operation for stone, 161
Volo, Surgeon Eccles' expedition to, 91

WATTIE, Surgeon, 21, 44, 83, 84
— report of, 58
Weller, Surgeon, illness of, 20
— 121, 122
— report of, 145
White, Mr., British Consul at Belgrade,
Williams, Mr., 15, 36, 77, 87, 92. 95, 98, 101
— report of, 98
Woods, Surgeon, 20, 68, 71, 72, 75, 99, 109
Wright, Mr. H., Hon. Sec., 1

YAYA PACHA, thanks to S. H. C., 190
Yenikeui, bad Government hospital accommodation at, 44
— establishment of S. H. depôt at, 45
Yhanilagh, the, Russian attack on, Kars district ambulance in attendance, 117
Young, Mr., Chief Commissioner of National Aid Society, 28, 66, 118
— his aid to S. H. ambulance at Porto Lagos, 28
Yussuf Bey, 99, 101

ZABIT PACHA, 27, 64
Zohrab, Consul, 99
— valuable services of, 101
— letter of, 109
— letter on the service rendered by S. H. and Lord Blantyre's hospitals in Asia, 130
— Reginald, 107, 108

ANALYSIS OF MEDICAL REPORTS.

BAR

BARKER, Mr., surgical report of Roumelian railway transport, 139
— — injuries to head, 139
— — carbolic acid for maggots in wounds, 139
— — case of shell injury of lower jaw, 139
— — bullet wound of temple, 139
— — — jaw, 139
— — injuries to chest, 140
— — non-penetrating wounds of chest, 140
— — penetrating wounds of chest, 140
— — wound in left triceps, 140
— — — front left chest, 140
— — — fifth and ninth ribs, 140
— — injuries to abdomen, 141
— — — upper extremity, 141
— — finger injuries, 141
— — injuries to lower extremities, 141
— — compound fractures, 142
— — injuries to joints, 142
— — — nerves, 142
— — complications in cases of gunshot injuries, 143
— — gangrene, 143
— — pyæmia, 143
— — frost-bite, 143
— — sword wounds, 143
— — bayonet wounds, 143
— — acute rheumatism, 143
— — pneumonia, 144
— — diarrhœa, 144
— — dysentery, 144
— — cholera, 144
— — ague, 144
— — small-pox, 144
— — typhus, 144
— — typhoid, 144
— — railway transport of wounded, 144

MAC

ECCLES, Mr., report on malarial poisoning, and its effect on wounds, 146
— — ague, 146
— — effects of atmosphere, 146
— — conditions favourable to malarial poisoning, 147
— — treatment, 147
— — typical case, 147
— — beneficial use of quinine, 148
— — general course of medical treatment, 148
— — rate of mortality during the late war, 148
— — scurvy, 149
— — gunshot wound of right leg, with complication of malarial poisoning, 149
— — compound comminuted fracture of humerus, with complication of malarial poisoning, 150
— — shell wound in buttock, with ague, 151
— — local effects of malarial poisoning, 152
— report of hospitals at Constantinople, 177
— — Turkish hospitals, 177
— — condition of the hospitals, 177
— — causes of tardy recovery of patients, 178
— — causes of imperfect treatment, 178
— — recommendations, 178

MACKELLAR, Mr. A. O., surgical report of, 164
— — injuries of the head, proportion large in consequence of mode of fighting, 164
— — reason why so few come under observation of surgeon, 164

MAC

Mackellar, Mr., report of (*continued*)
— — sick bearers, 164
— — case of trephining successful, 164
— — Dr. Sandwith's case, 164
— — shell wounds of the head, 165
— — shell wound of frontal region, 165
— — compound comminuted fracture of skull, 165
— — wound in right frontal region, 165
— — gunshot injuries of chest, 165
— — contusions and non-penetrating injuries from spent bullets, 165
— — penetrating wounds of chest, 166
— — seven wounds in one patient, 166
— — hernia of lung, 166
— — results of treatment, 166
— — wounds of upper extremity, 166
— — frequency of wounds in left hand and shoulder, 166
— — obliquity of wounds, 167
— — Mr. Longmore's explanation, 167
— — finger wounds, 167
— — large proportion of injuries to fingers, 167
— — self-mutilation, 167
— — intensity of cold, 167
— — field dressing, 168
— — difficulty of getting a Turk to take medicine, 168
— — ventilation, 168
— — probes and forceps, 168
— — plague of maggots, 168
— — Stromeyer's cushions, 169
— — plaster of Paris splints, 169
— — amputations of shoulder-joint, 169
— — — of arm, 169
— — excision of shoulder, 170
— — — of elbow-joint, 170
— — secondary excisions, 170
— — injuries of abdomen, 171
— — cases of, 171
— — wind contusion, 172
— — injuries of lower extremity, 172
— — gunshot fractures of thigh, 172
— — objections of the Turks to amputation, 172
— — Turkish surgeons, 173
— — conservatism, 173
— — injuries of the knee-joint, 174
— — Circassian surgical treatment, 174
— — results of amputation, 174
— — operations selected, 175
— — bayonet, sabre, and lance wounds, 175
— — injuries of arteries, 176
— — hæmorrhage, 176
— — barrack hospitals, 176
— — nursing, 176

PIN

McIVOR, Mr., surgical report of, 133
— — barrack hospital at Adrianople, 133
— — state of patients on admission, 133
— — wounds of the upper extremities, 134
— — fractures of the humerus, 134
— — fractures of the bones of the forearm, 134
— — bullet wounds of the wrist, 134
— — flesh wounds of the upper extremities, 135
— — bullet wounds of the lower extremities, 135
— — bullet wounds of the hip-joint, 135
— — fractures of the femur, 135
— — bullet wounds involving the knee-joint, 136
— — fractures of the bones of the leg, 136
— — bullet wounds involving ankle-joint, tarsal bones, &c., 136
— — injuries to toes, 136
— — gunshot injuries to skull, 137
— — bullet wounds of the face, 137
— — — neck, 137
— — — chest, 137
— — — abdomen, 137
— — treatment of wounds by bullets and fragments of shell, 137
— — dressings, 138
— — abscesses, 138

PINKERTON, Mr., surgical report of, 153
— — few wounded by sword or bayonet, 153
— — cuts or stabs fatal on the field, 153
— — the bayonet an inefficient weapon, 153
— — lance wounds, 154
— — nature of the ground on which fighting takes place greatly determining the situation and appearance of wounds, 154
— — bullet wounds, 154
— — wounds of entrance and exit, Mr. Longmore on, 154
— — fighting behind earthworks, 154
— — notes of surgical cases, 155
— — wounds of the upper extremities, 155
— — self-inflicted wounds, 155
— — cases of curious bullet wounds, 156
— — wounds in the neck, 156
— — eight wounds by one bullet, 156
— — loss of the entire lower jaw, 156
— — wound in head, 156
— — bullets in brain, 156
— — advantage of trained hospital bearers in selecting proper cases to remove from the field, 156
— — administration of chloroform, 157
— — — the Scotch style, 157

Pinkerton, Mr., report of (*continued*)
— — duties of a person administering chloroform, 157
— — Bryant's rule, 157
— — skin flaps in gunshot injury, 158
— — generally unfavourable result of surgical work in Russo-Turkish war, 158
— — dreadful condition of wounded during transport, 158
— — antiseptic condition of wounds, 158
— — Lister's, Mr., method, 158
— — Longmore's, Mr., criticism of it, 158
— — Dr. Pinkerton's first operation, 159
— — Foulis' bands for controlling hæmorrhage, 159
— — modes of operating, 159
— — sutures, 160
— — carbolic acid as an antiseptic precaution, 160
— — Teale's amputation unsuitable, 169
— — Dr. Vlathos' operation for stone, 161
— — — in favour of the high operation for stone, especially for children, 161
— — maggots in wounds, 161
— — danger of all forms of tourniquet which unduly constrict the limb, 162

Pinkerton, Mr., report of (*continued*)
— — Moffit's winged screw tourniquet, 162
— — Gooch's splints, 162
— — Stromeyer's triangular cushion in compound fracture, 162
— — paraffin for splints, 163
— — plaster of paris for splints, 163
— — soothing influence of tobacco on men suffering from the pain of wounds, 163
— — Lady Strangford's hospital, 163
— — women as nurses, 163

STIVEN, Mr., report on the Rustchuk and Stamboul New Barrack Hospital, 179
— — description of Rustchuk hospital, 179
— — sanitary condition of, 179
— — description of Stamboul hospital, 180

WELLER, Mr., surgical report of, 145
— — bullet wounds in the back, 145
— — — thigh, 145

www.ingramcontent.com/pod-product-compliance
Lightning Source LLC
Chambersburg PA
CBHW031830230426
43669CB00009B/1291